The Irish Cookbook

The

Irish

Cook

Book

Jp McMahon

Dairy-free ☼

Gluten-free ⚘

One-pot ⊖

Vegan ✻

Vegetarian △

Less Than 30 Minutes ⊕

Less Than 5 Ingredients ⊕

What is Irish Food?

> 'Cooking is like a language. You hear other people speak, you taste what other people cook, you read what they have to say and then you go and do it yourself.'
>
> Myrtle Allen, *The Ballymaloe Cookbook*, 1977

What is Irish food? For the most part, rightly or wrongly, Irish food – and Ireland – is associated with the potato. Yet, the potato came to Ireland relatively late in the country's history: it only truly became a staple for the poor in the late eighteenth and nineteenth centuries. It tells us next to nothing about the food that has been consumed by the people on this island. Ireland is an island with a rich food heritage dating back thousands of years. The popularity of the potato came about more out of economic and nutritional necessity than a desire for the vegetable. The potato was nutrient packed, it could be farmed in small areas and feed many, and its harvest could last six to nine months if the potatoes were stored correctly. However, the introduction of the potato and the subsequent famine, caused in part by the crop's collapse between 1846 and 1849, has erased much of Ireland's food history that came from our common consciousness.

Staple dishes associated with Irish food such as lamb stew and boxty only emerged in the space created after the famine. They are the after effects of this traumatic period. This is not to say they are less relevant to an enquiry into Irish food, but rather they cannot be the only story told. Irish food needs to be more than the sum of the last two hundred years (or even the last five thousand years of farming). We need to reconsider the past and change our attitude towards Irish food to create what the cuisine might be in the future.

In writing this book, I set out to investigate Irish food. I wanted to examine the history of food on the island to reclaim a food story that said much more than the one I was taught at school or heard as a young boy growing up in the 1980s. We should look back into history and bring forth the foodstuffs that brought people to this island, right back to the beginning, to the first settlers who migrated here with their rich diet of fish and wild food. This is where the answers reside. This is where, I believe, we will find the future of Irish food. Of course, I may be wrong, but in an age of unprecedented globalization, to pick a wild herb growing outside your front door is an act of revolution. It is an act that takes you back a couple of millennia and reconnects you with your local landscape. As J. P. Mallory writes in his book *The Origins of the Irish*, 'the earliest Irish were direct products of the land they occupied: no Irish geology = no Irish people'. This is not the answer to everything, but it is a good place to start. The land shaped us, and we in turn were shaped by it.

People lived on this island before written records. What do we know of their food culture? Only what we can glean from midden beds and archaeological finds from the north to the south of the island. But that is not to say that no food culture existed. Where there are people, there is food; and where there is food, there is a culture.

Migratory Influences

For me, Irish food is the sum of food consumed on this island regardless of what tribe, class or ethnic group cooked it. People eat to live, but they also eat to come together and express their culture. People travel, migrate and bring food with them wherever they go. The Celts, Vikings, Normans, Anglo-Saxons, French and Polish to name but a few, are some of the 'tribes' that made their way to Ireland and settled here, bringing with them new and different food traditions.

Of course, this pattern of migration has not stopped, nor will it ever do so. Presently, we are witnessing another mass immigration across Europe. This will undoubtedly alter our food culture over the next fifty years. Together with the Internet and the spread of information, our culinary culture is altering before our very eyes. Yet this does not mean we cannot learn from the past; that we cannot isolate certain elements and examine what it means for a food to be 'Irish'.

When the first people migrated to this island around 10,000 years ago, they ate out of necessity. Yet, these first peoples ate food that we still encounter today: oysters and seaweed, nuts and berries, sea and river fish. They also brought with them knowledge and traditions from other lands. They did not arrive with a blank slate at some Eden to start all over again. Irish food culture has always arisen out of what is to hand, what is growing on and in the ground. Nestled in all this is a hidden history – the story, or stories of Irish food, waiting to be uncovered.

Looking Back, Moving Forward

We must take our heads out of the sand and embrace the food treasures that make our island unique. Close your eyes and imagine large wild mussels bursting open over hot embers that light up the faces of those first settlers. Where is this recipe if not in the land that connects us back to those people? As with much of our oral tradition in literature, our oral tradition of food may be lost but it is not forgotten. We can find it in the landscape that surrounds us.

This cookbook looks back as well as forward. For some engaged in the industry, it will be too liberal and imaginative a view on Irish food. For others, it will be too conservative. Or it will be too contemporary an understanding of native ingredients (present history is always mired in contemporary trends). But if we do not look to our own larder (pantry), then where can we look? This book speaks of the past, but it also looks towards a future for Irish food based on the wealth of ingredients available on this island. The larder is perhaps the most central element that binds this book together, and this book creates as well as records, using our rich larder to forge a new Irish cuisine. There is no such thing as a pure national food (I am not a naive purist), an Irish food that exists outside space and time.

The task I set myself was to define an Irish food culture that arose principally from the island's indigenous ingredients, as well as some of those that made massive inroads into the country (namely, the potato). But what began as a project to define what surrounds us, turned into a project to understand what came before me as well.

This book is not a history of Irish food. No book is definitive. Rather, it is a present understanding of the lay of the land, what food in Ireland was, how it was used, how it was not and, ultimately, what Irish food can be. I hope you enjoy this journey of discovery. To understand the new Irish cuisine that has come about in recent years, we need to look backwards as well as forwards, to understand what food this island has given to us. We need to celebrate this food in our imaginations as well as our bellies!

What is Irish Food?

How to Use This Book

The purpose of this book is threefold. First, it looks at specific food found and consumed on the island of Ireland during distinct periods of time. In this case, the book is a historical record of food consumption from the moment people settled on this island to the present day. Secondly, it is a reflection on new trends of cooking in Ireland. These new trends focus on the primacy of the product and its specific geographic and temporal location. In other words, its *terroir*. The third intention of this book is to provide a contemporary record of the wild foods and seaweed used in new Irish cooking, both past and present. This book is thus a humble attempt to classify our wild food for a new generation and to inspire others to seek out, find and incorporate wild food into their lifestyles. In this last sense, the book is meant to educate and inspire people to examine their native wild ingredients and learn a little more about their landscape.

No one cookbook details the many uses of Irish wild food in cooking, taking in the historical and contemporary attitude towards wild food. Of course, there are many precedents that have paved the way to this point: *Wild and Free* (1978), written by Cyril and Kit Ó Céirín, is a wonderful example of how we have used wild food for centuries in Ireland. As I write this book, a signed copy of the republication of *Wild and Free* (2013) sits on my desk. It is signed by Kit with a dedication to my daughters, Heather and Martha. May they continue to carry the flame that has been passed to me.

In this book, I have not only sought to include or adapt old recipes (drawing on the wealth of archive material available in the National Library of Ireland), but also to find new configurations for ingredients that would have been available during certain periods. In this regard, I have taken poetic licence. This may annoy some historians of food. However, this book is written to challenge the histories we imagine and create new ones, from a creative desire to change the future. While I have used foodstuffs available during the different periods of history, I have sought to season the food in a contemporary manner. I have used oil, vinegar and salt wherever I deemed fit.

Regarding the wild food and seaweed used in this book, some may have difficulty sourcing some of these products. My advice to the reader is twofold: seek out local foragers and check out local markets for wild herbs. Feel free to substitute any of the wild herbs for cultivated herbs. Don't be put off making a dish merely because you cannot locate a specific herb or vinegar. A recipe is only ever a guideline and the recipes in this book are meant to encourage you to cook, not the opposite. With regard to seaweed, dried seaweed is now widely available in health shops and online (try the Wild Irish Seaweeds website). It has a very long shelf life so it stores well. As with the herbs, feel free to substitute different seaweeds as you please. If the recipe requires fresh seaweed, just rehydrate your dried seaweed and use accordingly. Dried seaweed comes whole or milled, so keep an eye on the type you need. I love to have a variety of milled seaweeds at home and use them to season everything from fish to lamb.

How to Use This Book

How to Use This Book

A Little History of Food in Ireland

Ireland was not always an island. Around 43 million years ago, two gigantic land masses collided. What resulted in this collision was the fusion of the northern and western parts with the southern and eastern parts of Ireland. Yet even at this point we would not have recognized the island – indeed, it was still connected to England and France. It was much closer to the present, around twenty thousand years ago, that the last land bridges from what are now Scotland, Wales, England and France finally submerged into the Irish Sea. This means that Ireland has only been an island (distinct in itself) for 0.02 per cent of its existence (which is next to nothing!). In another ten thousand years, we should expect to find ourselves joined to another country by some land bridge that resurfaces.

The first people to occupy Ireland date from around ten thousand years ago. There are trace remains from before this period, but there is currently no evidence that they settled here for a continued time. The savage cold spells of ice that covered Ireland preceding this period would more than likely have made the whole place uninhabitable. If people arrived and left, the ice removed any trace of their existence. Did anyone travel to Ireland before this time and settle here, however briefly? And where did the first people come from? England, Scotland, Wales, France, Spain and Scandinavia are all possible answers. Wherever they came from, it was a long time before any sort of distinct 'Irish' character emerged.

Ancient Forests

The flora and fauna that is unique to Ireland predates the arrival of the first humans. After the end of the last ice age, the first flowers and trees made their way to Ireland via the surrounding lands. There are more than 850 indigenous flora in Ireland, much fewer than England and France. This is probably due to our climate and the retreating ice. This is also the case for all our native fauna. Red deer and auroch (wild cattle) were important for Mesolithic diets in England but not in Ireland. They had to be brought here by people after the first settlers. While the trees and flowers came with the wind, the red deer and cows had to travel by boat.

Before the arrival of people, Ireland was completely covered with trees. Ireland's native trees include the oak, hazel, birch, ash, Scots pine, rowan and willow. The seeds of these trees were brought by birds and wind. Over millennia, people came to Ireland and brought with them other trees, such as horse chestnut, spruce, beech, larch, sycamore and fir. For me, these trees have been here so long, we might as well call them 'native'. Otherwise, at what point do we define something as native – when do we give it an Irish passport? This is the same for the people. If we only locate ourselves with the advent of Celtic people, then we miss out about eight thousand years of migration into Ireland. What about all those natives? What about their food traditions?

The First Migrants

Arriving to these shores from the last land bridges or by boat (we're still not sure), the first settlers encountered a great wooded land. We don't know why these hunter-gatherers, who would have made their way up through Northern Europe and Britain, came to Ireland. It could not have been for the weather or the richness of the land. Why then did people migrate to the island? Was it to escape persecution? To find new lands? All we know is that they came here and settled and made this island their home, from Mount Sandel in the north of the country to Lough Boora in the middle and Ferriter's Cove in the south-west.

Archaeological evidence shows that the early hunter-gatherers had a diverse diet: mammals, including bears and seals, fish and shellfish, and various wild plants and herbs. It is hard to find evidence of vegetal matter, but this is not to say these early settlers did not consume wild vegetables, sea herbs or seaweeds. Other foodstuffs are easier to determine because we have remains: bones discarded into fires and shells discarded by the sea are the two most common. Midden beds (heaps of shells) reveal much about the early people who came to Ireland. Information on diet also comes from the skeletal remains of people from the period. Finally, technological evidence, such as fish traps and stone tools, give us a hint to how people caught and ate their food.

Probably the first wild animal to be 'domesticated' in Ireland was the boar. These were brought over from abroad, most likely in boats with the hunters. They would roam freely, gorge themselves on hazelnuts, and be hunted when needed for food. The boars would continue to produce offspring and the population would be culled sustainably so that there was a constant supply of meat for the tribes. We would do well to adopt this method of animal husbandry now.

Because of the absence of available fauna in Ireland, and the location of many sites by rivers or estuaries, there was a considerable amount of fish in the Mesolithic diet. We know from archaeological sites that there was a plentiful supply of shellfish on the coast (from limpets and oysters to cockles and scallops). There are many wild species we still consume today. At the Mesolithic site in County Kerry (Ferriter's Cove), there is an abundance of fish such as cod, haddock, ling, whiting, wrasse and ray. Inland, in freshwater rivers, there are salmon, eel and brown trout. Fish remained a pivotal part of the Mesolithic diet until the advent of farming.

It is here that we start our food story, delving into the first foodstuffs of ancient Ireland. Growing up in Ireland, fish was never valued enough. It was a food for fasting, for the poor: something to eat when you didn't want to enjoy anything. Friday meant fish, which meant picking floury bones out of your mouth. How wrong I was about the role of fish in Irish food culture!

Temporary Settlements

Until the advent of farming, early colonists led a nomadic life, constructing temporary shelters according to the seasons. The oldest and most extensive Mesolithic site developed by hunter-gatherers is found at Mount Sandel in Coleraine, County Derry, in the north of the island. This site has carbon dating indicating an age of nine thousand years old, from about 7,000 BC.

The people who inhabited this site had a rich diet. We can tell they fed on many foods that are still common, such as shellfish and freshwater fish (from the nearby river Bann). The fish were probably caught using harpoons, nets or baited lines, while more complex fish traps may also have been used. Mesolithic fish traps, fashioned out of wooden posts and wattle panels and wicker baskets are known from other Irish sites. However, they also consumed animals that we no longer consider worthwhile for eating. Bear, squirrel and seal come to mind. Evidence for wooden racks,

A Little History of Food in Ireland

over which fish would have been dried or smoked to aid long-term storage, were also identified at Mount Sandel. In among all of this information, we can see how so much of what people now call 'New Irish Cuisine' took place during the formative years of the habitation of this island. Looking at Mount Sandel, we can see trace evidence of some of the first communal meals cooked over fire: roast salmon, burned hazelnut shells, smoked eel, as well as plenty of wild pig with watercress.

As well as Mount Sandel, there are also several other sites that tell us about our ancestor's food habits. From Ferriter's Cove in County Kerry and Belderrig in County Mayo to Lough Boora in County Offaly and Sutton in County Dublin, all offer us clues to the daily diet of the ancient people who settled in Ireland. Most settlements can be found on the coast, because this provided easy access to the sea on one side and to the land on the other. The earlier settlers loved their wild boar – and perhaps this testifies to our continued infatuation with the pig in Ireland. However, they also enjoyed fish such as bass and plaice. Seafood and game was supplemented with berries, fruits and nuts from the forest. Animals were also used for building dwellings – dried animal skins were stretched over wooden frames to create temporary settlements.

Watercress, wood sorrel, nettles and wild garlic also possibly formed part of the diet of these Mesolithic people. These plants all appeared with the retreat of the ice sheets. From the native trees, they could have picked hazelnuts and rowan berries as well as wild cherries, pears and crab apples. Juniper could have been used to flavour meat through the fire. I find these foods fascinating, considering we still eat many of them now. If I try to think about foods that make up the identity of Irish food, I could list a host of seaweeds, seeds, nuts, berries, lichen, fungi and wild greens. These foods form the backbone of a Mesolithic Irish food culture.

The Arrival of Domesticated Life

Farming changed Ireland. After its arrival, we shed the hunter-gatherer within us and became somewhat closer to the settled people we are now. Tribes could now plan to get through the long dark winter, saving seeds for the following year. They also started to build permanent settlements – to live in one place for most of their lives.

These Neolithic settlers brought new agricultural inventions that would change the face of the Irish landscape. Woodland was cleared to make way for fields and fuel. Animals were domesticated on pastures and enclosures. Cereals were planted, harvested and stored. Some historians argue that the agricultural revolution changed us for better and for worse. In the case of the former, we were free from being enslaved by the vicissitudes of the land: we were now in control. Yet, in the case of the latter, we left all our wild knowledge behind and left ourselves open to famine each time a crop failed. Whatever your judgement of the agricultural revolution, farming changed everything: from the way in which society was structured in Ireland, to our belief system, to the tools with which we shaped and crafted the land. It took four thousand years for the technology of farming to get to Ireland. The next six thousand years would largely be defined by that revolution. Considering more than 60 per cent of our landmass is given over to agriculture, you could argue that we are but a small baby step away from this ancient revolution.

It is impossible to pinpoint the exact moment when farming arrived. There is still much debate about whether immigrants originating from the Fertile Crescent in south-west Asia brought farming technology with them or whether the technology arrived and was adapted by the people who were already in Europe. (This is significant considering our conception of Europe now. It begs the question, were the first farmers of Europe immigrants and if this is so, why do we reject so many immigrants now?). It seems likely that farming or farmers arrived in waves, and there were many overlaps and interactions with the hunter-gatherers.

Neolithic Communities

Around 4,500 BC, Neolithic people began to arrive in Ireland. They brought with them new ways of living. Sheep, goats and grains were imported from south-west continental Europe. The population rose, and the style of housing changed. Great monuments were built. Around 4,300 BC, cattle arrived in Northern Ireland. The red deer was introduced from Britain about this time and thus offered a source of wild food to the first farming communities.

Agriculture proper (including the keeping of livestock and crop farming) has its beginnings in Ireland around 3,800 years ago at sites such as the Céide Fields in Connacht. This is one of the oldest Neolithic field systems in the world. This site is made up of small fields partitioned by dry-stone walls. The Céide Fields were farmed for several centuries between 3,700 and 3,200 BC. Neolithic farmers cultivated wheat and barley here and produced pottery that could carry milk and other types of dairy. Typical of these wares are wide-mouthed, round-bottomed bowls. These could also have been used for heating liquids or rendering fats for cooking.

During this period, what marks changes in the diet the most is the turn away from the sea. Fish falls away as an absolute necessity as people turned towards animals such as cattle and pigs and sheep and goat. Is this one reason why the modern Irish rejected fish for so long? Could a change that happened thousands of years ago still affect so many of us now?

As well as developing technologies of farming, these prehistoric people also evolved new techniques of cooking. Cooking food makes it easier to digest and thus, makes it more efficient and quicker to consume. Pottery and farming go hand in hand. When you start to produce more food than you can consume, you need to find a way to store it. Grooved ware pottery, which dates from around 2,500 BC in Ireland, indicates that this type of pottery may also have been used for fermentation because of its size. Could this be the start of the fermentation revolution that only recently returned to Ireland?

As well as the ever-useful pot, the Neolithic peoples built many complex monuments such as chamber tombs, standing stones and enclosures over hundreds of years. Standing stones, called dolmens, can still be found all over the country. The most prominent of them, Newgrange in County Meath, is a tomb that dates to 3,300–2,900 BC. These tombs and standing stones were constructed as sites to honour the dead. Newgrange also marks the winter solstice through the alignment of its entrance with the sunrise on the shortest day of the year. This fact illustrates a complex understanding of engineering and a knowledge of basic astrology which can be traced back to the advent of farming and the change in belief systems. Controlling the land means ownership, which means societal structure that results in the emergence of a class system and beliefs. Thus, food is inextricably linked to culture. Even clearing the woods for pasture required so-called 'axe factories' to produce more axes for the levelling of Ireland's ancient woodland.

The Beaker People and the Bronze Age

The first evidence of mead in Ireland comes from samples found in ceramics made by the Bell Beaker peoples (c.2,800–1,800 BC). Though alcohol could certainly have been made earlier, or occurred naturally, its residual evidence in pots marks the arrival of alcohol proper to Ireland. The arrival of this culture to Ireland is possibly marked by ceremonies (i.e. drinking parties!). Several historians have indicated that the introduction of new types of pottery is associated with a drinking culture.

A Little History of Food in Ireland

A Little History of Food in Ireland

A Little History of Food in Ireland

However, as well as bringing alcohol to Ireland, the Beaker people possibly introduced metallurgy. One thing that the Beaker people liked to do was drink and fight (as evidenced by the metal weaponry they created). It is not known whether the Beaker people came to Ireland, or whether a technology of making better beakers gradually arrived. We can never truly tell if previous inhabitants were wiped out, assimilated or died off. What did happen, however, is that food culture changed with each new technology.

Around four thousand years ago, Bronze Age technologies started to arrive in Ireland. These included the moulding of Ballybeg-type flat axes, and the beginnings of copper mining at Ross Island, Killarney and Mount Gabriel. As with the influx of previous technologies, these changed the way in which food was produced and consumed. With bronze, people could make better tools to hunt. Ceramic vessels were common for carrying, storing and heating liquids. They also created many more domestic tools. While we often focus on the jewellery of Bronze Age Ireland, it would also be useful to examine the ways in which the period changed our lives in the kitchen. Direct and indirect methods of cooking such as roasting, boiling and baking over open fires, which used ceramic vessels, spits and griddles, were all practised. In pits, there are remains of cattle and pigs that display marks of butchery.

In relation to cooking, the *fulachtai fia* (burned mounds) are the most enigmatic. There has been great difficulty interpreting their purpose with the absence of firm empirical evidence. However, the mounds are usually found near water, comprise of large quantities of heat-shattered stone and charcoal, and are situated next to an adjacent trough. This indicates that they may have been primarily cooking sites, though there are many with no animal bones present, so they could have been for beer-making or salt production or even leather treatment. Furthermore, they could have also been used to generate steam for bathing. Pit cooking, which points to social eating, played a pivotal part in the life of the tribe. Large cuts of meat wrapped in straw and slowly simmered would have fed many people. While *fulachtai fia* have been proven to work for cooking, this does not tell us the whole story. The only known written source dates to the seventeenth century, so the jury remains out. At one of our Food on the Edge events, beer was prepared in a *fulachtai fia* by cooking barley in a trough with the addition of hot stones to show that it was possible to do this using ancient technology. There is another theory afloat that sees people settling and farming barley to make beer, but I'll leave that one with you: we have enough drinking stories in our history already.

Aside from the *fulachtai fia*, one of the key pieces of agricultural equipment that dates from around 800 BC is the plough. The plough revolutionized farming. Though wooden ploughs had been used before this time, the new bronze plough did much to change the way people farmed and reduce the back-breaking duration of time they toiled the fields. Of course, the population grew, and more technologies arrived in Ireland that would continue to alter the way people ate. Interestingly, this period of culture in Ireland is defined by a shared relationship with the people that then occupied Britain. This should at least undercut any such notion that Ireland formed its culture separately to England. Constant migration between the countries is evidenced through all sorts of ritual behaviours such as burying the dead and leaving offerings to the Gods.

The Iron Age and the Celts

During the Iron Age (*c.*500 BC), Celtic influence in art (La Tène), language and culture begins to take hold in Ireland. The Celts loved fighting and alcohol as much as the Beaker people, and it is difficult to assess the true Celtic influence in Irish food and identity because of the lack of material evidence of a 'Celtic' invasion. How much did the Celts bring to Ireland, if they came at all? How much was already here from trading? Did we just gradually assume some type of Celtic identity (language and art) or was there an invasion? A lot of our thinking about the Celts arises from the nineteenth century when we were trying to forge an identity that was separate to our neighbours.

The Celtic peoples excelled at metalwork and with them came the introduction of pots and pans and tripods for cooking animals. Many similar iron tripods are still used for cooking lamb and goats today. The Celts were a sophisticated society, and their diet was rich with cultivated and wild foods. They ate and partied well! Bands of elite warriors roamed the country, looking for cattle to seize. Feasting, drinking and a whole load of swords define this period of Irish culture. Most of the earliest Irish literature (often purporting to be historical) comes from this period and pictures these roving bands upholding their own pastoral economy.

The Irish language is a Celtic branch of the Indo-European language family. It is no wonder that we looked back at these peoples as somewhat originary (in terms of their Irishness), because of the way they spoke. The legacy of their language is probably one of the most defining characteristics of Irish culture. This language filtered into books that became 'Irish' history for a long time. However, languages related to Irish may have been spoken since the Mesolithic period. It is most likely that language began to be formalized because of the complex culture that was arising, brought about by the social elites and rituals that governed that society in the rest of Europe. We were not some distant land learning how to speak by ourselves. We were part of a wider community in Europe that interacted and traded with each other.

Food, like art and weaponry, was a major cultural tool. To understand food, we need to understand the ways in which food is talked about and shared among people. As with language, food operates as a vehicle to bring people together. The Iron Age diet revolved around wheat and porridges made from barley or oats. Innovations of Celtic civilization include thrown-wheel pottery as well as rotary stones for grinding wheat. A pair of large decorated stones known as 'beehive querns' were used for grinding grains. Many of these have been found in the northern half of the country. Beer was the preferred drink of the Celts – although it was more an alcoholic gruel made of barley. As with the earlier settlers, these people made butter and cheese. Bog butter – butter preserved in earthenware and buried under the ground – still survives as a culinary tradition to this day. They also consumed vegetables such as parsnips, leeks and onions.

The open fire, in the middle of a circular hut, was the crux of the meal. Animals were roasted and braised and stews were cooked slowly in metal cauldrons over this fire. *Fulachtai fia* were possibly used to cook larger cuts of meat to feed more people during larger occasions. In terms of meat, the Celtic diet was mainly made up from beef, pork and mutton, though deer and hare also featured on the menu: roast venison and wild garlic would have been consumed. The Celts had many days that celebrated food, normally marking the seasons. Importantly, the Celts in Europe perfected the production of salt. Seasoning meat and curing it for a later date begins here in Irish food culture in a much more systematic manner.

Roman Influences

But at what point does a tradition begin? At what point can we say the people on this island became Irish? Since the beginning, since the Celts, since the Vikings, since the Normans, since the British? In the second century AD, Ptolemy's *Geographia* provides the earliest known written reference to habitation in the Dublin area, referring to a settlement in the area as Eblana Civitas. Though the Romans never invaded Ireland, there was much trade between the peoples of Ireland and those in present-day Wales, England and Scotland.

A Little History of Food in Ireland

We can assume that food trade also happened. In most popular accounts of Ireland, the Romans play no part. Yet we cannot deny their influence on certain aspects. J. P. Mallory jokes, 'Aside from major improvements to agriculture and stock-raising, and changes in settlement type, dress, ornament, tools, weapons, literacy, vocabulary, art and religion, what did the Romans ever do for Ireland?'. All joking aside, it is worthwhile to think about the influence of Roman food culture on Ireland, particularly with the advent of Christian missionaries. Changes occurred not only in religion, but in agriculture and settlement. Merchants travelled from Roman Britain to Ireland and traded. The remains of Roman ceramics have been discovered in Ireland. Did any of these ceramics contain garum? Were they used for carrying Irish milk?

Bánbhianna (white meat products, i.e. milk) were extremely important in the diet of the Irish at the turn of the new millennium. Milk was drunk fresh and soured and used to make cheese and butter. Butter would often be flavoured with herbs, flowers or in the bog. The milk left over from making butter (buttermilk) was regularly drunk to provide nourishment, and it would remain a table drink for the Irish throughout the ages, still nourishing farm and bog workers in the twentieth century.

By the fifth century, Roman Britons had brought Christianity to Ireland, and by the seventh century, many monasteries were dotted around Ireland. This was a golden age of Irish monastic influence, which peaked with the foundation of monastic schools by Columba and Brendan at Iona and Clonfert. Wild food such as nettles, sloe berries and hazelnuts were a key part of the monks' diet. They also planted orchards and kept bees to have a constant supply of fruit and honey. Another feature of their diet was the consumption of grains instead of meat and dairy products. Though grains had already been introduced to Ireland by the first farmers, the monks had their own system for farming around their monasteries. This development led to systematic methods of production and an increased productivity of the land. Each monastery had to be self-sufficient, so the building of lakes to stock with fish and the tilling of the land were essential for survival. A sour barley bread is characteristic of this time, which is associated with the asceticism of the monks. But it wasn't all doom and gloom when it came to food. The monks grew all manner of vegetables such as leeks, cabbages and different peas and beans. They cultivated fruits in their orchards and probably made mead and country-style wine. As late as the twelfth century, Cistern monks in Ireland created farms around their abbeys that were centres of excellence in agriculture and milling, producing enough food for everyone in the abbey.

The Brehon laws, in their written form, date from this time, but they were part of an oral Celtic tradition for many hundreds of years beforehand. Writing arrived with the monks in the seventh century, and it was their task to transcribe these rules. The 'Brehon' were judges who compiled the laws of the land. Ireland has one of the oldest systematic legal systems in the world. Food is mentioned many times in written accounts, generally in relation to property or to its use as a tribute for payment. Food was an articulation of social standing. Law tracts dating from the seventh and eighth centuries detail the types of foods guests were to be served if they visited your house. A guest could not be served food that was above or below their position. Beef, for example, was not a common occurrence for the average medieval traveller or labourer. It is not until the twentieth century that beef became something for everyone.

Arrival of the Vikings

According to records, the Vikings first came to Ireland in AD 795 when a group of likely Norwegian raiders plundered the island of Lambay. These early Viking raids were generally small in scale and quick. Vikings arrived, looted, took hostages to sell as slaves and then left again. The start of raids

A Little History of Food in Ireland

from the north marked the onset of two centuries of unrest that would interrupt what had been an era of burgeoning Irish Christian culture. What food traditions did these Norse invaders bring with them? We can well imagine pickled fish such as herring. The Vikings also loved wild mushrooms, and soups or broths made from these could have provided sustenance to the warriors as they plundered the land.

By the 840s, the Vikings had established several settlements. Records from the time detail their movements as they mounted attacks on the inland communities before retreating to their bases on the coast. Indeed, the Vikings founded many coastal towns, including a fortress at Dublin Bay (*Dubh Linn* – 'black pool'), where they landed in 852. After several generations of coexistence and intermarriage between the Gaelic and Norse communities, the population had blended so much as to establish the Norse-Gael, or Gall-Gael, peoples (*Gall* means 'foreign' in Old Irish).

In the early 900s many more towns were founded, including Cork, Limerick, Wexford and Waterford. All this profoundly affected the food culture of Ireland. The trade links that the Vikings established introduced Ireland to many 'foreign' ingredients such as olive oil, wine, spices and different herbs. In 902, the Vikings were pushed out of Ireland by the Irish king Muirecán, but the towns that they had established prospered and continued to trade with each other and the outside world, becoming an important part of the Irish economy.

The Norman Invasion

As with the Vikings, the arrival of the Normans in Ireland affected food and the culture of its consumption. With the Normans came many spices that had not been available on the island beforehand. The cultivation of pulses also increased and they became a staple part of the Irish diet. Peas, beans and lentils: all would still play their part eight hundred years later. The Normans also brought with them more systematic food production, particularly to the rich and fertile lands of the east. They intermarried with the Irish, which meant the food cultures mixed, too. More land meant more food, which meant exports – there were more items to trade for the many exotic foods that the Normans loved.

The native Irish (who were already a mixed bunch) took well to the Norman way of life. As well as increasing food production, the Normans introduced the open-field system and three-crop rotation. The open-field system was the traditional medieval system of farming in Europe, in which land was divided into strips and managed by an individual only in the growing season and was available to the community for grazing animals during the rest of the year.

In terms of what the Normans ate, many of the foodstuffs that had been important to the Celtic Gaels continued to provide sustenance, namely cattle and sheep. Milk and cheese production from these animals remained central to the way of life in Ireland. The Normans also introduced animals into Ireland: rabbits, fallow deer and pheasant and several freshwater fish. They loved hunting and fishing for sport. Gerald of Wales also mentions Ireland's wonderful lakes and fishes in his influential account of Ireland from 1188, *Topographia Hiberniae* (Topography of Ireland). This distinction, between those who pursued food for fun and those who barely had enough to eat, would continue to mark Ireland in terms of its food culture. On one side, wealthy landowners, mainly in the east, ate well, feasting on all sorts of meat and game, birds laden with spices and other exotic vegetables and fruits. On the other side, the 'native Irish' lived beyond the 'pale' (the area that is roughly Dublin today – 'pale' meaning 'palisade or fence') and subsisted on a paltry diet of dairy, bread and broths. What is clear though is that Irish food from this point on is a multifarious space, where the local meets the global: ginger, cinnamon,

A Little History of Food in Ireland

A Little History of Food in Ireland

saffron and nutmeg all date from this time, as well as almonds, grapes and walnuts. These continue to be used to the present day. Every time Irish people add almond flour or spices to their cake, they can thank the Normans for introducing them to the country.

The English Invasion

The wholesale invasion of Ireland by the English changed food culture again. By the time the English established control of the country, Norman and Gaelic food culture had fused together. The English added another layer. As well as the addition of new game birds such as pheasant, the English introduced the turkey and the potato. However, whatever sort of homogeneous space existed between the Norman and Gaels was fissured by British rule. The conquest of Ireland saw the growth in a land-owning English aristocracy whose sophisticated manners and palates advanced food culture disproportionately against the defeated indigenous Irish. Anglo-Norman lords or the remaining Gaelic lords (there were few) that adopted their customs followed suit. The food at this point was diverse and sophisticated but only for a certain sector of society. Up until the seventeenth century (before the advent of the potato in Ireland), for most people the staple foods were derived from grain and milk products. People consumed oats, barley, wheat and rye as well as milk, cheese and curds. Other popular foodstuffs were pig's blood and eggs. Meat such as pork, beef and lamb would have been something for the wealthy. The only reason the poor would have for killing a cow would be if it stopped giving milk. Accounts from the seventeenth century detail a people subsisting mostly on bread and milk, making bread from ground barley and peas. The damp weather in Ireland was not suitable for large-scale wheat growing so wheat bread was not a staple.

The eighteenth century sees the tradition of the 'big house' emerge. These houses, with their cooks and numerous staff, would compound the global nature of Irish food during this period. Sugar from the West Indies became a symbol of wealth and sophistication. Many products from all over the world were used in these kitchens. Looking at the few existing recipe books from this period shows the continued use of spices with oranges, lemons and many other exotic ingredients from afar. Ireland's position in the British Empire made it possible to receive food from almost anywhere in the world. Much of the information we have from this period comes from domestic recipe books kept by the women of the house. These manuscripts offer a fascinating window onto the food culture and domestic kitchens of the seventeenth and eighteenth centuries. A cookery manuscript from the papers of the Dillon family of Clonbrock, one of the first of the Anglo-Norman families to settle in Connaught, demonstrates the European character of Irish food from this period. They occupied their house from the twelfth to twentieth century.

Two types of produce dominate Ireland in the nineteenth century: beef and the potato. One left Ireland and fed the British Empire, the other remained and contributed to a famine that wiped out much of the indigenous population. Over 1 million people died of starvation during the famine and another million emigrated to places such as America and England. The Irish translation of the famine is more revealing. In Irish it is called 'The Great Hunger'. This for me (and for many other food historians) indicates that there was food in Ireland, it was just a case of distribution. The failure of the lumper potato left millions without their food source. In the years following the famine, the potato still played an important part; however, with the rise of the middle class a greater diversity of food did find its way to the market.

In the latter half of the nineteenth century, Ireland underwent a commercial transformation. The emerging bourgeois class purchased commodities such as tea, sugar and white bread from shops. This was the case in the city

A Little History of Food in Ireland

as well as in the small towns. Soda bread, the staple of our grandparents, which we imagine was made in Ireland since the ice age, only emerges in the latter half of the nineteenth century. Cheaper wheat from America combined with the invention of bicarbonate of soda (baking soda) and leftover buttermilk (from making butter) turned into our next staple. For most people after the famine, however, their diets were still made up of oats, Indian meal and potatoes. A survey from the period shows that few farm labourers ate any meat or fish regularly. Of course, the diet of coastal people was different, but for many, diversity did not arrive until much later. Writing in his book *Ireland* (1844), the German geographer Johan Georg Kohl observed: 'Many Irishmen have but one day on which they eat flesh, namely, on Christmas day. Every other day they feed on potatoes and nothing but potatoes.'

What did change in the nineteenth century was the government interest in the nutrition of its people. This occurred all over Europe. One change in Ireland saw the introduction in 1900 of domestic education as a compulsory subject for girls. Food was seen as a domestic science and the government hoped that by engaging women, families would eat better. Perhaps the greatest change in the nineteenth century in terms of our food culture was the opening of restaurants in Dublin in the 1860s. At first, these restaurants were run by foreigners (mostly French men) but in time this gradually changed. The Jammet Hotel and Restaurant, which opened in 1901, was one of the most famous of these. The restaurant, which served many of the most illustrious and notable people of the time (it closed in 1967) also represents the continued duality of Irish food in the twentieth century. Wealth and diversity on one side, with paucity and monotony on the other. It takes more than a restaurant to make a food culture, but a great legacy can be traced back to these first restaurants and how they changed our idea of food – especially presenting the idea that it could be a pleasurable activity.

However, private history is not the same as public history. When I first encountered Italian food in the late 1980s in Ireland, I thought it was the first time this food had come to Ireland. This was not the case. Not only did pasta and tomato sauce appear in Irish cookbooks of the 1950s but Italian cheese could be had in Dublin at the turn of the twentieth century. We need to be careful when establishing our food history, asking whose history we are talking about. There are many different food histories of Ireland and all are equally relevant. We cannot forget, when trying to establish our own identity in terms of food, that we are not alone. As Myrtle Allen writes:

> When we talk about an Irish identity in food, we have such a thing, but we must remember that we belong to a geographical and culinary group with Wales, England and Scotland as all countries share their traditions with their next-door neighbour.

The twenty-first century sees Irish food and its culture growing, in terms of its chefs, restaurants and the many producers who grow the fine produce that Ireland has always been noted for. We are growing more confident in terms of what we have and what we can do with it. For the first time, I think it would be fair to say that 'Irish cuisine' exists or is beginning to exist. With a focus on the sea and the land, we can begin to craft a food for the future. That being said, our food future needs to stay cognisant of the past; to the great waves of migration that changed Irish food again and again, over the past 10,000 years. The next food wave, whatever it will be, will come from the outside again. As an island, and the western-most point of Europe, we are pitched for the next great food revolution. Let's just hope it involves seaweed!

A Little History of Food in Ireland

Eggs and Dairy

Eggs and Dairy

'In ancient and medieval Ireland, milk and milk products, generally referred to as "bánbhia" or white meat, played a central role in the diet of the Irish people.'

Bríd Mahon, *Land of Milk and Honey: The Story of Traditional Irish Food and Drink*, 1991

Dairy has had a vital role in Ireland since the first Neolithic farmers. Before twentieth-century industrial agricultural production, most farmers kept a mix of dual-purpose cows (Shorthorn and Friesian) for both dairy and meat. Most milk was produced domestically and used in the family home. Butter was a valuable commodity, so it was usually sold (or used to pay rent or taxes) and rarely eaten by all. Every farmhouse churned their own butter and the diversity of butter was outstanding in comparison to today. The skimmed milk, left after the fat was removed from the milk, was fed back to the animals (now we feed it to ourselves with added vitamins and call it super-skimmed milk). This cycle of dairy farming dominated Ireland for thousands of years. Milk products were referred to as 'white meat' (*bánbhia*) and, because of the role cattle played in the economy, their red meat was seldom eaten, except at feasts or special occasions. Many milk products surfaced in Irish food history, from sour and ropy milk, to buttermilk and cheese. It is fair to say that after the potato, milk was one of the most important foodstuffs in Ireland. Of the many milks, there were *treabhantar* (fresh milk mixed with buttermilk) and *bainne clábair* (thick sour milk); not to mention the many versions of butter, curd and cheese made with milk. These would need a book to themselves! As Bríd Mahon observes in her book *Land of Milk and Honey* (1991), no other foodstuff 'was the subject of so many customs, traditions and superstitions'. Sour milk and buttermilk were favourite drinks and added to potatoes, cabbage and seaweed as a complete meal.

As well as the milking of the cow, goats and sheep were also kept for their milk. Though used predominantly in cheesemaking, the milk of these animals was an important addition to other foods, such as porridge. Keeping sheep was cheaper than keeping a cow, so the custom of sheep's milk often emerged in poorer places or places that were not suitable for keeping cattle, such as mountainous regions. A new tradition of sheep's milk, cheese and yogurt has emerged in recent years in Ireland, particularly in the west.

Eggs have been an important foodstuff in Ireland for thousands of years. Before the domestication of the chicken, people fed on eggs from wild birds, such as ducks, seagulls, puffins and quails. Large eggs would be boiled or roasted, while small eggs would be sucked out whole from the shell for a nutritious snack on the go. Following the arrival of chickens and other domestic fowl such as geese and ducks, eggs became a central part of the diet in Irish food culture. Chickens were rarely killed and always kept for their eggs. It seems every new wave of people that came to Ireland, from the Vikings and Normans to the English settlers, brought new ways of cooking eggs to the country. This practice continues nowadays with Polish and Brazilian people settling in Ireland and mixing aspects of their food culture with our own. From goose eggs that adorned medieval banquets to duck eggs for tired turf cutters, there can be no doubt that this amazing feat of natural engineering has fed many generations of people in Ireland. Growing up in the 1980s, I still knew a few families in Maynooth that kept chickens for eggs. When we visit Brooklodge Hotel in Macreddin Village, County Wicklow, my daughters gather their own eggs for their breakfast. I love to see their faces as they pick the eggs out of the straw. Though this is a treat for them, it's good to try and maintain the connection between the egg and the chicken.

Herb Omelette

Preparation and cooking: 5 minutes
Serves 1

3 eggs
15 g/½ oz (1 tablespoon) butter,
    plus extra for serving
a handful of chopped herbs (tarragon,
    chives, parsley or wild herbs)
sea salt

This omelette can be made with any seasonal herbs. I love to use the small leaves of wild garlic (ramps) when in season. Wild watercress is wonderful as well, or even nettles (blanch the nettles first to remove their sting).

Whisk the eggs together in a mixing bowl with a fork.

Heat the butter in a nonstick frying pan (skillet) over a medium–low heat until it begins to gently foam. Pour in the egg mixture and lift the pan to ensure the eggs cover the entire base of the pan. Cook gently for a minute until the eggs begin to set. Add the chopped herbs and remove from the heat.

Tip the omelette onto paper towels and roll into a cylinder. It should be yellow, without colour. Remove the paper towels. Rub the omelette with a little butter and season with sea salt.

Fried Eggs and Ceps

Preparation: 5 minutes
Cooking: 10 minutes
Serves 2

50g/2 oz (4 tablespoons) butter
2 tablespoons rapeseed (canola) oil
4 eggs
4 small ceps (porcini), cut into eighths
a few sprigs of fresh thyme
coarse (kosher) sea salt
toast, to serve

Heat half the butter and oil in a frying pan (skillet) large enough to fry all the eggs over a medium heat. Crack the eggs into the frying pan and cook for about 3 minutes until the white is set. Remove and allow the residual heat to cook the yolk. Season with a little coarse sea salt and set to one side somewhere warm while you cook the mushrooms.

In another frying pan, heat the remaining butter and oil. When the butter is gently foaming, add the ceps (porcini) and toss with the butter and oil. Add the thyme and cook for about 5 minutes until the mushrooms are soft. Season to taste.

Serve the eggs with the mushrooms and some toast.

Egg Salad Sandwich

Preparation: 15 minutes
Cooking: 10 minutes
Serves 4

6 eggs
50 g/2 oz (¼ cup) mayonnaise
2 spring onions (scallions), thinly sliced
2 tomatoes, diced
2 tablespoons chopped parsley
50 g/2 oz (4 tablespoons) butter (optional)
8 slices of brown bread
sea salt and freshly ground black pepper

Egg salad sandwiches were a staple of my childhood, particularly at family occasions. They were bound to appear on large plates, cut into triangles. On occasion, I remember very posh ones with watercress. Mustard or lemon juice can also be added for additional flavour. It is said that it is a peculiarly Irish thing to put butter and mayonnaise on the same sandwich!

Put the eggs in a large pan of cold water over a high heat, bring to the boil and cook for 5 minutes. Cool under cold running water and remove the shells.

Mix the mayonnaise, spring onions (scallions), tomatoes and parsley in a bowl. Dice (or smash)

the eggs, add them to the bowl and mix thoroughly. Season with salt and pepper.

Butter the bread (if you like) and spread some filling onto four of the slices. Cover with the other slices. Cut into triangles and serve.

Eggs and Dairy

Scrambled Eggs with Chorizo and Goat's Cheese

Preparation: 5 minutes
Cooking: 10 minutes
Serves 4

8 eggs
100 ml/3½ fl oz (scant ½ cup) milk
50 g/2 oz (4 tablespoons) butter
100 g/3½ oz Gubbeen chorizo, finely chopped
1 teaspoon finely chopped chives
1 tablespoon crème fraîche
50 g/2 oz St Tola cheese or other goat's cheese
sea salt
edible flowers and herbs, to garnish (optional)

Whisk the eggs together with the milk and season with sea salt.

Melt the butter in a frying pan (skillet) over a medium heat. When foaming, add the chorizo and fry for 2–3 minutes until nicely coloured.

Pour in the egg mixture and lightly scramble. Be careful not to overcook the eggs, reducing the heat if necessary.

When you're happy with the consistency, add the chives and crème fraîche.

Place some scrambled egg on each plate and crumble a little goat's cheese over each dish to serve.

See opposite –>

Eggs Baked in Ashes

Preparation and cooking: 20 minutes
Makes 2 eggs per person

2 eggs per person
toasted sourdough or soda bread, to serve

Put the eggs into the smouldering ashes of a fire and turn occasionally. Remove after 15–20 minutes, or less, depending on your liking.

They should be hard boiled by this time. Crack open and serve with some toasted sourdough or soda bread.

Bacon and Egg Tart

Preparation: 30 minutes, plus 1 hour chilling time
Cooking: 50 minutes
Serves 8

For the pastry
250 g/9 oz (2 cups) plain (all-purpose) flour, plus extra for dusting
125 g/4½ oz (1 stick plus 1 tablespoon) butter
½ teaspoon sea salt
1 egg

For the filling
4 rashers (slices) streaky (regular) bacon
4 eggs
300 ml/10 fl oz (1¼ cups) single (light) cream
2 spring onions (scallions), finely diced
sea salt

There are many egg tarts in the Irish tradition, especially with leeks and cheese. A vegetarian equivalent of this tart can be made by replacing the bacon with mushrooms. If you have any wild or cultivated herbs to hand, simply chop them up and add them to the filling.

To make the pastry, add the flour and butter to a large mixing bowl and mix together using your fingertips until it resembles breadcrumbs. Add the salt and then the egg and enough chilled water to form a stiff dough. When the dough comes together, wrap in cling film (plastic wrap) and refrigerate for 1 hour.

Preheat the oven to 200°C/400°F/ Gas Mark 6. Grease a 23-cm/ 9-inch diameter fluted tart pan.

On a floured work surface, roll out the pastry to a disc as large as your pan and use it to line the pan. Line the pastry case (shell) with

baking (parchment) paper and fill with baking beans (pie weights) or dried beans. Blind bake in the preheated oven for 10–15 minutes, then remove the paper and weights. Reduce the oven temperature to 170°C/340°F/Gas Mark 3½.

To make the filling, grill (broil) or fry the bacon and cut it into strips. Whisk the eggs together with the cream in a medium mixing bowl. Add the bacon and spring onions (scallions) and season to taste.

Pour the mixture into the tart case (shell) and bake in the preheated oven for 30–35 minutes until set.

　　　Eggs and Dairy

Eggs and Dairy

Scotch Eggs

Preparation: 20 minutes
Cooking: 8 minutes, plus 10 minutes per batch
Serves 6

8 eggs
300 g/11 oz sausages, the meat removed
    from its casings
a small handful of chives, chopped
a small handful of parsley, chopped
freshly grated nutmeg
150 g/5 oz (3 cups) fresh breadcrumbs
flour, for dredging
rapeseed (canola) oil, for deep-frying
sea salt

Scotch eggs are boiled eggs encased in sausage meat and breadcrumbs and then fried. Originating in England in the later eighteenth century, the first recipe appeared in Maria Rundell's *A New System of Domestic Cookery* (1806). They were a typical picnic food for the Anglo-Irish upper classes when out hunting. Though less popular nowadays, they still pop up on restaurant menus around the country.

Put six of the eggs into a pan filled with cold water, bring to the boil and boil for 3 minutes. Cool the eggs under cold running water and then remove the shells.

Place the sausage meat in a bowl and add the chopped herbs. Season with salt and a little nutmeg.

Dredge the boiled eggs in flour and then encase in the sausage meat. Roll in the flour once again and shake off any excess.

Whisk the remaining two eggs in a bowl. Dip the boiled eggs into the bowl and then roll in the breadcrumbs. Shake off the excess crumbs.

Add the oil to a deep-fat fryer and heat to 175°C/350°F, or until a cube of bread browns in 30 seconds. Fry the eggs in the heated oil, in batches if necessary, for 8–10 minutes until brown and crispy.

See opposite –>

Quail's Eggs with Smoked Eel and Asparagus

Preparation: 15 minutes
Cooking: 15 minutes
Serves 4

8 quail's eggs
100 g/3½ oz smoked eel
50 g/2 oz (¼ cup) mayonnaise
1 teaspoon chopped parsley
lemon juice, to taste
8 asparagus spears, woody ends removed
50 g/2 oz (4 tablespoons) butter,
    room temperature
4 slices of brown soda bread
sea salt and freshly ground black pepper

I like to serve this combination of ingredients on brown soda bread, but they also make a great salad. Quail's eggs were once difficult to source, but now there are a number of small quail farms which supply both the eggs and the birds. 12 Quail Farm in County Leitrim is run by a mother and daughter team and they produce high quality eggs. We get our smoked eel from Lough Neagh, where they have been fishing eel for thousands of years (see Eel, page 146).

Bring a large pan of water to a boil, add the eggs and cook for 2–3 minutes, depending on how you like your yolk cooked. Cool under cold running water and then remove the shells.

In a small bowl, combine the smoked eel, mayonnaise, parsley and lemon juice. Season with salt and pepper and mix.

Heat a ridged griddle (grill) pan over a high heat. Add the asparagus and grill for 3–4 minutes until tender.

Rub with a little butter, season with sea salt.

Cut each asparagus spear into four and cut the quail's eggs in half.

Butter the soda bread and spread some of the smoked eel mixture on top of the bread. Place the asparagus spears on top and finish with the quail's eggs.

Eggs and Dairy

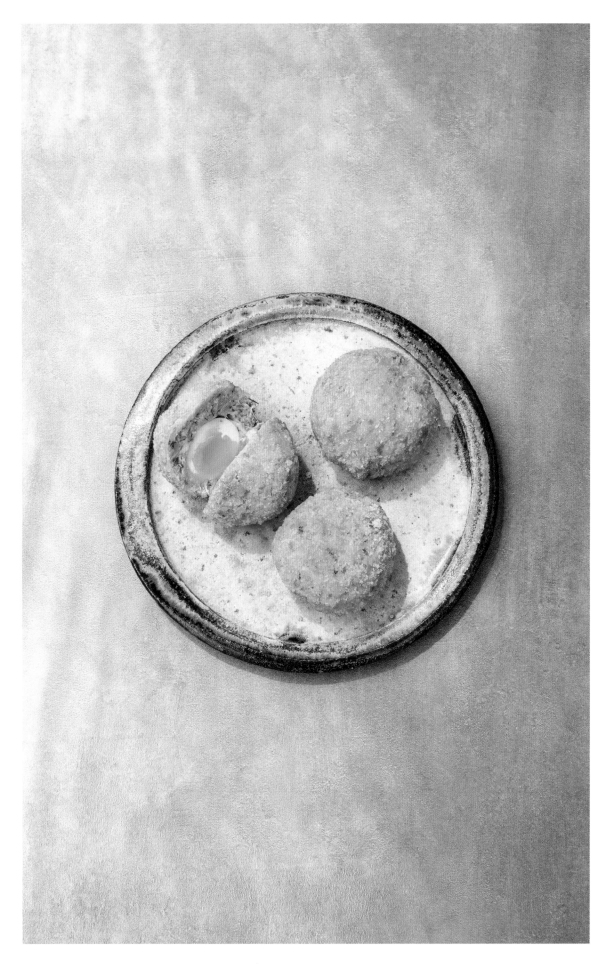

Eggs and Dairy

Butter and Buttermilk

Butter has a long and deep history in Irish food culture. From thousand-year-old bog butter to the beautiful and rich taste of contemporary cultured butter made by Cuinneog in County Mayo, butter is probably the product that most people associate with Irish food, after the potato. Indeed, butter's marriage with the potato only furthers the association of these two foods. Nothing is more beautiful than new season potatoes with butter and sea salt. Before the potato, there were oatcakes, which seemingly were so hard and abrasive they needed plenty of butter to help people swallow them. We owe our beautiful butter to the luscious grass that grows in Ireland. This in turn is produced by all the rain, so we have something to thank the weather for.

It's unfortunate that most of us no longer get to experience the process of making butter. Making your own butter is not difficult and it's something that many Irish women of past generations would have done. In his book *Teague Land: or A Merry Ramble to the Wild Irish* (1698), John Dunton claims to have observed the most sensational butter churning performance, wherein the sweat from the woman's arm pits drips into the churn. Whatever the veracity of this tale, it does demonstrate the physicality of butter-making in seventeenth-century Ireland. Nowadays, most butter tastes the same due to the homogenization of the process.

Buttermilk (*bláthach*) is a by-product of making butter. Once a drink in its own right (especially on hot days cutting turf), buttermilk is now consigned to being the principal ingredient in Irish soda bread. However, buttermilk is a unique ingredient in Irish food culture. In the past it would have been naturally soured, due to the cultured state of the product. I love to use it for dressing fish, or as a sauce for shellfish. Mix equal quantities of cream and buttermilk, season with sea salt and split with a herb oil. Buttermilk is also great as a marinade for meats such as poultry, pork and wild game, such as duck, pheasant and venison. The lactic acid in the milk helps to tenderize the meat and retain moisture. It also allows added flavours (such as herbs or spices) to permeate throughout the meat to ensure a fuller flavour. Juniper is a great spice to combine with buttermilk when marinating chicken or rabbit.

To Make Your Own Cultured Butter

Preparation: 30 minutes, plus overnight resting time
Makes 1 litre/34 fl oz (4¼ cups)

1 litre/34 fl oz (4¼ cups) double (heavy) cream
2 tablespoons buttermilk or natural live yogurt
5 g/⅛ oz (1 teaspoon) salt

Mix everything together in a large bowl, cover and leave at room temperature overnight, or longer if you want a more pronounced flavour.

In the morning, transfer to the refrigerator until cold. Remove and whisk the cream until the solids separate from the liquids.

Strain the buttermilk from the butter (it should yield 300 ml/10 fl oz/1¼ cups). Wash the butter in clean cold water to remove the last of the buttermilk.

Add more salt if needed and work the butter with wet hands on a clean chopping board to remove the last of the liquid.

Roll the butter and refrigerate until hard enough to serve.

See opposite ->

Eggs and Dairy

Eggs and Dairy

Herb and Seaweed Butters

Butter is a great vehicle for flavour. Compound butters are good for adding additional layers of flavours to a dish, whether it be seaweed for a fish dish or wild garlic (ramps) butter for a vegetable dish. Anything can be added to compound butter, from herbs to seaweed (dried or fresh) to fresh flowers (marigolds, violas, borage, etc.). All will add colour and flavour to whatever dishes you use them over. I love to make wild garlic butter when in it's in season, but dill, fennel and parsley all make a nice herb butter. If using seaweed, I prefer to use dried milled seaweed as fresh adds too much moisture to the butter. Milled dillisk (dulse) or nori is best in my opinion. Potatoes with wild garlic butter and crab claws with seaweed butter are two of my favourites. Simply add whichever flavourings you like before rolling the butter (see page 36).

Turf-smoked Butter

To make this butter, you'll need to have access to a turf fire. Build a fire with wood or charcoal and allow to burn down low. Place some turf on the fire. When it starts to smoke, put the butter in a metal bowl, cover it loosely with aluminium foil, and place over the smoke for 4–5 minutes. Make sure the butter doesn't completely melt. You want the smoke to cool enough just to kiss the outside of the butter. Place the butter in a food processor with a whisk and whip the butter. Season with salt and place in a tub or a piping (pastry) bag. Turf butter works well with grilled salmon or mackerel.

How to Make Your Own Yogurt

Preparation: 10 minutes, plus cooling
Cooking: 10 minutes, plus overnight
Makes 1 litre/34 fl oz (4¼ cups)

1 litre/34 fl oz (4¼ cups) full-fat (whole) milk
15 g/½ oz (1 tablespoon) live cultured yogurt

Yogurt is another by-product of milk, which is produced with the addition of a live bacterial culture. It is said to have been invented in Mesopotamia around 5,000 BC, and the practice of yogurt-making would have travelled to Ireland with the first farmers, who brought cows, sheep and goats into the country. There are many small producers now making wonderful sheep's and goat's yogurt. Velvet Cloud in County Mayo and The Galway Goat Farm in County Galway spring to mind as probably the best new producers. I love the gentle acidity, as well the cold freshness, that yogurt brings to a dish. I often use yogurt with chicken or pork instead of making a sauce. Hanging yogurt (through muslin/cheesecloth) is a great way to make it thicker and richer. We often do this with sheep's yogurt before serving with charred summer vegetables, such as courgettes.

Heat the milk in a large pan over a medium heat to 82°C/180°F. Maintain the temperature for 2–3 minutes, stirring occasionally to avoid the milk burning.

Cool the milk to 43°C/110°F and add the cultured yogurt. Place the yogurt in a heatproof container and seal.

Place in the oven at 43°C/110°F overnight, or for 8–12 hours, to allow the yogurt to ferment and thicken.

When the yogurt is thick, allow to cool and refrigerate for up to a couple of weeks.

Eggs and Dairy

Cheese

The Irish farmhouse cheese revival began in 1978, with Veronica Steele producing her cheese in Milleens in County Cork. It was the year I was born. I have heard stories of her cheese making its way to Myrtle Allen's Ballymaloe House (the first restaurant in the country to champion farmhouse cheese) by bus unaccompanied – one bus to Cork City and then the driver would put the cheese on another bus from West Cork to East Cork. This was the rebirth of the cheese industry in Ireland. Real cheese, I mean. Two women on opposite sides of Cork with a passion for a product that spoke of place: Myrtle Allen and Veronica Steele. The Irish food movement that continues now owes everything to those two brave ladies who sought to revitalize our artisan food industry. One could safely say that this was the beginning of contemporary Irish food.

But cheesemaking in Ireland predates this revolution and was an important part of life for early farming communities. It is said that cheesemaking began in the monasteries, but there is evidence that cheese was made in pre-Christian Ireland. That the monks from Ireland brought the secrets of making hard and soft cheese to France and further afield from the sixth and seventh centuries onwards is another story that circulates. If it's to be believed, all French cheese owes its origin to the emigration of Irish monks. Regardless of these stories, we do have descriptions of cheese in monastic and secular records during the latter part of the first millennium. The twelfth-century text *The Vision of Mac Conglinne* details not only information on the Irish medieval diet, but also speaks of cheesemaking and the making of curds. The consumption of curds and whey has been popular throughout Irish history. Curds were also made from boiling sweet and sour milk together or adding buttermilk into warm milk. Curds were so popular that they were (like butter and cattle) used as currency. The nutritious leftover whey was drunk, and was also said to have curative properties.

After the departure of the monks, cheesemaking did not fare as well in Ireland and had all but died out after the constant warring with the English. Though the consumption of curds and whey did continue due to the large amount of milk peasants consumed, cheesemaking suffered greatly. It did however continue in some farmhouses, with several types of cheese being made for domestic consumption. In the late 1600s, the English bookseller and writer John Dunton described the latter practice among peasants in Connemara in his book *Teague Land: or A Merry Ramble to the Wild Irish* (1698). Unfortunately, these cheeses do not seem to have acquired the same reputation as their French, Spanish and Italian counterparts did.

Despite a few intermittent revivals before the twentieth century, we focused more on butter than on cheese. Saying that, cheddar and other types of cheese were made in Ireland during the twentieth century, but nothing of the calibre that Mrs Steele brought back to this country. For me, learning about farmhouse cheese in my early twenties (particularly through Sheridan's cheesemongers in Galway City), the holy trinity always hailed from West Cork: Milleens, Gubbeen and Durrus. All these cheeses are still made now. We use them daily in the restaurant. But there are others now, so many others: Cashel Blue, St Tola goat's cheese, Kearney Blue, Cáis na Tíre, Young Buck and Rockfield sheep's cheese. I could go on. Farmhouse cheese is now available in many countries. So, go out and search your own area and see what sort of cheese you can find. It will enrich your experience and give you a better sense of your own place. Much of the American Farmhouse cheese movement owes itself to an ongoing dialogue with many small Irish cheesemakers.

Eggs and Dairy

Making Fresh Curds

Preparation: 5 minutes
Cooking: 15 minutes
Makes 500 g/1 lb 2 oz (2 cups)

500 g/1 lb 2 oz (2 cups) whole (full-fat) milk
1 teaspoon rennet
sea salt

Curds are made by adding rennet to warm milk. The rennet causes the milk to split or separate into curds and whey. Though the curds can be pressed and turned into cheese, they can also be eaten fresh or slightly sour. Whey can be used for broths and sauces – as with buttermilk, I find its acidity useful to balance a dish.

To make curds, put the milk into a pan over a medium heat and heat for about 5 minutes until warm. Remove from the heat and add the rennet. Cover the milk and allow to curdle for 10 minutes.

Cut the curds and return to the heat. Heat gently for about 3 minutes until the whey is clear.

Strain through a piece of muslin (cheesecloth) and season with sea salt. Reserve the whey to use as a sauce (see page 379).

Cream Cheese with Nettles

Preparation: 15 minutes, plus 10 minutes resting and a few hours chilling
Cooking: 10 minutes
Serves 4

500 ml/17 fl oz (generous 2 cups) whole (full-fat) milk
250 ml/8 fl oz (1 cup) double (heavy) cream
1 teaspoon rennet
75 g/2¾ oz stinging nettle leaves
extra virgin rapeseed (canola) oil
sea salt

To serve
Herb Oil (see page 351) of your choice
edible flowers such as marigolds

Cream cheese is produced not only by adding cream to whipped curds, but also from 'creaming' the cheese. The main different between curds and cream cheese is the texture.

Put the milk and cream into a pan over a medium–low heat and warm gently. Remove from the heat and add the rennet. Cover the milk and allow to curdle for 10 minutes. Strain through a piece of muslin (cheesecloth) and reserve the whey. Whip the curds until smooth. Add a little of the whey if needed. Season with some sea salt.

Bring a pan of water to the boil and blanch the nettle tips for 1–2 minutes. Refresh in iced water. Lay out a rectangle of cling film (plastic wrap). Lay the nettle leaves on the cling film. Season with sea salt. Spoon the cream cheese on top of the leaves and roll into a cylinder. Refrigerate for 2–3 hours until firm.

Unroll the cylinder, brush with a little oil and season with sea salt. Carve into rounds, drizzle with some Herb Oil, if desired, and garnish with flowers.

Milleens with Roasted Hazelnuts

Preparation and cooking: 30 minutes
Serves 4

1 wheel of Milleens cheese
50 g/2 oz hazelnuts, roasted and crushed
crusty bread, to serve
edible flowers, to garnish (optional)

Preheat the oven to 180°C/350°F/ Gas Mark 4.

Put the wheel of cheese into a small ovenproof dish and bake in the preheated oven for 10–15 minutes until the cheese melts.

Cover with the roasted and crushed hazelnuts. Serve with some lightly toasted crusty bread.

See opposite –>

Eggs and Dairy

Eggs and Dairy

Cheese Custard

Preparation: 5 minutes
Cooking: 15 minutes
Serves 4

200 ml/7 fl oz (scant 1 cup) double
   (heavy) cream
200 g/7 oz good-quality Irish cheddar
   cheese or a hard sheep's cheese, cubed
6 eggs
sea salt

We use this custard to fill little shortcrust pies, but it's also beautiful spread on toasted sourdough bread.

If you have a Thermomix, add all the ingredients to the bowl and cook at 70 °C/158 °F until the custard is set.

Otherwise, bring the cream and cheese to the boil in a small pan over a medium heat. Remove from the heat and blend the mixture with a small immersion blender.

Whisk the eggs together and then add them gradually to the warm cream mixture. Cook the mixture in a heatproof bowl over a pan of simmering water for 20 minutes, or until the mixture thickens. Season to taste.

Allow to cool and spoon into a tub or a piping (pastry) bag.

Porridge

'The children of inferior grades are to be fed on porridge or stirabout made of oatmeal on buttermilk or water taken with stale butter and are to be given a bare sufficiency; the sons of chieftains are to be fed to satiety on porridge made of barley meal upon new milk, taken with fresh butter, while the sons of kings and princes are to be fed on porridge made of wheaten meal upon new milk, taken with honey.'

W. Neilson Hancock et al., *Ancient Laws of Ireland*, Vol. 2, 1869

The first Irish farmers brought grain to Ireland. Little did they know that 1,500 years later many Irish people would sustain themselves on porridge, often three times a day. Like the potato, grains have suffered in Irish history due to their association with poverty. From the first farmers to the first monks and abbots, grains played a central role in building a community. Because of the weather, wheat did not grow well in Ireland. Our damp climate has always hampered its production, and while wheat production existed in Ireland before the first century AD, the technology to grow it more effectively came over to us from Roman Britain.

Wheat may not have done well in the Irish climate, but oats, barley and rye flourished. Oats came to Ireland somewhere around 500 BC. They suited the inclement Irish weather and thrived in poor soil. Oats were usually eaten in the form of a gruel or porridge. Often, they were mixed with butter or buttermilk to provide a more rounded meal. In his sixteenth-century *History of Ireland*, Edmund Campion described 'oatmeal and butter' being combined. It may be a minor crop in relation to wheat, barley and rye, but oats provided sustenance to most pastoral folk. Though porridge can be made with many different grains (such as barley and wheat), it is most often associated in the Irish imagination with oats. As well as adding butter and buttermilk, honey, salt and sheep's milk could also be added to porridge. Medieval monks were known to top their porridge with all sort of wild and cultivated fruits, from apples to blackberries. Oats also went into making the bread and cakes that contributed to the daily diet of the rural poor. They now feature on many menus and in people's homes as a 'health food' or dessert ingredient. Oat milk is also produced in Ireland for both home and abroad. It is a better dairy-free option than less-sustainable almond milk.

'Stirabout' is just another name for porridge in Ireland. As with all oat porridges, flavouring very much depends on the person making the porridge: milk, butter, cream, honey, sugar, yogurt, fresh or dried fruit are all fair game. My grandfather made his only with milk. I think I remember him adding brown sugar, but I could be wrong! Porridge oats take approximately three times as much liquid. I like to soak them overnight to shorten the cooking time.

A Fair White Porridge Made with Sheep's Milk

Preparation: 5 minutes, plus soaking time
Cooking: 5 minutes
Serves 4

200 g/7 oz (2¼ cups) rolled oats
200 ml/7 fl oz (scant 1 cup) sheep's milk
50 g/2 oz (¼ cup) sheep's yogurt
sea salt

This porridge was mentioned in the twelfth-century text *The Vision of Mac Conglinne*. I grew up eating porridge on cold winter mornings in the 1980s. Cooking oats in milk or water until soft and creamy – that was the only porridge I knew. However, when I began looking into Irish food, I realized how central the oat was, not only as a breakfast, but as a meal in itself.

Put the oats in a medium pan and cover with 200 ml/7 fl oz (scant 1 cup) slightly salted water. Leave to soak overnight.

The following morning, add the milk (the oats will have soaked up the water). Cook the oats over a medium heat for about 5 minutes until the porridge becomes soft and creamy. Season with some sea salt. Remove from the heat.

Serve with a spoon of sheep's yogurt on top.

Note
Medieval monks combined their porridge with honey and hazelnuts from the woods to create a delicious, textured meal. To recreate this, whisk 2 tablespoons of honey or apple syrup into your porridge and top with some roasted hazelnuts and a dollop of fermented cream. Another good variation for this porridge is to add 2½ tablespoons Nettle Purée (see page 87) once cooked.

Smoked Eel Porridge

Preparation: 10 minutes, plus overnight soaking time
Cooking: 5 minutes
Serves 4

200 g/7 oz (2¼ cups) rolled oats
200 ml/7 fl oz (scant 1 cup) milk
100 g/3½ oz smoked eel, chopped
50 g/2 oz (¼ cup) fermented cream
3 tablespoons thinly sliced spring onions (scallions)
sea salt

It's unfortunate that porridge is not used more as a savoury ingredient. Smoked eel and oats work very well together.

Put the oats in a medium pan and cover with 200 ml/7 fl oz (scant 1 cup) slightly salted water. Leave to soak overnight.

The following morning, add the milk (the oats will have soaked up the water). Cook the oats over a medium heat for about 5 minutes until the porridge becomes soft and creamy. Season with some sea salt. Remove from the heat.

Serve alongside the eel with a spoon of fermented cream and sprinkle on some spring onions (scallions).

Eggs and Dairy

Granola with Sheep's Yogurt and Rhubarb Compote

Preparation: 10 minutes
Cooking: 30 minutes
Serves 4

4 tablespoons rapeseed (canola) oil
225 g/8 oz (⅔ cup) local honey
350 g/12 oz (4 cups) rolled oats
150 g/5 oz (1 cup) pumpkin seeds
100 g/3½ oz (⅔ cup) sunflower seeds
50 g/2 oz (⅓ cup) hazelnuts
4 tablespoons linseeds (flaxseed)
sea salt, to taste

For the rhubarb compote
750 g/1 lb 10 oz (6 cups prepared) rhubarb,
   trimmed and cut into even pieces
100 g/3½ oz (½ cup) caster (superfine) sugar
½ teaspoon dried rose petals (optional)

To serve
100 g/3½ oz (½ cup) sheep's yogurt
   (I use Velvet Cloud)
fresh berries
edible flowers

To make the granola, preheat the oven to 150°C/300°F/Gas Mark 2.

Mix the oil and honey in large bowl. Add all the remaining ingredients and mix well until everything is coated. Spread out over two baking sheets and bake in the preheated oven for 15–20 minutes or until the oats are golden in colour.

Meanwhile, to make the compote, combine all the ingredients with 100 ml/3½ fl oz (scant ½ cup) of water in a pan and stew over a medium heat for 25–30 minutes, or until the compote has a nice glossy consistency.

To serve, spoon some rhubarb compote into a bowl and top with the granola, a dollop of yogurt, fresh berries and edible flowers.

See opposite –>

Porridge with Sweet Apples

Preparation: 10 minutes, plus overnight soaking time
Cooking: 15 minutes
Serves 4

200 g/7 oz (2¼ cups) rolled oats
200 ml/7 fl oz (scant 1 cup) milk
2 apples, cored and cut into wedges
3 tablespoons honey
sea salt

The Middle Ages in Ireland saw plenty of oats, honey, butter and apples. This is my little tribute to the medieval monks of Ireland, who undoubtedly lived a somewhat difficult and parsimonious life.

Put the oats in a medium pan and cover with 200 ml/7 fl oz (scant 1 cup) slightly salted water. Leave to soak overnight.

The following morning, add the milk (the oats will have soaked up the water). Cook the oats over a medium heat for about 5 minutes until the porridge becomes soft and creamy. Season with some sea salt. Remove from the heat and whisk in a little of the honey.

Meanwhile, cook the apples. Preheat the oven to 180°C/350°F/Gas Mark 4.

Put the apple wedges onto a baking sheet lined with baking (parchment) paper and brush with a little more of the honey. Roast in the preheated oven for 5–10 minutes until soft and caramelized, turning the apples halfway through the baking time and brushing the other side with the remaining honey. Season with a little sea salt.

Serve the porridge in warmed bowls with the caramelized apples.

Eggs and Dairy

Vegetables

Vegetables

'The earliest historical sources in Ireland abound with references to the fertility of the land. In the saga literature, which relates tales of the kings of Ireland, their successful reigns are mirrored by bountiful harvests of fruits and vegetables.'

Regina Sexton, *A Little History of Irish Food*, 1998

The Irish are not generally known for their love of vegetables. Growing up, I was not treated to an assortment of wondrously vegetal and fruity foodstuffs. Vegetables were something you ate with meat or fish, not something you considered as things in themselves. But this has changed in the last twenty years. No only are we embracing different vegetables, but we are also trying to cook them with more care. As a nation, we constantly overcooked our vegetables. However, most vegetables need little or no cooking, and it is a great shame to deprive ourselves of the great nutrients that this food contains. It is important to treat vegetables with as much respect as meat or fish. Peeling or cooking a carrot is as complicated as perfectly cooking a steak. All vegetables should be cooked with great care. They should never be just thrown into a pot and boiled until soft. The more time you spend with your vegetables, the nicer they will taste. Memories of my nana cooking cabbage for 45 minutes will haunt me forever. It is almost as if we were afraid of them. Yet, the future is much brighter.

Because of our temperate climate, Ireland has great soil for growing vegetables (this has always been the case, even since the sixth century). The country plays host to so many wonderful small vegetable farms, many of them organic or focusing on heritage varieties of vegetables. This is the future of Irish vegetables, with tradition and diversity playing a part in helping us to create interesting food. Long ago, everyone planted their own vegetables (or at least planted them communally) in small gardens. Interestingly, the first poem in the English language to mention gardening references the 'herbys o yrlonde'. It was entitled 'The Feat of Gardening' (1440–1450) and was written by Master Jon Gardener. This poem is testament to not only the historical nature of gardening in Ireland but also the lyrical appreciation of growing one's own food:

> In the month of April
> Set & sow them everywhere
> Herbs to make both sauce & sew
> Thou shall have them here and there
> Of all the herbys of yrlonde
> Here thou shall know many one
> Pellitory, Dittander, Rue & Sage
> Clary, Thyme, Hyssop and Borage
> Mint, Savory, Town cress & Spinach
> Lettuce, Calamint, Avance & Borage

We still import too many vegetables into Ireland. While it seems logical to import what we cannot grow (such as citrus fruit and many stone fruits, such as lemons and avocados), it strikes me as bizarre that we import potatoes, root vegetables and other vegetables that grow well here. To really capitalize on our beautiful land, we need to focus on our local environment and the bounties it gives us. The root of the local food movement resides in the soil, literally. Wherever you find yourself on this small planet of ours, search out local vegetable growers who focus on organic or heritage varieties of vegetables: these people care about the soil and its future.

Braised Lettuce with Beef and Stout Stock

Preparation: 5 minutes
Cooking: 1 hour 30 minutes
Serves 4

500 g/1 lb 2 oz beef bones
rapeseed (canola) oil
2 onions, halved
a few sprigs of rosemary and thyme
250 ml/8 fl oz (1 cup) stout
1 litre/34 fl oz (4¼ cups) beef stock (broth)
4 baby gem lettuces or other lettuces
   suitable for cooking
sea salt

Preheat the oven to 200°C/400°F/ Gas Mark 6.

Rub the bones with a little rapeseed (canola) oil and place on a baking pan with the onions. Roast in the preheated oven for about 40 minutes until nicely caramelized.

Place the onions and bones in a pan and discard the fat. Cover with the stout and the beef stock (broth) and add the herbs. Simmer for 45 minutes and then strain.

Halve the baby gem. Warm a little oil in a frying pan (skillet) over a medium heat and fry the lettuce until nicely coloured. When you're happy with the colour, add the stock and simmer for a few minutes until softened. Season to taste.

Creamed Spinach with Nutmeg

Preparation: 5 minutes
Cooking: 15 minutes
Serves 4

25 g/1 oz (2 tablespoons) butter
25 g/1 oz (3 tablespoons) plain
   (all-purpose) flour
400 ml/14 fl oz (1⅔ cups) milk
1 bay leaf
100 ml/3½ fl oz (scant ½ cup) double
   (heavy) cream
freshly grated nutmeg, to taste
325 g/11½ oz (12 cups) spinach, washed
   and any tough stems removed
sea salt
ground white pepper

Make a roux by melting the butter in a medium pan over a medium–low heat and whisking in the flour, a little at a time, for about 2 minutes until you have a paste.

In a separate medium pan, warm the milk with the bay leaf.

Pour the milk over the roux and whisk until the sauce is smooth. Add the cream and continue to cook for about 5 minutes until the sauce has thickened. Season with the nutmeg and white pepper and remove the bay leaf.

Bring a pan of salted water to the boil, add the spinach, bring back to the boil and blanch for 1–2 minutes. Remove from the pan and wring the excess water out of the spinach.

Chop the spinach and season with salt.

Add the spinach into the pan with the sauce and heat over a low heat, stirring occasionally, until warm, then serve.

Spinach with Hazelnuts and Wild Garlic

Preparation and cooking: 10 minutes
Serves 4

50 g/2 oz (3½ tablespoons) butter
200 g/7 oz (7 cups) spinach, washed
50 g/2 oz (1 cup) wild garlic (ramps) leaves
50 g/2 oz (½ cup) hazelnuts, roasted
   and crushed
sea salt

Warm the butter in a large frying pan (skillet) over a medium heat.

Remove any tough stems from the spinach, add to the pan and coat with the butter. After a minute or two the spinach will begin to wilt.

Add the wild garlic (ramps) leaves and hazelnuts and cook for a minute until the spinach and garlic leaves are a green colour.

Remove from the heat and season with sea salt.

Vegetables

Steamed Asparagus Wrapped in Sea Lettuce

Preparation and cooking: 5 minutes
Serves 4

16 asparagus spears, trimmed
25 g/1 oz fresh sea lettuce
extra virgin rapeseed (canola) oil
tarragon vinegar (see Herb or Fruit Vinegar,
    page 352), to taste (optional)
sea salt

Most people don't realize that asparagus is a native plant to Ireland, though the wild variety does not quite stand up to the cultivated kind. It takes three years to get the ground ready for asparagus, so it is definitely a labour of love to grow. Drummond House, in County Louth, grow wonderful asparagus. It's a pity the season is so short. However, it's worth waiting for every year, as local asparagus (wherever it is grown in the world) tastes superior to the kind that travels halfway round the world to get to us. The combination of sea lettuce with asparagus works well together. If you can't source fresh sea lettuce, use any dried seaweed sheets. Rehydrate in cold water before using.

Brush the asparagus with oil and wrap it in the sea lettuce. Season with sea salt.

Put the asparagus into a steamer and steam for 2–3 minutes. Remove from the heat and dress with the tarragon vinegar, if using.

See opposite –>

Asparagus with Lemon

Preparation and cooking: 10 minutes
Serves 4

50 g/2 oz (3½ tablespoons) butter
16 asparagus spears, trimmed
juice of 1 lemon
sea salt

Melt the butter in a large pan over a medium heat for about 1 minute until it begins to foam.

Add the asparagus spears and cook for 3–4 minutes, or until the spears turn bright green, then add 3½ tablespoons of water and cook for 1–2 minutes until tender.

Season with lemon juice and salt.

See image on page 165.

Battered Salsify Fried in Beef Dripping

Preparation and cooking: 20 minutes
Serves 4

4 salsify, peeled and quartered
500 g/1 lb (2½ cups) beef dripping
plain (all-purpose) flour, for dusting
sea salt

For the batter
125 g/4½ oz (generous 1 cup) plain
    (all-purpose) flour
¾ teaspoon fast action dried (active dry) yeast
a pinch of sea salt
275 ml/9¾ fl oz (generous 1 cup) ale or lager

To make the batter, combine the flour, yeast, salt and beer in a bowl and whisk until smooth. Set aside.

Bring a large pan of salted water to the boil over a high heat. Add the salsify quarters and cook for about 5 minutes until tender. Remove from the water and pat dry with paper towels.

Heat the beef dripping in a frying pan (skillet) over a medium heat.

Roll the salsify quarters in the flour, dip them in the batter until coated and fry in the beef dripping for 3–4 minutes until golden brown.

Season with salt before serving.

Vegetables

Vegetables

Broad Bean Salad

Preparation: 20 minutes
Cooking: 15 minutes
Serves 4

1 kg/2¼ lb (8 cups) broad (fava) beans,
  in their pods (shells)
100 g/3½ oz streaky (regular) bacon
1 head of butterhead lettuce, broken
  into leaves
3½ tablespoons extra virgin rapeseed
  (canola) oil
5 teaspoons apple cider vinegar
4 sardines, in oil, cut into bite-sized pieces
4 eggs, hard-boiled, shelled and quartered
2 tablespoons chopped parsley
sea salt

A version of this recipe is included in Florence Irwin's *The Cookin' Woman: Irish Country Recipes* (1949). As with peas, broad beans have a long history of use in Irish cooking since the Middle Ages.

Remove the beans from their pods (shells). Bring a large pan of salted water to the boil over a high heat and blanch the beans for about 3 minutes. Refresh in iced water and peel.

Fry the bacon in a frying pan (skillet) over a low heat for a few minutes on each side until crispy. Dry the bacon with paper towels to remove the excess fat, then dice into thin strips.

To serve the salad, put the lettuce leaves into a large salad bowl and dress with the oil, vinegar and sea salt. Arrange the rest of the ingredients on top of the lettuce and garnish with the parsley.

See opposite –>

Charred Courgettes with Pumpkin Seeds

Preparation and cooking: 15 minutes
Serves 4

2 courgettes (zucchini)
rapeseed (canola) oil
tarragon vinegar (see Herb or Fruit Vinegar,
  page 352), or another vinegar of your choice
sea salt

To serve
pumpkin seeds, toasted in a little oil
parsley, chopped

Rub the courgettes (zucchini) all over with oil, then char them with a chef's blowtorch or over the flame of a burner on the hob (stove).

Chop the courgettes into bite-sized pieces.

Season with salt and tarragon vinegar, and garnish with the pumpkin seeds and chopped parsley.

Brussels Sprouts with Smoked Bacon

Preparation: 10 minutes
Cooking: 10 minutes
Serves 4

125 g/4½ oz smoked streaky (regular)
  bacon, finely chopped
450 g/1 lb Brussels sprouts, peeled
  and trimmed
2 tablespoons finely chopped parsley

Put the bacon in a frying pan (skillet) over a medium–high heat and fry for about 5 minutes until crispy.

Bring a medium pan of salted water to a boil, add the sprouts, bring back to a boil and cook for about 5 minutes until tender.

Add the sprouts to the pan with the bacon and toss together.

Garnish with the chopped parsley.

Vegetables

Peas with Butter and Mint

Preparation and cooking: 15 minutes
Serves 4

1 kg/2¼ lb peas, podded (shelled)
1 teaspoon sugar
15 mint leaves, plus extra to garnish (optional)
50 g/2 oz (4 tablespoons) butter
sea salt

Peas (*Pisum sativum*) have been eaten in Ireland since medieval times, especially field peas, which could be dried and preserved, for harsher times. Garden peas are a more recent addition to the Irish diet, arriving possibly in the sixteenth century.

Bring a medium pan of water to the boil over a high heat and blanch the peas with the sugar and mint for about 3 minutes. Strain through a sieve and discard the mint.

Transfer the peas to a serving dish and combine with the butter and salt. Garnish with a few fresh mint leaves if desired.

See opposite –>

Peas and Broad Beans with Sheep's Cheese

Preparation and cooking: 20 minutes
Serves 4

250 g/9 oz (1¾ cups) podded (shelled) peas
250 g/9 oz (1¾ cups) podded (shelled) broad (fava) beans
100 ml/3½ fl oz (scant ½ cup) extra virgin rapeseed (canola) oil
100 ml/3½ fl oz (scant ½ cup) apple balsamic vinegar
100 g/3½ oz semi-hard sheep's cheese (about 6 months old), sliced
herbs and flowers (wild, if possible, such as marigold flowers and bitter cress), to serve
sea salt

Prepare a large bowl half-filled with water and ice cubes.

Bring a medium pan of salted water to the boil, add the peas and broad (fava) beans, bring back to the boil and blanch for 1 minute. Refresh in the ice-cold water and strain.

Season the peas and beans with the oil, vinegar and some salt. Put into a bowl and cover with the cheese slices. Finish with some herbs and flowers.

Broccoli with Hazelnut Sauce

Preparation and cooking: 15 minutes
Serves 4

450 g/1 lb (2 cups prepared) broccoli, cut into nice florets
extra virgin rapeseed (canola) oil, for drizzling
apple cider vinegar, to taste
sea salt

For the hazelnut sauce
150 g/5 oz (1⅓ cups) hazelnuts, toasted
250 ml/8 fl oz (1 cup) extra virgin rapeseed (canola) oil
1 clove garlic, crushed
3 tablespoons apple balsamic vinegar
sea salt

If you can get your hands on baby broccoli (broccolini) or purple sprouting broccoli, use it instead of regular broccoli as it makes a more elegant dish. Standard balsamic vinegar can be used instead of apple balsamic if it is difficult to source.

Put all the ingredients for the hazelnut sauce into a food processor and blend into a rough paste. Season to taste with sea salt and adjust the consistency of the sauce if desired (you can make it looser with a little more oil or water).

Bring a medium pan of salted water to the boil, add the broccoli florets, return to the boil and blanch for 2–3 minutes. Drain and dress with the oil, vinegar and sea salt. If you have a chef's blowtorch, you can use it to give the florets a slight char.

Serve the broccoli florets and hazelnut sauce in two separate bowls.

Vegetables

Cauliflower in Cheese Sauce

Preparation: 5 minutes
Cooking: 35 minutes
Serves 4

1 cauliflower, trimmed of green leaves
   and cut into florets
500 ml/17 fl oz (generous 2 cups) milk
freshly grated nutmeg, to taste
1 bay leaf
50 g/2 oz (3½ tablespoons) butter
50 g/2 oz (⅓ cup) plain (all-purpose) flour
150 g/5 oz (1⅓ cups prepared) good-quality
   farmhouse cheddar cheese, grated
sea salt and freshly ground black pepper

I first tasted cauliflower with cheese sauce when I was a fifteen-year-old chef working in Maynooth College. I can't imagine the sauce was made with an Irish farmhouse cheese, but for me this is now the only way. Still, tasting that cauliflower and cheese back then opened my eyes to a world of gastronomy.

Preheat the oven to 180°C/350°F/ Gas Mark 4. Half-fill a large bowl with water and ice cubes.

Bring a large pan of salted water to the boil, add the cauliflower florets, return to the boil and blanch for 1 minute. Remove the florets from the water and refresh in the ice-cold water.

To make the sauce: put the milk, nutmeg and bay leaf into a medium pan over a medium heat and heat for 3–4 minutes until warm. Meanwhile, in a separate medium pan, make a roux by melting the butter over a medium–low heat and whisking in the flour, a little at a time, for a few minutes until you have a paste.

Add the milk, a ladle at a time, and whisk continuously until you have a thick sauce. Fold 100 g/3½ oz (scant 1 cup) of the cheese into the sauce. Simmer for a few minutes, then season with salt and pepper.

Put the cauliflower florets into an ovenproof dish and cover with the sauce. Sprinkle the rest of the grated cheddar over the sauce.

Bake in the preheated oven for 20 minutes until golden brown. Remove and discard the bay leaf before serving.

See opposite –>

Cauliflower Poached in Milk with Smoked Pork Fat

Preparation and cooking: 20 minutes
Serves 4

1 cauliflower, trimmed of green leaves
750 ml/25 fl oz (3 cups) milk
1 bay leaf
15 g/½ oz (3¾ teaspoons) smoked pork fat
   (it can be saved after cooking smoked
   bacon), melted
sea salt and freshly ground black pepper

Preheat the grill (broiler).

Put the cauliflower, milk and bay leaf into a large pan and cover with a suitable lid. Place over a high heat, bring to the boil, then reduce the heat and simmer for 10 minutes. The cauliflower should still have a bite and be able to stand upright.

Remove the cauliflower from the milk, brush with the melted smoked pork fat and place under the grill (broiler) for a few minutes, or until nicely caramelized. You can also roast the cauliflower in the oven on a medium heat until browned.

Season with salt and pepper, being mindful that the bacon fat will already be salty.

Vegetables

Red Cabbage with Apples, Raisins and Spices

Preparation: 15 minutes
Cooking: 20 minutes
Serves 4

50 g/2 oz (4 tablespoons) butter
1 onion, sliced
1 red cabbage, shredded
1 teaspoon ground allspice
freshly grated nutmeg, to taste
150 ml/5 fl oz (⅔ cup) red wine
3½ tablespoons red wine vinegar
2 tablespoons honey
2 apples, peeled, cored and cut into cubes
75 g/2¾ oz (½ cup) raisins
sea salt and freshly ground black pepper

Melt the butter in a large pan over a medium heat. Add the onion, cabbage, allspice and nutmeg and fry for 5–7 minutes until the onion is soft and translucent.

Add the wine, vinegar and honey and a little water if needed and simmer for 3–5 minutes until the cabbage has softened.

Add the apples and raisins and simmer for a few minutes until the apples are tender.

Season with salt and pepper and remove from the heat.

See opposite –>

Cavolo Nero with Rose Vinegar

Preparation and cooking: 10 minutes
Serves 4

75 g/2¾ oz (5½ tablespoons) butter
200 g/7 oz cavolo nero (lacinato kale), stems trimmed
3 tablespoons Wild Rose Vinegar (see page 352)
sea salt

Cavolo nero (lacinato kale) is a variety of cabbage that grows well in Ireland and has populated Irish menus in the last number of years. For a nice variation with a traditional twist, add freshly grated nutmeg and lemon instead of the rose vinegar. You can also use different types of cabbage (such as savoy or hispi) for some classic buttered greens.

Warm the butter in a large frying pan (skillet) over a medium–low heat until it foams.

Blanch the cavolo nero (lacinato kale) in a large pan of boiling water for a few seconds, then transfer it immediately to the foaming butter. Heat the cabbage briefly until wilted, then add the vinegar.

Season with sea salt and serve.

See image on page 129.

Cabbage with Nutmeg

Preparation: 10 minutes
Cooking: 30 minutes
Serves 4

1 × 1-kg/2¼-lb green pointed (hispi) cabbage
75 g/2¾ oz (5½ tablespoons) butter
120 ml/4 fl oz (½ cup) chicken stock (broth)
120 ml/4 fl oz (½ cup) double (heavy) cream
freshly grated nutmeg, to taste
sea salt and freshly ground black pepper

Remove the outer leaves from the cabbage, trim the stalk and quarter the cabbage.

Bring a large pan of salted water to the boil over a high heat, add the cabbage, return to the boil and cook for 2–3 minutes. Remove the cabbage from the water and pat dry with paper towels.

Melt the butter in a large pan over a medium heat, then add the cabbage quarters and caramelize the cut sides of each quarter.

Add the chicken stock (broth) and cream, bring to the boil and season with nutmeg, salt and pepper. Cook for about 15 minutes until the cabbage is tender. Serve.

Vegetables

Vegetables

Spelt with Leeks

Preparation: 10 minutes
Cooking: 1 hour 5 minutes
Serves 4

50 g/2 oz (4 tablespoons) butter
3 leeks, thinly sliced
leaves of a few sprigs of thyme, chopped
1 bay leaf
350 g/12 oz (2 cups) spelt grains
250 ml/8 fl oz (1 cup) cider (hard cider)
750 ml/25 fl oz (3 cups) vegetable stock (broth)
2 tablespoons chopped parsley
sea salt

Spelt was an important staple in parts of Europe from the Bronze Age to medieval times. It grew well in poor soil, so suited the Irish climate.

Melt half the butter in a large frying pan (skillet) over a medium heat. Fry the leeks with the thyme and bay leaf for about 5 minutes until nice and soft. Add the spelt grains and cook for a minute, then add the cider and bring to the boil.

Add the stock (broth) and simmer for 40 minutes–1 hour until the spelt is cooked and tender. Add a little more water if required.

Remove from the heat and fold in the remaining butter and parsley. Season before serving.

See opposite –>

Leek and Oatmeal Soup

Preparation: 10 minutes
Cooking: 1 hour
Serves 4

50 g/2 oz (3½ tablespoons) butter
8 leeks, sliced
750 ml/25 fl oz (3 cups) chicken stock (broth)
750 ml/25 fl oz (3 cups) milk
50 g/2 oz (⅓ cup) pinhead (steel-cut) oats
100 ml/3½ fl oz (scant ½ cup) double (heavy) cream
chives, finely chopped, to garnish
sea salt

This traditional Irish soup (*brotchán roy*) uses leeks, oats and milk. These three ingredients are central to Irish 'Gaelic' cooking. Some recipes include spices such as mace, nutmeg and black pepper. The inclusion of these ingredients represents a fusion of Irish and outside influences. References to brotchán appear in the ninth-century manuscript *The Monastery of Tallaght*, in which it is described as a meal for the monks.

Melt the butter in a large pan over a low heat and add the leeks. Season with sea salt and cook for about 15 minutes until soft but without adding any colour to the leeks.

In a separate large pan, combine the chicken stock (broth) and milk with the oats. Cook over a low heat – stirring continually to prevent the oats sticking to the pan or forming lumps – for about 45 minutes.

Blend the oat mixture together with an immersion blender and strain through a fine sieve.

Add the cream, then pour the warm oat liquid over the leeks and simmer for 10 minutes.

Pour into bowls and garnish with a sprinkle of chives.

Young Leeks in Seaweed Butter

Preparation: 10 minutes, plus chilling time
Cooking: 5 minutes
Serves 3

5 g/⅛ oz dried sea lettuce
250 g/9 oz (2¼ sticks) butter
dash of apple cider vinegar
6 young leeks
sea salt

To make the butter, rehydrate the sea lettuce briefly in cold water, then squeeze it dry and finely chop. Blend with the butter in a food processor. Wrap the butter in cling film (plastic wrap) and leave to set in the refrigerator (you will make more than you need, so store any leftovers for later use).

Bring a pan of salted water to the boil over a high heat, add a dash of vinegar and poach the leeks whole for about 5 minutes until tender.

Season the leeks with sea salt and serve with the seaweed butter.

Vegetables

Onions Roasted in Pork Fat with Thyme

Preparation and cooking: 25 minutes
Serves 4

50 g/2 oz (⅓ cup) pork fat, melted
4 onions, peeled, topped and tailed (trimmed)
a few sprigs of thyme
sea salt

Warm the pork fat in a large frying pan (skillet). Place the onions in the fat and add the thyme. Turn the onions to coat them in the fat and cook for 5–7 minutes until they are nicely browned all over. Reduce the heat and cover, allowing the onions to cook slowly for a further 15 minutes until cooked through and tender.

Remove from the pan and allow to cool, then season with sea salt and serve.

See opposite –>

Onion Soup with Cider and Cheese

Preparation: 15 minutes
Cooking: 1 hour 55 minutes
Serves 4

100 g/3½ oz (7 tablespoons) butter
10 onions, sliced
a few sprigs of thyme
4 sage leaves
350 ml/12 fl oz (1½ cups) cider (hard cider)
2 litres/70 fl oz (8½ cups) chicken stock (broth)
150 g/5 oz (1⅓ cups prepared) mature cheddar cheese, grated
sea salt

Melt the butter in a large pan over a low heat. When foaming, add the onions, thyme and sage and season with sea salt. Cook the onions for about 40 minutes, stirring occasionally, until nicely browned. Add the cider and cook for about 15 minutes until reduced by half.

Add the chicken stock (broth), reduce the heat to a simmer and cook for 1 hour. Remove the herbs and add more stock or water if required.

Return to the heat to warm gently, divide among four warmed bowls and scatter with the grated cheddar. Stir before serving.

Young Carrots Cooked in Butter

Preparation and cooking: 10 minutes
Serves 4

100 g/3½ oz (7 tablespoons) butter
a bunch of young carrots, unpeeled but trimmed, about 12 in total
parsley, finely chopped, to garnish
sea salt

Put the butter with a little water in a large pan over a medium heat for 2–3 minutes until melted. Add the carrots to the pan and cover. Cook the carrots for 5–7 minutes until they are tender, adding a little water at a time if needed.

Remove the carrots from the pan, season with sea salt and garnish with finely chopped parsley.

Carrots and Ginger

Preparation and cooking: 15 minutes
Serves 6

100 g/3½ oz (7 tablespoons) butter
450 g/1 lb baby carrots, trimmed
250 ml/8 fl oz (1 cup) ginger wine or
  (hard) cider infused with ginger
1 teaspoon grated ginger
1 teaspoon paprika
2 tablespoons honey
50 g/2 oz (2 cups) watercress or chervil,
  to garnish
sea salt

This nineteenth-century recipe reflects the coming together of Gaelic and British colonial concerns. Traditional ingredients such as carrots, honey and butter are combined with paprika and ginger, which would have been imported from the Far East. Much nineteenth-century cooking in Ireland demonstrates a confluence of these two worlds coming together.

Melt half the butter in a large pan over a medium heat, add the carrots, and cook for a few minutes, turning occasionally.

Add the ginger wine, ginger, paprika, honey and a little water. Reduce the heat to a simmer and cook the carrots for 3–4 minutes until softened but still with a bite.

Add the remaining butter to make a nice glaze.

Season with sea salt and garnish with some watercress or chervil.

See opposite –>

Carrots in Chicken Stock with Chives

Preparation and cooking: 10 minutes
Serves 6

6 carrots, chopped into rounds
500 ml/17 fl oz (generous 2 cups)
  chicken stock (broth)
50 g/2 oz (3½ tablespoons) butter, cubed
1 tablespoon finely chopped chives
sea salt

Put the carrots into a medium pan over a medium heat and cover with the chicken stock (broth) and butter. Bring to a simmer and cook for about 5 minutes, until soft.

Season with sea salt and garnish with the chives. Strain if desired.

Baby Carrots with Buttermilk and Tarragon Oil

Preparation and cooking: 10 minutes, plus cooling time
Serves 4

24 baby carrots, trimmed
500 ml/17 fl oz (generous 2 cups) carrot juice
100 ml/3½ fl oz (scant ½ cup) buttermilk
2 tablespoons tarragon oil (see Herb Oil,
  page 351)
sea salt

Put the carrots into a medium pan and cover with the carrot juice. Bring to a simmer over a medium heat and cook for about 5 minutes until tender. Remove from the heat.

Transfer the carrots to a serving dish and season with sea salt.

When the remaining juice has cooled, add the buttermilk. Stir the sauce with the tarragon oil until it splits and serve.

Vegetables

Vegetables

Kohlrabi and Beetroot Salad

Preparation: 10 minutes
Serves 4

2 kohlrabi, grated or julienned
2 beetroot (beets), grated or julienned
50 g/2 oz (2 cups) watercress
1 tablespoon chopped parsley
100 ml/3½ fl oz (scant ½ cup) extra virgin rapeseed (canola) oil
2 tablespoons apple cider vinegar
1 tablespoon honey
fennel fronds, to garnish (optional)
sea salt

Most Irish people I meet have never encountered a kohlrabi before. It sits somewhere between the cabbage and radish family. This recipe is adapted from Florence Irwin's book *The Cookin' Woman: Irish Country Recipes* (1949). I feel kohlrabi is much underused in Irish cooking, considering it grows so well here.

Lightly salt the kohlrabi and beetroot. Combine the salted vegetables with the watercress and parsley in a salad bowl or large platter.

Make a dressing by mixing the oil, vinegar, honey and a pinch of sea salt in a bowl, then pour it over the vegetables and toss together. Garnish with fennel fronds, if using.

See opposite –>

Goat's Curd with Salt-baked Beetroot and Hazelnut Dressing

Preparation: 10 minutes
Cooking: 1 hour
Serves 4

500 g/1 lb 2 oz (2 cups) sea salt
100 g/3½ oz goat's curd
4 beetroot (beets)

For the dressing
3½ tablespoons light rapeseed (canola) oil
3½ tablespoons hazelnut oil
2 tablespoons apple cider vinegar
1 tablespoon honey
sea salt

Beetroot (beets) and goat's cheese are popular in Irish salads. Salt baking is popular with seafood, but I find it works well with vegetables, too. In this recipe, I don't cover the beetroot with salt, which is often done.

Preheat the oven to 160°C/325°F/Gas Mark 3.

To bake the beetroot (beets), make 4 mounds with the salt in a baking dish and place a beetroot on top of each. Bake in the preheated oven for 1 hour, until you can pass a knife through the beetroot.

When they are cool enough to handle, peel and cut into wedges.

Put all the dressing ingredients into a bowl and whisk. Season to taste and adjust as desired.

Dress the beetroot and serve with the goat's curd.

Parsnip and Apple Soup

Preparation: 15 minutes
Cooking: 35 minutes
Serves 4

50 g/2 oz (3½ tablespoons) butter
2 onions, chopped
a few sprigs of rosemary, thyme and sage
1 kg/2¼ lb (about 10) parsnips, chopped
500 g/1 lb 2 oz (about 3) Bramley apples or other cooking apples, peeled, cored and chopped
1.5 litres/50 fl oz (6¼ cups) chicken stock (broth)
250 ml/8 fl oz (1 cup) double (heavy) cream
sea salt

Melt the butter in a large pan over a medium heat, add the onions and herbs, and cook for about 5 minutes until the onions are soft and translucent.

Add the parsnips and apples and season with salt. Cook for 5 minutes, then add the chicken stock (broth). Simmer for 20–25 minutes until the parsnips are soft.

Remove the herb sprigs, then add the cream and blend the soup with an immersion blender until smooth and strain through a sieve.

Return to the heat to warm gently before serving.

Vegetables

Parsnips in Butter

Preparation: 5 minutes
Cooking: 20–25 minutes
Serves 6

6 parsnips, chopped
50 g/2 oz (3½ tablespoons) butter
1 teaspoon sugar
3 sage leaves, torn
sea salt

In the past, butter was used less frequently than it is today for cooking. Pork fat was a common fat for cooking vegetables. If you like, you can use pork fat (lard) instead of butter in this recipe.

Preheat the oven to 200°C/400°F/Gas Mark 6.

Bring a large pan of water to the boil over a high heat, add the parsnips, bring back to the boil and blanch for about 2 minutes. Drain.

Put the parsnips into a roasting pan with the butter, sugar, sage and salt.

Roast in the preheated oven for about 20 minutes, turning them halfway through, until nicely caramelized.

Swede and Smoked Bacon Soup

Preparation: 15 minutes
Cooking: 45 minutes
Serves 4

1 tablespoon rapeseed (canola) oil
100 g/3½ oz smoked bacon, diced
2 onions, diced
2 bay leaves
3 sage leaves, plus extra to garnish
500 g/1 lb 2 oz (3½ cups prepared) swede (rutabaga), diced
250 g/9 oz (1⅔ cups prepared) potatoes, diced
1.5 litres/50 fl oz (6¼ cups) chicken stock (broth)
60 g/2¼ oz (¼ cup) sour cream, to serve
sea salt

The Irish-American community call swede (rutabaga) 'yellow turnip'. It is an important vegetable in Irish cooking all over the world.

Heat the oil in a large pan over a medium heat, add the bacon and fry for about 10 minutes until nicely caramelized.

Add the onions, bay leaves and sage and fry for a few minutes, then add the swede (rutabaga) and potatoes and cook for a further 5 minutes.

Cover with the chicken stock (broth) and simmer for 20–25 minutes until the vegetables are soft.

Blend the soup with an immersion blender until smooth and strain through a fine sieve. Adjust the seasoning and thickness of the soup, adding more stock or water if needed.

Return to the heat to warm gently before serving with sage leaves and some sour cream on top.

See opposite –>

Mashed Swede with Black Pepper

Preparation: 15 minutes
Cooking: 20 minutes
Serves 4

1 large swede (rutabaga), peeled and cubed
2 potatoes, peeled and cubed
100 g/3½ oz (7 tablespoons) butter, cubed
sea salt and freshly ground black pepper

Bring two separate medium-sized pans of salted water to the boil, add the swede to one pan and the potatoes to the other, and cook for about 15 minutes or until tender.

Strain both vegetables into a colander and allow them to sit to remove excess water.

Press them through a potato ricer along with the cubes of butter. Season the mashed vegetables with salt and pepper and serve.

Vegetables

Vegetables

Kohlrabi Roasted in Butter and Hay

Preparation: 10 minutes
Cooking: 45 minutes
Serves 4

100 g/3½ oz (7 tablespoons) butter, cubed
4 kohlrabi, peeled
3 tablespoons apple cider vinegar
a small handful of hay
sea salt

Preheat the oven to 190°C/375°F/Gas Mark 5.

Melt the butter in a large frying pan (skillet) over medium heat. When foaming, add the kohlrabi. Baste for 3–4 minutes in the foaming butter, keeping the butter a warm nutty colour – if needed, reduce the heat to prevent the butter burning or becoming black.

When the kohlrabi is a nice colour, add the vinegar and heat for a few minutes.

Place the hay in the bottom of an oven tray and arrange the kohlrabi in the hay. Roast in the preheated oven for 45 minutes until the kohlrabi are tender, basting them occasionally in the butter and vinegar mixture. Keep this sauce in a warm place.

To serve, carve the kohlrabi. Brush them with a little of the warm butter and vinegar sauce, and season with a little sea salt.

See opposite –>

Jerusalem Artichoke Soup

Preparation: 15 minutes
Cooking: 25 minutes
Serves 4

30 g/1 oz (2½ tablespoons) pork fat or dripping, for frying
2 onions, chopped
15 Jerusalem artichokes (sunchokes), peeled and chopped
2 medium Rooster or Yukon Gold potatoes, peeled and chopped
2 cloves garlic, crushed
2 litres/70 fl oz (8½ cups) chicken stock (broth)
250 ml/8 fl oz (1 cup) double (heavy) cream
sea salt

To serve
2 tablespoons hazelnut oil
25 g/1 oz (¼ cup) hazelnuts, roasted

Soup made from Jerusalem artichokes (sunchokes) appears in many Irish cookbooks. Interestingly, Jerusalem artichokes are not originally from Jerusalem and are not in fact artichokes. They hail from South America and are part of the sunflower family. This soup is often referred to as 'Palestine soup' in old cookbooks. Confit pheasant leg is a nice topping for this soup – you can shred the meat and place it on top of the soup.

Warm the pork fat in a large pot over a medium heat. Add the onions and fry for 3–5 minutes until softened.

Add the Jerusalem artichokes (sunchokes) and potatoes. Season with sea salt and then add the garlic. Cook for 5 minutes until the vegetables have a nice colour.

Add the chicken stock (broth). Everything should be covered – if more liquid is required, top up with a little water. Simmer for about 15 minutes until the potatoes are soft.

Add the cream and adjust the seasoning if needed.

Blend the soup with an immersion blender until smooth, then strain through a fine sieve.

Return to the heat to warm gently, ladle into warmed bowls and drizzle with some hazelnut oil. To finish, grate some hazelnuts over the soup.

Vegetables

Vegetables

Squash and Oyster Mushrooms

Preparation: 10 minutes
Cooking: 25 minutes
Serves 4

2 small pumpkins or butternut squash
rapeseed (canola) oil
a few sprigs of thyme
150 g/5 oz oyster mushrooms, thickly
   sliced and scored
25 g/1 oz (1¾ tablespoons) butter
2 tablespoons finely chopped parsley
edible flowers and fresh herbs such as parsley,
   fennel, sage or thyme, to serve (optional)
sea salt

Preheat the oven to 200°C/400°F/
Gas Mark 6.

Halve the squash horizontally
and scoop out the seeds. In a
roasting pan, coat the squash with
oil, season with salt and add the
thyme. Put into the preheated oven
and roast for about 25 minutes or
until soft.

Meanwhile, heat a little oil in a
frying pan (skillet) over a medium
heat and fry the mushrooms for
about 5 minutes. Add the butter
towards the end of the cooking
time and finish with parsley.

Place the mushrooms in the centre
of each piece of squash. Garnish
with some fresh herbs and serve.

See opposite –>

Celeriac in Brown Butter

Preparation: 10 minutes
Cooking: 50 minutes
Serves 4

rapeseed (canola) oil
1 celeriac (celery root), peeled
150 g/5 oz (1¼ sticks) butter, cubed
a few sprigs of thyme
sea salt

Preheat the oven to 180°C/350°F/
Gas Mark 4.

Heat a little rapeseed (canola) oil in
a flameproof casserole (Dutch oven)
over a medium heat, add the celeriac
(celery root) and cook, turning it
occasionally, for 2–3 minutes until
nicely browned all over.

Reduce the heat and add the butter
and thyme. Allow the butter to

foam, baste the celeriac and cook,
basting occasionally, for 15–20
minutes until it has a nice golden
colour. Add a little water to stop
the butter browning.

Transfer to the preheated oven
and bake for 30 minutes, basting
occasionally.

Remove from the oven, carve the
celeriac, season and serve.

Celeriac with Yellow Chanterelles and Onion Sauce

Preparation: 15 minutes
Cooking: 1 hour 45 minutes
Serves 4

1 celeriac (celery root), cut into 8 wedges
25 g/1 oz (2 tablespoons) butter
50 g/2 oz yellow chanterelles
10 g/¼ oz Pickled Ramsons (see page 356)
a few sprigs of thyme
sea salt

For the onion sauce
6 small onions, sliced
3½ tablespoons rapeseed (canola) oil
500 ml/17 fl oz (generous 2 cups) chicken
   stock (broth)
sea salt

Preheat the oven to 220°C/425°F/
Gas Mark 7.

Toss the onions with the oil in
a baking dish and roast in the
preheated oven for 25–30 minutes
until nicely caramelized. Transfer
the onions to a colander to drain.

Put the onions into a large pan
with the chicken stock (broth) and
simmer over a medium–low heat
for 1 hour. Remove the onions and
simmer the stock over a medium
heat for about 15 minutes until
reduced by half or the consistency
of a loose glaze. Season to taste.

Meanwhile, bring a medium pan
of salted water to the boil, add the
celeriac (celery root) and simmer
for 15 minutes until you can pass a
knife through it. Drain and season
with salt.

Melt the butter in a frying pan
(skillet) over a medium heat and
fry the mushrooms briefly with
some thyme. Season to taste.

To serve, divide the celeriac
between warm bowls, top with the
mushrooms and garnish with some
ramsons (ramps). Finish with the
onion sauce.

Vegetables

Potatoes

What was Irish food like before the advent of the potato? For many, Irish food without the perennial 'spud' (this British word for the potato comes from 'spade') is inconceivable. But for most of the time that people consumed food on this island, there were no potatoes. Each era of Irish food has been marked by different foods, but oats and milk were certainly more widespread before the arrival of the potato.

The potato more than likely came to Ireland in the seventeenth century. The first record of potato farming is from 1606 in County Down, however, it is possible that the potato was planted earlier, in the late 1500s. One seventeenth-century commentator, John Stevens, noted how potatoes with sour milk was the 'chief part' of the diet of the native Irish. Regardless of when it arrived, by the nineteenth century the potato was ubiquitous, providing the staple food of the poor. This situation was not unique to Ireland. The potato contributed to the population boom that occurred in Europe during this time, as for such a small vegetable, it was packed full of vitamins and minerals, and provided much-needed energy.

The ending of diversity in Irish food was not only due to the potato's arrival but also because the native Irish had only restricted access to the land due to colonization by the English. Probably the most notable historical incident associated with the potato is the famine (or the Great Hunger, as it's called by the Irish). You would imagine that following the failure of the potato crop during a number of years in the 1840s, there was no food in Ireland to feed people. Nothing could be further from the truth. There was plenty of food in Ireland. It was just not available to the starving tenement farmers and peasants who had relied solely on the potato to feed themselves. More food was exported out of Ireland during the famine than before it. Masses of corned beef and barley left the island to feed people elsewhere. The potato was therefore a blessing and a curse for the Irish people. A small patch of potatoes could feed a family, but overreliance meant that the failure of the crop contributed to the deaths of a million people and the emigration of as many between 1845 and 1851.

The potato's role as a stereotype of Irish food has obscured other valuable products. However, it has fed many and it will continue to dominate the dinner table in many Irish homes worldwide. As Regina Sexton writes in her *A Little History of Irish Food* (1998), Irish people could communicate using the potato as a vehicle for introduction and invitation. Like most of their generation, my grandparents ate potatoes every day. Luckily, we now have new cooks and chefs cooking the potato in myriad interesting ways. The future is bright for the humble spud.

A Potato Crisp Sandwich

Preparation: 5 minutes
Serves 1

15 g/½ oz (1 tablespoon) butter, room temperature
2 slices of white 'batch' bread (shop-bought, or see page 302) or regular sliced pan
1 individual packet of good-quality potato crisps (chips)

The crisp sandwich was a staple when we were growing up as kids in the 1980s. I think it perfectly encapsulates the Irish infatuation with bread and potatoes. Aer Lingus (the national airline) now sell them on board to assemble yourself. I am told it can only be made with white sliced pan or batch bread so no fancy bread here, please! Supremely comforting, I will always greet a crisp sandwich with great nostalgia.

Spread the butter on both slices of bread. Lay the potato crisps (chips) on top of one slice and cover with the other. Cut in half and serve.

Potatoes Cooked in Seawater

Preparation: 5 minutes
Cooking: 25 minutes
Serves 6

1 kg/2¼ lb (about 10 medium) potatoes
enough seawater to cover the potatoes

To serve
100 g/3½ oz (7 tablespoons) butter, melted
3 tablespoons chopped parsley
coarse (kosher) sea salt

If you want to give the potatoes a salt crust, leave the potatoes in the pan until the water has completely evaporated. Though this technique is popular in the Canary Islands, Portugal and the South of France, it seems to have emerged out of necessity in the west of Ireland.

Put the potatoes into a large pan and cover with seawater. Bring to the boil over a high heat, reduce the heat and simmer for about 20 minutes until the potatoes are soft.

Remove the potatoes from the pan and cut in half. Drizzle with some melted butter, garnish with the parsley and season with a little coarse sea salt.

Making Your Own Chips

Preparation: 10 minutes
Cooking: about 15 minutes per batch
Serves 4

rapeseed (canola) oil, for deep-frying
6 large Rooster or Yukon Gold potatoes, cut into finger-sized lengths
fine sea salt

In Ireland, we seem to have some aversion to deep frying things at home. Yet, we have no problem consuming deep-fried food. Chips (French fries) are the supreme achievement of a complex cooking process. Crispy on the outside, fluffy on the inside – I cannot imagine a greater culinary gift.

Preheat the oil in a deep-fat fryer to 140°C/275°F.

Lower the potatoes into the pre-heated oil with a slotted spoon and blanch, in batches if necessary, for about 10 minutes until soft. You should be able to pass a cocktail stick (toothpick) through the potato. They will be pale. Remove and drain on paper towels. Allow the oil to return to temperature between batches.

Increase the deep-fat fryer temperature to 180°C/340°F.

Return the chips to the oil and fry again, in batches if necessary, for 4–5 minutes until brown and crispy. Remove from the oil and stand in the basket for a moment to let the excess oil drip off.

Tip the chips into a suitable bowl and season liberally with sea salt.

See image on page 157.

Mashed Potatoes

Preparation: 15 minutes
Cooking: 25 minutes
Serves 6

1.2 kg/2 lb 6 oz (about 10 medium) potatoes, peeled and cubed
450 g/1 lb (4 sticks) butter, cubed
sea salt

There is no easy way to say this: the best mash has the most butter! I like to make my mash with a ratio of close to 2:1, that is, two parts potatoes to one part butter. If this seems excessive, then you're obviously not attuned to the subtleties of the beautiful marriage that this combination makes.

Put the potatoes into a large pan of salted water and bring to the boil over a high heat. Reduce the heat and simmer for about 15 minutes until soft. Strain.

Pass the potatoes through a drum sieve with the butter and season.

Note
Make greened potatoes during the summer season by blending a large handful of fresh herbs such as dill, chives, chervil and wild garlic (ramps) with rapeseed (canola) oil and then rippling through the mashed potatoes before serving.

Vegetables

Colcannon

Preparation: 20 minutes
Cooking: 25 minutes
Serves 6

1 kg / 2¼ lb (about 10 medium)
   potatoes, peeled
250 g/9 oz (2¼ sticks) butter,
   room temperature
100 ml/3½ fl oz (scant ½ cup) milk
6 spring onions (scallions), thinly sliced
15 g/½ oz (¼ cup prepared) parsley,
   finely chopped
sea salt

Colcannon is a traditional Irish dish originally made from leftover potatoes combined with cabbage, kale or other greens. The word 'colcannon' possibly derives from the Welsh for 'leek soup' (*cawl cennin*), which also contains potatoes. The dish likely originated from combining leftover potatoes with leeks and water to form a new meal. It receives one of its first modern-day mentions in 1735, when the Welshman William Bulkely dined on a dish called 'Coel Callen' in Dublin and wrote about it in his diary. There are many variations of colcannon, with cabbage, spring onion (scallion) and parsley all playing their part. In her book *Irish Country Recipes* (1937), Florence Irwin describes the making of mashed potatoes with nettles. In coastal areas, seaweeds were folded into potatoes. The dish was the subject of a famous nineteenth-century folk song:

> Did you ever eat colcannon when 'twas made with yellow cream?
> And the kale and pratties blended like the picture in a dream?
> Did you ever take a forkful, and dip it in the lake
> Of the heather-flavoured butter that your mother used to make?
> Oh, you did; yes, you did. So did he and so did I,
> And the more I think about it, sure the more I want to cry.
> Ah, God be with the happy times, when troubles we had not
> And our mothers made colcannon in the little three-legged pot.

Put the potatoes into a large pan and cover with water. Bring to the boil over a high heat, then simmer for about 20 minutes until soft.

When soft, strain and press through a drum sieve with the butter. Season with sea salt.

Meanwhile, bring the milk to the boil in a small pan, add the spring onions and simmer for 4–5 minutes until the onions are tender, then fold into the potatoes.

Check the seasoning and finally fold in the chopped parsley.

See opposite –>

Champ

Preparation: 10 minutes
Cooking: 20 minutes
Serves 6

1.2 kg/2 lb 6 oz (about 10 medium)
   potatoes, peeled
300 g/11 oz (2¾ sticks) butter,
   room temperature
150 ml/5 fl oz (⅔ cup) milk
4 leeks, thinly sliced
25 g/1 oz chives, finely chopped
sea salt

Some may argue that the difference between champ and colcannon is purely semantic. Both are made from potatoes and some type of greens. It may come down to whether cabbage is used, but I have found versions of both that include cabbage. In her *Irish Traditional Cooking* (1995), Darina Allen includes some wonderful variations, including Claragh champ (with peas) and leek and crispy onion champ (made with beef dripping). Cally is a Dublin version of champ made with green onions. Pandy was yet another variation which was often served to children.

Put the potatoes in a large pan and cover with water. Bring to the boil, then reduce the heat and simmer until soft, about 10 minutes. Strain and pass through a drum sieve with half the butter. Season.

Put the other half of the butter in a medium pan over a low– medium heat.

When the butter is foaming, add the leeks and sweat until soft. Add the milk and heat gently.

Fold the leek mixture into the potatoes, ensuring there are no lumps. Check the seasoning and fold in the chopped chives.

Vegetables

Vegetables

Potato Croquettes

Preparation: 30 minutes
Cooking: 20 minutes, plus about 2 minutes
frying per batch
Serves 6

800 g/1¾ lb (about 7 medium)
    potatoes, peeled
30 g/1 oz (2 tablespoons) butter, melted
50 g/2 oz (scant ½ cup prepared)
    cheddar cheese, grated
1 egg, beaten
3½ tablespoons milk
25 g/1 oz (⅓ cup) finely chopped parsley
rapeseed (canola) oil, for deep-frying
sea salt

To coat
150 g/5 oz (1¼ cups) plain (all-purpose) flour
2 eggs, beaten
150 g/5 oz (2 cups) dry breadcrumbs

Steam the potatoes for about 20 minutes until soft. Allow to cool a little, then lightly mash and combine them with the butter, cheese, egg, milk, parsley and salt in a bowl. Chill until cold.

Shape the chilled potato mixture into small balls or logs. The size of these croquettes is up to you.

Heat the oil in a deep-fat fryer to 180°C/350°F or until a cube of bread browns in 30 seconds. Place the flour, eggs and breadcrumbs in three separate bowls.

Coat the croquettes first by rolling them in the flour and shaking off any excess, then dipping them in the beaten eggs and finally rolling them in the breadcrumbs.

Fry in the preheated oil, in batches, for about 2 minutes until golden brown all over, then remove and drain on paper towels. Allow the oil to return to temperature between batches.

Curried Potatoes

Preparation: 20 minutes
Cooking: 25 minutes
Serves 6

25 g/1 oz (1¾ tablespoons) butter
1 onion, diced
1 clove garlic, very finely chopped
2 teaspoons good-quality curry powder
    (or your own spices ground into a powder)
1 bay leaf
250 ml/8 fl oz (1 cup) vegetable stock (broth)
750 g/1 lb 10 oz (about 7 medium) potatoes,
    peeled and diced
250 ml/8 fl oz (1 cup) double (heavy) cream
3 tablespoons chopped coriander (cilantro)
lemon juice, to taste
sea salt and freshly ground pepper

Curry powder arrived in Ireland in the eighteenth or nineteenth century, due to the influence of the British Empire and Irish soldiers stationed in India. Soldiers stationed in garrisons in the west of Ireland often had some curry spice to hand. In my research for this book, I came across a nineteenth-century curry recipe from Westport (County Mayo). Many curry recipes survive and can be found in cookbooks in the early twentieth century. This recipe is based on one that appears in Maura Laverty's *Full & Plenty: Classic Irish Cooking* (1960). I added a little cream and coriander to give it a richer, aromatic taste.

Melt the butter in a large pan over a medium heat. When it starts to foam, add the onion and garlic and fry for about 5 minutes until the onion starts to soften.

Add the curry powder, bay leaf and a little stock (broth). Allow the mixture to simmer for 5 minutes.

Add the potatoes and remaining stock. Cover and allow to simmer over a low heat for about 10 minutes, until the potatoes are tender but not too soft.

Add the cream, bring to the boil and allow to simmer for 5 minutes.

Remove from the heat and add the chopped coriander (cilantro). Season with salt, pepper and lemon juice.

Potato and Kale Soup

Preparation: 15 minutes
Cooking: 40 minutes
Serves 4

75 g/2¾ oz (5½ tablespoons) butter
2 leeks, chopped
freshly grated nutmeg
750 g/1 lb 10 oz (about 7 medium) potatoes,
    peeled and chopped
1.5 litres/50 fl oz (6¼ cups) chicken
    stock (broth)
200 g/7 oz curly kale, stems removed
250 ml/8 fl oz (1 cup) double (heavy) cream
sea salt and white pepper

This soup takes two very common Irish ingredients and marries them with two common spices used in Irish cooking: white pepper and nutmeg. As I have said elsewhere in the book, Irish food of the past few hundred years is an amalgamation of home-grown food stuffs with spices that come from afar. As well as nutmeg, mace was also a popular addition to potato soup. You can leave out the kale if desired and keep in the spices.

Melt the butter in a large pan over a medium heat. Add the leeks and season with freshly grated nutmeg, salt and white pepper. Cover the pan and cook the leeks for about 15 minutes until softened.

Add the potatoes, cover with the stock (broth) and bring to a simmer. Cook for about 15 minutes until the potatoes are soft. Add the kale and cook for 1 minute.

Blend the soup with an immersion blender until smooth.

Add the cream and return to the heat to warm gently. Adjust the seasoning as desired and serve.

Potatoes Roasted in Duck Fat

Preparation: 10 minutes
Cooking: 45 minutes
Serves 6

1 kg/2¼ lb (about 10 medium)
    potatoes, peeled
100 g/3½ oz (½ cup) duck fat
leaves from a few sprigs of thyme
sea salt

In this recipe I use duck fat, but goose fat, pork fat or beef dripping can also be used. All these fats will give a different flavour and I think it's interesting to experiment with different types of fats. Different herbs will also help, such as rosemary or sage. In many recipes, flour is added to make the potatoes extra crispy, however I find this addition unnecessary.

Preheat the oven to 180°C/350°F/ Gas Mark 4.

Put the potatoes into a large pan of salted water and bring to the boil. When the water comes to the boil, strain the potatoes.

Melt the fat in a large flameproof, ovenproof dish with the thyme.

When the fat is hot, place the potatoes in the fat and ensure they get an even coating. Season with sea salt.

Roast in the preheated oven for 30–40 minutes until soft in the middle, turning them every 5–10 minutes to help them brown evenly.

Potatoes with Mint and Parsley

Preparation: 5 minutes
Cooking: 20 minutes
Serves 6

1 kg/2¼ lb new potatoes
100 g/3½ oz (7 tablespoons) butter, cubed
a handful of mint and parsley, finely chopped
sea salt

Bring a large pan of salted water to the boil, add the potatoes and simmer for about 15 minutes until soft. Strain and return to the pan.

Add the butter to the pan and cover until melted.

At the last minute add the herbs and serve.

See image on page 237.

Potato Gratin with Cheddar

Preparation: 20 minutes, plus 30 minutes
infusing time
Cooking: 50 minutes
Serves 6

400 ml/14 fl oz (1⅔ cups) milk
400 ml/14 fl oz (1⅔ cups) double
 (heavy) cream
2 cloves garlic
1 bay leaf
freshly grated nutmeg
8 black peppercorns
50 g/2 oz (3½ tablespoons) butter
1 kg/2¼ lb waxy potatoes, peeled and sliced
250 g/9 oz (2¼ cups prepared) Irish
 farmhouse cheddar cheese, grated
sea salt

Put the milk and cream into a pan with the garlic, bay leaf, nutmeg and black peppercorns. Bring to the boil. Remove from the heat and allow to infuse for about 30 minutes. Strain through a fine sieve.

Meanwhile, preheat the oven to 180°C/350°F/Gas Mark 4. Grease the base and sides of an ovenproof dish with the butter.

Layer the potatoes in the prepared dish with half the cheese and a little salt. Pour the cream and milk mixture over the potatoes and finish with the rest of the cheese.

Bake in the preheated oven for 45 minutes.

See opposite –>

Coddled Potatoes

Preparation: 15 minutes
Cooking: 25 minutes
Serves 4

100 g/3½ oz bacon, diced
2 onions, sliced
450 g/1 lb (about 8 small) potatoes, peeled
500 ml/17 fl oz (generous 2 cups)
 pork stock (broth)
2 tablespoons chopped parsley
sea salt and freshly ground black pepper

Fry the bacon in a large frying pan (skillet) over a medium heat. Once the fat has melted from the bacon, add the onions. Cook for 5–10 minutes until the bacon is nice and crisp and the onions begin to colour.

Add the potatoes and fry for a minute, then add the stock (broth). Simmer for about 15 minutes until the potatoes are tender.

Add the chopped parsley, remove from the heat and season to taste with salt and pepper.

Potatoes with Milk and Herring

Preparation: 10 minutes
Cooking: 30 minutes
Serves 4

6 potatoes, peeled
1 litre/34 fl oz (4¼ cups) milk
1 bay leaf
4 herring fillets
sea salt
2 tablespoons chopped parsley, to garnish

In the eighteenth century, the English agronomist Arthur Young observed in *A Tour in Ireland* that, 'the food of the poor is potatoes, milk and herring'. This recipe evokes the austerity of peasant food of the period.

Put the potatoes, milk and bay leaf into a large pan over a medium heat, bring to a simmer and cook for about 20 minutes until the potatoes are soft. Remove the potatoes from the milk and set aside in a warm place.

Poach the herring fillets in the milk for 2–3 minutes until cooked.

Return the potatoes to the milk to warm them. Remove and discard the bay leaf.

Place the potatoes and herring on a plate and pour enough milk over them to keep them moist. Season to taste and garnish with the parsley.

Hasselback Potatoes with Smoked Bacon and Beer

Preparation: 20 minutes
Cooking: 45 minutes
Serves 6

1 kg/2¼ lb (about 20 small) potatoes, peeled
250 g/9 oz smoked streaky (regular)
  bacon rashers (slices), or enough to wrap
  the potatoes
120 ml/4 fl oz (½ cup) beer
sea salt

Preheat the oven to 180°C/350°F/ Gas Mark 4.

Make as many slices into each potato as you can without cutting all the way through. Wrap each potato in bacon and place in a roasting pan.

Pour the beer over the potatoes and season with a little salt (not too much as the bacon is already salted). Roast in the preheated oven for 45 minutes or until the potatoes are tender.

See opposite –>

Boxty

Preparation: 20 minutes
Cooking: 20 minutes, plus 10 minutes
per batch
Serves 4

300 g/11 oz (about 3 medium) potatoes,
  peeled and cubed
300 g/11 oz (about 3 medium) potatoes,
  peeled and grated
250 ml/8 fl oz (1 cup) buttermilk
1 teaspoon sea salt
250 g/9 oz (2 cups) plain (all-purpose)
  flour, sifted
1 teaspoon baking powder
butter, for frying

The traditional Irish potato pancake known as boxty is associated with many different parts of Ireland, though the north-west seems to lay most claim to it. Longford and Leitrim play a major part in the story of boxty, but many other counties also have the tradition. The most common way of making boxty consisted of combining grated raw potato and mashed potato with flour and frying it. Later recipes added bicarbonate of soda (baking soda) to help it rise and buttermilk for moisture. Often an egg is added for texture. Nowadays, the mixture is fried in a pan, but in the past it would have been cooked directly on the hotplate of a range. As with colcannon and champ, there is no set way of making boxty and it depends on the equipment one has to hand: pan boxty, boiled boxty, griddle boxty and loaf boxty are some regional variations.

Put the cubed potatoes in a medium pan of salted water, bring to the boil and cook for about 15 minutes until soft. Strain and mash.

Lightly salt the grated potatoes and squeeze them in your hands to remove the excess starch. Combine both potatoes with the buttermilk and salt in a large bowl.

Add the flour and baking powder and mix thoroughly.

Heat a little butter in a frying pan (skillet) over a medium heat and spoon in the mixture in the shape of small pancakes. Cook the pancakes in batches for about 5 minutes each until nicely browned, turn over and cook a further 5 minutes until the other side is browned.

Vegetables

Vegetables

Potato Farls

Preparation: 20 minutes
Cooking: 30 minutes
Serves 4

500 g/1 lb 2 oz (about 4 medium) potatoes,
    peeled and cut into halves or quarters,
    depending on their size
100 g/3½ oz (1 cup) rye flour, plus a little
    extra for rolling
1 teaspoon bicarbonate of soda (baking soda)
50 g/2 oz (½ cup) rolled oats
3½ tablespoons milk
50 g/2 oz (4 tablespoons) butter, softened,
    plus a little extra for frying
sea salt

To serve
25 g/1 oz (1¾ tablespoons) butter
100 g/3½ oz black pudding (blood sausage),
    sliced and grilled (broiled) until crispy
    (optional)

Part bread, part potato, potato farls (or fadge) were traditionally served as part of an 'Ulster' breakfast of eggs, bacon and black pudding (blood sausage). The word 'farl' comes from the Scots Gaelic word 'fardel', meaning 'fourth'. The bread was scored into four before frying to make it easier to share. Before the advent of white flour and bread soda, farls were made with oats and butter.

Put the potatoes into a pan of salted water over a high heat, bring to the boil and simmer for about 10 minutes until the potatoes are tender. Don't allow the potatoes to become mushy as they will absorb too much water. Drain the potatoes and leave to dry out for a few minutes before pressing them through a drum sieve.

Sift the rye flour with the bicarbonate of soda (baking soda) and add to the potatoes. Add the rolled oats and milk and season with sea salt. Knead the dough until it comes together, adding a little more flour if necessary.

Divide the dough into two halves. Traditionally, each half is shaped into one large round, rolled into a flat circular shape and cut into four, but you can also divide and shape the dough into individual patties.

Heat a little of the butter in a heavy-based frying pan (skillet). Fry the individual patties or all four quarters of the one large round for about 3 minutes on both sides until nicely browned.

Serve with some butter and black pudding (blood sausage), if using.

See opposite –>

Potato Cakes

Preparation: 10 minutes
Cooking: about 10 minutes per batch
Makes 10–12 cakes

450 g/1 lb (4 medium) potatoes, cooked
    and mashed
75 g/2¾ oz (scant ⅔ cup) self-raising flour
    (all-purpose flour mixed with ½ teaspoon
    baking powder), sifted, plus extra for
    dusting (optional)
1 egg, beaten
25 g/1 oz (1¾ tablespoons) butter, melted
rapeseed (canola) oil, for frying
sea salt

Potato cakes are usually made with leftover mashed potato. Though there are plenty of variations and many regional recipes, they are always made up of potatoes, flour, butter and egg. Many recipes include spring onions (scallions) and nutmeg, but these can be left out. In some recipes, spices or herbs such as parsley or caraway seeds are added. Potato cakes were often served at breakfast time instead of bread. This is not surprising considering the difficulty with growing wheat in Ireland. Potato bread, as potato cakes were often called, served as a substitute. As well as going well with The Full Irish breakfast (see page 246), they also pair well with smoked fish such as mackerel, eel and salmon, along with sour cream.

In a large mixing bowl, combine the potatoes, flour and a pinch of sea salt. Add enough of the egg and butter to form a firm dough.

Shape into 10–12 potato cakes either with your hands or by rolling the mixture out with a little additional flour.

Warm some oil in a large frying pan (skillet) over a medium–low heat and fry the cakes, in batches if necessary, for about 5 minutes until nicely browned, then turn over and fry the other side for a further 5 minutes until nicely browned.

Note
Regional variations of potato cakes include bacon, oats and apples. Add seaweed to the cakes to give them a nice coastal flavour. I like to add dried milled dillisk (dulse) to mine.

Vegetables

Vegetables

Seaweed, Wild Plants and Fungi

'There are several hundred edible plants and fruits and fungi growing wild in these islands. [...] The last century and a half has brought about a remarkable change in eating habits, the decrease in the use of wild harvest being one significant aspect.'

Cyril and Kit Ó Céirín, *Wild and Free: Cooking from Nature*, 1978

Ireland has a wonderful tradition of using wild food, despite it being somewhat of an undercurrent to the main tradition of meat and vegetables. It is difficult to assess clearly why wild food suffered so much in Irish history, though we could argue that fish and shellfish have experienced a similar fate until recently. From talking to foragers and seaweed pickers whose families have been picking the stuff for generations, many cite the famine as a defining schism in our understanding of wild food. If you could not afford to buy or grow your food, you were forced to go and search for food in the wild. This type of thinking created a negative connotation around the procurement of food from the wild. The stigma of picking your own wild food (whether seaweed, herbs or mushrooms) has persisted, though this is not only the case in Ireland. It seems the more developed and wealthy different areas of the world have become, the more their interest in and value of wild food has diminished accordingly. I think we are now at least four or five generations removed from the experience of wild food. Of course, in recent years, wild food has returned to the foreground, undoubtedly spurred on by the revolution in Nordic food. Wild food is an integral part of what I consider Irish food to be in terms of its past and present. It marks it out as different and allows me to engage with the specific terroir of my local landscape. Wild food cuts through the homogenization of much contemporary processed food. Let us hope its future is bright.

Seaweed Salsa

Preparation: 10 minutes
Serves 4

10 g/¼ oz fresh sea lettuce, diced
10 g/¼ oz fresh dillisk (dulse), diced
5 g/⅛ oz fresh nori, diced
extra virgin rapeseed (canola) oil
Seaweed Vinegar (see page 352)
sea salt

This salsa can be used as a condiment for fish and vegetables. I particularly love it over a freshly opened sea urchin or some raw scallops. It also goes well with poached white fish, such as cod, monkfish or ling. In terms of vegetables, try it with freshly grilled asparagus or even over some new season boiled potatoes.

Mix the seaweeds together in a suitable bowl.

Season to taste with the oil, vinegar and salt. Use immediately.

Peasant's Jelly

Preparation: 5 minutes
Cooking: 25 minutes, plus setting time
Serves 4

100 g/3½ oz fresh carrageen moss

Adapted from *The Cookin' Woman: Irish Country Recipes* (1949). The lady who gave Florence Irwin the recipe said she 'gave it [the seaweed] a good boil'. It goes well with wild game or poached chicken.

Put the carrageen moss into a medium pan and cover with water. Bring to the boil over a medium heat and simmer for 15–20 minutes until soft.

Strain, place the liquid in bowls or cups and refrigerate until set. This will keep for a few days in the refrigerator.

Sloke

Preparation: 5 minutes
Cooking: 1 hour
Serves 4

200 g/7 oz fresh nori or 35 g/1¼ oz dried
   (if using dried, rehydrate in cold water for
   30 minutes)
100 ml/3½ fl oz (scant ½ cup) double
   (heavy) cream
100 g/3½ oz (7 tablespoons) butter
lemon juice, to taste
sea salt and freshly ground black pepper

Sloke is another name for nori. You can get it straight off the rocks during May and September. In her book, *The Cookin' Woman: Irish Country Recipes* (1949), Florence Irwin includes two recipes for sloke, one from County Down and the other from County Donegal. She recommends the sloke be eaten with oat cakes, fried bacon or with a dinner of mutton and potatoes. Sloke is also used to make Laverbread (see page 272).

Put the nori into a medium pan, cover with water and simmer for about 1 hour until the mixture is a soft pulp.

Put the cream into a small pan over a medium–low heat and bring to the boil. Fold the cream and butter into the seaweed. Season with salt and pepper and lemon juice and serve.

Wild Garlic and Hazelnut Pesto

Preparation: 15 minutes
Makes about 575 g/1¼ lb (2 cups)

150 g/5 oz (1⅓ cups) wild garlic (ramps)
300 ml/10 fl oz (1¼ cups) extra virgin
   rapeseed (canola) oil
75 g/2¾ oz (⅔ cup) hazelnuts, toasted
75 g/2¾ oz (¾ cup prepared) good-quality
   farmhouse cheddar cheese, cubed
apple cider vinegar, to taste
sea salt

This pesto is delicious served with rib-eye steak.

Put the wild garlic (ramps) and oil into a food processor. Blend roughly and then add the hazelnuts and cheese. Blend again until smooth.

Season with vinegar and sea salt. Pour into a suitable container and cover with oil until ready to use. Store in the refrigerator for up to 1 month. The pesto also freezes well for up to a year.

Nettle Purée

Preparation: 10 minutes
Cooking: 10 minutes
Serves 6

25 g/1 oz (2 tablespoons) butter
1 onion, diced
250 g/9 oz stinging nettle tips
tarragon vinegar (see Herb or Fruit Vinegar,
   page 352), to taste (optional)
sea salt

Nettles should be picked before the end of May because once they seed, they become coarse and are not good for your stomach. I like to stir this through porridge (see page 43) or use it as a sauce for white fish. Nettles also pair well with soft fresh cheese, such as curd. Try the purée with fresh goat's curd and caramelized oats.

Heat the butter in a medium pan over a medium heat and fry the onion until soft and translucent, about 5 minutes. Add the nettle tips and cook briefly until they wilt. Do not overcook as your purée will lose its vibrant colour.

Transfer to a food processor, blend (adding a little water if needed), then pass through a fine sieve.

Season to taste with salt and tarragon vinegar, if using (I usually hold back on seasoning with vinegar until the last moment as it tends to discolour the purée).

If you want to thicken your purée, hang it in a muslin cloth (cheesecloth) overnight.

Vegetables

Nettle Soup

Preparation: 20 minutes
Cooking: 30 minutes
Serves 4

100 g/3½ oz (7 tablespoons) butter
2 onions, diced
1 leek, chopped
a few sprigs of thyme and rosemary
200 g/7 oz (1 large) potato, diced
1 litre/34 fl oz (4¼ cups) vegetable
  stock (broth)
200 g/7 oz stinging nettles, washed,
  leaves picked
100 g/3½ oz (3½ cups) spinach, washed
25 g/1 oz wild garlic (ramps), optional
25 g/1 oz sea beet (optional)
100 ml/3½ fl oz (scant ½ cup) double
  (heavy) cream
sea salt

When I was young, I never knew you could eat nettles. Then I found a book called *Wild and Free*. It was published the year I was born: 1978. It detailed how the Irish people of the early Christian era enjoyed a nettle broth for sustenance. Indeed, nettles have been eaten in Ireland since the Bronze Age. Of course, this was long before the potato came to Ireland, so oats were used to thicken the soup. It was probably more of a gruel, a rough pottage, made simply from butter, oats, milk and nettles. Wild leeks and wild garlic (ramps) would also have been used. Most nettle soup nowadays is thickened with potato instead of oats. I find the addition of spinach leaves or wild sea beet helps the flavour of the soup because nettles can be quite astringent. Chopped bacon can be added for those who want to add substance to the dish.

Melt the butter in a large pan over a medium heat. When it starts to foam, add the diced onions and chopped leek. Season with a little sea salt. Add the thyme and rosemary. Cook for about 5–7 minutes until translucent.

Add the chopped potato. Fry for a further minute, then add the vegetable stock (broth). Bring to the boil and simmer for about 15 minutes until the potato is soft.

Add the nettles, spinach, wild garlic and sea beet (if using). Simmer for a minute and then blend with an immersion blender until smooth. Press through a fine sieve.

Add the cream and return to the heat until warm. Season to taste.

See opposite –>

Sea Kale with Hollandaise

Preparation: 5 minutes
Cooking: 10 minutes
Serves 4

25 g/1 oz (1¾ tablespoons) butter
150 g/5 oz sea kale, stems removed
sea salt

For the hollandaise sauce
300 g/11 oz (2¾ sticks) butter
4 egg yolks
1 tablespoon lemon juice
sea salt

The late Myrtle Allen (the grandmother of Irish cuisine) also had a version of this dish, served on soda bread. Sea kale is a type of cabbage that grows in sandy coastal areas around Ireland. Many country houses had sea kale in their gardens due to the difficulty in finding it. Darina Allen (Myrtle's daughter-in-law) grows sea kale in her walled garden at Ballymaloe House in County Cork.

To make the hollandaise sauce, first clarify the butter by heating it in a medium pan over a low heat for 3–5 minutes until melted and straining out the milk solids through a fine sieve lined with muslin (cheesecloth).

Place the eggs yolks and lemon juice in a heatproof bowl over a pan of simmering water. Add a spoonful of water and whisk.

Gradually add the clarified butter, whisking continuously, until an emulsion forms. Season to taste. If the sauce is too thick, thin it with a little warm water.

Heat the butter in a large frying pan (skillet) over a medium heat, add the sea kale and heat for a few minutes until wilted, adding a little water to soften. Season with sea salt and serve with the hollandaise sauce.

Vegetables

Vegetables

Sorrel Salad with Pickled Oyster Mushrooms

Preparation and cooking time: 10 minutes, plus cooling time
Serves 4

250 ml/8 fl oz (1 cup) malt vinegar
3½ tablespoons apple balsamic vinegar
75 g/2¾ oz (⅓ cup) caster (superfine) sugar
1 teaspoon juniper berries
250 g/9 oz (4 cups prepared) oyster mushrooms, sliced
350 g/12 oz (14 cups) mixed sorrel leaves (greens)
extra virgin rapeseed (canola) oil, to taste
sea salt

This salad is best made with a mixture of sorrel leaves (greens), such as sorrel, sheep's sorrel and wood sorrel.

To pickle the mushrooms, put the vinegars, sugar, 3½ tablespoons of water and the juniper into a large pan over a high heat and bring to the boil. Add the mushrooms and return to the boil. Remove from the heat and allow to cool.

To make the salad, dress the sorrel leaves with salt and oil. Put the leaves into a salad bowl and place the pickled mushrooms in the centre. Season the mushrooms with a little salt if desired.

Wild Mushroom Barley

Preparation: 10 minutes
Cooking: 35 minutes
Serves 2

2 tablespoons olive oil
2 shallots, finely chopped
2 cloves garlic, very finely chopped
150 g/5 oz mixed wild mushrooms
200 g/7 oz (1 cup) barley
100 ml/3½ fl oz (scant ½ cup) cider (hard cider)
450 ml/15 fl oz (scant 2 cups) vegetable stock (broth)
50 g/2 oz (4 tablespoons) butter, cubed
a handful of chervil, chopped

This is made in the same manner as risotto, by slowly incorporating one ladle of stock at a time.

Heat the oil in a medium pan over a medium heat and fry the shallots and garlic for about 2 minutes until soft. Add the mushrooms and fry for 3 minutes, then add the barley and cook for 1 minute, ensuring the barley is evenly coated.

Pour in the cider and bring to the boil. Add the vegetable stock (broth), gradually one ladle at a time, stirring continuously until it all has been absorbed and the barley is tender, about 25 minutes.

Add the butter cubes to the barley and stir until emulsified. Fold in the chopped chervil and spoon the barley onto warmed plates.

Yellow Chanterelles in Duck Fat and Thyme

Preparation: 5 minutes
Cooking: 6 minutes
Serves 4

25 g/1 oz (¼ cup) duck fat, melted
25 g/1 oz (1¾ tablespoons) butter
300 g/11 oz yellow chanterelles, halved or quartered
a few sprigs of thyme
sea salt

All mushrooms work well with duck fat and woody herbs such as rosemary and thyme. Some of my favourites include chanterelles, ceps, oyster and hedgehog mushrooms. The aroma that emanates from freshly cooked mushrooms when fried in duck fat and thyme is heavenly.

Heat the duck fat and butter in a medium pan over a medium heat. When hot, add the mushrooms and thyme and fry for about 5 minutes until the mushrooms have softened.

Season with some sea salt. Strain lightly with a sieve to remove the excess fat.

Cep and Hazelnut Salad with Sheep's Cheese

Preparation: 10 minutes
Serves 4

300 g/11 oz fresh ceps (porcini)
100 ml/3½ fl oz (scant ½ cup) extra virgin
   rapeseed (canola) oil
2 tablespoons apple balsamic vinegar
100 g/3½ oz hard sheep's cheese, grated
50 g/2 oz (½ cup) hazelnuts, roasted
   and crushed
a small handful of chervil, leaves picked nicely
sea salt

Ceps and hazelnuts go together like tomato and basil. Though the Italians would like to lay claim to the combination, both ceps and hazelnuts have grown together in Ireland for centuries.

Slice the ceps (porcini) very thinly and arrange them in a circular shape on each of the plates.

Mix the oil and vinegar together and season with sea salt. Dress the ceps with the vinaigrette and season with more salt if needed.

Scatter the cheese and hazelnuts over the mushrooms. Garnish with the chervil and serve immediately.

Wild Mushroom Soup

Preparation: 10 minutes
Cooking: 25 minutes
Serves 4

75 g/2¾ oz (5½ tablespoons) butter
2 onions, diced
750 g/1 lb 10 oz wild mushrooms
150 ml/5 fl oz (⅔ cup) mead (or a dry white
   wine if not available)
1 litre/34 fl oz (4¼ cups) vegetable
   stock (broth)
150 ml/5 fl oz (⅔ cup) double (heavy) cream
sea salt

This soup dates back to the time of the Vikings, who brought their love of all things wild (in terms of food!) to Ireland. If you want to make this soup and don't have wild mushrooms to hand, you can substitute them with button mushrooms or a mixture of different cultivated exotic mushrooms.

Heat the butter in a large pan over a medium heat. When foaming, add the onions and mushrooms and cook for 5 minutes until the onions begin to soften.

Add the mead to the pan and cook off the alcohol. Add the stock (broth), bring to the boil and simmer for 15 minutes.

Add the cream and blend with an immersion blender. Season to taste and return to the heat to warm gently before serving.

Mushroom and Sherry Broth

Preparation: 10 minutes
Cooking: 1 hour 10 minutes
Serves 4

2 tablespoons rapeseed (canola) oil
500 g/1 lb 2 oz mixed mushrooms
1 onion, diced
2 celery stalks, diced
2 cloves garlic, crushed
a few sprigs of thyme and rosemary
1 bay leaf
75 ml/2½ fl oz (⅓ cup) dry sherry
a small handful of parsley
sea salt

Heat the oil in a frying pan (skillet) over a medium heat. When hot, add the mushrooms, onion, celery, garlic, thyme, rosemary and bay. Cover the pan and cook for 5 minutes until the onion is soft.

Add the sherry and bring to the boil. Cover everything with water and simmer for 1 hour. Remove from the heat and add the parsley.

Allow to cool, then strain. Discard the solids. Warm before serving.

Vegetables

Wild Mushroom and Walnut Tart

Preparation: 30 minutes, plus 1 hour chilling time
Cooking: 50 minutes
Serves 8

For the pastry
225 g/8 oz (1¾ cups) plain (all-purpose) flour, sifted, plus extra for dusting
125 g/4½ oz (1 stick plus 1 tablespoon) butter, cubed, plus extra for greasing
25 g/1 oz (¼ cup) walnuts, toasted and blended into a fine powder
½ teaspoon sea salt
1 egg yolk

For the filling
1 tablespoon rapeseed (canola) oil
1 onion, finely diced
2 cloves garlic, very finely chopped
400 g/14 oz yellow chanterelles, big ones halved
300 ml/10 fl oz (1¼ cups) double (heavy) cream
4 eggs, whisked
1 teaspoon thyme, finely chopped
sea salt

This tart can be made with different wild mushrooms. However, I find the smaller varieties work better.

To make the pastry, rub the flour and butter together in a mixing bowl until they form a crumb. Add the walnut powder, salt and egg yolk and enough chilled water to make a stiff dough. When the dough comes together, wrap in cling film (plastic wrap) and refrigerate for 1 hour.

Preheat the oven to 170°C/340°F/ Gas Mark 3½. Grease a 30-cm/ 12-inch-diameter fluted tart pan and line with the pastry.

Dust a work surface with some flour and roll out the pastry in a circle large enough to line the pan. Line the pan with the pastry, then line the pastry with baking (parchment) paper and fill with baking beans (pie weights) or dried beans.

Blind bake in the preheated oven for 10–15 minutes, then remove the paper and weights.

For the filling, heat the oil in a medium pan over a medium heat, add the onion and garlic and fry for about 5 minutes until soft. Add the mushrooms and season with sea salt, then cook for about 5–10 minutes until soft.

Add the mushroom filling to the tart case (shell). Whisk the cream, eggs and thyme together and pour over the mushrooms.

Return to the oven and bake for 25 minutes or until set.

See opposite –>

Wild Mushroom Purée

Preparation: 15 minutes
Cooking: 25 minutes
Serves 4

1 tablespoon rapeseed (canola) oil
1 onion, chopped
1 clove garlic, very finely chopped
250 g/9 oz wild mushrooms
a sprig of thyme
150 ml/5 fl oz (⅔ cup) chicken stock (broth)
100 g/3½ oz (scant ½ cup) sour cream
sea salt

I like to make this with ceps (porcini) or king oyster mushrooms, but you can use any large meaty mushroom. It goes extremely well with pork, especially pork chops or pork belly.

Heat the oil in a frying pan (skillet) over a medium heat. When hot, add the onion and garlic and fry for about 5 minutes until soft. Season with a little salt, add the mushrooms and thyme and cook for a further 5 minutes until the mushrooms are soft.

Add the chicken stock (broth) and bring to the boil. Reduce the heat to a simmer and cook for about 15 minutes until the liquid has reduced a little.

Remove the mushrooms from the heat and blend into a smooth purée in a food processor. Press it through a fine sieve if desired.

Fold in the sour cream and season to taste.

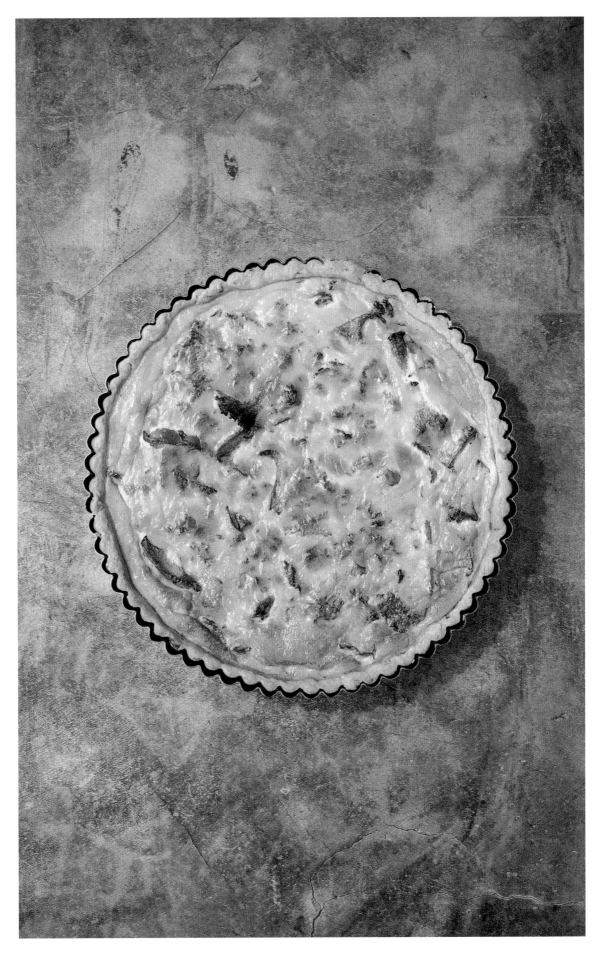

Vegetables

Shellfish

Shellfish

'In these days, when attention has been so directed towards the cultivation of the common kinds of eatable shellfish, it is surprising that the importance of certain others for food has been hitherto almost entirely overlooked. We understand the good qualities of oysters, cockles and a few other kinds, [...] but some equally as nutritious (which are universally eaten on the Continent) are seldom, if ever, seen in our markets, or are only used locally as food, and the proper modes of cooking them are scarcely known.'

M.S. Lovell, *The Edible Mollusca of Great Britain and Ireland*, 1867

Shellfish, since ancient times, has held a central place in Irish food culture. It was a vital food for the earliest inhabitants of Ireland. We can well imagine the first hunter-gatherers who arrived more than 10,000 years ago feasting from the rich resources that the seas had to offer. Cracking open oysters and urchins and cooking mussels on the fire are some of the images that come to my mind. Many midden beds contain the shells of mussels, oysters, scallops and other shellfish, proving they offered nutriment for the first peoples of Ireland.

Those settling along the coast had access to vast amounts of wild shellfish. Filled with a rich meaty and saline protein, oysters were a superfood for people on the go. Many of these midden beds display evidence of the vast quantity of oysters eaten. Combined with seaweed, they provided a nutritious meal for the hunter-gatherer. The native oyster, which has been at home in Ireland for many thousands of years, is still consumed today and exported all over the world. I love to eat this oyster as naturally as possible, just adding a little sea lettuce for taste, texture and colour, and some extra virgin rapeseed (canola) oil. Oysters were not only eaten raw in ancient times. Smoking oysters in hay, as other fish and shellfish, dates back to Neolithic times. As well as augmenting the taste of the oyster, it helped preserve the shellfish.

I don't know if anyone eats limpets (*bairneachs*) now. Traditionally, they were a food for the poor. They would be hacked off the rocks with a special chisel (*eisitean*) and cooked in water, or formed the base for a broth or soup. Darina Allen includes a recipe in her book *Irish Traditional Cooking* (1995) for Limpet soup from County Kerry. And in his book, M.S. Lovell also provides a recipe for limpet soup. Interestingly, the latter author says to remove the seaweed attached to the limpets. However, Darina Allen reports that the people of Cape Clear would leave the seaweed attached to the limpets. Limpets were probably also boiled in seawater and eaten straight up as they are in other European countries. Perhaps it is our proximity to the sea that makes us turn away from it, or maybe farming offered more security.

As with fish, we have a mixed relationship with shellfish. Much of what we land is exported – indeed, several fisheries only export their shellfish. Except for those in small pockets along coastal towns, many people express an aversion to seafood. Of course, we do have festivals that celebrate the oyster and other shellfish, but outside these occasions, many turned to the land instead. Why it this so? I suppose we could blame everyone except ourselves – the lack of fishing boats and good ports, the EU with their quotas, the British colonization of Ireland – but in truth, until we fall in love with shellfish, it will continue to be exported in vast numbers. We, as a people, need to learn to love our own shellfish.

Saying that, every Irish cookbook produced in the last hundred years (and even earlier) contains recipes for shellfish, from oysters to mussels, and clams to lobster. The oldest oyster recipes I came across date from the eighteenth century. They were pickled or fried in beef dripping. The recipes in this section showcase the diversity of our relationship to shellfish: raw, cooked, deep-fried and pickled. There is very little we don't do with shellfish. Looking forward to the future, I'd love to see Irish shellfish finally achieve its central place in the canon of Irish cuisine. Given its central role in New Nordic cuisine, maybe young Irish chefs will begin to showcase more fish and shellfish on their menus.

Oysters

Every September we have festivals that celebrate the native oyster. They are only available from September to April (months with an 'r'), as their flavour changes in the summer as they spawn. Ireland is also now a home for the Pacific oyster, which arrived in the 1960s to help sustain the wild population. While some regard the native as superior, for me, they have different uses and flavours. The Pacific oysters grown around the coasts of Ireland all have their own unique terroir. It's a shame that we continue to divide them in terms of their origin: if you had been living in Ireland since the 1960s and your children and their children lived there, wouldn't they be Irish by now? Of course. So, if you're in Ireland, celebrate both oysters, with Irish garnishes such as fresh seaweed (sea lettuce and pepper dulse) and pickled elderflower or more traditional ones such as lemon, and onions in red wine vinegar. You'll find both all over the country.

Oyster Pie

Preparation: 20 minutes, plus chilling time
Cooking: 50 minutes
Serves 8

For the pastry
250 g/9 oz (2 cups plus one tablespoon) plain (all-purpose) flour
250 g/9 oz (2¼ sticks) cold butter, cubed
1 egg, for glazing
sea salt

For the filling
50 g/2 oz (4 tablespoons) butter
2 onions, diced
50 g/2 oz (⅓ cup) plain (all-purpose) flour
1 teaspoon ground mace
250 ml/8 fl oz (1 cup) double (heavy) cream
250 ml/8 fl oz (1 cup) milk
1 bay leaf
24 oysters, shucked, with their liquid reserved
lemon juice, to season
sea salt and freshly ground black pepper

Oyster pie featured on many 'big house' menus. I came across numerous oyster pie recipes in old cookbooks, dating back to the eighteenth century. It contained black pepper, mace, lemon, butter and the yolks of hard-boiled eggs. Again, these recipes demonstrate the confluence of two worlds: the native with the exotic. We have to remember that all spices that travelled to Ireland during this period travelled from the Middle East or even further afield in some cases.

For the pastry, sift the flour into a bowl and rub in the butter. Add the salt and enough cold water to bring the dough together. Wrap in cling film (plastic wrap) and refrigerate for 1 hour.

Preheat the oven to 170°C/340°F/ Gas Mark 3½.

To make the filling, melt the butter in a medium pan over a medium–low heat, add the onion and gently fry the onion for about 5 minutes until softened. Add the flour with the mace and cook for 2–3 minutes to form a roux.

Meanwhile, put the cream and milk with the reserved oyster liquid and bay leaf into a separate medium pan over a medium heat and heat for about 5 minutes until warm.

Pour gently over the roux, whisking. Continue to whisk to avoid any lumps. Season with lemon juice and sea salt.

Roll out enough pastry to cover a deep pie dish measuring 20–25 cm/8–10 inches. Arrange the oysters on the bottom of the pie dish and pour over the sauce. Cover with the pastry and make a few incisions to allow the heat to escape.

Brush the pastry with the egg and bake in the preheated oven for 25–30 minutes until the pastry is golden brown.

Oysters Fried in Beef Dripping

Preparation: 10 minutes, plus 2 hours
soaking time
Cooking: 5 minutes
Serves 4

16 oysters, shucked
150 ml/5 fl oz (⅔ cup) buttermilk
250 g/9 oz (1¼ cups) beef dripping

For breadcrumbed oysters
150 g/5 oz (1¼ cups) plain (all-purpose) flour
250 g/9 oz (2½ cups) dry breadcrumbs
sea salt

For battered oysters
150 g/5 oz (1¼ cups) plain (all-purpose) flour
150 g/5 oz (1¼ cups) cornflour (cornstarch)
300 ml/10 fl oz (1¼ cups) sparkling water

For the herb mayonnaise
120 g/4 oz (½ cup) good-quality mayonnaise
2 tablespoons chopped herbs of your choice

Oysters fried in beef dripping were popular in the eighteenth and nineteenth centuries. This recipe is adapted from the *O'Donovan Family Recipe Book* (1713). Any herb mayonnaise will work – try dill or fennel.

Soak the oysters in the buttermilk for 2 hours in the refrigerator.

Meanwhile, mix together the mayonnaise and chopped herbs in a small bowl, or blend in a food processor until smooth.

For the breadcrumbed oysters, season the flour on one plate and put the breadcrumbs on another.

Dry off the oysters with paper towels. Dust with the flour and then return to the buttermilk. Finally, coat in the breadcrumbs.

For battered oysters, whisk together the flours and water. Pat the oysters dry, then dust with a little flour and dip into the batter.

Heat the beef dripping in a shallow pan over a high heat until it reaches 175°C/350°F or a cube of bread browns in 30 seconds. Fry the oysters for 1–2 minutes on each side until crispy.

Serve with the herb mayonnaise.

See opposite –>

Oysters and Whiskey

Preparation: 15 minutes
Cooking: 2 hours 15 minutes
Serves 4

8 oysters, shucked
extra virgin rapeseed (canola) oil, to serve

For the whiskey broth
2 onions, halved horizontally but unpeeled
1 litre/34 fl oz (4¼ cups) chicken stock (broth)
2 cloves garlic
2 sprigs of thyme
75 ml/2½ fl oz (⅓ cup) whiskey
Seaweed Vinegar (see page 352)
sea salt

To make the broth, grill the onions in a dry pan over a medium heat until completely charred. Peel and place in a pan with the rest of the broth ingredients. Bring to the boil over a high heat, then reduce the heat to low and simmer for 2 hours. Strain and season to taste with salt and vinegar.

Put two oysters into four warmed bowls. Ladle the warm broth over the oysters. Top with a few dots of extra virgin rapeseed (canola) oil.

Hay-smoked Oysters

Preparation: 5 minutes
Cooking: 5 minutes
Serves 4

a handful of hay
12 oysters
extra virgin rapeseed (canola) oil
sea salt

Throwing shellfish into a smouldering fire to force them open is a very old method of cooking. This slight cooking would give it a smoky flavour.

Place the hay in a smoking box and place the oysters on top. Cover the box and place over a direct heat. Smoke the oysters for a couple of minutes until they open slightly.

Remove from the box and pop off the top shell with a small knife. Be careful not to spill the liquid in the oyster. Dress the oyster with a few drops of oil, season and serve.

Shellfish

Shellfish

Oysters with Wild Garlic Butter

Preparation: 15 minutes
Cooking: 2 minutes
Serves 4

8 oysters
brown soda bread, to serve

For the wild garlic butter
450 g/1 lb (4 sticks) butter, room temperature
75 g/2¾ oz (⅔ cup) wild garlic (ramps)
apple cider vinegar, to taste
sea salt

Put the butter and wild garlic (ramps) into a food processor and blend together. Season with the vinegar and salt. Form into a cylinder by wrapping in a piece of cling film (plastic wrap) and refrigerate until required.

Preheat the grill (broiler). Shuck the oysters and detach from the shell. Place a knob (pat) of the butter into each oyster. Grill (broil) the oysters for about 2 minutes until the butter begins to bubble.

Serve with some brown soda bread.

See opposite –>

Oysters Stewed in Butter

Preparation: 5 minutes
Cooking: 5 minutes
Serves 4

50 g/2 oz (4 tablespoons) butter
12 oysters, shucked with their liquid reserved
ground mace, to taste
100 ml/3½ fl oz (scant ½ cup) double (heavy) cream
ground white pepper, to taste
sea salt

This recipe can be dated back to c.1775 and represents a typical way of cooking oysters. Because oysters had to travel from the coast, most recipes pickled or cooked them due to the possibility of bacteria. The Irish writer Jonathan Swift, known for writing *Gulliver's Travels* (1726) famously wrote, 'It was a bold man that first ate an oyster.'

Melt the butter in a medium pan over a very low heat until it begins to gently simmer. Add the oysters, season with the mace, white pepper and sea salt and cook for a minute until just cooked and curling at the edges. Remove the oysters from the pan and keep in a warm place.

Add the cream and the oyster liquid to the pan, increase the heat to medium, bring to the boil and whisk. Return the oysters to the sauce and serve.

Scallops in Their Shells Cooked Over Turf

Preparation and cooking: 15 minutes
Serves 4

1 small piece of turf
4 scallops in their shell
Burnt Hay Oil (see page 351), to taste (optional)
Seaweed Vinegar (see page 352), to taste
sea salt

Light a charcoal fire and place the turf piece among the hot charcoals. When the turf starts to smoke, place the scallop shells on a wire rack over the charcoal and turf. Cook the scallops for about 5 minutes until they slightly open. Remove the scallops from the grill and open fully.

Remove the entire contents from the shell, reserving the liquid.

Separate the scallop meat from the roe and intestines. Strain the reserved liquid and season with a little oil and vinegar.

Cut each scallop lengthwise into four. Season the scallop meat with sea salt and place back in the warm shell. Pour a little of the reserved broth over each scallop and serve.

Shellfish

Shellfish

Raw Scallops with Apple and Kohlrabi

Preparation: 20 minutes
Serves 4

1 apple
1 kohlrabi
extra virgin rapeseed (canola) oil, to taste
apple cider vinegar, to taste
8 scallops, cleaned and roe removed
dill leaves, to garnish (optional)
sea salt

Using a mandoline or very sharp knife, slice the apple and the kohlrabi, and then cut into discs roughly the same size of the scallops with the aid of a circular pastry cutter. Place on a tray and dress with some oil, salt and vinegar.

Slice the scallops into four thin slices each and arrange them on plates with the apple and kohlrabi discs. I like to alternate each one to form a nice shape.

Drizzle with a little more oil if required and garnish with some dill leaves (if using).

See opposite –>

Scallops Poached in Brown Butter

Preparation: 15 minutes
Cooking: 10 minutes
Serves 4

200 g/7 oz (1¾ sticks) butter
8 scallops, cleaned and roe removed
juice of 1 lemon
1 tablespoon finely chopped parsley
sea salt and freshly ground black pepper

Put the butter into a large pan over a medium heat and simmer until the butter caramelizes. Remove from the heat. Strain the butter if desired, but I like the caramelized nutty butter bits left at the bottom.

While the butter is still warm, place the scallops into the butter and leave for 5 minutes. They will cook in the residual heat of the butter. If you want them more cooked, simply put the pan of brown butter over a low heat. However, be careful not to over-poach the scallops.

To serve, slice the scallops in half and place the two scallops (four halves) on each plate.

In a small bowl, mix together the brown butter, lemon juice, black pepper, parsley and sea salt. Pour over the scallops.

Scallops with Black Pudding

Preparation and cooking: 10 minutes
Serves 4

8 scallops, cleaned and roe removed
2 tablespoons rapeseed (canola) oil
8 slices of black pudding (blood sausage)
50 g/2 oz (4 tablespoons) butter
a few sprigs of thyme
sea salt

Scallops and black pudding are a classic Irish combination and represent our take on surf and turf. The tenderness of the scallop meat marries well with the rich, succulent blood pudding. Often, if I can get my hands on fresh blood, I make a sauce to go with the scallops. I like to pan-fry the scallop on one side only as otherwise it tends to dry out.

Season the scallops with sea salt.

Heat the oil in a large frying pan (skillet) over a medium–low heat. Fry the scallops and black pudding (blood sausage) on one side for about a minute until nicely caramelized.

Add the butter and thyme. Baste the scallops and black pudding slices for 1 minute.

Turn the scallops and black pudding over and remove the pan from heat. Allow to warm in the pan briefly and then serve.

Shellfish

Shellfish

Queen Scallops in Beer Batter

Preparation: 5 minutes
Cooking: 2 minutes per batch
Serves 4

rapeseed (canola) oil, for deep-frying
150 g/5 oz (1¼ cups) plain (all-purpose) flour,
    plus a little extra for dusting
1 teaspoon baking powder
300 ml/10 fl oz (1¼ cups) beer
250 g/9 oz queen scallops, roe removed
sea salt
a few lemon wedges, to serve

Put the oil into a deep-fat fryer and heat to 180 °C/350 °F, or until a cube of bread browns in 30 seconds.

Meanwhile, whisk the flour, baking powder and beer together until smooth. Season with sea salt.

Dredge the scallops in flour and then dip into the batter.

Fry the scallops in the preheated oil, in batches if necessary, for about 2 minutes until nice and crispy. Allow the oil to return to temperature before adding the next batch.

Serve with some lemon wedges.

Mussels

Though most mussels we eat now are farmed in the many bays and inlets of Ireland, wild mussels have been an easily obtainable food source since Mesolithic times (5,500 BC). Hunter-gatherers would have hand-harvested mussels off the rocks at low tide and cooked them over fire or in skin bags full of water heated by small pebbles. As with oysters, many midden beds containing mussel shells have been unearthed all around the country, showing that people have consumed mussels throughout Irish history. Mussel shells dating from around the Mesolithic period have been found at Baylet on Inch Island in County Donegal. The simple combination of mussels and seaweed represents two foodstuffs available to the first peoples that inhabited Ireland. Close your eyes and picture the first 'Irelander' sitting on the beach, steaming mussels open over a fire and combining them with fresh dillisk (dulse). I do not think we could find a more resolute image to represent Irish food, in terms of its past, present and future. Next time you have the opportunity to build a fire on the beach try tossing some wild mussels into the embers and eating them with a little rapeseed (canola) oil and herb or seaweed vinegar.

Mussels and Dillisk

Preparation: 10 minutes
Cooking: 5 minutes
Serves 4

200 ml/7 fl oz (scant 1 cup) cider (hard cider)
1 onion, quartered
1 clove garlic, very finely chopped
1 kg/2¼ lb mussels, scrubbed and debearded
extra virgin rapeseed (canola) oil
Seaweed Vinegar (see page 352), to taste
sea salt
10 g/1 oz dried dillisk (dulse), rehydrated
    in cold water, to garnish

Put the cider, onion and garlic in a large saucepan over a high heat and bring to the boil. Add the mussels and cover. Steam for 1–2 minutes until they open. Discard any that do not.

Drain through a colander, reserving the cooking liquid.

Shell the mussels and dress with a little of the reserved cooking liquid, some oil, salt and a little vinegar.

Place the mussels in a bowl and garnish with the dillisk (dulse).

Mussels in a Smoked Butter Sauce

Preparation: 15 minutes
Cooking: 20 minutes
Serves 4

500 ml/17 fl oz (generous 2 cups) cider (hard cider)
1 onion, roughly chopped
1 clove garlic, smashed
a few sprigs of thyme
500 g/1 lb 2 oz mussels, scrubbed clean
250 g/9 oz (1 cup plus 2 tablespoons) smoked Irish butter, cubed
a few sprigs of chervil, to serve
extra virgin rapeseed (canola) oil, to serve
sea salt

Put the cider, onion, garlic and thyme into a pan over a medium heat and bring to the boil. Add the mussels, cover and cook for 1–2 minutes.

Strain the sauce, transfer to another pan over a medium heat and cook for 10–15 minutes until reduced by half.

Meanwhile, pick the mussels from their shells. Discard any that are unopened.

When the sauce is reduced, blend the butter into the sauce and season to taste.

Divide the mussels among four bowls and pour over the sauce. Garnish with a little chervil and add a drizzle of extra virgin rapeseed (canola) oil.

Mussel and Saffron Broth

Preparation: 15 minutes
Cooking: 20 minutes
Serves 8

50 g/2 oz (4 tablespoons) butter, cubed
2 onions, chopped
2 cloves garlic, very finely chopped
a few sprigs of thyme
250 ml/8 fl oz (1 cup) white wine
a few saffron strands
500 ml/17 fl oz (generous 2 cups) fish stock (broth)
2 kg/4½ lb mussels, scrubbed clean
3 tablespoons chopped parsley
sea salt and freshly ground black pepper

Saffron has a long history of use in Irish cooking. Writing in her book *In an Irish Country Kitchen* (1993), Clare Connery observes that saffron was used to colour mussel soup. Darina Allen includes a mussel and saffron soup in her *Traditional Irish Cooking* (1995).

Put a large pan over a medium heat and add the butter. When it begins to foam, add the onions, garlic and thyme. Cook for about 5 minutes until the onion softens.

Add the wine, saffron and the fish stock. Bring to the boil and cook for a few minutes to reduce.

Add the mussels, cover and cook for 2–3 minutes until all the mussels have opened. Discard any that do not open.

Remove from the heat and add the parsley. Season with pepper. Ladle into warmed bowls.

Mussels with Stout

Preparation: 10 minutes
Cooking: 10 minutes
Serves 4

1 tablespoon rapeseed (canola) oil
1 onion, diced
1 clove garlic, very finely chopped
1 sprig of thyme
50 g/2 oz (4 tablespoons) butter, cubed
250 ml/8 fl oz (1 cup) stout
1 kg/2¼ lb mussels, scrubbed clean
sea salt

Warm the oil in a large frying pan (skillet) over a medium heat. Add the onion, garlic and thyme and season with sea salt. After a minute, add the butter. When it has melted, add the stout, bring to the boil and cook for 5 minutes to burn off the alcohol.

Add the mussels and cover. Steam for 1–2 minutes until all the mussels open. Remove from the heat, discard any that do not open and serve.

Shellfish

Mussels with Tarragon Mayonnaise and Brown Bread

Preparation and cooking: 15 minutes
Serves 4

250 ml/8 fl oz (1 cup) cider (hard cider)
1 onion, chopped
2 cloves garlic, very finely chopped
a few sprigs of tarragon
1 kg/2¼ lb mussels, scrubbed clean
brown bread, to serve

For the tarragon mayonnaise
120 g/4 oz (½ cup) good-quality mayonnaise
2 tablespoons chopped tarragon leaves

Put the cider, onion, garlic and tarragon into a large pan over a medium heat and bring to the boil. When boiling, add the mussels and cover. Steam for 1–2 minutes or until the mussels open, then remove from the heat. Discard any that are unopened.

Mix together the mayonnaise and chopped tarragon in a small bowl, or blend in a food processor until smooth.

Serve the mussels with the mayonnaise and brown bread.

See opposite –>

Sea Urchins

Sea urchins are rare in Ireland today due to overfishing in the 1970s. As with much of our shellfish, we sold much of it to the French and Spanish. But there are a few producers now farming sea urchins in Ireland. We source ours from Mungo Murphy in Connemara, who also farm abalones, sea cucumber and seaweed. If you're ever in Ireland, do visit them to learn about sea urchins. For me, sea urchins should be eaten immediately after opening, but they can also be boiled in seawater for 1–2 minutes first. Because of their saline nature I love to pair them with seaweed. However, they work well with many sauces, from butter to tomato.

To open a sea urchin, using a pair of sharp scissors, make a cut from its mouth to the edge of the urchin. Then, holding the urchin in one hand, cut around the top of the sea urchin, being careful not to damage the gonads below. Remove the top of the urchin and then clean in-between each gonad. If not serving immediately, place on some crushed ice.

Sea Urchins with Buttermilk and Tarragon

Preparation: 5 minutes
Serves 4

4 sea urchins
2 tablespoons buttermilk
2 tablespoons tarragon oil
   (see Herb Oil, page 351)
sea salt

Open the sea urchins with a pair of sharp scissors (see above). Cut in a circular fashion and be careful not to damage the gonads.

Mix the buttermilk and the tarragon oil and season lightly with sea salt. Pour the dressing over the urchin and serve.

Shellfish

Shellfish

Shellfish Steamed over Seaweed

Preparation: 10 minutes
Cooking: 10 minutes
Serves 4

a few sheets of fresh kelp
2 kg/4½ lb mixed shellfish (mussels,
  clams, cockles, razor clams, winkles/
  periwinkles, etc.)
extra virgin rapeseed (canola) oil
Seaweed Vinegar (see page 352),
  or any vinegar of your choice
sea salt

Steaming shellfish is a great way to retain its succulence. By adding seaweed to the water, you can impart its flavour into the shellfish. This is also a great way of cooking flat fish, such as turbot and sole.

Line the inside of a bamboo steaming basket with some of the seaweed. Place the mixed shellfish evenly on top (you may have to steam in batches). Cover the shellfish with the rest of the seaweed. Place the lid on top.

Bring a pan of water to the boil and top with the basket. Steam the shellfish for 5–10 minutes, until they open.

Transfer the shellfish to a bowl and dress with oil, vinegar and salt.

An Irish Shellfish Salad

Preparation: 10 minutes
Cooking: 15 minutes
Serves 4

16 large mussels, scrubbed clean
16 surf clams, scrubbed clean
4 langoustines (Dublin Bay prawns),
  split lengthwise
4 scallops, roe removed
4 oysters, shucked
extra virgin rapeseed (canola) oil
Seaweed Vinegar (see page 352),
  or another vinegar of your choice
sea salt

To garnish
a selection of wild sea herbs
15 g/½ oz (about ½ cup) fresh sea lettuce
15 g/½ oz fresh nori

For me, the combination of the shellfish below represents a taste of the west of Ireland. However, any shellfish can be used, depending where you are in the world. Seek out your local shellfish. As with the shellfish, any local sea herbs or seaweed can use used. Alternatively, use dried seaweed and rehydrate in cold water.

Light a charcoal fire or barbecue grill. Place the mussels and clams over the hot embers for 4–5 minutes. When they open, remove from the grill. Reserve in a warm place.

Put the langoustines (Dublin Bay prawns) onto the grill, shell side down, for about 5 minutes until the meat cooks ever so slightly. Reserve with the mussels and clams.

Place the oysters and scallops (both lightly oiled) on the grill and cook on one side for about 5 minutes until they have a nice colour.

Season all the shellfish with oil, salt and vinegar, then serve on a platter with the seaweed and the sea herbs.

Cockles and Breadcrumbs

Preparation: 15 minutes
Cooking: 10 minutes
Serves 4

250 ml/8 fl oz (1 cup) cider (hard cider)
1 onion, quartered
1 clove garlic, crushed
a few sprigs of thyme
1 kg/2¼ lb cockles
50 g/2 oz (4 tablespoons) butter, melted
100 g/3½ oz (2 cups) fresh breadcrumbs
a handful of chopped parsley
sea salt

Preheat the grill (broiler).

Put the cider into a large pan over a medium heat and add the onion, garlic and thyme. Bring to the boil, add the cockles and cover. Steam for 1–2 minutes, or until the cockles open. Strain and reserve the liquid.

Remove the cockles from their shells.

Combine the melted butter with the breadcrumbs and parsley. Season to taste.

Place each cockle in its shell in a heatproof dish with a little of the reserved liquid and cover with the breadcrumbs. Grill (broil) the cockles for 1–2 minutes until the crumbs are crispy.

See opposite –>

Shellfish

Cockles, Clams and Kale Cooked in Dry Cider

Preparation and cooking: 15 minutes
Serves 4

250 ml/8 fl oz (1 cup) dry cider (hard cider)
1 onion, diced
1 clove garlic
1 bay leaf
350 g/12 oz cockles
350 g/12 oz clams
75 g/2¾ oz (1 cup prepared) kale, stems removed and leaves chopped into bite-sized pieces
chopped parsley or chervil, to serve

Put the cider into a large pan with the onion, garlic and bay leaf. Bring to the boil and then add the cockles, clams and kale.

Cover and steam over a medium heat for 90 seconds, or until all the shellfish has opened. Discard any that have not opened. Eat immediately.

See opposite –>

Cockles in Butter with Samphire

Preparation and cooking: 10 minutes
Serves 4

50 g/2 oz (4 tablespoons) butter
1 kg/2¼ lb cockles
150 g/5 oz (1 cup) samphire (sea beans)
sea salt

Melt the butter in a large pan with 250 ml/8 fl oz (1 cup) of water. When boiling, add the cockles and cover the pan with a suitable lid. Steam over a medium heat for 1–2 minutes until all the clams have opened.
Strain and toss the samphire (sea beans) through the cockles. Season with sea salt.

Cockles and Smoked Bacon

Preparation: 10 minutes
Cooking: 10 minutes
Serves 4

1 tablespoon rapeseed (canola) oil
1 onion, finely diced
500 ml/17 fl oz (generous 2 cups) cider (hard cider)
500 g/1 lb 2 oz cockles
4 rashers (slices) smoked streaky (regular) bacon

Preheat the grill (broiler).

Heat the oil in a large pan over a medium heat, add the onion and fry for about 5 minutes until softened and then add the cider. When it comes to the boil, add the cockles and cover. Cook for 1–2 minutes.

Remove from the heat and strain the cockles through a sieve, reserving the liquid. Return the liquid to the heat and reduce by half.

Meanwhile, grill (broil) the bacon until crispy. Dice the bacon and add to the cider and onion mixture.

Shell the cockles and mix with the bacon, cider and onion.

Shellfish

Live Razor Clams

Preparation: 30 minutes
Serves 4

16 razor clams, alive and very fresh
extra virgin rapeseed (canola) oil
Herb Vinegar (see page 352), or another
   vinegar of your choice
sea salt

Razor clams are bivalves, similar to mussels and clams, though their flesh is white and tender and resembles squid. They are found buried in the sand and are plentiful in the west of Ireland. They need to be harvested at low tide and rinsed well before steaming.

Rinse the clams in cold running water for 20 minutes.

Using a small knife, open the razor clams. Discard the mouth and intestine. Briefly rinse the meat.

Slice the meat (it should still be wriggling) into bite-sized pieces.

Dress with some oil, vinegar and salt. Eat immediately.

Razor Clams with Cider and Rosemary

Preparation and cooking: 10 minutes
Serves 4

250 ml/8 fl oz (1 cup) cider (hard cider)
1 shallot, chopped
2 cloves garlic, crushed
4 sprigs of rosemary
500 g/1 lb 2 oz razor clams
sea salt
chopped chives, to garnish

As well as working with cider and woody herbs, razor clams pair nicely with most seaweeds and sea vegetables. Pepper dulse seaweed is a beautiful accompaniment to this recipe. I also love to serve them with gooseberries in the late summer.

Put the cider, shallot, garlic, and rosemary into a large pan and bring to the boil. Add the razor clams and cover.

Steam for 1 minute, or until all the clams open. Season and serve garnished with chives.

See opposite –>

Connemara Clams with Pumpkin and Cider

Preparation: 10 minutes
Cooking: 40 minutes
Serves 4

1 medium orange pumpkin
a few sprigs of rosemary
250 ml/8 fl oz (1 cup) cider (hard cider)
2 shallots, chopped
20 large clams
125 g/4½ oz (1 stick plus 1 tablespoon) butter
rapeseed (canola) oil
sea salt

Preheat the oven to 180°C/350°F/ Gas Mark 4.

Cut the pumpkin into wedges and scoop out the seeds. Season with sea salt and rosemary and roast in the preheated oven for 35–40 minutes until tender.

Meanwhile, put the cider into a large pan over a medium heat, add the shallots and heat until boiling. Add the clams and cook for 5–10 minutes until they open.

Remove the clams from the pan and separate the meat from the shells.

Strain the cider through a sieve and transfer to a small pan. Return to the boil and simmer for 5–10 minutes to reduce a little, then add the butter to the cider and blend with an immersion blender until smooth. Return the sauce to the heat to warm through.

To serve, place a warm wedge of pumpkin with some clams on a plate. Spoon over the warm sauce.

Shellfish

Crab with Smoked Cheese Custard

Preparation: 20 minutes, plus chilling time
Cooking: 15 minutes
Serves 4

250 g/9 oz crabmeat
extra virgin rapeseed (canola) oil
zest and juice of 1 lemon
sea salt

For the cheese custard
150 ml/5 fl oz (⅔ cup) double (heavy) cream
150 ml/5 fl oz (⅔ cup) milk
100 g/3½ oz (scant 1 cup prepared) Irish smoked cheese, grated
4 egg yolks
chopped chives and seaweed powder, to garnish (optional)

To make the custard, add the cream, milk and cheese to a medium pan over a medium heat and bring to the boil. Remove from the heat.

Meanwhile, bring a separate medium pan of water to the boil.

Add the egg yolks to a large heatproof bowl and gradually pour the hot cream mixture over the eggs, whisking all the time to avoid scrambling. Place the bowl over the pan of simmering water and cook for about 20 minutes until the custard thickens. Transfer to a blender and blend until smooth. Season to taste.

Pick through the crabmeat for shell and season with the oil, lemon juice, lemon zest and salt.

Place the crab in the bottom of four bowls and pour the custard over the top. Refrigerate for 2 hours until set. Serve garnished with chopped chives and seaweed powder, if you wish.

See opposite –>

Crab with Curry Mayonnaise and Pineapple

Preparation: 25 minutes
Cooking: 15 minutes
Serves 4

For the crab
500 g/1 lb 2 oz crabmeat, picked through for shell
1 apple, cored, peeled and diced
1 celery stick, diced
2 teaspoons chopped chervil
100 ml/3½ fl oz (scant ½ cup) extra virgin rapeseed (canola) oil
grated zest and juice of 1 lemon
sea salt

For the mayonnaise
250 g/9 oz (generous 1 cup) mayonnaise
1 teaspoon curry powder
lemon juice, to taste

For the pineapple
1 pineapple, peeled, cored and sliced
100 g/3½ oz (½ cup firmly packed) soft brown sugar
juice of 1 lime

Walking down Dublin's Moore Street with my nana, I always wondered where all the pineapples came from and who ate them. The Irish, it seems, have a penchant for pineapple. I think one of the unique features of Irish food in the second half of the twentieth century is its ability to take our own indigenous ingredients and combine them with exotic elements such as bananas and pineapple. Interestingly, pineapple and banana were grown in glasshouses in Kylemore Abbey in Connemara in the later nineteenth century. The Victorian Walled Garden was developed along with the Castle and contained twenty-one heated glasshouses and a workforce of forty gardeners. Though the combination of crab with curry and pineapple seems outlandish, it perfectly encapsulates a particular epoch of Irish food, namely, the 1970s and the 1980s.

Preheat the oven to 180°C/350°F/ Gas Mark 4.

For the crab, mix all the ingredients together, season with salt and set aside.

To cook the pineapple, put the pineapple rings onto a baking sheet and sprinkle the brown sugar and lime juice over them. Turn the rings and repeat the process.

Roast in the preheated oven for 15 minutes. Allow to cool slightly.

Mix the mayonnaise with the curry powder and lemon juice.

To serve, put a few roasted pineapple rings on each plate, divide the crab meat among them and top with a dollop of the mayonnaise.

Shellfish

Shellfish

Crab Claws with Seaweed and Samphire

Preparation: 5 minutes
Cooking: 5–10 minutes
Serves 4

35 g/1¼ oz (2 tablespoons) butter
12 cooked crab claws, shells removed
Seaweed Vinegar (see page 352) or apple
    cider vinegar, to taste
50 g/2 oz (⅓ cup) samphire (sea beans)
25 g/1 oz (¼ cup) fresh sea lettuce
sea salt

Melt the butter in a large pan over a medium heat. When it starts to foam, reduce the heat, add the crab claws and heat for 3–5 minutes until the crab claws are warmed through.

Season with sea salt and Seaweed Vinegar.

Place the crab claws on a platter and garnish with the samphire (sea beans) and sea lettuce.

See opposite –>

 # Potted Crab

Preparation: 10 minutes, plus chilling time
Cooking: 5 minutes
Serves 4

300 g/11 oz fresh crabmeat, picked
    through for shell
grated zest and juice of 1 lemon
a pinch of ground mace
freshly grated nutmeg
250 g/9 oz (2¼ sticks) butter
sea salt
toasts, to serve

In a bowl, mix the crabmeat with the lemon zest and juice, mace and a good grating of nutmeg. Season with sea salt.

Melt the butter in a medium pan over a medium heat until it separates. Strain the clarified butter through a piece of muslin (cheesecloth) into a jug (pitcher) or small bowl and discard the solids.

Mix half the butter through the crabmeat, check the seasoning, and then place the crab into small ramekins. Spoon the remaining clarified butter over the crabmeat. Cover and refrigerate until set, for at least 1 hour and up to 24 hours.

Remove half an hour before serving. Serve the potted crab with toasts.

 # Whole Crab Cooked in Seaweed and Seawater

Cooking: 15 minutes
Serves 2

enough seawater to cover the crabs
a handful of fresh seaweed (kombu or
    sugar kelp)
2 live crabs

Crabs are not the only shellfish that work well in seawater: lobster, clams, mussels and cockles all benefit from being cooked in saltwater. Be careful with the seasoning though, as no salt should be required after cooking in saltwater. Seaweed enriches the cooking of any shellfish, lending an umami quality, especially if using any of the kelp family.

Bring the seawater and the seaweed to the boil in a large pan over a high heat. Drop the crabs into the boiling water and reduce the heat to a simmer. Cook for 15 minutes.

Dress the crabs: crack off the claws and legs and remove their meat. Place the crabs on their back and separate the crab body from the central part of the crab by putting your hands under the base of the crab and pushing upwards until you hear it break. Remove the spongy 'dead men's fingers' and discard. Drain any excess water from the shell of the crab and remove the stomach sac and hard membranes inside the shell. Serve.

Shellfish

Shellfish

Brown Crab and Linseed Crackers

Preparation: 30 minutes, plus 2 hours
resting time
Cooking: 20 minutes
Serves 4

250 g/9 oz brown crabmeat, picked through
   for shell
1 Irish apple, finely diced
1 shallot, finely diced
1 celery stalk, peeled and leaves removed,
   finely diced
small handful of mixed herbs such as flat leaf
   parsley, fennel, chervil, dill, finely chopped
sea salt

For the crackers
300 g/11 oz (1¾ cups) brown
   linseeds (flaxseed)
1 tablespoon honey
½ teaspoon sea salt

For the mayonnaise
2 egg yolks
1 tablespoon apple cider vinegar
1 teaspoon Irish mustard
250 ml/8 fl oz (1 cup) light rapeseed
   (canola) oil
sea salt

To make the crackers, mix the linseeds (flaxseed) with 200 ml/ 7 fl oz (scant 1 cup) of water, the honey and salt in a bowl. Leave to sit for 2 hours, stirring regularly, until the mix thickens.

Preheat the oven to 140°C/275°F/ Gas Mark 1. Spread the linseed mix very thinly over a silicone baking mat. Bake for 20 minutes in the preheated oven until completely dry. Once cool, break into pieces.

To make the mayonnaise, put the egg yolks with the vinegar and mustard into a large mixing bowl. Whisk until combined. Gradually add in the oil, slowly, to make sure it emulsifies with the egg.

When all the oil has been combined, check the mayonnaise for seasoning. If the mayonnaise is too thick, you can add a few teaspoons of water.

In a large bowl, combine the crabmeat with the diced apple, shallot and celery. Add the mayonnaise and mix thoroughly. Finally, add the herbs and again check the seasoning. You want to make sure the acidity and salt levels are right.

To serve, fill four ramekins with the crab and garnish with some herbs. Serve the crackers on the side.

Potted Shrimp

Preparation: 15 minutes, plus chilling time
Cooking: 5 minutes
Serves 4

200 g/7 oz (1¾ sticks) butter
500 g/1 lb 2 oz brown shrimp, cooked, shelled
   and deveined (don't worry if they break up)
1 teaspoon Herb Vinegar (see page 352),
   or another vinegar of your choice
dill, finely chopped, plus extra to serve
sea salt
toast, to serve

The brown shrimp I use are seasonal. They are fished off the Aran Islands. I would avoid using imported shrimp for this recipe. To cook the shrimp, just blanch briefly in water for 1 minute and then drop into a bowl of iced water to stop the cooking process.

Melt the butter in a large pan over a medium–low heat and simmer until the milk solids separate. Strain the clarified butter through a piece of muslin (cheesecloth) into a jug or small bowl. Allow to cool.

In a large bowl, combine the shrimp with the vinegar and dill and season with a little sea salt.

Divide the shrimp among 4 ramekins, pressing them in tightly.

Divide the clarified butter among the ramekins and refrigerate to set, about 1 hour and up to 24 hours.

To serve, remove from the refrigerator and allow to come up to room temperature. Garnish with a little more dill and serve with some toast.

See opposite –>

Shellfish

Shellfish

Langoustines Baked on Rock Salt

Preparation: 5 minutes
Cooking: 35 minutes
Serves 4

1 kg/2¼ lb (4 cups) rock salt
12 large langoustines (Dublin Bay prawns)

Preheat the oven to 180°C/350°F/ Gas Mark 4.

Put the rock salt into an ovenproof dish and bake in the preheated oven for 30 minutes.

Remove the salt from the oven and place the langoustines (Dublin Bay prawns) on the salt. Return to the oven and bake for 3–5 minutes or until the langoustines are cooked.

Crack the langoustines open and serve immediately.

<u>Note</u>
You can flavour the salt with any herbs, spices, seaweed or citrus. Just add to the salt before baking.

See opposite –>

Langoustines and Rosemary

Preparation: 15 minutes
Cooking: 5 minutes
Serves 4

8 langoustine (Dublin Bay prawn) tails
  (heads reserved for stock)
8 large rosemary twigs
extra virgin rapeseed (canola) oil
sea salt

<u>For the rosemary salt</u>
80 g/3 oz (¼ cup) sea salt
20 g/¾ oz (⅔ cup) rosemary leaves

To make the rosemary salt, put the rosemary leaves and salt into a food processor and blend, then pass through a fine sieve.

Light a charcoal fire or grill. (The langoustines/prawns can also be cooked with a chef's blowtorch.)

Shell the langoustines and skewer them with the rosemary twigs. Rub the langoustines with a little oil and season lightly with the rosemary salt.

Lay the langoustines on the hot grill on their backs and cook for 3–5 minutes until nicely charred.

Remove from the grill and brush lightly with additional oil and season with a little more rosemary salt. Serve immediately.

Langoustines Cooked in Blackcurrant Leaves

Preparation and cooking: 15 minutes
Serves 4

16 blackcurrant leaves
16 large langoustines
  (Dublin Bay prawns), peeled
extra virgin rapeseed (canola) oil
blackcurrant vinegar (see Herb or Fruit
  Vinegar, page 352, optional)
sea salt

Blackcurrants have a long history of growing in Ireland, particularly in the south of the country. Blackcurrant leaves have a fruity aromatic flavour that is quite unique and I love using them to wrap fish and shellfish before cooking. It is similar to wrapping food in vine leaves.

Preheat the grill (broiler).

Bring a small pan of water to the boil and blanch the blackcurrant leaves briefly.

Season the langoustines (Dublin Bay prawns) with oil, salt and vinegar (if using). Wrap the langoustines with the blackcurrant leaves. Tie or skewer them, if necessary.

Grill (broil) the langoustines for about 5 minutes, or until the tail meat turns opaque. Serve immediately.

Shellfish

Lobster

Though lobster is now seen as a preserve of the rich, coastal people in Ireland have fed off them for centuries. Like many food products, lobsters would have been caught and then sold (instead of eaten) because of the price they fetched. Many eighteenth-century household accounts show the demand for lobster among the landed class. Yet, this is not to say other people did not eat them. I have spoken to people from the Aran Islands who told me they got sick of eating them due to the amount they ate. This is perhaps the tragedy of many island people, who preferred to eat the food of the land, instead of the sea. Despite this, Irish lobster is revered in France and further afield.

Lobster Soup

Preparation: 15 minutes
Cooking: 2 hours
Serves 4

2 live lobsters
2 litres/70 fl oz (8½ cups) fish stock (broth)
50 g/2 oz (4 tablespoons) butter
2 onions, diced
2 leeks, nicely chopped
1 bay leaf
a few sprigs of rosemary and thyme
4 rashers (slices) smoked streaky (regular) bacon, diced
2 carrots, chopped
2 celery stalks, diced
250 ml/8 fl oz (1 cup) white wine
parsley, to garnish
sea salt

In her book, *Traditional Irish Cooking* (1995), Darina Allen transcribes a Lobster Soup from the Pakenham Mahon Papers at Strokestown Park in County Roscommon. It shows the use of lobster very far inland.

Preheat the oven to 180°C/350°F/ Gas Mark 4. Fill a large bowl with cold water and ice cubes.

To kill the lobsters, drive a knife into the centre of their heads. Blanch in a large pan of boiling water for 5 minutes. Refresh in the iced water. When cold, remove the meat from the tail and claws and reserve.

Put the shells onto a baking sheet and roast in the preheated oven for 25 minutes.

Put the roasted lobster shells into a large pan and cover with the fish stock (broth). Bring to the boil and simmer for 1 hour. Strain and reserve the liquid.

Meanwhile, melt the butter in a large pan over a medium heat and add the onions, leeks and herbs. Cover and cook for 5–7 minutes until the onions are soft. Add the bacon, carrots and celery and fry for a few minutes. Add the wine and simmer for 5–10 minutes until reduced by half.

Cover the vegetables with the reserved stock and simmer until cooked to your liking. Remove the bay leaf and herbs.

Add the lobster meat to the soup and garnish with some chopped parsley. Ladle into warmed bowls.

See opposite –>

Lobster in a Salt Crust

Preparation: 5 minutes
Cooking: 20 minutes
Serves 1

2 egg whites
1 kg/2¼ lb (4 cups) coarse (kosher) sea salt
1 live lobster

Preheat the oven to 180°C/350°F/ Gas Mark 4. Combine the egg whites and the salt in a mixing bowl.

To kill the lobster, drive a knife down through the top of its head. Place the lobster on a baking sheet and cover with the egg and salt mix.

Bake in the preheated oven for 15–20 minutes until the salt is golden brown.

Allow to cool slightly and then crack open the salt. Split the lobster and crack open the claws.

Shellfish

Shellfish

Lobster and Whiskey

Preparation and cooking: 15 minutes
Serves 2

2 live lobsters
100 ml/3½ fl oz (scant ½ cup) whiskey
5 black peppercorns
a sprig each of thyme and rosemary
200 ml/7 fl oz (scant 1 cup) double
   (heavy) cream
50 g/2 oz (4 tablespoons) cold butter, cubed
sea salt
edible flowers and herbs, to garnish (optional)

Lobster and whiskey cooked in cream is called 'Dublin Lawyer'. There are many variations of this dish in different Irish cookbooks. In some, the whiskey is poured over the lobster and it is set alight.

Bring a large pan of salted water to the boil over a high heat. To kill the lobsters, drive a knife into the centre of their heads. Plunge them into the boiling water for 4–5 minutes. Remove from the water and allow to rest.

In a small pan, bring the whiskey, peppercorns and herbs to the boil and set alight. When the flame goes out, add the cream and boil for a few minutes until it thickens slightly. Strain, then add in the cold butter and season with some salt.

Split the lobsters in half and crack open their claws. Serve with the sauce and garnish with edible flowers and herbs, if you wish.

Alternatively, you can reserve the claws for another recipe and just use the tails. Remove the tails from their shells and extract the digestive tract. Chop up the meat and fold it into the sauce.

Note
You can also make a delicious sauce for lobster with Madeira and nutmeg. Bring 150 ml/5 fl oz (²/₃ cup) Madeira and 150 ml/ 5 fl oz (²/₃ cup) chicken stock (broth) to the boil, then simmer for 5 minutes. Whisk in 250 g/ 9 oz (2¼ sticks) cubed butter and season with freshly ground nutmeg and sea salt. Serve with lobster as above.

See opposite –>

Lobster with Spices

Preparation: 10 minutes
Cooking: 10 minutes
Serves 2

2 teaspoons mixed spices such as nutmeg,
   cloves, black pepper and/or mace
100 g/3½ oz (7 tablespoons) butter, softened
2 live lobsters
sea salt

This recipe dates to c.1780 and encapsulates the landed gentry's penchant for spices, which would have signified a certain degree of wealth and prestige.

Pound the spices in a mortar with a pestle until a smooth powder. Mix with the butter in a small bowl.

Preheat the grill (broiler). Fill a large bowl with cold water and ice cubes.

Bring a large pan of water to the boil over a high heat. To kill the lobsters, drive a knife into the centre of their heads. Blanch them for 3 minutes in the boiling water and refresh in the iced water.

Split the lobsters in half and brush with the spiced butter. Grill (broil) the lobsters under the preheated grill for a few minutes until caramelized.

Crack open the claws and remove the flesh. Season and serve.

     Shellfish

Shellfish

Poached Lobster with Butter and Cider Sauce

Preparation: 10 minutes
Cooking: 20 minutes
Serves 1

1 live lobster

For the sauce
500 ml/17 fl oz (generous 2 cups)
   cider (hard cider)
1 onion, quartered
1 clove garlic
a few sprigs of rosemary and thyme
250 g/9 oz (2¼ sticks) butter, cubed
apple cider vinegar, to taste
sea salt

To make the sauce, put the cider into a medium pan over a medium heat. Add the onion, garlic, rosemary and thyme and bring to the boil for 10–15 minutes until reduced by half. Strain, add the butter and blend with an immersion blender until smooth. Season with a little sea salt and vinegar.

Bring a large pan of salted water to the boil over a high heat. To kill the lobster, drive a knife into the centre of its head. Poach the lobster in the boiling water for 5 minutes until the shell is bright red.

To serve, cut the lobster in half and crack open the claws. Serve with the cider sauce.

Deep-fried Squid with Garlic and Parsley

Preparation and cooking: 10 minutes
Serves 4

4 cloves garlic
250 ml/8 fl oz (1 cup) extra virgin rapeseed
   (canola) oil, plus extra for deep-frying
4 whole squid
100 g/3½ oz (¾ cup) plain (all-purpose) flour
2 tablespoons finely chopped parsley,
   plus extra to garnish
sea salt

Put the garlic with the oil into a food processor and blend until smooth, then strain through a fine sieve.

Heat the oil in a deep-fat fryer to 180°C/350°F, or until a cube of bread browns in 30 seconds.

Clean the squid and score the tubes. Slice into thin strips. Dredge the squid through the flour and shake off any excess.

Fry the squid in the deep-fat fryer for 45 seconds until golden brown. Shake off the excess oil before transferring to a large bowl.

Season with the garlic oil, salt and chopped parsley.

See opposite –>

Baby Squid with Baby Onions

Preparation: 15 minutes
Cooking: 30 minutes
Serves 4

16 baby (pearl) onions
extra virgin rapeseed (canola) oil
malt vinegar, to taste
16 baby squid, cleaned
flat leaf parsley, chopped
sea salt

Preheat the oven to 180°C/350°F/ Gas Mark 4.

Put the onions onto a baking sheet and bake in the preheated oven for 25–30 minutes until soft. Allow to cool slightly, then peel and halve the onions. Dress with oil, salt and vinegar.

Meanwhile, preheat the grill (broiler).

Season the squid with sea salt and grill (broil) on each side for about 1 minute until cooked.

Dress the squid with oil and vinegar. Place them on a plate and arrange the onions on top. Garnish with some parsley.

Shellfish

Shellfish

Charred Octopus with Seaweed Glaze

Preparation: 15 minutes
Cooking: 1 hour 15 minutes
Serves 8

1 octopus

For the seaweed glaze
100 g/3½ oz (scant ⅓ cup) honey
100 ml/3½ fl oz (scant ½ cup) water
   (from the cooking of the octopus)
15 g/½ oz (1 tablespoon packed) soft
   light brown sugar
15 g/½ oz (1 tablespoon) butter
1 teaspoon dried milled seaweed
apple cider vinegar, to taste
sea salt

Squid can be used as an alternative to octopus in this dish. The squid will cook a lot quicker, so if using, just glaze the squid and grill or roast. This is lovely served with the Cavolo Nero with Rose Vinegar on page 58.

To cook the octopus, put it into a large pan of water over a medium heat and bring to the boil. Reduce the heat and simmer gently for 45 minutes–1 hour until the tentacles are soft and you can easily insert a knife into the thickest part of a tentacle. Remove from the pan and cut off the tentacles. Discard the head and reserve some of the cooking water.

For the glaze, put all the ingredients (except the vinegar and salt) into a small pan over a medium heat and bring to the boil. Simmer gently for 5–10 minutes until reduced to a nice glaze. Season to taste with salt and vinegar.

Preheat the grill (broiler). Brush the octopus tentacles with the glaze.

Grill (broil) the octopus for a couple of minutes until crispy, basting occasionally with the glaze.

See opposite –>

Monica Sheridan's Shellfish Soup

Preparation: 15 minutes
Cooking: 30 minutes
Serves 4

25 g/1 oz (1¾ tablespoons) butter
1 onion, chopped
2 cloves garlic, crushed
1 large potato, peeled and chopped
1.25 litres/44 fl oz (5¼ cups) fish stock (broth)
1 bay leaf
a pinch of saffron
1 kg/2¼ lb mixed shellfish (mussels, clams
   and cockles), scrubbed clean
10 g/¼ oz dried dillisk (dulse), rehydrated
   and chopped
100 ml/3½ fl oz (scant ½ cup) double
   (heavy) cream
small bunch of parsley, chopped
sea salt

This recipe, which is based on a French potato soup, is adapted from Monica Sheridan's *The Art of Irish Cooking* (1965). Interestingly, it contains saffron and seaweed, which represent the two sides of Irish cooking: one that looks out into the world and the other that focuses on the land at home. Sheridan strains her soup and adds the shellfish back in (so it's more of a broth), but I prefer not to. Sheridan was a cook, writer and television host in the 1960s and did much to teach people about food in general. Her irreverent humour brought much joy, and changed many people's attitudes to Irish food. Her books include *Monica's Kitchen* (1963), *The Art of Irish Cooking* (1965) and *My Irish Cookbook* (1965), all of which are still relevant today. Irish food owes her a great debt.

Melt the butter in a large pan over a medium heat. Add the onion, garlic and potatoes and fry for about 5 minutes until the onion is soft. Add the fish stock (broth) with the bay leaf and saffron. Bring to the boil and simmer for about 15 minutes until the potatoes are soft.

Add the shellfish and seaweed, cover and cook for 5–10 minutes until the shellfish have opened. Discard any that don't.

Stir in the cream and the parsley and season. Serve in warmed bowls.

Shellfish

Freshwater Fish

Freshwater Fish

For centuries, rivers have been an important food source for Irish people. From the first settlers to the anglers of today, these same rivers still provide us with food. Mount Sandel, one of the earliest settlements in Ireland, was settled due to the abundance of salmon and eels at the site. Most subsequent settlements and towns were built around rivers, whether at its mouth or along it. Communities, and therefore economies, grew around rivers as there was a constant source of food from the river fish. As well as wild salmon and brown trout, eel provided sustenance to the earliest inhabitants of Ireland. At Lough Boora in County Offaly, Mesolithic settlers fed on eels and hazelnuts to sustain themselves. For me, these are the three central freshwater fish that are tied to Ireland's food history. The salmon holds a particularly important place in Irish history. As well as being an important foodstuff, the salmon was also a vibrant symbol of knowledge. It appears in many of the sagas and heroic tales of the ancient Irish, such as in the Fenian Cycle. In one story, the salmon eats nine hazelnuts that fall into the Well of Wisdom (*an Tobar Segais*) from nine hazel trees that surrounded the well. By eating these nuts, the salmon gained all the world's knowledge. While cooking the salmon for an older poet, Fionn mac Cumhaill burns his thumbs on the crispy fat of the salmon and thereby gains its knowledge.

Nowadays most people fish for fun, rather than to eat, and we no longer rely on our rivers and lakes as a reliable food source like we once did. However, eating river fish is a great way of stepping back in time. River fish also pairs well with the wild food you find around it, such as nettles, garlic and watercress. Saying this, the Irish people's proclivity for salmon has not abated. Wild salmon is a rare treat in Ireland nowadays due to low stocks, and we often only see one or two a year come into the restaurant. Though the debate continues regarding the pros and cons of farmed salmon, (including organic farmed salmon, which we use in our restaurants), our appetite for it continues.

Turf-smoked Salmon

Smoking salmon over turf was quite common in Ireland. Though now most producers favour oak and other woods, I love the taste of turf-smoked salmon. Turf fires were widespread in cottages and it would have made perfect sense to preserve the fish over the smoke of the fire. Before smoking the fish, it needs to be brined in a salt water solution. This helps to keep the fish moist while smoking. Fishermen in the west of Ireland often smoked salmon that they had just caught over the smouldering turf fires on their boats. These fires would have been in three-legged pots.

Wild Salmon 'Poached' in Clay

Preparation: 5 minutes
Cooking: 30 minutes
Serves 6

1 × 5 kg/11 lb salmon
rapeseed (canola) oil
herbs and lemon (optional)
clay, as needed
sea salt

In her book, *The Art of Irish Cooking* (1965), Monica Sheridan mentions how a man cooked a salmon in mud over a turf fire. She says it was the 'nicest salmon I have ever eaten'. Baking fish or vegetables in clay (or mud) is an age-old way of cooking, being particularly good because it traps the moisture into the fish, thereby keeping it nice and succulent. It is still a popular method in Greece and southern parts of Italy.

Lay the whole salmon onto a baking sheet. Remove the fins, brush with oil and season with salt. If you want to put any aromatics such as herbs or lemon into the belly of the salmon, now is the time to do it. Mix the clay with water until it is the consistency of a paste.

Preheat the oven to 180°C/350°F/ Gas Mark 4. Cover the salmon completely and bake in the oven for 30 minutes.

Remove from the oven and rest for the same time. Crack open the clay and serve.

Poached Wild Salmon

Preparation: 5 minutes
Cooking: 25 minutes
Serves 4

500 ml/17 fl oz (generous 2 cups) cider (hard cider)
30 g/1 oz (1½ tablespoons) honey
1 bay leaf
1 side of wild salmon, pin-boned
sea salt

To serve
50 g/2 oz (4 tablespoons) butter
coarse (kosher) sea salt
a handful of watercress

Put 500 ml/17 fl oz (generous 2 cups) of water, the cider, honey and bay leaf into a pan (a fish kettle is probably best) large enough to accommodate the salmon. Add a handful of salt and bring to the boil.

Reduce the heat so that the water is at a bare simmer, then place the fish in the water and poach for 10 minutes. Remove it from the water.

Melt the butter in a small pan over a medium–low heat. Brush the salmon with the melted butter and season with coarse sea salt.

Garnish with the watercress.

Grilled Wild Salmon Steaks with Parsley Butter

Preparation: 15 minutes, plus chilling time
Cooking: 15 minutes
Serves 4

50 g/2 oz (4 tablespoons) butter
4 wild salmon steaks
watercress, to serve
sea salt

For the parsley butter
100 g/3½ oz (7 tablespoons) butter,
   at room temperature
2 tablespoons chopped parsley
juice of 1 lemon

If you can't source wild salmon steaks, use organic salmon fillets instead. Just pay attention to the cooking time if the fillet is thicker.

To make the parsley butter, put all the ingredients into a food processor and blend until smooth. Roll into a cylinder with the aid of cling film (plastic wrap). Chill in the refrigerator for at least 45 minutes to set.

Preheat the grill (broiler) or put a griddle pan over medium–high heat. Melt the butter in a small pan over a medium–low heat.

Brush the salmon with the melted butter and season with sea salt. Place under the preheated grill or onto the griddle pan and cook for 10–15 minutes, depending on steak thickness, until they reach a core temperature of 58°C/136°F on a meat thermometer.

Slice a round of parsley butter and place on the top of each salmon steak. Garnish with some watercress.

See opposite –>

Wild Salmon with Scapes and Pickled Wild Garlic Buds

Preparation: 15 minutes
Cooking: 15 minutes
Serves 4

1 tablespoon rapeseed (canola) oil
4 × 150-g/5-oz wild salmon fillets
350 g/12 oz (3 sticks) butter, cubed
500 ml/17 fl oz (generous 2 cups) cider
   (hard cider)
2 bay leaves
wild garlic vinegar (see Herb or Fruit Vinegar,
   page 352), to taste (optional)
20 garlic scapes, trimmed
pickled wild garlic buds
   (see Pickled Ramsons, page 356)
sea salt

This recipe not only celebrates the salmon but also the wild garlic (ramps) season. If you missed it, not to worry, as it comes every year! Garlic scapes are extremely popular now and can be found in most markets in Ireland.

Preheat the oven to 180°C/350°F/ Gas Mark 4.

Heat the oil in a large frying pan (skillet) over a medium heat. Season the salmon with sea salt and fry on the skin side for about 5 minutes until crispy. Remove from the frying pan and discard the excess oil.

Place the fish on a baking sheet with a little of the butter on top of each fillet.

Pour the cider into a medium pan over a high heat, add the bay leaves, bring to the boil and heat for about 15 minutes or until reduced to 300 ml/10 fl oz (1¼ cups).

Remove from the heat and add the rest of the butter to the sauce. Blend with an immersion blender until smooth. Season with salt and vinegar, if using.

Meanwhile, put the fish into the preheated oven for 3–5 minutes until cooked to your liking.

Bring a medium pan of salted water to the boil over a high heat, then blanch the garlic scapes for 1 minutes. Remove from the water and season with salt.

To serve, place the salmon and scapes on the plates and pour the sauce over the scapes. Garnish with some pickled wild garlic buds.

Freshwater Fish

Salmon with New Potatoes, Spinach and Cider Cream

Preparation: 10 minutes
Cooking: 45 minutes
Serves 4

280 g/10 oz new potatoes
5 tablespoons rapeseed (canola) oil
4 × 150-g/5-oz salmon fillets
50 g/2 oz (4 tablespoons) butter
200 ml/7 fl oz (scant 1 cup) cider (hard cider)
200 ml/7 fl oz (scant 1 cup) double (heavy) cream
100 g/3½ oz (3½ cups) baby spinach
sea salt

Preheat the oven to 180°C/350°F/Gas Mark 4.

Put the new potatoes into a large pan of salted water over a high heat, bring to the boil and boil for about 15 minutes, or until you can pierce them with a knife. Cool under cold running water. Pat dry with paper towels and quarter.

Warm 1 tablespoon of the oil in an ovenproof frying pan (skillet). Place the salmon, skin side down, in the pan. Fry for about 5 minutes until the skin is crispy. Add the butter and baste until the top of the salmon is no longer translucent. Transfer the salmon in the pan to the preheated oven for 6–8 minutes or until the salmon is cooked to your liking.

Meanwhile, pour the cider into a medium pan over a medium heat and heat for about 10 minutes until reduced by half. Add the cream and reduce again for a further 10 minutes or so until you achieve a sauce consistency. Season to taste.

Heat the remaining oil in a separate frying pan. Fry the potatoes for 5–10 minutes until nicely caramelized, then add the spinach and cook briefly for about 1 minute until the spinach wilts.

To serve, place the potatoes and spinach on the base of each plate. Place the salmon on top of the potatoes and pour the sauce around the salmon.

Dill-cured Salmon with Horseradish Cream

Preparation: 10 minutes, plus minimum 24 hours curing time
Serves 4

80 g/3 oz (⅓ cup) granulated sugar
120 g/4 oz (½ cup) coarse (kosher) sea salt
1 large bunch of dill
1 side of salmon, pin-boned

For the horseradish cream
125 g/4½ oz (½ cup) crème fraîche
1 tablespoon freshly grated horseradish
sea salt

Combine the sugar, salt and dill, then spread the mix over the salmon. Place the salmon on a tray, wrap in cling film (plastic wrap) and place in the refrigerator. Cure for at least 24 hours. You can place a weight on top of the salmon to cure it quicker. Up to 48 hours is fine. Rinse the salmon before serving. You can also leave it another day in the refrigerator after rinsing.

When ready to serve, mix the crème fraîche with the horseradish and season. Slice the salmon and serve with the horseradish cream.

Note
It's also possible to cure salmon in the same way using fresh horseradish. Replace the dill in the recipe with 3 tablespoons freshly grated horseradish, and serve with some sheep's yogurt and watercress. Try using toasted fennel seeds in a cure for salmon, too – I like to brush the salmon with beer first when doing this.

See opposite –>

Freshwater Fish

Smoked Salmon with Cream Cheese and Trout Roe

Preparation: 10 minutes
Serves 4

100 g/3½ oz (scant ½ cup) cream cheese
100 g/3½ oz (scant ½ cup) crème fraîche
1 tablespoon chopped dill
250 g/9 oz smoked salmon, thinly sliced
50 g/2 oz trout roe
1 tablespoon Pickled Ramsons (see page 356)
extra virgin rapeseed (canola) oil

Combine the cheese and crème fraîche in a small mixing bowl with the dill, reserving a little dill for finishing the plate.

Lay the salmon on a platter and place the cream cheese mixture in the centre. Garnish with the trout roe and ramsons. Finish with a little oil and fresh dill.

Soused Wild Salmon with Spices

Preparation: 10 minutes, plus chilling time
Cooking: 5 minutes plus 2 days pickling time
Serves 8

200 ml/7 fl oz (scant 1 cup) malt vinegar
100 g/3½ oz (½ cup) granulated sugar
2 teaspoons mustard seeds
1 teaspoon whole allspice berries
2 teaspoons coriander seeds
2 whole cloves
1 teaspoon ground ginger
1 bay leaf
1 piece of cinnamon
1 wild salmon, filleted and pin-boned

Put all the ingredients apart from the salmon into a medium pan with 200 ml/7 fl oz (scant 1 cup) water. Place over a medium heat and bring to the boil. Remove from the heat and allow to cool.

Place the salmon in a suitable lidded container.

Pour the pickling liquid over the salmon, cover and refrigerate for 48 hours.

Remove the salmon from the liquid to serve.

Brown Trout with Leeks

Preparation: 15 minutes
Cooking: 20 minutes
Serves 2

2 medium or 1 large brown trout, scaled and gutted
extra virgin rapeseed (canola) oil
small bunch of lovage
4 leeks, trimmed of their tops and sliced into 2-cm/¾-inch rounds
200 g/7 oz (1¾ sticks) butter, cubed
500 ml/17 fl oz (generous 2 cups) cider (hard cider)
sea salt

Lovage is a herb related to celery. It has a similar taste. If you cannot locate it, you can use flat-leaf parsley instead. You can also use white wine instead of cider for a lighter taste. If the trout is big, just use one.

Preheat the oven to 180°C/350°F/ Gas Mark 4.

Make a few diagonal incisions on each side of the fish, rub with oil and season with salt. Stuff the belly of the fish with some of the lovage.

Place the leeks upright on a large roasting pan. Dot the butter around the leeks. Place the rest of the lovage on top of the leeks and top with the fish. Pour over the cider.

Bake the fish in the preheated oven for 20 minutes, basting occasionally. Allow to rest for 5 minutes before serving.

To serve, place the fish and the leeks on a large serving platter. Blend the butter and cider together and spoon the sauce over both.

See opposite –>

Freshwater Fish

Trout Meunière á la Monica Sheridan

Preparation and cooking: 15 minutes
Serves 4

4 trout fillets
plain (all-purpose) flour, for dredging
100 ml/3½ fl oz (scant ½ cup) clarified butter
lemon juice, to taste
2 teaspoons chopped parsley
sea salt and freshly ground black pepper

This recipe is adapted from Monica Sheridan's book *The Art of Irish Cooking* (1965). Her original recipe contains no measurements and is more of a prose poem written with gusto! The word 'meunière' means 'miller's wife'. Thus, to cook something à la meunière was to cook it by first dredging it in flour. French methods of cooking were imported into Ireland from at least the eighteenth century onwards, particularly in aristocratic (landed gentry) country houses and estates. A lot of these cooking methods, as Regina Sexton has observed, were 'an indirect statement of the family's ambitions of status, good standing and taste'. The use of French terms still continues in many Irish restaurants today, which makes a case for our continued fascination with French cooking.

Put the flour into a bowl and season with salt and pepper. Dredge the trout fillets in the seasoned flour.

Heat the clarified butter in a large frying pan (skillet) over a medium heat.

Fry the trout fillets for 5–6 minutes, turning once, until golden brown.

Season with salt and lemon juice and garnish with the parsley.

Baked Brown Trout Stuffed with Herbs and Lemon

Preparation: 15 minutes
Cooking: 18 minutes
Serves 1

50 g/2 oz (4 tablespoons) butter, plus a little extra to rub the outside of the fish
4 shallots, chopped
50 g/2 oz (1 cup) fresh breadcrumbs
grated zest and juice of 1 lemon
1 tablespoon chopped chives
1 tablespoon chopped parsley
1 brown trout, scaled and gutted, with the central bone removed
sea salt

The brown trout (*Salmo trutta*) or *breac donn* (Irish) is a native Irish species of freshwater fish. It's probably the most common river fish that is eaten in Ireland. I think the medium-sized fish are best for cooking.

Preheat the oven to 180°C/350°F/ Gas Mark 4.

Melt the butter in a medium pan over a medium heat, add the shallots and fry for about 2 minutes until translucent. Add the bread-crumbs and the lemon juice and zest. Remove from the heat and fold in the fresh herbs. Season the mixture with sea salt.

Stuff the fish with the stuffing and tie with some twine to keep the stuffing in place. Rub the outside of the fish with a little butter and season with sea salt. Put into a roasting pan and bake in the preheated oven for 15 minutes.

Brown Trout with a Warm Kale and Barley Salad

Preparation: 10 minutes

Cooking: 30 minutes

Serves 4

250 g/9 oz (1¼ cups) barley

100 ml/3½ fl oz (scant ½ cup) extra virgin
   rapeseed (canola) oil, plus extra for frying
   and oiling the fish

2 leeks, sliced into rounds

1 teaspoon fennel seeds

150 g /5 oz (2 cups prepared) kale, stems
   removed and leaves cut in pieces

25 g/1 oz (½ cup prepared) tarragon, chopped

2 tablespoons apple balsamic vinegar

4 brown trout fillets

1 bay leaf

sea salt

Put the barley into a medium pan, cover with water and season with salt. Bring to a simmer and cook over a medium–low heat for about 25 minutes until tender.

Meanwhile, preheat the oven to 180°C/350°F/Gas Mark 4.

Heat some oil in a frying pan (skillet) over a medium–low heat, add the leeks and fennel seeds and fry for about 5 minutes until tender. Add the kale and a little water, then cover and allow the kale to steam for a further 5 minutes until tender.

Remove from the heat and mix together with the barley and tarragon. Season to taste.

Blend the oil and vinegar and dress the barley and kale mixture.

Rub the trout fillets with some oil and season with salt. Bake on a baking sheet in the preheated oven for 5–7 minutes until the fish is opaque.

Serve the fish with the barley and kale salad.

Fried Pollan

Preparation and cooking: 15 minutes

Serves 4

4 pollan, gutted and scaled

plain (all-purpose) flour, for dusting

rapeseed (canola) oil, for frying

lemon wedges, for serving

sea salt and freshly ground black pepper

Pollan is a river fish found in Lough Neagh. In her book *The Cookin' Woman: Irish Country Recipes* (1949), Florence Irwin recounts that fishmongers would be heard crying, 'Pollan alive and kicking in the cart'. Pollan was usually fried in flour, but it was on occasion also used for soup. Lough Neagh Pollan is now recognized as a Protected Food Name (PFN) under EU law. Pollan is making a comeback and can be found on menus in the more adventurous restaurants.

Dust the fish in flour.

Heat a little oil in a frying pan (skillet) over a medium heat and fry the fish on both sides, for 5–6 minutes total, until cooked.

Season with salt and pepper before serving with lemon wedges.

Freshwater Fish

Pike with Gooseberries and Sherry

Preparation: 10 minutes
Cooking: 30 minutes
Serves 4

300 g/11 oz (2 cups) green gooseberries,
    topped and bottomed (trimmed)
1 shallot, finely diced
100 ml/3½ fl oz (scant ½ cup) fino sherry
75 ml/2½ fl oz (⅓ cup) sherry vinegar
75 g/2¾ oz (⅓ cup firmly packed) soft
    brown sugar
4 × 150-g/5-oz pike fillets
sea salt
edible flowers, to garnish (optional)

Put the gooseberries and shallot into a medium pan with the sherry, sherry vinegar and brown sugar. Bring to the boil over a medium heat and simmer for 20–25 minutes until you achieve a light jammy consistency.

Bring a large pan of salted water to the boil over a medium heat, add the pike, reduce to a simmer and poach for 3–5 minutes, depending on your preference.

Garnish the pike fillets with edible flowers if you wish, and serve with a generous spoonful of gooseberries.

See opposite –>

Whole Pike Wrapped in Bacon with Sage Stuffing

Preparation: 20 minutes
Cooking: 25 minutes, plus resting time
Serves 4

1 pike
16 rashers (slices) smoked streaky
    (regular) bacon

For the stuffing
100 g/3½ oz (7 tablespoons) butter,
    plus extra for greasing
1 onion, finely diced
2 tablespoons finely chopped sage
100 g/3½ oz (2 cups) fresh breadcrumbs
sea salt

The idea of wrapping a fish in rashers (bacon) is a strange one, but it seems to have been practised occasionally in Ireland. The fat of the pork helps keep the fish moist and imparts the unique flavour of pork fat (lard) into the fish. Pork fat was a common cooking fat in Ireland before the introduction of cooking oils, such as sunflower and olive oil, in the twentieth century.

Preheat the oven to 180°C/350°F/ Gas Mark 4. Grease a roasting pan.

To make the stuffing, melt the butter in a frying pan (skillet) over a medium–low heat. Add the onion and sage and season with sea salt. Cook for about 5 minutes until the onion is soft. Remove from the heat and fold in the breadcrumbs. Leave to cool slightly.

Fill the cavity of the pike with the stuffing. Wrap the pike in the bacon rashers (slices), leaving the head and tail exposed. Depending on the size of the fish, you may not need all the rashers.

Lay the fish on the greased pan and roast in the preheated oven for 20 minutes, or until the core temperature of the fish reaches 55°C/130°F on a meat thermometer. Remove from the oven and allow to rest for 5 minutes.

Freshwater Fish

Whole Carp with New Potatoes and Pickled Beetroot

Preparation: 20 minutes
Cooking: 30 minutes
Serves 4

1 kg/2¼ lb new potatoes, scrubbed clean
150 g/5 oz (1¼ sticks) butter, cubed
2 carp, gutted and scaled
1 tablespoon apple balsamic vinegar,
   or to taste
extra virgin rapeseed (canola) oil
sea salt

For the pickled beetroot
4 medium beetroot (beets), cooked and peeled
300 ml/10 fl oz (1¼ cups) apple cider vinegar
100 g/3½ oz (½ cup) granulated sugar
a few sprigs of thyme

Carp is an oily freshwater fish. There are four types of carp in the rivers of Ireland. Because of the low water temperatures, they don't grow to a great size, but I find the small ones better to cook with. One large carp can be used in the recipe, however. Carp can be fished throughout the summer months. Due to their strong flavour, they work well with potatoes and pickled vegetables. Unfortunately, most Irish people don't eat them, though they're a favourite for many of my Polish friends.

Preheat the oven to 180°C/350°F/Gas Mark 4.

Put the potatoes into a large pan and cover with water. Season the water with salt and bring to the boil over a high heat. Reduce the heat to a simmer and cook for about 20 minutes until you can pass the point of a knife through the potatoes. Strain and reserve a little of the water in the pan.

Melt the butter in the pan with the reserved water. When it begins to boil, add the potatoes and toss through the butter emulsion. Season with some sea salt.

Meanwhile, to pickle the beetroot (beets), quarter the cooked beetroot, place it in a heatproof bowl and season with sea salt. Bring the vinegar, 200 ml/7 fl oz (scant 1 cup) of water and the sugar to the boil in a pan over a medium heat. Let cool slightly.

Pour the pickling liquid over the beetroot and allow to cool completely.

To cook the fish, rub both sides with some oil and season lightly with salt. Place on a hot griddle (grill) pan and grill both sides for about 1 minute each until the skin is crispy (you can also skip this step and put it straight into the oven).

Transfer the fish to a roasting pan, put it into the oven and cook for 5–7 minutes or until the core temperature of the fish reaches 45°C/113°F on a meat thermometer. Remove from the oven and transfer to paper towels to absorb the excess fat.

Brush the top of the carp with some apple balsamic vinegar. Season with a little more salt. Serve the dish family-style on separate dishes.

See opposite –>

Perch Baked in Milk with Bay Leaf and Mace

Preparation: 10 minutes
Cooking: 20 minutes
Serves 4

150 g/5 oz (1¼ sticks) butter
2 perch, trimmed of their fins
350 ml/12 fl oz (1½ cups) milk
2 bay leaves
1 blade of mace
sea salt

Preheat the oven to 180°C/350°F/Gas Mark 4. Grease the bottom of a baking dish large enough to fit both the fish.

Rub the fish with the remaining butter and season with sea salt. Place the two fish in the dish then pour the milk into the dish. Add the bay leaves with the mace and cover the dish.

Bake in the preheated oven for 20 minutes. Remove from the oven and allow to stand for 5 minutes.

Remove the fish from the dish, discard the bay leaves and the mace and blend the sauce to emulsify the milk and butter. Pour the sauce over the fish and serve.

Freshwater Fish

Eel

Archaeologists have found evidence of eel fishing dating back to the Bronze Age. In ancient times, the most efficient way of fishing for eel would have been trapping, using stationary wooden fish traps at the mouth of freshwater streams during their migration into the sea. Eels could also be caught using a three-pronged spear. In the Middle Ages, eels were a source of protein for the poor. Eel weirs were established, and though eel consumption has declined, Lough Neagh in Northern Ireland is the home of the largest wild-caught eel fishery in Europe. Eel fishing has been a major industry on the lough for centuries. Since 1960, Lough Neagh Fishermen's Co-operative manage the fishery. It now manages the production of around 400 tonnes of eels annually and exports internationally. The eel is brined and then smoked traditionally. This is where we source all our smoked eel. I find it unfortunate that most people do not want to engage with eel nowadays. No doubt this is due to it receiving poor treatment in their childhood, being overcooked and tasteless. Boiled eel in a heavy white sauce does not sound appetizing in the least. Eels were also associated with poverty (as was most fish). It is time we re-evaluate our attitude towards eel. Though eel stocks are low and most commercial fishing is not allowed, you can source it responsibly and try it. Smoked eel is a real delicacy whose taste is tied to Irish history.

☼ ✄ ⊖ ⊕

How to Smoke an Eel

Preparation: 10 minutes, plus chilling time
Cooking: 1 hour plus 24 hours soaking and drying time
Serves 4

1 kg/2¼ lb eel, gutted
50 g/2 oz (3 tablespoons) rock salt
a small handful of wood chips

You will need a smoker to make this recipe. They can be bought relatively cheaply (they are widely available online), but if you can't get hold of one, you can buy eel ready-smoked. Smoked eel is wonderful in salad, folded into mashed potatoes or made into Potato Cakes (see page 148). In Aniar, we serve it with a light potato mousse. The key is to contrast the strong flavour of the eel with a neutral or light flavour.

Salt the eel for at least 12 hours in a suitable tray in the refrigerator. Turn the eel frequently.

Rinse the salt off the eel and dry with a cloth. Return to the refrigerator and allow to dry for a further 12 hours.

Set up the smoker following the manufacturer's instructions and smoke the eel over a low smoke for 1 hour or until cooked through.

Note

Eels are mostly smoked vertically, with a hook tied around their head so that it doesn't break off. If you only have a horizontal box smoker, the eels will smoker faster because they will be closer to the smoke. Keep an eye on the amount of smoke and heat coming from the smoker. I use a horizontal box smoker for hot smoking all our fish in the restaurant.

Collared Eel

Preparation: 15 minutes
Cooking: 35 minutes
Serves 4

1 large eel, boned but not skinned
apple cider vinegar
sea salt and freshly ground black pepper

For the herb and spice mix
2 teaspoons finely chopped marjoram
2 teaspoons finely chopped thyme
2 teaspoons finely chopped sage
½ teaspoon freshly grated nutmeg
½ teaspoon mace
2½ teaspoons sea salt

While the original practice of collaring was confined to the pig – a boned and rolled neck of pork (or 'collar') that was tied with string and poached – the term became associated with the technique of boning and rolling many different foodstuffs, including eels. An all but forgotten practice, collared eel appears in many country house recipe books from the seventeenth and eighteenth centuries. Mace is a spice often used in cooking of the time. It is the lacy red aril that covers nutmeg seeds. After being hand-picked and removed from the seed, it is dried and becomes brown. You can buy ground mace, or it can be found in whole blades. Until the nineteenth century, it was only available from the so-called 'Spice Islands', located in Indonesia. It is fascinating to think of the distance that mace needed to travel in order to get to Ireland. It is still a popular spice, though limited mostly to baking.

To prepare the herb and spice mix, combine the fresh herbs with the spices and salt in a mixing bowl.

Season the flesh side of the eel with the mix and then roll up the eel as tightly as you can and secure with kitchen string or tape.

Bring a large pan of salted water to the boil and reduce to a simmer.

Place the eel in the water and poach for 25–30 minutes until the meat starts to fall apart. Gently remove the eel from the water.

To store the eel, mix half the cooking liquid with equal parts vinegar and boil. Put the collared eel into the pickling liquid and store until needed.

Eel and Onion Soup

Preparation: 10 minutes
Cooking: 1 hour 5 minutes
Serves 4

100 g/3½ oz (7 tablespoons) butter
500 g/1 lb 2 oz (about 4) onions, sliced
a few sprigs of thyme
1 blade of mace or 1 teaspoon ground mace
1.5 litres/50 fl oz (6¼ cups) ham water
    (water leftover from cooking ham),
    or stock (broth) of your choice
200 g/7 oz fresh or smoked eel, cut into
    bite-sized pieces
a bunch of herbs, such as tarragon, parsley,
    dill and chervil, chopped together
sea salt

If using fresh eel, you'll need to skin, clean and fillet them. Alternatively, you can use smoked eel fillets – I usually use them for ease. If using smoked eel, the eel can be added at the very end because it is already cooked. If using fresh fillets, 5–10 minutes cooking time is sufficient.

Melt the butter in a large pan over a medium heat. Add the onions and season with sea salt. Add the thyme and mace and fry over a low heat for 20 minutes until the onions are nicely caramelized.

Add the ham water, bring to the boil, reduce the heat and simmer for 45 minutes. If using fresh eel, add it in the last 5–10 minutes of the cooking time. Remove from the heat. Alternatively, add the smoked eel after removing the pan from the heat.

Add the herbs, adjust the seasoning and serve.

Smoked Eel and Potato Salad

Preparation: 15 minutes
Cooking: 20 minutes
Serves 4

750 g/1 lb 10 oz waxy potatoes, peeled
    and cubed
100 g/3½ oz smoked eel, flaked
1 red onion, finely diced
4 gherkins (pickles), finely diced, plus some
    of the liquid
100 g/3½ oz (½ cup) mayonnaise
parsley, finely chopped
sea salt

Bring a large pan of salted water to the boil over a medium heat, add the potatoes and simmer for about 15 minutes until cooked but still having a bite. Strain and cool.

Combine all the ingredients in a large bowl. Mix together and season with salt and a little vinegar from the gherkins (pickles) according to your taste.

See opposite –>

 # Smoked Eel and Potato Cakes

Preparation: 25 minutes
Cooking: 4 minutes, plus 2–3 minutes
per batch
Serves 4

rapeseed (canola) oil, for deep-frying
800 g/1¾ lb (about 7 medium)
    potatoes, peeled, cooked and mashed
1 onion, finely chopped
250 g/9 oz smoked eel
15 g/½ oz (¼ cup prepared) chopped parsley
plain (all-purpose) flour, for dusting
sea salt

Heat 1 tablespoon of oil in a small pan over a medium heat and fry the onion for 3–4 minutes until translucent. Drain any excess oil.

Heat the oil in a deep-fat fryer until the oil reaches 180°C/350°F, or until a cube of bread browns in 30 seconds.

In a large bowl, combine the potato, eel, onion and parsley, season to taste and mix together thoroughly. Shape the mixture into golf-ball sized balls.

Pat dry with paper towels and dust the balls in flour. Ensure they are completely dry before dusting, as any water will cause them to split.

Fry the balls, in batches if necessary, in the hot oil for 2–3 minutes until golden brown and crispy. Allow the oil to return to temperature between batches. Drain on paper towels and serve.

 # River Fish and Mushroom Broth

Preparation: 25 minutes
Cooking: 1 hour 25 minutes
Makes 2 litres/70 fl oz (8½ cups)

2 tablespoons rapeseed (canola) oil
2 fennel bulbs, diced
2 leeks, sliced
1 onion, diced
2 bay leaves
2 sprigs of thyme
500 ml/17 fl oz (generous 2 cups) cider
    (hard cider)
50 g/2 oz dried mixed wild mushrooms
1 kg/2¼ lb river fish, such as pike or perch,
    roughly chopped and rinsed
sea salt

Heat the oil in a large pan over a low heat, add the fennel, leeks and onion and fry for 10 minutes until the vegetables are soft.

Add the bay leaves and thyme and season with sea salt. Add the cider and dried mushrooms and bring to the boil.

Place the fish in the pan and cover with water. Return to the boil, then reduce the heat to a simmer. Allow to simmer for 1 hour.

Strain through a sieve lined with a piece of muslin (cheesecloth). Season to taste and serve.

Freshwater Fish

Freshwater Fish

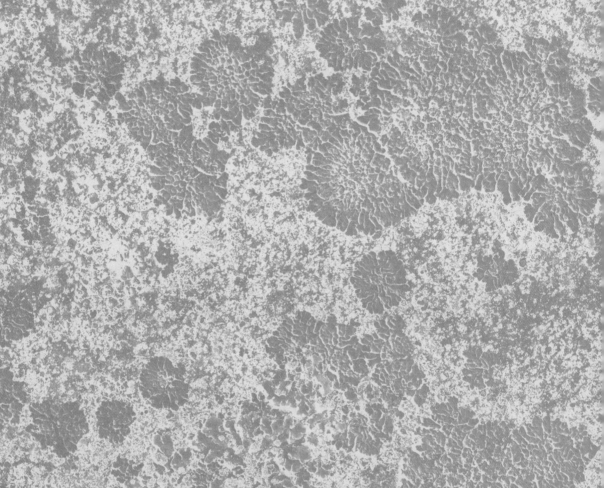

Saltwater Fish

Saltwater Fish

You'd be forgiven for thinking that Ireland is not an island surrounded by the sea, given our relationship with seafood. As a nation, we have under-appreciated the sea and its wonderful bounty. Growing up, all I ever ate was bony whiting, floured to the point of gruel. No wonder many of my generation didn't like fish. Why was this so? What happened to our relationship with fish? Historically, this was not always the case. Coastal communities have long set up by the sea because of its nourishment. In the case of Ireland, I can only imagine that colonialism and religious conflict affected our access and the way in which we valued sea fish. Access to ports for deep-sea fishing was not something the native Irish had, especially during the contested period of colonization by the English. Ireland became a breeding ground for cattle for the British Empire (we exported beef by the tonne). Thus, a lot of the fish that appeared in recent Irish food recipes are small fish that swim closer to shore such as mackerel and herring. However, salted ling (and other salted fish) does feature prominently in the south, so fishing was done, just not on a scale large enough to feed an entire population. Talking to people who lived by the sea, I understand that the absence of fish in my diet did not mean the absence of fish in all diets. Coastal communities have lived off the sea out of necessity since the very first settlers came to Ireland. But this necessity does constitute a food culture. Roasting whole fish over the fire, curing and smoking mackerel over smouldering turf: these are wonderful images for Irish food and should hold a firm place in our imagination as much as the potato or beef.

However, fish's association with abstinence did not help its image. Also, and because of this, fish became wrapped up with the image of poverty. As with shellfish, before the twentieth century, produce of the sea was generally given less value than produce from the land. One could argue that this has always been the case everywhere since the agricultural revolution. People began to feed themselves from the land and hence turned away from the sea. The land offered more security. Those living by the coast enjoyed the seafood, but those that did not had little access. It is worth remembering that all the first Irish communities settled by the sea, so when thinking about Irish food and its legacy, we need to re-evaluate the role of the sea. Irish food has a long history and often recent times (the last two hundred to three hundred years) blinds us from seeing further back into our past: into the many meals that have been enjoyed by the sea.

As well as not appreciating the quality of fish we get in Ireland, we do not seem to understand that fish in its raw state is a truly beautiful thing. Raw mackerel is delicious with a little apple balsamic vinegar (which is produced in Ireland), as is lightly salted halibut with pickled elderflowers. Cod is another fish that is suited to a raw or lightly cooked state. I always urge the students of our cookery classes in Aniar to at least taste raw fish: it won't kill you! Memories of eating overcooked fish will haunt my youth forever, but that does not mean that the future of Irish seafood is bleak. Cooking fish delicately is the only way to go. There are too many stories in Ireland of people being fed fish that was overcooked, and I can certainly contribute a few. Fish on Friday and during Lent is what I remember. I am glad those days are gone. Now, when I roast a whole turbot with seaweed, I think back through the entire history of Irish food and know that it has its place there. The sea is a wonderful resource with an abundance of wild food. We need to treasure it so that it may continue to be there and feed us for the next thousand years.

Fried Cod's Roe

Preparation: 10 minutes
Cooking: 35 minutes
Serves 4

450 g/1 lb whole cod's roe, in membrane
1 clove garlic
2 teaspoons apple cider vinegar
1 small white onion, quartered
a few sprigs of thyme
a few lemon wedges, to serve
sea salt

To fry the roe
plain (all-purpose) flour, for dredging
50 g/2 oz (4 tablespoons) butter

Though seldom eaten nowadays, fried cod's roe is a nutritious meal. In James Joyce's *Ulysses* (1922), one of the central characters, Leopold Bloom, delights in 'fried hencods' roes'. Though the pungent flavour appeals to his senses, it may not appeal to many younger eaters.

To poach the cod's roe, lightly salt and wrap the cod's roe in a piece of muslin (cheesecloth) and tie at each end. Alternatively, salt and wrap in cling film (plastic wrap). Fill a medium pan with water and add the garlic, vinegar, white onion, thyme and some sea salt. Bring the water to the boil over a medium heat and reduce to a simmer. Add the cod's roe and poach for 25 minutes or until firm. Remove from the water and cool.

Slice the cod's roe into rounds and dredge in flour.

Heat the butter in a frying pan (skillet) over a medium heat and fry the cod's roe for 3–4 minutes until nicely browned.

Serve with some lemon wedges.

Creamed Salted Cod

Preparation: 15 minutes, plus soaking time
Cooking: 20 minutes, plus overnight soaking time
Serves 4

500 g/1 lb 2 oz salt cod
400 g/14 oz (about 4 medium) potatoes, peeled and diced
500 ml/17 fl oz (generous 2 cups) milk
2 cloves garlic, thinly sliced
1 bay leaf
100 ml/3½ fl oz (scant ½ cup) single (light) cream
3½ tablespoons olive oil
a whole nutmeg, for grating
toast and bitter greens, to serve

Creamed salted cod was popular in Ireland in the mid-twentieth century, appearing in many cookbooks of the day, such Monica Sheridan's *The Art of Irish Cooking* (1965). In this recipe, I add a potato to give a little more substance to the dish. Ideally, the creamed fish is served on toast, but it would also have been served with potatoes and rice. The process of creaming fish was used for smoked haddock and salted ling, too. This blending of fish with milk and olive oil originates in the south of France, namely in Roussillon, Languedoc and Provence. However there are many European variations in places such as Spain, Portugal, Italy and even as far north as Denmark and Finland.

Soak the cod in water overnight. Remove from the water and rinse.

Put the potatoes into a large pan and cover with water. Bring to the boil over a medium heat and simmer for about 15 minutes until soft. Strain.

Meanwhile, put the cod into a separate large pan with the milk, garlic and bay leaf and simmer for 10 minutes. Strain and reserve the milk.

Put the potatoes and cod into a food processor with the cream and olive oil. Grate a little nutmeg into the mix and blend, adding enough of the reserved milk to make a nice purée.

Serve on some toast with bitter greens.

Cod with Saffron and Tomatoes

Preparation: 15 minutes
Cooking: 40 minutes
Serves 4

1 tablespoon rapeseed (canola) oil
1 onion, finely diced
2 cloves garlic, crushed
150 g/5 oz (about 3 small) potatoes,
    peeled and diced
1 bay leaf
175 ml/6 fl oz (¾ cup) sherry
a good pinch of saffron
350 ml/12 fl oz (1½ cups) fish stock (broth)
1 × 400-g (14-oz) can of chopped
    tomatoes, blended
600 g/1 lb 5 oz cod fillet, skinned
    and boned, cut into bite-sized pieces
2 tablespoons parsley
sea salt and freshly ground black pepper

Saffron has been used in Irish cooking for the last few hundred years. Though this recipe derives from a Mediterranean style of cooking, similar recipes appear in many Irish cookbooks of the mid to late twentieth century. For me, it demonstrates the influence of European modes of cooking after World War II. Ireland became a member of the Council of Europe in 1949 and joined the United Nations in 1955. The country began to look outwards again after decades of economic stagnation. Because the fish cooks quickly, always put it in near the end to ensure the flavour and texture of the fish is still there.

Heat the oil in a large pan over a medium heat, add the onion and garlic, cover and cook for about 5 minutes until soft and nicely coloured. Season with a little salt.

Add the potatoes and bay leaf and cook for a few minutes. Then add the sherry, saffron and fish stock (broth). Cook for about 15 minutes until the potatoes are nearly tender.

Add the tomatoes, reduce to a simmer and cook for 15 minutes. In the last minute, add the fish and cook for 1 minute. Add the chopped parsley and season to taste with salt and pepper.

See opposite –>

Cod, Peas, Barley and Cavolo Nero

Preparation: 15 minutes
Cooking: 25 minutes
Serves 2

2 tablespoons rapeseed (canola) oil
1 onion, diced
100 g/3½ oz (½ cup) barley
300 ml/10 fl oz (1¼ cups) vegetable
    stock (broth)
75 g/2¾ oz (½ cup) green peas
75 g/2¾ oz (5½ tablespoons) butter, cubed
300 g/11 oz cod fillet, cut in two, skin on
a small handful of cavolo nero (lacinato kale),
    stems removed
sea salt

Heat 1 tablespoon of the oil in a large pan over a medium heat, add the onion and fry for about 3 minutes until translucent. Add the barley and fry for 2 minutes. Add the vegetable stock (broth) in stages. When the barley is soft, after about 20 minutes, add the peas. Finally, add 50 g/2 oz (4 tablespoons) of the butter.

Meanwhile, season the fish with salt and leave for 10 minutes.

Heat the remaining oil in a large heavy-based frying pan (skillet) over a medium heat. Put the fish into the pan, skin side down, and heat for 1–2 minutes until the skin is crispy, then add the remaining butter. Baste the fish continuously with the butter.

Cook the fish until the core temperature reaches 50 °C/122 °F on a meat thermometer. If the fillet is large, you may want to put it in the oven preheated to 180 °C/350 °F/Gas Mark 4 for 2–3 minutes. Don't allow the butter to burn. Keep it a nice brown colour.

To serve, blanch the cavolo nero (lacinato kale) in a pan of boiling water for 30 seconds. Season and place it on the bottom of the plate. Spoon the barley onto the plate. Place the fish on the barley.

Saltwater Fish

Saltwater Fish

Beer-battered Hake with Chips and Wild Garlic Mayonnaise

Preparation and cooking: 15 minutes,
plus resting time
Serves 4

250 ml/8 fl oz (1 cup) beer
125 g/4½ oz (1 cup) plain (all-purpose) flour,
   plus a little extra for dusting
¾ teaspoon fast action dried (active dry) yeast
rapeseed (canola) oil, for deep-frying
4 hake fillets, skin removed
sea salt

To serve
chips (French fries) (see page 75)
Wild Garlic Mayonnaise (see page 383)

Combine the beer, flour and yeast in a bowl and whisk until smooth. Set aside and leave at room temperature for 15 minutes.

Preheat the oil in a deep-fat fryer until the oil reaches 175°C/350°F, or until a cube of bread browns in 30 seconds.

Dust the hake in flour and then dip into the batter.

Fry the fish fillets in the oil for 4–8 minutes, depending on the size of the fillets, until they float and are crispy. Remove and shake off the excess oil.

Serve with chips (French fries) and Wild Garlic Mayonnaise.

See opposite –>

Whole Hake with Wild Green Sauce

Preparation: 5 minutes
Cooking: 20 minutes
Serves 4

1 medium hake, gutted and scaled,
   fins removed
sea salt

For the wild green sauce
150 g/5 oz (4–5 cups) wild green herbs such as
   wild garlic (ramps), fennel, sorrel, watercress
175 ml/6 fl oz (¾ cup) extra virgin rapeseed
   (canola) oil, plus extra for oiling the fish
3½ tablespoons apple cider vinegar

This sauce can be made with any green herbs, wild or cultivated. Just pick a selection of three or four that you like and blend together.

Preheat the oven to 200°C/400°F/ Gas Mark 6.

Rub the fish with a little oil and season with sea salt. Roast in the preheated oven for 15–20 minutes or until the core temperature of the fish reaches 45°C/115°F on a meat thermometer.

Remove from the oven and rest in a warm place for 5 minutes.

To make the sauce, put the herbs, oil and vinegar into a food processor and blend. Season with sea salt.

Brill and Wild Garlic

Preparation: 10 minutes
Cooking: 20 minutes
Serves 4

1 medium brill, fins removed
100 g/3½ oz (scant 1 cup) wild garlic
   (ramps) leaves
100 g/3½ oz (7 tablespoons) butter, cubed
200 ml/7 fl oz (scant 1 cup) cider (hard cider)
sea salt

Preheat the oven to 180°C/350°F/ Gas Mark 4.

Wrap the top of the fish with the wild garlic (ramps) leaves. Put the butter cubes on top of the garlic and season with sea salt. Place in a baking pan and pour the cider around the fish.

Bake in the preheated oven for 15–20 minutes until the fish comes away easily from the bone.

      Saltwater Fish

Saltwater Fish

Pollock with Hazelnut Crumb

Preparation and cooking: 15 minutes
Serves 4

500 g/1 lb 2 oz pollock fillet, cut into 4 pieces
50 g/2 oz (4 tablespoons) butter, melted
dill vinegar (see Herb or Fruit Vinegar,
    page 352, optional)
25 g/1 oz (½ cup) fresh breadcrumbs
25 g/1 oz (¼ cup) hazelnuts, ground
2 teaspoons chopped dill
sea salt

I like to serve this with a sorrel leaf salad.

Preheat the oven to 200°C/400°F/
Gas Mark 6.

Line a baking sheet with grease-proof (wax) paper and place the 4 pieces of fish on the sheet. Brush the fish with a little of the melted butter and season with salt and a little of the vinegar, if using.

Combine the breadcrumbs, ground hazelnuts and dill in a bowl.

Cover the fish with the crumb. Drizzle the remaining butter over the top.

Bake in the oven for 7 minutes.

Sea Trout with Mustard and Hazelnut Dressing

Preparation: 25 minutes
Serves 1

100 g/3½ oz sea trout fillet, skinned and
    pin-boned
25 g/1 oz (⅔ cup) small sea beet leaves
    (or baby spinach or chard), to serve

For the dressing
100 ml/3½ fl oz (scant ½ cup) extra
    virgin rapeseed (canola) oil
1½ tablespoons hazelnut oil
3 tablespoons apple cider vinegar
1 teaspoon Dijon mustard
1 teaspoon honey
sea salt, to taste

For the dressing, whisk the ingredients together to form an emulsion.

Slice the trout thinly. Season lightly with salt and leave for 15 minutes.

Dress the fish with the dressing and garnish with the sea beet leaves.

Stuffed Haddock

Preparation: 10 minutes
Cooking: 15 minutes
Serves 4

50 g/2 oz (4 tablespoons) butter, melted,
    reserving a little for brushing the fish
125 g/4½ oz (2¾ cups) fresh breadcrumbs
2 cloves garlic, very finely chopped
2 tablespoons chopped parsley
1 teaspoon chopped thyme leaves
rapeseed (canola) oil, for brushing
2 × 500-g/1-lb 2-oz haddock fillets
sea salt

Preheat the oven to 180°C/350°F/
Gas Mark 4.

To make the stuffing, combine the melted butter with the breadcrumbs, garlic and herbs until it comes together.

Brush oil on the skin side of the fish fillets and season both sides with sea salt.

Place the stuffing on the flesh side of one of the fillets and cover with the other fillet. Ensure the skin side of the fillet is facing upwards. Brush the top fillet with the remaining butter.

Tie the fish with kitchen string (twine) and bake in the preheated oven for 15 minutes.

Smoked Haddock with Poached Egg and Nutmeg

Preparation: 10 minutes
Cooking: 40 minutes
Serves 4

500 ml/17 fl oz (generous 2 cups) milk
1 bay leaf
freshly grated nutmeg, to taste
400 g/14 oz smoked haddock
50 g/2 oz (4 tablespoons) butter
1 leek, chopped
50 g/2 oz (generous ⅓ cup) plain
  (all-purpose) flour
4 eggs
soda bread, to serve

Bring the milk, bay leaf and nutmeg to a simmer in a large pan over a medium heat. Poach the haddock for 6–8 minutes until the fish is opaque. Remove the haddock from the milk and flake into a bowl.

To make a sauce, heat the butter in a small pan over a medium heat, add the leeks and fry for about 5 minutes until soft, then add the flour and heat, stirring continuously, for 2 minutes to make a roux. Pour in the milk and heat for 5–10 minutes until it thickens to a sauce. When thick enough, remove from the heat and add the flaked haddock.

Bring a large pan of water to the boil over a high heat and poach the eggs for 3–5 minutes until cooked to your liking.

Serve the haddock on the soda bread with an egg on top. Finish with a little freshly grated nutmeg.

Whole Roast Turbot with Fennel and Seaweed

Preparation: 15 minutes
Cooking: 15 minutes
Serves 4

1 whole turbot
rapeseed (canola) oil
1 fennel bulb
50 g /2 oz dried kelp, rehydrated in cold water
250 ml/8 fl oz (1 cup) dry cider (hard cider)
150 g/5 oz (1¼ sticks) butter, cubed
tarragon vinegar (see Herb or Fruit Vinegar,
  page 352, optional)
a handful of fennel fronds
sea salt

Preheat the oven to 200°C/400°F/Gas Mark 4. Trim the turbot of its fins and tail. Oil the top and bottom of the fish and season with sea salt.

Halve the fennel lengthwise and shave it on a mandoline. Put the fennel and seaweed into a large roasting pan and dress with a little oil and vinegar, if using. Season with sea salt. Pour the cider over the fennel and seaweed. Add the butter cubes and lay the fish on top.

Roast in the preheated oven for about 15 minutes until the flesh turns opaque and flakes from the bone. Remove the fish from the oven and allow to rest.

Peel the skin from the fish and garnish with the fennel fronds.

Ling with Potatoes

Preparation: 15 minutes
Cooking: 15 minutes
Serves 4

1 kg/2¼ lb (9 medium) potatoes, peeled
250 ml/8 fl oz (1 cup) milk
500 g/1 lb 2 oz ling, cut into pieces
125 g/4½ oz (1 stick plus 1 tablespoon) butter
sea salt

Ling are long, cod-like fish. Salted ling and potatoes was a typical peasant dish, particularly in the south of Ireland. If fuel was scarce, the ling would be placed over the boiling potatoes to save on cooking fuel.

Put the potatoes into a large pan and cover with salted water. Bring to the boil over a high heat and simmer for about 15 minutes until tender.

Meanwhile, warm the milk in a medium pan over a medium–low heat, add the ling and poach for 3 minutes until the flesh is opaque. Strain and reserve the milk.

Drain and mash the potatoes with the reserved milk and the butter. Fold in the ling pieces and season to taste.

Saltwater Fish

Sea Bream in a Dillisk Salt Crust

Preparation: 20 minutes
Cooking: 15 minutes
Serves 4

light rapeseed (canola) oil, for greasing
  and drizzling
1 kg/2¼ lb (3½ cups) salt
4 teaspoons milled dillisk (dulse)
4 egg whites
1 whole sea bream
25 g/1 oz (about 1 cup) fresh dillisk (dulse)
Seaweed Vinegar (see page 352)
coarse (kosher) sea salt

Preheat the oven to 180°C/350°F/ Gas Mark 4. Grease a roasting pan with some oil.

For the salt crust, mix the salt with the milled dillisk (dulse) and egg whites.

Trim the fish of all its fins and place in the prepared pan. Cover the fish with the salt crust. Roast in the preheated oven for 15 minutes.

Dress the fresh dillisk in a small mixing bowl with oil, salt and vinegar.

Crack open the salt crust and lift the fish away from the crust. Peel back the skin and remove the four fillets. Serve with the dressed dillisk.

See opposite –>

Plaice and Sea Herbs

Preparation: 20 minutes
Cooking: 20 minutes
Serves 4

50 g/2 oz (⅔ cup) fresh kelp (kombu)
50 g/2 oz (⅔ cup) fresh sugar kelp
75 g/2¾ oz (5½ tablespoons) butter
1 large plaice, trimmed
100 g/3½ oz (about 2⅓ cups) wild sea herbs
  (sea beet, sea purslane, samphire/sea beans,
  arrow grass, orache)
extra virgin rapeseed (canola) oil
Seaweed Vinegar (see page 352)
sea salt

Nothing represents Irish food better than the combination of wild fish with the sea herbs that grow all along the coast. The saline flavour of these herbs lends the dish a natural salty and crunchy character. Plaice is of ancient Irish stock and has been eaten in Ireland since the early settlers cooked it over open fires. Bones are found at many early settlements.

Preheat the oven to 180°C/350°F/ Gas Mark 4.

Lay the kelps in a large roasting pan. Rub the butter into all sides of the fish and season liberally with the sea salt. Lay the fish on top of the seaweed. Pour some water into the pan until it reaches up to the sides of the fish. Bake in the preheated oven for 15–20 minutes or until the flesh comes easily away from the bone.

Place the sea herbs in a mixing bowl and season with oil, vinegar and salt.

To serve, lift the skin of the fish off the fillets and remove the top two fillets. Remove the bone to expose the bottom fillets. Place all the fillets on a large warm dish and lay the seasoned sea herbs on top of the fillets. To finish, sprinkle some more rapeseed (canola) oil over the entire dish.

Saltwater Fish

John Dory with Leeks

Preparation: 10 minutes, plus resting time
Cooking: 20 minutes
Serves 4

1 John Dory
4 leeks
3 cloves garlic, crushed
a few sprigs of tarragon
100 g/3½ oz (7 tablespoons) butter, cubed
250 ml/8 fl oz (1 cup) cider (hard cider)
extra virgin rapeseed (canola) oil
juice of 1 lemon
sea salt

Trim the John Dory of its fins with a pair of sharp scissors. Score the fish. Oil the fish and season with salt. Allow to stand at room temperature for 20 minutes.

Preheat the oven to 180°C/350°F/Gas Mark 4.

Slice the leeks and rinse. Put the leeks into the bottom of a roasting pan. Place the garlic and tarragon on the leeks with the butter. Lay the fish over the leeks. Pour the cider around the fish.

Bake in the preheated oven for 15–20 minutes or until the flesh comes easily away from the bone. Allow to rest for a few minutes before serving.

Season with oil, lemon juice and sea salt.

See opposite –>

Deep-fried Ray Wings

Preparation and cooking: 15 minutes, plus overnight soaking time
Serves 2

2 ray wings, trimmed and quartered
250 ml/8 fl oz (1 cup) buttermilk
rapeseed (canola) oil, for deep-frying
100 g/3½ oz dry breadcrumbs
100 g/3½ oz plain (all-purpose) flour, for dusting
sea salt

Soak the ray wings overnight in buttermilk. This will help tenderize them.

The following day, preheat the oil in a deep-fat fryer until the oil reaches 180°C/350°F, or until a cube of bread browns in 30 seconds. Dry off the wings and reserve the buttermilk.

Dredge in the flour and then return to the buttermilk. Finally, coat each piece in breadcrumbs.

Fry the ray wings in the hot oil for 4–8 minutes, depending on their size, until they float and are crispy. Remove and shake off excess oil.

Wrasse and Onions

Preparation: 15 minutes
Cooking: 20 minutes
Serves 4

100 g/3½ oz (7 tablespoons) butter
2 cloves garlic, crushed
a few sprigs of thyme
1 wrasse, gutted and scaled
4 onions, sliced
3½ tablespoons apple cider vinegar
sea salt

Of the five wrasse species, Ballan wrasse (*Labrus bergylta*) is the largest and swims among the rocks close to shore, feeding off mussels and limpets. Salted wrasse with white sauce was once a typical Christmas Eve dish on the Aran Islands.

Preheat the oven to 180°C/350°F/Gas Mark 4.

Melt half the butter in a small pan over a low heat with the garlic and a little of the thyme. Strain the butter through a sieve, reserving the butter and the garlic and thyme.

Place the reserved garlic and thyme in the belly of the fish. Brush the fish with the butter and season with sea salt. Transfer the fish to a roasting pan and roast in the preheated oven for 10–15 minutes until cooked and the flesh is opaque.

Meanwhile, for the onions, melt the remaining butter in a medium pan over a medium heat and fry the onions for about 10 minutes until soft and nicely browned. Season with salt, thyme and the cider vinegar. Adjust the seasoning if desired.

Serve the fish with the onions.

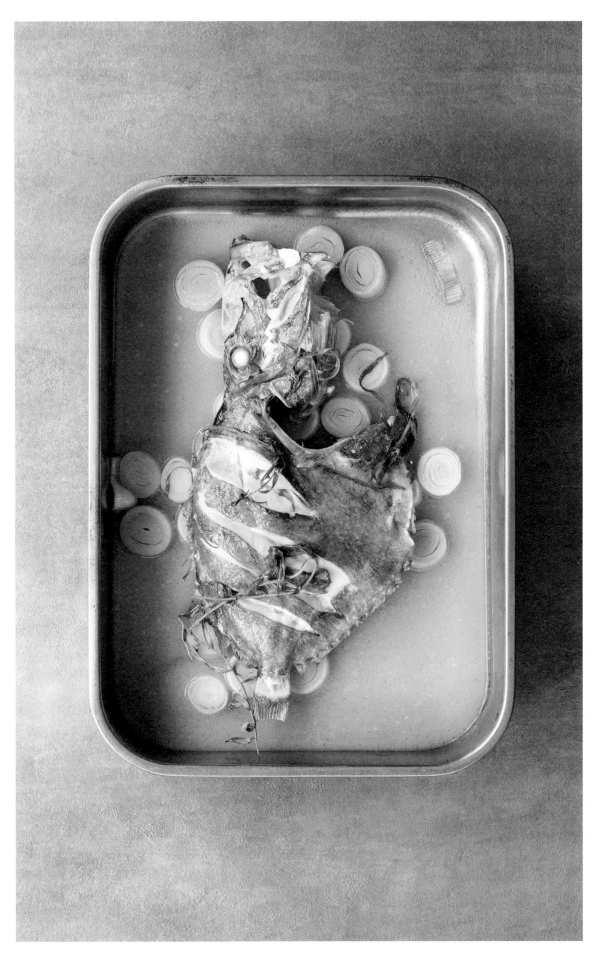

Saltwater Fish

Monkfish with Brandy and Mushrooms

Preparation: 10 minutes
Cooking: 30 minutes
Serves 4

1 tablespoon rapeseed (canola) oil,
  plus extra if needed
4 × 150-g/5-oz monkfish fillets
50 g/2 oz (4 tablespoons) cold butter, diced
a few sprigs of thyme
250 g/9 oz mushrooms, quartered if large
2 tablespoons brandy
200 ml/7 fl oz (scant 1 cup) double
  (heavy) cream
1 tablespoon finely chopped chives
sea salt
Asparagus with Lemon (see page 50), to serve

Preheat the oven to 180°C/350°F/ Gas Mark 4.

Heat the oil in a large frying pan (skillet) over a medium heat. Season the fish with salt, and when the oil is hot, fry the fish on one side for about 2 minutes until the fish is starting to turn opaque. Add the butter and thyme, reduce the heat so the foaming butter doesn't burn and baste the fish for 2 minutes.

Place the fish in a small roasting pan and pour the butter over the fillets. Transfer to the preheated oven and cook for 3–5 minutes, depending on your liking. Remove from the oven and keep warm.

In the meantime, add the mushrooms to the pan and fry over a medium heat until nicely coloured. You may need a little more oil. Deglaze the frying pan with the brandy and heat for a few minutes to burn off the alcohol. Add the cream and reduce for 15–20 minutes until it is thick enough to coat the back of a spoon. At the last minute, add the chives and season the sauce with sea salt.

Serve the roasted monkfish with the mushroom and brandy sauce and the Asparagus with Lemon.

See opposite –>

Monkfish Cheeks with Leeks

Preparation: 10 minutes
Cooking: 15 minutes
Serves 4

75 g/2¾ oz (5½ tablespoons) butter
4 tablespoons rapeseed (canola) oil
2 leeks, thinly sliced in rounds
8 medium monkfish cheeks
a few sprigs of thyme
Herb Vinegar (see page 352), optional
sea salt

To garnish
wild leek oil (see Herb Oil, page 351), optional
three-cornered leek flowers (optional)

To cook the leeks, add 25 g/1 oz (1¾ tablespoons) of the butter to a frying pan (skillet) with 2 tablespoons of oil over a medium heat. When warm, add the leeks, season with a little sea salt, reduce the heat to low and cook for about 15 minutes until tender and without colour. If the leeks need a little moisture, add a teaspoon of water as required. Check the seasoning.

Meanwhile, to fry the monkfish cheeks, season the cheeks with salt. In frying pan big enough to hold the eight cheeks, warm the remaining oil over a medium heat. When the oil is hot, put the cheeks into the frying pan and cook for 3–4 minutes until nicely brown on one side, then add the reaming butter and the thyme. Allow the butter to foam and go slightly brown. Baste the other side of the cheeks for 3–4 minutes until no longer opaque.

Remove from the pan and rest in a warm place for 3–5 minutes. Drain the excess fat from the cheeks by laying them on some paper towels.

To serve, spoon some leek mixture into the centre of each warm plate. Place two cheeks on top of the monkfish leeks. Garnish with a little wild leek oil and a few three-cornered leek flowers, if using.

Saltwater Fish

Saltwater Fish

Red Mullet with Lovage en Papillotte

Preparation: 10 minutes
Cooking: 15 minutes
Serves 4

2 whole red mullets, scaled and gutted
rapeseed (canola) oil
25 g/1 oz lovage leaves, with stems
lovage vinegar (see Herb or Fruit Vinegar, page 352) to taste, or another vinegar of your choice
sea salt

Both red mullet and lovage appear in the early months in Ireland and work well together. The celery-like taste of lovage lifts the flavour of the fish. *En papillotte* is a French term for wrapping fish in paper before baking. In this way the fish steams and moisture is retained. While it works well with any whole small fish, it also suits small fillets of fish.

Preheat the oven to 180°C/350°F/Gas Mark 4.

Rub the fish with some oil and season with sea salt. Place a few of the lovage leaves inside the belly of the fish.

Lay each fish on a sheet of baking (parchment) paper and place the remaining lovage on top of the fish. Dress with a little vinegar.

Fold the edge of the baking paper over so it resembles a parcel. Make sure the edges are sealed. You can wrap it again with aluminium foil to help stop the steam escaping. This will help keep the flesh moist.

Bake in the preheated oven for 10–15 minutes. Open the parcels and serve immediately.

See opposite –>

Connemara Sole with Brown Butter and Sage

Preparation: 10 minutes
Cooking: 15 minutes
Serves 4

4 Connemara sole (witch)
extra virgin rapeseed (canola) oil
100 g/3½ oz (7 tablespoons) butter
6 sage leaves
sea salt
dill vinegar (see Herb or Fruit Vinegar, page 352), to taste, or another vinegar of your choice
boiled new potatoes, seasoned with coarse (kosher) sea salt and oil

This small variety of flounder called 'witch' is plentiful off the west coast of Ireland. Unfortunately, its name doesn't exactly do the fish any justice. Someone decided somewhere that is should be rechristened: Connemara sole. Now it has a new lease of life. It is a beautiful piece of fish and it roasts whole very well.

Preheat the oven to 180°C/350°F/Gas Mark 4. Line a roasting pan big enough to hold the 4 fish with baking (parchment) paper (you may need to use two pans).

Rub the top side of the fish with oil and season well with sea salt. Place them in the lined pan(s) and roast the fish in the preheated oven for 5 minutes.

In the meantime, put the butter in a small pan over a medium–low heat with the sage leaves. Swirl the butter and allow it to froth. When the butter becomes nutty (you'll see the colour change), remove the pan from the heat and add a good few dashes of the dill vinegar.

The amount of vinegar added is to taste, so if you like more acid with your fish, then be my guest.

Remove the fish from the oven and pour the brown butter over the fish. Return the fish to the oven and bake for a further 10 minutes, or until the flesh comes cleanly away from the bone. You can check with a fork.

Serve immediately with boiled new potatoes.

Saltwater Fish

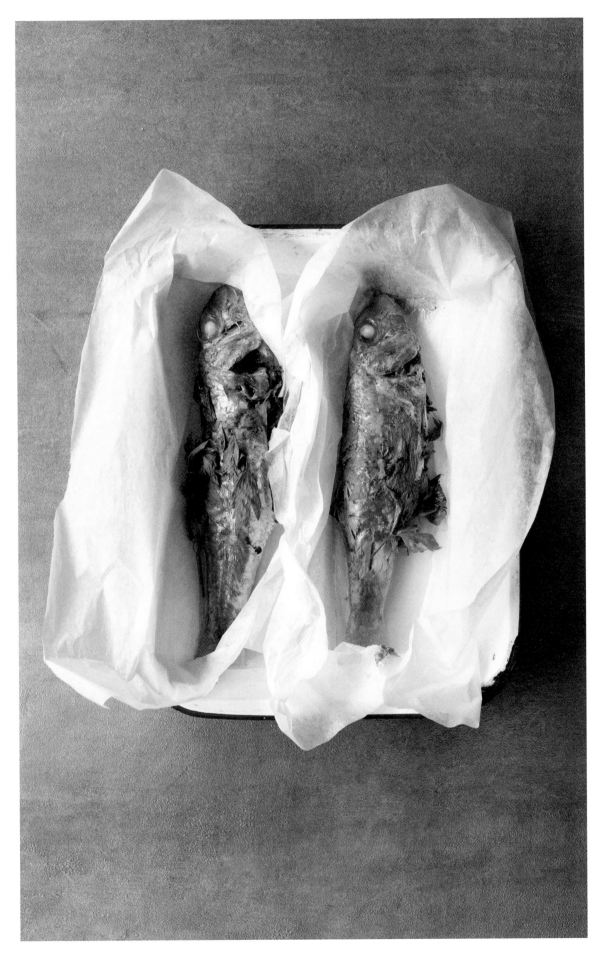

Saltwater Fish

Sole with Anchovy Paste

Preparation: 10 minutes
Cooking: 15 minutes
Serves 4

1 whole sole, trimmed with top skin removed
a few sprigs of thyme, leaves finely chopped
boiled potatoes, to serve

For the paste
100 g/3½ oz anchovies
2 cloves garlic
250 ml/8 fl oz (1 cup) extra virgin rapeseed
   (canola) oil, plus extra for greasing
2 tablespoons apple cider vinegar

This is based on a recipe from Maura Laverty's *Traditional Irish Cookbook*. Though Laverty includes a few more ingredients such as cheese and breadcrumbs, I loved the simplicity of the sole with the anchovy paste. Anchovy paste is likely descended from the Roman fermented fish sauce, garum. It is a part of the cuisines of Great Britain (Worcestershire sauce), the Philippines and Vietnam and thus takes in the colonial aspect of Irish cooking. If you don't want to make the anchovy paste, there are some great ones you can purchase from a delicatessen and in larger supermarkets.

Preheat the oven to 180°C/350°F/ Gas Mark 4.

For the anchovy paste, put all the ingredients into a food processor and blend until smooth.

Oil the bottom of an ovenproof dish and place the sole in the dish. Spread the anchovy paste on top of the sole and garnish with the thyme. Bake in the preheated oven for 10–15 minutes until the flesh is opaque.

Serve with some boiled potatoes.

Slip Sole with Salt-marsh Sauce

Preparation: 10 minutes
Cooking: 5 minutes
Serves 4

4 slip soles, trimmed of their skirt
1 tablespoon rapeseed (canola) oil
50 g/2 oz (4 tablespoons) butter, cubed
sea salt

For the sauce
150 g/5 oz (about 3 cups) sea herbs, picked
250 ml/8 fl oz (1 cup) extra virgin rapeseed
   (canola) oil
2 tablespoons apple cider vinegar
sea salt, to taste

A slip sole is a small sole. My fishmonger Stefan Griesbach (who runs Gannet Fishmongers in Galway) introduced them to me many years ago. In this recipe, I use all the sea herbs I can find in the marsh (samphire/ sea beans, orache, sea aster, sea beet, sea radish, sea purslane). If you can't source sea herbs, use any selection of herbs, such as parsley, fennel, chives.

To make the sauce, put all the ingredients into a food processor and blend until smooth. Adjust seasoning as desired. If the sauce is too thick, thin it down with a little more oil (it depends on your own preference). This sauce should keep for a week in the refrigerator and can be frozen for up to six months.

To fry the fish, season with sea salt on both sides. Heat the oil in a large frying pan (skillet). Place the sole in it, skin side down, and fry for 1–2 minutes, then add the butter. Allow to foam. Baste the other side of the fish for a further 1–2 minutes until it is cooked and the flesh is opaque.

Serve the fish with the green salt-marsh sauce on the side.

Herring with English Mustard

Preparation and cooking: 5 minutes
Serves 4

4 herring fillets
1 teaspoon English mustard
sea salt

Preheat the grill (broiler).

Rub the fish with the mustard and grill (broil) for 2–3 minutes until the flesh is opaque.

Season with sea salt and serve.

Saltwater Fish

Kippers

Kippers are herrings that have been butterflied, salted and cold smoked. Once popular on the breakfast table, both in Ireland and in England (particularly on Fridays), they are seldom consumed nowadays. They have fallen out of favour since the 1970s with the advent of more and more processed breakfast cereals. Because of their oily character, they are extremely good for one's health. The phrase 'kippering' refers to the process of salting and smoking the fish. 'Red' herrings get their name from being heavily smoked. Grilled with a little butter, kippers can be served on toast with scrambled eggs for breakfast. They can also be cut into strips and marinated in oil and vinegar before serving as a starter (appetizer) or as a snack with a nice glass of wine. In the west of Ireland, they were often eaten with potatoes and buttermilk. Because they were salted and smoked, they would have lasted a long time in a cool place.

Herring Cooked in the Embers of a Turf Fire

Preparation and cooking: 15 minutes
Serves 4

8 herring, whole, gutted
extra virgin rapeseed (canola) oil
wild garlic vinegar (see Herb or Fruit Vinegar, page 352), or another vinegar of your choice
50 g/2 oz (¼ cup) sour cream, to serve
sea salt

This is a very old way of cooking herring. Utensils such as metal pans or prongs were used to cook the fish. Cooking the fish over embers is similar to the Basque way of cooking fish.

Light a fire and allow it to burn down until the embers are red hot.

Season the herring with sea salt. Thread a long metal skewer through each one.

Grill the herring over the embers for 6–8 minutes until cooked with the skin nicely browned and the flesh opaque.

Dress with a little oil and vinegar and serve with the sour cream.

Mackerel Tartare with Cucumber and Orache

Preparation: 20 minutes
Serves 4

2 mackerel, filleted and pin-boned
1 cucumber, finely diced
fresh sea lettuce, diced
extra virgin rapeseed (canola) oil
Seaweed Vinegar (see page 352), or another vinegar of your choice
sea salt
orache tips, washed, to serve

Skin the mackerel fillets and gently separate the flesh. Mix together with the cucumber and sea lettuce. Season to taste with the oil, salt and vinegar.

To serve, divide the dressed mackerel among four plates. Garnish with the orache tips and finish with a few drops of rapeseed (canola) oil.

Soused Mackerel in Cider and Juniper

Preparation: 5 minutes, plus curing
and chilling times
Cooking: 10 minutes
Serves 4

4 mackerel fillets, central bone removed
2 teaspoons juniper berries
200 ml/7 fl oz (scant 1 cup) cider (hard cider)
200 ml/7 fl oz (scant 1 cup) apple cider vinegar
60 g/2¼ oz (⅓ cup) granulated sugar
sea salt

To serve
Rhubarb Compote (see page 44)
50 g/2 oz (¼ cup) sheep's yogurt

Sousing, or pickling, fish is a great way to extend the season. Salting the fish will also ensure the fish has a longer shelf life. Feel free to use beer or wine instead of cider and to change the spices or add fresh herbs.

Lightly salt the mackerel fillets and cure for 30 minutes in the refrigerator.

Toast the juniper berries briefly in a dry pan to release their aroma.

To make a pickling liquid, put the cider, vinegar, sugar and juniper into a medium pan over a medium heat and bring to the boil. Remove from the heat. Cool slightly.

Place the mackerel, skin side up, in a suitable tray. Pour the pickling liquid over the mackerel, making sure to cover the fish. Cover and refrigerate, allowing to cool completely.

Serve with the Rhubarb Compote and sheep's yogurt.

See opposite –>

Mackerel with Sorrel Sauce

Preparation: 10 minutes
Cooking: 23 minutes
Serves 4

4 mackerel fillets
sea salt

For the sauce
350 ml/12 fl oz (1½ cups) fish stock (broth)
150 ml/5 fl oz (⅔ cup) white wine
1 shallot, finely diced
1 bay leaf
200 ml/7 fl oz (scant 1 cup) double
   (heavy) cream
75 g/2¾ oz (3 cups) fresh sorrel
25 g/1 oz (1 cup) spinach, washed
50 g/2 oz (¼ cup) yogurt

For the sorrel sauce, put the fish stock (broth), white wine, shallot and bay leaf into a wide pan over a medium heat and simmer for 15–20 minutes until the liquid is reduced by half. Strain and add the cream. Bring to the boil.

Preheat the grill (broiler).

Put the cream mixture with the sorrel, spinach and yogurt into a food processor and blend until smooth. Season with sea salt.

Grill (broil) the mackerel for 2–3 minutes until the flesh is opaque and serve with the sorrel sauce.

Smoked Mackerel Pâté

Preparation and cooking: 10 minutes
Serves 4

5 smoked mackerel fillets
100 g/3½ oz (generous ⅓ cup) crème fraîche
   or sour cream
100 g/3½ oz (generous ⅓ cup) sheep's yogurt
2 tablespoons chopped chervil, fennel and dill
Herb Vinegar (see page 352, optional)
sea salt
toast or crackers, to serve

Pick the flesh from the mackerel. Combine the flesh in a bowl with all the other ingredients. Do not over mix.

Season to taste with vinegar, if using, and salt.

Serve with some toast or crackers.

Saltwater Fish

Deep-fried Pilchards Rolled in Barley Flour

Preparation and cooking: 10 minutes
Serves 4

rapeseed (canola) oil, for deep-frying
100 g/3½ oz (⅔ cup) barley flour
500 g/1 lb 2 oz pilchards
1 lemon, cut into wedges
sea salt

Heat the oil in a deep-fat fryer until the temperature reaches 180°C/350°F, or a cube of bread browns in 30 seconds.

Put the flour into a shallow dish and season with sea salt.

Dredge the pilchards in the seasoned flour, then fry in the hot oil for 3–5 minutes until crispy.

Season with sea salt and serve with the lemon wedges.

See opposite –>

Sprats with Drawn Butter

Preparation: 5 minutes
Cooking: 15 minutes
Serves 4

100 g/3½ oz (7 tablespoons) butter
200 g/7 oz (1⅔ cups) plain (all-purpose) flour
1 teaspoon paprika
200 g/7 oz sprats
rapeseed (canola) oil, for deep-frying
sea salt and freshly ground black pepper

To serve
50 g/2 oz watercress
2 lemons, quartered

Melt the butter slowly in a pan over a medium heat, skimming off any scum that floats to the top. Set aside.

Combine the flour with the paprika in a large bowl, season with a pinch of salt and pepper and dust the sprats in the seasoned flour.

Heat the oil in a deep-fat fryer until the temperature reaches 180°C/350°F, or a cube of bread browns in 30 seconds.

Fry the sprats in batches for about 5 minutes, until crispy.

Serve with the drawn butter, watercress and lemon quarters.

Whiting in Batter

Preparation and cooking: 15 minutes
Serves 4

rapeseed (canola) oil, for deep-frying
150 g/5 oz (1¼ cups) plain (all-purpose) flour, plus extra for dredging
150 ml/5 fl oz (⅔ cup) water
1 teaspoon baking powder
4 whiting fillets
sea salt

Growing up, whiting was our go-to fish. We would eat it on Friday and it would be dredged in flour, then fried in butter. I hated the bones. I was afraid of the fish. Thankfully, trips to Spain taught me there was more to fish than whiting. Saying that, when in season, whiting is a great fish, The following recipe is adapted from Monica Sheridan's *The Art of Irish Cooking* (1965). In the recipe, she deep-fries the fish in a batter with baking powder. The batter protects the fish and keep it moist and tender (unlike the whiting of my youth).

Heat the oil in a deep-fat fryer until the oil reaches 180°C/350°F, or a cube of bread browns in 30 seconds.

Combine the flour, water, baking powder and a pinch of salt to make a loose batter. Put some extra flour in a plate for dredging.

Dredge the whiting first in the flour and then dip them into the batter.

Fry the whiting in the hot oil for about 5 minutes until crispy.

Saltwater Fish

Kedgeree

Preparation: 10 minutes
Cooking: 15 minutes
Serves 4

150 g/5 oz (¾ cup) long-grain rice
75 g/2¾ oz (5½ tablespoons) butter
1 onion, diced
1 teaspoon cayenne pepper
2 eggs, hard-boiled, quartered
2 tablespoons chopped parsley
a few lemon wedges, to serve
sea salt

For the poached haddock
500 ml/17 fl oz (generous 2 cups) milk
1 bay leaf
3 juniper berries
450 g/1 lb smoked haddock fillet

Kedgeree is a fish breakfast dish usually consisting of smoked haddock, boiled rice, eggs and curry powder. The original dish was vegetarian and came from India, but by the time it arrived in Victorian Britain, it had changed from being made from vegetables and rice to smoked fish and rice. Yet, the inclusion of rice and spices shows how food taste travelled and changed with imperialism and colonialism. A breakfast of the 'big house', kedgeree will be found occasionally on hotel menus around the country.

Cook the rice in a pan of boiling water following the package directions until soft. Strain and combine with half the butter.

Meanwhile, for the poached haddock, put the milk with the bay leaf and juniper berries into a large pan over a medium heat, bring to a simmer and poach the haddock for 2 minutes until the flesh is opaque. Remove the fish from the milk and skin, debone and flake.

Heat the remaining butter in a small pan over a medium heat and fry the onion with the cayenne pepper for about 5 minutes until soft.

In a large bowl, combine all the ingredients. Garnish with the lemon wedges.

See opposite –>

Fishcakes with Oatmeal Coating

Preparation: 20 minutes
Cooking: 30 minutes
Makes 8

500 g/1 lb 2 oz (about 4 medium)
    potatoes, peeled
250 g/9 oz salmon fillet
250 g/9 oz smoked white fish fillet,
    such as haddock or coley
25 g/1 oz (1¾ tablespoons) butter
1 onion, finely diced
2 tablespoons chopped parsley
2 tablespoons chopped tarragon
2 tablespoons chopped chervil
pinhead (steel-cut) oats, to coat the fishcakes
rapeseed (canola) oil, for deep-frying
sea salt

I've made many fishcakes over my career. Often, they were made with the trimmings from all the fish. At home, I make them with salmon and smoked fish to give them both taste and texture. Bound together with potato, they are always comforting. They can be coated with breadcrumbs if you prefer. I prefer to deep-fry the fishcakes, but they can also be shallow-fried in a frying pan (skillet).

Put the potatoes into a medium pan and cover with water. Bring to the boil over a medium heat and simmer for about 15 minutes until soft. Remove from the water, dry and mash or put through a potato ricer. Season with sea salt.

Meanwhile, bring a large pan of water to the boil and reduce to a simmer. Lower the fish into the water and poach for 5 minutes until the flesh is opaque. Remove from the water and dry. Flake the fish and season with sea salt.

Melt the butter in a small pan over a medium heat and add the onion. Season with sea salt and cook for about 5 minutes until the onion is translucent.

Combine all the ingredients in a bowl with the chopped herbs. Check the seasoning. Shape into 8 patties and coat in the oats.

Heat the oil in a deep-fat fryer until the oil reaches 180°C/350°F, or a cube of bread browns in 30 seconds. When hot, carefully lower the fishcakes into the oil and fry for a few minutes until golden brown. Alternatively, heat 3–4 tablespoons of rapeseed (canola) oil in a frying pan over a medium–high heat and fry the fishcakes for about 5 minutes on each side until golden brown.

Saltwater Fish

Seafood and Seaweed Chowder

Preparation: 25 minutes
Cooking: 1 hour 25 minutes, plus
standing time
Serves 4

<u>For the stock</u>
2 tablespoons rapeseed (canola) oil
1 onion, diced
1 carrot, diced
1 celery stalk, diced
250 ml/8 fl oz (1 cup) dry cider (hard cider)
25 g/1 oz dried kelp or kombu
3 cloves garlic, peeled
2 bay leaves
a few sprigs of thyme
500 g/1 lb 2 oz mussels, scrubbed clean
500 g/1 lb 2 oz clams, scrubbed clean

<u>For the chowder</u>
25 g/1 oz (1¾ tablespoons) butter
1 onion, finely chopped
600 g/1 lb 5 oz (about 9 medium)
    potatoes, cubed
2 leeks, diced
250 ml/8 fl oz (1 cup) double (heavy) cream
300 g /11 oz pollock fillet, skinned and boned,
    cut into small chunks
sea salt

<u>To garnish</u>
chopped dill
finely milled nori

I give this classic Irish fish soup a little twist with the addition of seaweed.

To make the stock (broth), heat the rapeseed (canola) oil in a large pan over a medium heat. Add the onion, carrot and celery and sauté for about 10 minutes until they start to caramelize. Pour over the cider and cook for a couple of minutes. Pour in 1 litre/34 fl oz (4¼ cups) of water and add the seaweed, garlic, bay leaves and thyme. Bring to the boil, then turn the heat down and simmer for 40 minutes.

To finish, cook the mussels and clams in the stock for 3–5 minutes until they open. Remove from the stock and place them in a suitable container, discarding any that haven't opened. When cool enough to handle, pick the meat from the shells and discard the shells. Strain the stock through a fine sieve.

For the chowder, melt half of the butter in a large saucepan over a medium heat. Add the onion and sauté for 3–4 minutes until translucent. Add the potatoes and leeks and stir to mix. Add the seaweed stock. Season to taste. Bring to the boil, then turn down the heat and simmer for about 15 minutes until the vegetables are tender. Add the cream and warm through. Add the pollock and cook for 2 minutes. Finally, add the mussel and clam meat and remove from the heat. Allow to stand for 5 minutes.

To serve, fold the chopped dill through the chowder and divide among four warmed bowls. Garnish with a sprinkle of milled nori.

See opposite –>

Smoked Coley and Mussel Soup

Preparation: 20 minutes
Cooking: 40 minutes
Serves 4

250 ml/8 fl oz (1 cup) white wine
a few sprigs of thyme
500 g/1 lb 2 oz mussels, scrubbed clean
500 ml/17 fl oz (generous 2 cups) milk
1 bay leaf
500 g/1 lb 2 oz smoked coley, skinned
    and boned
50 g/2 oz (4 tablespoons) butter
2 onions, chopped
2 leeks, chopped
3 potatoes, peeled and chopped
100 g/3½ oz smoked bacon, chopped
500 ml/17 fl oz (generous 2 cups)
    fish stock (broth)
250 ml/8 fl oz (1 cup) single (light) cream
chopped parsley, to garnish

Smoked coley is another fish on the wane in Ireland. Occasionally, I encounter it on breakfast menus in hotels. As with haddock, try to seek out naturally smoked fish that has not been dyed.

In a large pan over a medium–high heat, bring the wine and thyme to the boil and steam the mussels for 3–5 minutes until they open. Strain the liquid and reserve. Pick the mussels from their shells. Discard the shells and any that do not open. Reserve the meat for the soup.

Bring the milk and bay leaf to a simmer in a large pan over a medium heat. Poach the coley for 4–5 minutes. Strain the liquid through a fine sieve and reserve. Flake the meat and set aside.

Heat the butter in a large pan over a medium heat and fry the onions, leeks and potatoes for about 5 minutes to soften. Add the bacon and fish stock and simmer for 10–15 minutes until the potatoes are soft. Add the reserved liquid and the cream and heat for a couple of minutes until warm.

Add the fish and mussel meat, divide among four warmed bowls and garnish with parsley.

Saltwater Fish

Saltwater Fish

A Fish Pie

Preparation: 25 minutes
Cooking: 1 hour 15 minutes
Serves 4

1 kg/2¼ lb (9 medium) potatoes, peeled
    and cut into even-sized pieces
200 g/7 oz (1¾ sticks) butter, cubed
700 ml/24½ fl oz (3 cups) fish stock (broth)
100 ml/3½ fl oz (scant ½ cup) cider
    (hard cider)
500 g/1 lb 2 oz white pollock fillet, skinned
500 g/1 lb 2 oz smoked haddock fillet, skinned
50 g/2 oz (4 tablespoons) butter
50 g/2 oz (scant ½ cup) plain
    (all-purpose) flour
200 ml/7 fl oz (scant 1 cup) double
    (heavy) cream
a handful of dill and chives, finely chopped
sea salt

Put the potatoes into a large pan and cover with cold water. Season with salt and bring to the boil over a high heat. Reduce to a simmer, cook for about 15 minutes until tender and strain. Push the potatoes through a drum sieve and fold in the butter. Season with sea salt.

Meanwhile, put the fish stock (broth) and cider into a large pan over a medium heat and bring to a simmer. Add the fish and simmer for 5 minutes, then lift out with a slotted spoon. Flake into a bowl.

Preheat the oven to 200°C/400°F/ Gas Mark 6.

Melt the butter in a medium pan over a medium–low heat and stir in the flour. Cook for about 3 minutes until the flour is no longer raw. Gradually whisk in the stock. Add the cream and bring to the boil, then simmer for about 20 minutes until thickened.

Add the flaked fish to the sauce and add the herbs. Check the seasoning. Pour the mixture into a suitable baking dish and top with the mashed potato. Furrow the top of the potatoes. Bake in the preheated oven for 30 minutes or until the top is golden.

See opposite –>

Sea Mammals and Seabirds

'In one of the largest islands, called Owey, they used to kill a great number of seals which they salted for winter and were so fond of it as to prefer it to any other meat.'

Cited in Joseph C. Walker, 'Memoir of the Armour and Weapons of the Irish', 1788

Sea mammals such as seals are no longer eaten in Ireland, though they once were. In the research for this book, I came across a reference to salted seal in Donegal in the eighteenth century in Bríd Mahon's *Land of Milk and Honey*. In the eastern part of Canada, seal is still popular, particularly in Newfoundland. Did the Irish emigrants bring their penchant for seal meat over when they left their homeland? Seal remains were found at many castles around Ireland in the Middle Ages, even at Maynooth Castle (outside Dublin, where I grew up). These remains dates from the thirteenth to the fifteenth century. Why did we stop eating seal and other sea animals? Was it a cultural or religious shift? You may also wonder why I am discussing these animals in a book on Irish food if neither can be eaten or sourced in this country. For me, it's important to recognize our food history and where we have come from. The first settlers of Ireland (the people who inhabited Ireland for three thousand years until the agricultural revolution) ate all kinds of sea mammals.

Seabirds were also once part of the native Irish diet. Puffins and other seabirds such as auks made up the diet of many island people in the south of the country such as Skellig and Blaskets. Today, puffins are now a protected species under Irish law, so you won't be able to eat them in Ireland. In Iceland, puffins are still hunted and eaten. They are roasted like pigeons, or cured and dried and then shaved into thin slices.

Saltwater Fish

Poultry

Poultry

In general, poultry is defined as domesticated birds, such as chicken, turkey, duck, geese and other birds that are raised for their eggs and meat. As with wild game, there is a rich tradition throughout the ages of rearing poultry for food. I recommend that you always use poultry certified free-range that has not been restricted to cages and was given access to the outdoors.

Chicken

'In Galway it was believed that the rooster should be killed [on the 11th November] before sundown, and the rooster that fathered the most chicks should be the one chosen. The blood should be spilled in the four corners of the house, proceeding in a clockwise direction, and the last of the blood should be used to form a pool in the centre of the kitchen [this was done to keep away evil spirits].'

Niall Mac Coitir, *Ireland's Birds: Myths, Legends and Folklore,* 2015

It is hard to tell when exactly chickens arrived in Ireland, though they are noted in various myths and folk tales. Their presence in Ireland goes back possibly to the Iron Age or even further. Both cocks or roosters and hens are mentioned in stories of Irish monks and by the Norman writer Gerald of Wales. Chicken in Ireland was not always as pervasive as it is now. Having a chicken on a farm to supply eggs was both economical and vital for the survival of the family. Chicken was not a common dish because the eggs were valuable. Usually, it was the cock that was killed. Eating a chicken was a luxury. From something central to feeding people off the land, it has now turned into a cheap source of protein for all.

Since World War II, chicken has become the most consumed species on the planet. In Ireland, about 180,000 are slaughtered a day. That is a phenomenal 66 million a year. Much of this chicken is of low quality in terms of taste and is often sold below cost. However, there are some excellent producers of organic and free-range chicken dotted around Ireland. We source our chicken from Ronan Byrne, aka The Friendly Farmer. Ronan's chickens live outdoors all the time (hence the term 'pasture reared') and for up to nine to twelve weeks: this is twice the age of a caged chicken's life. Ronan's philosophy of good chicken husbandry affects in a very positive manner the state and taste of the chicken that we use in Aniar, Cava and Tartare. We want strong, healthy chickens that have good skin and bone structure. Ronan's chickens are housed in large chicken coops and are free to roam in and out as they desire. They have plenty of space, good food and natural light. Due to all this (and more), the chickens are a lot bigger and better than most shop-bought chickens. There is no excuse for buying poor-quality chicken. By and large we consume too much chicken. If we were to pay more for chicken and eat it less often, the state of the chicken industry would be a lot better. Eat chicken once or twice a week, not every day. Expect to pay more for a free-range chicken than you would for a caged chicken. If it's cheap, then something is wrong with the system that produces the chicken. If you live in the United States, where regulations are less strict and you may pay more for a 'free-range' or 'cage-free' label that is not necessarily humanely raised, look for poultry with an Animal Welfare Approved, Certified Humane or American Humane Certified label. Perhaps in this way we can learn from the past: chicken should be an animal that we value, not something only produced to placate our hunger.

Chicken and Wild Mushroom Broth

Preparation: 10 minutes
Cooking: 2 hours
Serves 4

1 × 1.5-kg/3-lb chicken
2 onions, quartered
2 carrots, chopped
1 leek, sliced
1 celery stalk, chopped
100 g/3½ oz mixed wild mushrooms
4 tablespoons cream sherry
a large sprig of rosemary
a few lovage leaves
sea salt
extra virgin rapeseed (canola) oil,
    to serve (optional)

Chicken broth was a staple of many Irish people's diets and many have fond memories of their grandmother cooking chicken broth over the fire. In this recipe, I have added wild mushrooms and lovage with a dash of cream sherry (every Irish home would have some) but it can be made with any vegetables you may have to hand. It's important you don't boil your broth because this will make it cloudy. Often, the chicken would have been taken from the broth, shredded and added back in. You can do this if you like, but I think chicken sandwiches are a better bet!

Place all the ingredients into a large pan and cover with water. Bring to a gentle boil and then reduce to an absolute simmer. Simmer for 2 hours.

Strain, season with sea salt and serve. If you like, finish with some extra virgin rapeseed (canola) oil.

Cream of Chicken Soup with Nutmeg and Caraway Seeds

Preparation: 20 minutes
Cooking: 25 minutes
Serves 4

50 g/2 oz (4 tablespoons) butter
2 onions, diced
4 leeks, sliced
2 celery stalks, diced
1 bay leaf
2 teaspoons caraway seeds
1 clove garlic, very finely chopped
50 g/2 oz (generous ⅓ cup) plain
    (all-purpose) flour
1 litre/34 fl oz (4¼ cups) chicken
    stock (broth)
2 chicken breasts, skinned and diced
500 ml/17 fl oz (generous 2 cups) milk
150 ml/5 fl oz (⅔ cup) double (heavy) cream
freshly grated nutmeg, to taste
2 tablespoons chopped tarragon, to serve
sea salt

Melt the butter in a large pan over a medium heat. When it begins to foam, add the onions and the leeks and fry for about 5 minutes until soft. Add the celery, bay leaf, caraway seeds and garlic and cook for a further minute. Finally, add the flour and cook for 2 minutes to form a paste.

Cover with the chicken stock (broth) and bring to the boil. Reduce the heat and simmer for 15 minutes, then add the chicken. Poach for 5 minutes until the chicken is cooked through.

Add the milk and cream and some freshly grated nutmeg. Using an immersion blender or food processor, blend the soup until smooth. Strain through a fine sieve if desired (I like to do this to make the soup even more silky smooth). Season to taste.

Return the soup to the heat for a few minutes until warm. To serve, ladle into warmed bowls and garnish with some chopped tarragon.

Yellow Broth

Preparation: 20 minutes
Cooking: 40 minutes
Serves 4

50 g/2 oz (4 tablespoons) butter
1 onion, chopped
2 celery stalks, chopped
2 carrots, chopped
100 g/3½ oz (⅔ cup) pinhead (steel-cut) oats
2 litres/70 fl oz (8½ cups) chicken stock (broth)
250 ml/8 fl oz (1 cup) double (heavy) cream
1 tablespoon chopped parsley
sea salt

Otherwise known as *brothchán buidhe*, this broth would have provided nourishment to a whole family by using the leftover chicken carcass to produce another meal.

Melt the butter in a large pan over a medium heat and add the vegetables. Cook for about 10 minutes until nicely caramelized. Add the oats and cook for a further few minutes.

Add the stock (broth) and simmer for 30 minutes. Season before serving, either as it is, or strain the broth through a fine sieve if you prefer.

Add the cream and parsley.

See opposite –>

Chicken Thighs with a Plum Glaze

Preparation: 10 minutes, plus marinating time
Cooking: 35 minutes
Serves 4

12 chicken thighs
sea salt

For the glaze
6 plums, halved and stoned (pitted)
1 onion, finely diced
150 ml/5 fl oz (⅔ cup) cider (hard cider)
100 ml/3½ fl oz (scant ½ cup) chicken stock (broth)
60 g/2¼ oz (⅓ cup) granulated sugar
4 tablespoons apple cider vinegar

To make the plum glaze, combine all the glaze ingredients in a medium pan over a medium heat and bring to the boil. Reduce the heat to low and simmer for 15–20 minutes until reduced. Blend and strain through a sieve. Adjust the seasoning if desired.

Season the chicken thighs and marinate with the plum glaze, preferably for a few hours in the refrigerator.

Preheat the oven to 180°C/350°F/Gas Mark 4.

Put the chicken into a roasting pan and roast in the preheated oven for 15 minutes, basting occasionally.

Chicken Legs Stuffed with Black Pudding

Preparation: 15 minutes
Cooking: 40 minutes
Serves 2

1 × 200-g/7-oz log of black pudding (blood sausage)
1 egg white
2 chicken legs, deboned and cartilage removed
sea salt

Preheat the oven to 180°C/350°F/Gas Mark 4.

Blend the black pudding (blood sausage) in a food processor with the egg white.

Season the chicken legs and place on a sheet of cling film (plastic wrap). Place the pudding stuffing in the middle of the legs and roll into a tight cylindrical shape. Wrap in aluminium foil.

Roast the chicken in the preheated oven for 35–40 minutes until it reaches a core temperature of 65°C/150°F on a meat thermometer and the juices run clear.

Poultry

Chicken Stew with Dumplings

Preparation: 20 minutes
Cooking: 30 minutes
Serves 4

1 chicken, cut into 8 pieces
15 g/½ oz (2 tablespoons) plain
    (all-purpose) flour
2 tablespoons rapeseed (canola) oil
15 g/½ oz (1 tablespoon) butter
1 onion, chopped
4 sage leaves
a sprig each of rosemary and thyme
2 carrots, chopped
250 ml/8 fl oz (1 cup) cider (hard cider)
1 litre/34 fl oz (4¼ cups) chicken
    stock (broth)
1 teaspoon sea salt
freshly ground black pepper
chopped flat leaf parsley, to garnish

For the dumplings
350 g/12 oz (2¾ cups) plain
    (all-purpose) flour, sifted
50 g/2 oz (4 tablespoons) cold butter, grated
1 teaspoon baking powder
350 ml/12 fl oz (1½ cups) milk
sea salt

Though dumplings have fallen out of favour in contemporary Irish food, many recipes for stews with dumplings appear in twentieth-century cookbooks.

Season the chicken pieces with all the salt and some pepper and coat in the flour.

Heat the oil over a medium–high heat in a large heavy-bottomed pan or casserole dish (Dutch oven) and fry the chicken pieces, in batches, for about 5 minutes until golden brown all over. Set the chicken aside and wipe out the pan.

Melt the butter in the pan and add the onion, sage, rosemary and thyme. Fry for 3–4 minutes until the onion is soft then add the carrot. Deglaze the pan with the cider and bring to the boil.

Return the chicken and juices to the pan and cover with the stock (broth). Simmer over a medium–low heat for about 25–30 minutes until the chicken is cooked through with no signs of pink and the juices run clear.

Meanwhile, to make the dumplings, combine the flour and butter in a bowl with the baking powder and salt. Add the milk to make a loose dough. Add tablespoonfuls of the dumpling mixture to the pan with the chicken for the last 5–10 minutes of the cooking time, flipping the dumplings halfway through so they cook on both sides. Add the parsley and serve.

See opposite –>

Chicken Breasts with Cider Cream and Juniper

Preparation: 10 minutes
Cooking: 35 minutes
Serves 2

2 chicken breasts, skin on, inner fillet removed
2 tablespoons rapeseed (canola) oil
50 g/2 oz (4 tablespoons) butter
a few sprigs of thyme
175 ml/6 fl oz (¾ cup) cider (hard cider)
6 juniper berries, crushed
175 ml/6 fl oz (¾ cup) double (heavy) cream
sea salt

Preheat the oven to 180 °C/350 °F/ Gas Mark 4.

Season the chicken breasts with a little sea salt. Warm the oil in a large frying pan (skillet) over a medium–high heat. When hot, put the chicken breasts into the pan, skin side down. After a minute, check to see if the skin is nice and brown. If you're happy with the colour, reduce the heat to medium and add the butter and the thyme. Baste the top side of the chicken breasts (don't turn them over) for about 5 minutes until opaque.

Remove the chicken from the pan and put into the preheated oven, skin side up, for 10 minutes until cooked through and the juices run clear.

Discard the butter in the pan and add the cider and juniper berries. Bring to the boil and cook for about 10 minutes until reduced by half. Add the cream and cook for a further 10 minutes, or until reduced by half again or the sauce is thick enough to coat the back of a spoon.

Carve the chicken breasts and spoon the sauce over them.

Note
I also like to make a cream sauce with brandy and green peppercorns to serve with chicken breasts cooked in this way. Follow the technique for the sauce here, but add 3 tablespoons of brandy and 6 green peppercorns in place of the cider and juniper berries.

Poultry

Hay-smoked Chicken with Wild Mushroom Barley

Preparation: 10 minutes
Cooking: 35 minutes
Serves 2

2 chicken breast supremes
150 g/5 oz hay
2 tablespoons rapeseed (canola) oil
2 shallots, finely chopped
2 cloves garlic, finely chopped
150 g/5 oz wild mushrooms
250 g/9 oz (1¼ cups) barley
120 ml/4 fl oz (½ cup) dry white wine
750 ml/25 fl oz (3 cups) chicken stock (broth)
50 g/2 oz (4 tablespoons) butter, cubed
2 teaspoons chopped chervil or parsley
sea salt

This recipe calls for chicken supremes – this is the whole chicken breast, with skin and bones, along with the first joint of the wing attached. However, it can also be made with regular chicken breasts.

Season the chicken breasts with salt. Put the hay into a smoke box, add the chicken and smoke for about 15 minutes until it reaches a core temperature of 65°C/150°F on a meat thermometer. Remove and rest for at least 5 minutes.

For the barley, heat the oil in a large pan over a medium heat and add the shallots, garlic and wild mushrooms. Season with a little salt. Add the barley and cook for 1 minute, ensuring the barley is evenly coated. Add the white wine and bring to the boil.

Add the chicken stock (broth), one ladle at a time, until it has been absorbed by the barley. Continue to add the stock gradually until all of it has been absorbed. Add the butter cubes to the barley and stir through until melted. Add the chopped herbs to the barley and stir through.

Spoon the barley onto two warmed plates. Slice the chicken lengthwise and serve on top of the barley.

See opposite –>

Chicken with Morels and Cider

Preparation: 10 minutes
Cooking: 40 minutes
Serves 4

2 tablespoons rapeseed (canola) oil
4 chicken breasts, skin on
50 g/2 oz (4 tablespoons) butter
a few sprigs of thyme
150 ml/5 fl oz (⅔ cup) cider (hard cider)
1 shallot, diced
100 g/3½ oz morels, soaked in water and dried
250 ml/8 fl oz (1 cup) double (heavy) cream

Morels are an exquisite wild mushroom and are quite expensive. Any other wild or cultivated mushroom can be used instead of morels if you can't source them. Oyster or chestnut mushrooms will work well.

Preheat the oven to 180°C/350°F/Gas Mark 4.

Heat the oil in a large frying pan (skillet) over a medium–high heat. Season the chicken breasts on both sides, and add them, skin side down, to the pan. Fry the chicken for about 5 minutes until the skin is nicely browned. Add the butter and thyme and allow the butter to foam. Baste the chicken for a couple of minutes but do not turn it over.

Transfer the chicken to a roasting pan and pour over the butter.

Deglaze the frying pan with the cider over a medium heat. Add the shallot and morels and cook for about 15 minutes until the cider has reduced by half. Add the cream and reduce for 10–15 minutes until the sauce coats the back of a spoon.

Meanwhile, cook the chicken in the preheated oven for 7 minutes until cooked through. Remove the chicken from the oven and serve with the morel and cider sauce.

Poultry

Poultry

Roast Chicken Wrapped in Bacon

Preparation: 15 minutes
Cooking: 1 hour 5 minutes
Serves 4

1 whole chicken
50 g/2 oz (4 tablespoons) butter,
    slightly melted
freshly grated nutmeg
enough rashers (slices) of streaky
    (regular) bacon to cover the chicken
sea salt
Bread Sauce (see page 380), to serve
chopped herbs, to garnish (optional)

For the stuffing
100 g/3½ oz (7 tablespoons) butter
1 onion, diced
1 teaspoon chopped thyme
150 g/5 oz (3 cups) fresh breadcrumbs
2 tablespoons chopped parsley

Preheat the oven to 180°C/350°F/
Gas Mark 4.

To make the stuffing, melt the
butter in a frying pan (skillet)
over a medium heat and add the
onion and thyme. Cook for about
5 minutes until the onion is soft.
Tip into a large mixing bowl
and combine with the remaining
stuffing ingredients. Season
to taste.

Stuff the cavity of the chicken,
then brush it with butter and
season with salt and nutmeg. Cover
the entire bird with the bacon and
put into a roasting pan. Roast in the
preheated oven for about 1 hour.
After 30 minutes, add 150 ml/
5 fl oz (⅔ cup) water to the base
of the pan to help keep the bacon
moist. Serve with Bread Sauce and
garnish with herbs if you wish.

See opposite –>

Roast Chicken Stuffed with Oysters

Preparation: 15 minutes
Cooking: 1 hour 20 minutes, plus resting time
Serves 4

1 whole chicken
50 g/2 oz (4 tablespoons) butter, softened
3 oysters, blended together with their juices
green salad, to serve
sea salt

For the stuffing
75 g/2¾ oz (5½ tablespoons) butter
1 onion, finely chopped
100 g/3½ oz (2 cups) fresh breadcrumbs
12 oysters, chopped, juices reserved

The combination of meat with oysters appears often in recipes from the
eighteenth and nineteenth century in the upper echelons of Irish society.
Oysters with chicken and lamb (and indeed much more) seemed to be
a favourite with the landed classes. Blending oysters to make a glaze for
meat provides a marked salinity to any roast. Roast beef also works well
with an oyster glaze.

Preheat the oven to 160°C/325°F/
Gas Mark 3.

To make the stuffing, melt the
butter in a medium pan over
a medium heat, add the onion,
and fry for 3–4 minutes until
translucent. Season with a little
salt. Remove the pan from the
heat and add the breadcrumbs
and oysters. Mix thoroughly until
combined. If the breadcrumbs
are a little dry, add a little of the
oyster juices.

Stuff the cavity of the chicken and
put it into a suitable casserole dish
(Dutch oven). Rub the butter
over the chicken and season with
sea salt.

Roast for 30 minutes in the
preheated oven, then brush with
oyster juice. Roast for a further
30 minutes, basting occasionally.
Increase the oven temperature
to 200°C/400°F/Gas Mark 6
and cook the chicken for a further
15 minutes until nicely browned.

Remove from the oven and allow
to stand for 10 minutes. Serve with
some crisp green salad leaves.

Poultry

Chicken Cooked in Mud

Known as Tinker's Chicken, this recipe is mentioned in Monica Sheridan's *The Art of Irish Cooking* (1965). Travellers roaming around Ireland would cover a chicken in mud and then place it in a hole in the ground. The hole would then be filled with earth and a fire would be set on top. A few hours later, when the fire died down, the chicken would be dug up and cracked open with a hatchet. The feathers and the skin would be stripped away to reveal the soft white flesh of the chicken. According to Sheridan, travellers would have cooked both hedgehogs and fish using the same method.

Theodora FitzGibbon's Roast Chicken with Honey and Curry

Preparation: 5 minutes
Cooking: 25 minutes
Serves 4

115 g/4 oz (1 stick) butter
75 ml/2½ fl oz (⅓ cup) honey
2 teaspoons mustard
2 teaspoons curry powder
1 chicken, jointed
sea salt

This recipe is inspired by the great Irish food writer Theodora FitzGibbon. FitzGibbon was an early pioneer of Irish food, writing many books on the subject. She also wrote several books on the cuisines of other countries. Her writing is still relevant today and provides me with much inspiration for the future of Irish food.

Preheat the oven to 180°C/350°F/ Gas Mark 4.

Melt the butter in a medium pan over a medium heat. Mix in the honey, mustard, curry powder and salt.

Coat the chicken with the mixture and lay the pieces in a roasting pan. Roast in the preheated oven for 15–20 minutes.

Chicken Hearts with Poached Egg and Wild Garlic

Preparation and cooking: 20 minutes
Serves 2

2 eggs
a handful of chicken hearts
50 g/2 oz (4 tablespoons) butter
rapeseed (canola) oil
a few sprigs of thyme
sea salt
10 wild garlic (ramps) flowers and leaves, to serve

Bring a large pan of salted water to a simmer over a medium heat and poach the eggs for 4–5 minutes until the white is set. Lift the eggs out of the water with a slotted spoon and place on some paper towels to absorb the excess water.

Clean the chicken hearts and season. Melt the butter with the oil in a medium pan, add the hearts and thyme and fry over a medium heat for 1–2 minutes. They will cook very quickly. I recommend medium rare. Cut the hearts in two and season with sea salt.

To serve, place the eggs in the centre of two plates and season with some sea salt. Arrange the hearts around the egg. Decorate with some wild garlic leaves and flowers.

Goose

Goose was traditionally cooked in Ireland around the end of September (the feast of Michaelmas). The geese were put out on the grass in late spring and then finished on the grain that was left over after the harvest. There are many mentions in seventeenth-century poems of the benefits of eating goose at Michaelmas. Goose was traditionally cooked in the fire in a 'Dutch oven' (a cast iron pot with a lid). Turf was placed on the lid and replaced as it burned. This would have imbued the goose with a scent of turf. In her book, *Land of Milk and Honey* (1991), Bríd Mahon describes a goose baked in 'blue clay' in the fire in Blackloin, County Cavan. This sounds like an amazing way to cook a goose, because (as with salt baking) none of the moisture could escape from the goose. This type of process demonstrates the rich culinary heritage at the heart of Irish cooking and counters Louis M. Cullen's assertion that Irish cooking (or the Irish diet) was 'retarded' and backwards in terms of its complexity.

Goose Stuffed with Potatoes Cooked over a Turf Fire

Preparation: 15 minutes
Cooking: 3 hours 30 minutes, plus resting time
Serves 8

1.5 kg/3¼ lb (13 medium) potatoes, peeled
150 g/5 oz (1¼ sticks) butter
1 onion, chopped
a handful of sage, chopped
1 × 6–7-kg/13–15-lb goose
50 g/2 oz (¼ cup) goose fat, melted
bitter greens, to serve
sea salt

If you don't have a turf fire, place a 'sod' of turf (a palm-sized piece of turf) in your oven and preheat the oven to 160°C/325°F/Gas Mark 3.

Place the potatoes into a large pan with salted water over a high heat, bring to the boil, then reduce the heat and simmer for about 20 minutes until soft. Strain the water and mash the potatoes. Season with sea salt.

Melt the butter in a frying pan (skillet) over a low heat and fry the onion and sage for 3–4 minutes until the onion is translucent.

In a bowl, combine the onion and sage with the mashed potato. Mix well and check the seasoning.

Place the potato stuffing in the cavity of the goose and sew shut with some kitchen string (twine).

Rub the goose with the goose fat and season with sea salt. Place in a roasting pan and roast in the oven for approximately 3 hours or until the core temperature reaches 72°C/160°F on a meat thermometer. This may take a little longer, so I always like to use a thermometer to be exact. Baste the bird occasionally. To imbue the goose with a turf smell, burn the turf slightly every 20 minutes with the aid of a chef's blowtorch.

Rest the goose for 25 minutes before carving. Serve with the stuffing and some bitter greens.

Duck

'In medieval times it was usual to boil a duck with turnips or with parsley and sweet herbs or a sauce of clarified butter, seasoned with spices. […] In parts of Ireland it was traditional to cook the duck with berries of juniper, known in Irish as "iúr creige".'

Bríd Mahon, *Land of Milk and Honey*, 1991

We produce wonderful ducks in Ireland, both in the north and the south of the country. Enough now, that we actually export many to China! My favourite is reared in a place called Skeaghanore, in West Cork. Located near the sea, the Hickey family have been rearing ducks (and geese) since the mid-1990s. I don't know if it's the magic of West Cork or the way these ducks are reared on a natural diet of corn that makes their meat so succulent. It's probably a combination of both: the unique terroir of the south-west of Ireland mixed together with excellent animal husbandry. I love the idea of the ducks breathing in the sea air, feeding off the land over time to produce a meat that is tender and with a rich fat that rivals our best butter.

All domestic ducks descend from the wild mallard, which landed in Ireland long before people got here. For some reason, ducks were domesticated much later than the chicken. Maybe it was because we had so many wild ducks and other birds in Ireland. Or maybe it was because the chicken gave us eggs as well. Thus, much of the literature around ducks in Ireland before the fifteenth century refers to the wild variety, which were hunted in abundance since the arrival of hunter-gatherers. Wild ducks pop into many Irish myths, including the tales of Fionn mac Cumhaill (he seems to have liked his food – remember the salmon of knowledge on page 132). However, because of the proximity of ponds and lakes to monasteries, many types of wild duck, such as teal, became semi-domesticated by monks. In this way, a food supply was nearby in case of shortage or famine. Whole roast duck is a wonderful affair and a great meal to share with friends and family.

Duck Liver Pâté with Gin and Juniper

Preparation: 15 minutes
Cooking: 25 minutes, plus chilling time
Serves 4

200 g/7 oz (1¾ sticks) butter, cubed
a few sprigs of thyme and rosemary
1 onion, diced
rapeseed (canola) oil, for frying
500 g/1 lb 2 oz duck livers, trimmed of sinew and chopped
4 tablespoons double (heavy) cream
75 ml/2½ fl oz (⅓ cup) gin
a few juniper berries, crushed
sea salt
sourdough bread and gooseberry chutney, to serve

For the topping
150 g/5 oz (1¼ sticks) butter
thyme leaves
a few juniper berries

Put 25 g/1 oz (1¾ tablespoons) of the butter with the thyme and rosemary into a medium pan over a medium heat and fry the onion for about 5 minutes until soft and translucent.

Wipe the pan clean, add a little oil and then add the livers. Season with sea salt. Cook for 6–8 minutes until nice and brown, then add the cream, gin and juniper and cook for a further few minutes. Don't overcook the liver. You can remove the liver while the cream and gin are reducing if needed.

Put the liver mix into a food processor and blend, adding the remaining butter one cube at a time, until the mixture is nicely emulsified. Check the seasoning.

Pass the mixture through a fine sieve, then place the pâté in a bowl or individual ramekins and chill while you make the butter topping.

Melt the butter with the thyme and juniper in a small pan over a medium heat for about 10 minutes until the milk solids have separated from the butter. Strain through a fine sieve lined with a piece of muslin (cheesecloth) and then pour over the pâté. Chill until set.

Serve with some sourdough bread and gooseberry chutney.

See opposite –>

Poultry

Duck Breasts with Port and Redcurrant Sauce

Preparation: 10 minutes
Cooking: 20 minutes
Serves 4

2 tablespoons rapeseed (canola) oil
4 duck breasts
50 g/2 oz (4 tablespoons) butter
a few sprigs of thyme
sea salt

For the sauce
100 g/3½ oz (7 tablespoons) butter
2 shallots, chopped
1 bay leaf
150 ml/5 fl oz (⅔ cup) port
200 g/7 oz (¾ cups) fresh redcurrants
250 ml/8 fl oz (1 cup) chicken or duck
  stock (broth)
sea salt

Preheat the oven to 180°C/350°F/ Gas Mark 4 if you like your duck more than medium-rare.

To make the sauce, melt 25 g/1 oz (1¾ tablespoons) of the butter in a medium pan over a medium heat and fry the shallots for 2–3 minutes until soft. Add the bay leaf and port, bring to the boil and let simmer for about 10 minutes until reduced by half. Add the redcurrants and stock (broth). Bring to a simmer and cook for about 4 minutes until the berries are plump and have burst. Remove the bay leaves then blend the sauce with an immersion blender and strain through a sieve. Return to the boil and reduce a little. Add the remaining butter, stir in until melted and season with salt.

Meanwhile, to cook the duck breasts, heat a frying pan (skillet) over a medium heat with the oil. Score the duck breasts and season liberally with salt. Place the breasts into the pan, skin side down. Cook the duck breasts for 6–8 minutes until the fat has rendered out of the skin. Add the butter and thyme and baste for a further 3–4 minutes, turning the breasts occasionally.

If you want the duck cook more than medium-rare, transfer to the preheated oven for a few minutes.

Pour a little of the sauce onto a plate, slice a duck breast and place on top.

Note
I also like serving duck breast cooked in this way with a rhubarb sauce, made by stewing together 400 g/14 oz diced rhubarb, 1 finely diced onion, 25 g/1 oz (1¾ tablespoons) melted butter, 75 g/2¾ oz (⅓ cup firmly packed) soft brown sugar, 75 ml/2½ fl oz (⅓ cup) apple cider vinegar, 150 ml/5 fl oz (⅔ cup) cider (hard cider), 3 toasted juniper berries, 1 bay leaf and a pinch of sea salt. You can either leave the sauce chunky or blend it (removing the bay leaf and juniper berries first).

See opposite –>

Poultry

Spiced Duck with Potato and Sage Stuffing and Apple Sauce

Preparation: 30 minutes
Cooking: 1 hour 45 minutes, plus resting time
Serves 4

500 g/1 lb 2 oz (about 8 medium) potatoes, peeled
1 whole large duck
a little duck fat
1 onion, diced
1 teaspoon finely chopped sage
sea salt

For the apple sauce
100 g/3½ oz (½ cup firmly packed) soft brown sugar
100 ml/3½ fl oz (scant ½ cup) dry sherry
750 g/1 lb 10 oz (about 5) cooking apples, peeled, cored and roughly chopped
a little fresh grated ginger, to taste

For the spice mix
1 teaspoon juniper berries
1 teaspoon coriander seeds
1 star anise
1 teaspoon fennel seeds

Preheat the oven to 180°C/350°F/Gas Mark 4.

Boil the potatoes in a large pan of salted water over a medium–high heat for about 15 minutes until you can pass a knife through them. Strain and mash.

Meanwhile, for the apple sauce, dissolve the sugar in the sherry in a medium pan over a medium heat. Add the apples and fresh ginger. After it comes to the boil, reduce the heat to a simmer and stew for about 5 minutes until the apples are soft. Put into a food processor and blend until smooth.

For the spice mix, toast the spices in a dry pan for a few minutes and blend in a spice grinder. Add salt to taste. Keep in an airtight jar.

Heat the duck fat in a small pan over a medium heat and fry the onion with the sage until soft and translucent. Combine with the mash potatoes to make the stuffing.

For the duck, stuff the duck with the potato stuffing. Score the skin and season it with the spice mix. Roast in the preheated oven for 1 hour 30 minutes or until a core temperature of 65°C/150°F is reached on a meat thermometer. Allow to rest for 10 minutes before carving.

See opposite –>

Duck Leg Cooked in Its Own Fat with Parsnip and Apple Purée

Preparation: 15 minutes, plus 6 hours minimum curing time
Cooking: 2 hours
Serves 4

For the confit duck
1 teaspoon each caraway seeds, coriander seeds and juniper berries
a few sprigs of thyme and rosemary, chopped
2 bay leaves, torn
4–6 duck legs
1 head of garlic, unpeeled
enough duck fat to cover the legs, warmed
sea salt and freshly ground black pepper

For the parsnip and apple purée
2 parsnips, peeled and diced
1 potato, peeled and diced
1 apple, peeled, cored and diced
350 ml/12 fl oz (1½ cups) milk
50 g/2 oz (4 tablespoons) butter

This way of cooking duck legs is also known as confit and was popularized in France, particularly the south-west. 'Confit' comes from the old French *confire* and means 'to preserve'. However, the practice of preserving duck legs in fat was common all over Europe. Many other cuts of meats from pork belly to lamb shoulder can be confited. The meat cooks slowly, retaining moisture and flavour. It is usually salted first, often with spices.

For the duck legs, toast the spices and blend in a spice grinder. Mix with the herbs and season. Sprinkle liberally over the duck legs and leave to cure in the refrigerator for at least 6 hours or overnight.

Preheat the oven to 140°C/275°F/Gas Mark 1.

Wipe off the cure and put the duck legs into a deep ovenproof dish. Place the head of garlic beside them and cover with the duck fat.

Cover and roast in the oven for 2 hours or until the duck legs are tender.

Meanwhile, make the purée. Put the parsnip, potato and apple into a pan and cover with the milk. Put the pan over a medium heat, bring to a simmer and cook for 20 minutes, until the vegetables are tender. Add the butter and blend with an immersion blender until smooth. Season to taste.

Poultry

Poultry

Wild Game

Wild Game

'The fawn and the deer
and every kind of game
is there,
The red-fox a-leaping,
the badger and the
yellow hare.
The music of the hounds
and the horns a blow-ing,
And with the rise of the
sun you would lift up
your heart.
There are gentlemen
on steeds and horsemen
being tried,
Hunting all through other
until comes the night'

Antoine Ó Raifteirí, 'Killeadan,
or County Mayo'

Some of the first foods eaten by the earliest settlers of Ireland include wild birds and other game. There are bone remains in Ireland of mallard (wild duck) and pigeon (squab). Mallards were the first species of wild duck on the island of Ireland. Bones from this ancient duck were found at the Mesolithic sites of Mount Sandel (County Derry) and Lough Boora (County Offaly). All duck, bar one exception, descend from mallard (the Muscovy duck is a large breed of wild duck that originates from Central and South America). Mallard season takes off in Ireland from September onwards. Because of their size, mallard roast quickly and can be pan-fried on the crown (with the two breasts attached to the bone). When we eat these birds today, we are engaging in an eight thousand-year-old tradition that has taken place on the island of Ireland.

From Clare to the Midlands, to Wicklow in the east, Ireland is a wonderful place for game. Unfortunately, throughout the ages, wild birds (and deer) were generally preserved for the elite who hunted them for game. As well as hunting deer and wild birds, they would have also looked for wild boar and badgers. As Fergus Kelly observes in his book *Early Irish Farming* (2000), complex laws divided the deer among the hunting party and the person who owned the land. A seventh- or eighth-century law text dictates that while the owner of the hounds got the haunch, the landowner received the belly. There are probably few people left today who hunt for their own food as opposed to hunting for sport. However, game has enjoyed a recent resurgence in Ireland today, due to its popularity among those interested in wild food and hunters who have started to sell them directly to restaurants. My family never hunted, and I have only recently engaged in the activity. I am not a great shot, though I do relish the act of trying to hunt for my own food, something most of us never have to do anymore. Several of the hunters I know do the job commercially and supply ourselves and other restaurants in the west of Ireland. Our game supplier Eamonn Giblin, based in County Clare, supplies us with the most wonderful assortment of birds and venison. There is nothing more beautiful than cooking game over an open fire. If you're looking for an Irish barbecue tradition, then look no further than to an open turf fire with an array of birds hanging over it and a few loins of venison under a grill of smouldering juniper branches.

Venison

'Beith ag ithe na feola fiadh agus an fheoil-fhiadh ar an gcnoc go foil'

'Eat your venison while the deer is still on the mountain' (an old Irish saying)

The word 'venison' originally applied to any furred game caught in the wild, but now it only applies to deer. There is a rich tradition of eating deer in both Ireland and the rest of the UK. Red deer were introduced into Ireland by early farmers. In his twelfth-century *Topography of Ireland*, Gerald of Wales spoke highly of the quality of Irish red deer. Fallow deer followed with the arrival of the Anglo-Normans (first mentioned in 1213, a licence was granted to the archbishop of Dublin to bring thirty fallow deer from England). Finally, sika deer arrived in the nineteenth century. They were introduced to County Wicklow by Lord Powerscourt and subsequently escaped, causing the population of sika deer to soar into the tens of thousands. Nowadays, deer farms supply Northern Ireland and England with venison all year round, but I prefer the wild variety, which is only available from late autumn (fall) to late winter. Deer meat should be hung for between twelve and twenty-two days before eating. This process helps tenderize the meat and develops its flavour. Historically, before the advent of the refrigerator, the meat would have been rubbed with ginger and black pepper to keep the flies away. Venison is an extremely lean meat. A common way to cook it in the past involved larding it (sewing pork fat through the meat). This would keep the meat nice and moist. Venison pies were very popular from the Middle Ages up to the nineteenth century. In a 1605 recipe, the author recommended a thick rye and lard pastry to enclose slowly cooked venison meat that was spiced with ginger and cinnamon. Spices and game have gone hand in hand for centuries. For me, venison loin or fillet (tenderloin) should always be cooked rare and then well rested in a warm place. It pairs well with autumnal fruits (blackberries, apples and plums) and goes wonderfully with salt-baked beetroot (beets). You should cook venison loin as you would a steak, in a pan with a little oil over a high heat, then finish with some butter to baste and a sprig of thyme or some juniper berries. If you can buy it on the bone, you can make a wonderful venison sauce in the same manner that we make duck sauce. Nowadays, I prefer to shun the spices that have dominated the flavour of game to get to the true taste of the meat. One could argue that this is not historically accurate, but new histories are always created from turning our back on some of the ways of old. I offer recipes that include and exclude spices.

Venison Tartare with Blackberries

Preparation: 15 minutes
Serves 4

300 g/11 oz venison loin, sinew removed
1 tablespoon finely chopped shallot
10 g/¼ oz (¼ cup prepared) chives, finely chopped
extra virgin rapeseed (canola) oil, to season
apple balsamic vinegar, to season
sea salt, to season

To serve
40 g/1½ oz (¼ cup) blackberries, halved
wood sorrel, to garnish (or use parsley)

Finely chop the venison loin. Put the meat into a medium-sized bowl and add the shallot and chives. Mix together and season with the oil, vinegar and salt.

Divide the mixture among four plates and garnish with the blackberries and wood sorrel.

Venison Pies

Preparation: 35 minutes, plus overnight
marinating and 1 hour chilling time
Cooking: 2 hours 35 minutes
Serves 4

For the pastry
200 g/7 oz (1²/₃ cups) plain (all-purpose)
    flour, sifted, plus extra for dusting
1 teaspoon sea salt
100 g/3½ oz (7 tablespoons)
    cold butter, cubed
1 egg yolk, plus 1 egg, beaten separately
    for brushing

For the filling
500 g/1 lb 2 oz venison shoulder, diced
200 ml/7 fl oz (scant 1 cup) cider (hard cider)
a few sprigs of thyme, sage and rosemary,
    finely chopped
50 g/2 oz (4 tablespoons) butter
1 onion, diced
50 g/2 oz (generous ⅓ cup) plain
    (all-purpose) flour
300 ml/10 fl oz (1¼ cups) beef stock (broth)
sea salt

Meat pies have always had a strong presence in Irish and British cuisine. Food writer Colman Andrews wrote in *The Country Cooking of Ireland* (2009) that pies were inspired by 'economic restrictions' to use leftovers and to extend what meat was available. However, they also dominate the recipe books of the 'big houses' of the landed aristocracy. For food historian Regina Sexton, pies (and puddings and roasts) were 'emerging as emblems of traditional British cookery'. Their appearance in books demonstrates how many 'elite Irish' saw themselves in the same tradition.

The night before, marinate the venison in the cider and herbs.

The next day, to make the pastry, combine the flour and salt in a mixing bowl. Rub in the butter and then add one egg yolk. Add just enough ice-cold water to bring the dough together. Wrap in cling film (plastic wrap) and allow to rest in the refrigerator for at least 1 hour. When ready, roll out the dough on a floured surface and cut into 8 rounds using a 20–25-cm/ 8–10-inch pastry cutter. Transfer 4 rounds to a baking sheet lined with baking (parchment) paper.

Meanwhile, make the filling. Melt the butter in a large pan over a medium heat and fry the onion for about 5 minutes until soft.

Strain the cider from the venison. Add the venison to the pan and brown all over. When browned,

add the flour and cook for a minute, then add the cider and beef stock (broth). Reduce the heat and cook for 2 hours until the venison is extremely tender. Remove from the heat and allow to cool.

Preheat the oven to 180°C/350°F/ Gas Mark 4.

Place one-quarter of the venison mixture in the middle of each of the pastry rounds on the baking sheet. Brush the sides with a little water and cover with the remaining pastry rounds. Make a small hole in the centre of each pie to allow steam to escape. Brush each pie with the remaining egg and crimp the edges with a fork.

Bake in the preheated oven for 30 minutes or until the filling is hot and the pastry is nicely browned.

See opposite –>

☼ �

Venison Broth

Preparation: 20 minutes
Cooking: 5 hours
Serves 6

2 kg/4½ lb venison bones
1.5 kg/3¼ lb venison shoulder, cubed
about 75 ml/2½ oz (⅓ cup) rapeseed
    (canola) oil
2 onions, chopped
2 leeks, chopped
2 carrots, chopped
2 celery stalks, chopped
a bouquet garni of thyme, sage, parsley,
    rosemary and bay leaf
sea salt

Preheat the oven to 200°C/400°F/ Gas Mark 6.

Put the venison bones into a roasting pan and roast in the preheated oven for about 40 minutes until nicely browned.

Cook the venison in batches. Heat 2 tablespoons of the oil in a large pan over a medium heat, add the venison shoulder without crowding the pan, season with sea salt and fry for about 5 minutes, until nicely browned. Remove the venison from the pan and set aside.

Repeat with the remaining venison – you may need more oil depending on how many batches you fry.

In the same pan, heat a tablespoon of oil, add the vegetables and cook for about 10 minutes until nicely browned.

Return the meat to the pan with the bones and herbs. Add enough water to cover everything, bring to the boil, reduce the heat and simmer for 3–4 hours. Strain and serve (you can use the meat for pies or croquettes).

Wild Game

Wild Game

Venison and Cauliflower Purée

Preparation: 15 minutes
Cooking: 25 minutes, plus resting time
Serves 4

2 tablespoons rapeseed (canola) oil
400 g/14 oz venison loin, trimmed of sinew
100 g/3½ oz (7 tablespoons) butter
a few sprigs of thyme
venison jus (see Lamb Jus, page 379), warmed

For the cauliflower purée
1 cauliflower, cut into florets
450 ml/15 fl oz (scant 2 cups) milk
100 ml/3½ fl oz (scant ½ cup) double
    (heavy) cream
coarse (kosher) sea salt

Preheat the oven to 200°C/400°F/
Gas Mark 4.

To make the cauliflower purée, add the cauliflower to a large pan with the milk and cream, bring to a simmer and cook for 5–7 minutes until the cauliflower is soft. Strain the milk from the cauliflower and reserve. Blend the cauliflower in a food processor. Add enough milk to make a smooth purée. Season and pass through a fine sieve.

To cook the venison, heat the oil in a large ovenproof frying pan (skillet) over a high heat.

Season the venison loin. When the oil is smoking hot, add the venison and brown evenly on all sides. Add the butter and thyme and cook for about 10 minutes until the butter caramelizes. Reduce the heat and baste the loin for a few minutes.

Transfer to the preheated oven and cook for 5 minutes. Remove from the oven and rest for 5 minutes.

To serve, carve the loin and serve with the purée and warmed jus.

See opposite –>

Venison and Barley Stew

Preparation: 15 minutes
Cooking: 2 hours 45 minutes
Serves 8

2 tablespoons rapeseed (canola) oil
2 onions, sliced
2 carrots, chopped
1 leek, sliced
a few sage leaves
2 cloves garlic, very finely chopped
2 kg/4½ lb venison shoulder, diced
3 litres/105 fl oz (12½ cups) beef stock (broth)
450 ml/15 fl oz (scant 2 cups) beer
200 g/7 oz (1 cup) barley
sea salt

Heat the oil in a large stewpot over a medium heat and fry the onions, carrots and leek for about 10 minutes until the vegetables are lightly caramelized. Add the sage leaves and garlic.

Season the venison with sea salt and add to the pan. Brown the meat all over.

Add the stock (broth) and beer, bring to the boil, then reduce the heat to a simmer. Cook for 1 hour 30 minutes, then add the barley and cook for a further 1 hour. Ensure the venison meat is tender before removing the stew from the heat. Remove the sage leaves and season to taste.

Salt-baked Venison

Preparation: 15 minutes
Cooking: 20 minutes, plus resting time
Serves 4–6

500 g/1 lb 2 oz (4 cups) plain
    (all-purpose) flour
300 g/11 oz (1 cup) sea salt
75 g/2¾ oz (5½ tablespoons) butter, melted
1 venison loin, trimmed of sinew

This is a traditional way of cooking deer which keeps the meat moist. Dry spices such as fennel or coriander seeds can be added to the paste.

Preheat the oven to 200°C/400°F/
Gas Mark 6.

In a large mixing bowl, combine the flour and salt, then mix in enough water to bind and form a dough. Knead the dough until it comes together smoothly.

Rub the melted butter over the venison. Roll out the dough and wrap it around the venison. Ensure there are no gaps in the dough.

Bake on a baking sheet in the preheated oven for 15–20 minutes. Remove and rest for 10 minutes before carving.

Wild Game

Wild Game

Haunch of Venison with Plums, Port and Cinnamon

Preparation: 15 minutes, plus 1 hour
marinating time
Cooking: 2 hours, plus resting time
Serves 8

1 × 3-kg/6½ lb haunch of venison, on the bone
500 ml/17 fl oz (generous 2 cups) venison
   or beef stock (broth)
150 ml/5 fl oz (⅔ cup) port
12 plums, halved and stoned (pitted)
1 bay leaf

For the marinade
75 ml/2½ fl oz (⅓ cup) apple balsamic vinegar
1 teaspoon ground cinnamon
75 g/2¾ oz (⅓ cup firmly packed)
   soft brown sugar
50 g/2 oz (4 tablespoons) butter, melted
sea salt and freshly ground black pepper

The haunch is the back leg of the venison. It can be treated the same as a leg of lamb for most recipes. Serve with wilted greens, such as chard.

Combine all the ingredients for the marinade in a mixing bowl and mix thoroughly. Brush the haunch of venison with the marinade and allow to stand at room temperature for 1 hour.

Preheat the oven to 160°C/325°F/Gas Mark 3.

Put the venison into a roasting pan and roast in the preheated oven for 1 hour 15 minutes.

Add the stock (broth), port, plums and bay leaf to the pan and roast for a further 45 minutes, basting the venison intermittently with the liquid, until it reaches a core temperature of 60°C/140°F on a meat thermometer.

Allow to rest for 10 minutes before carving.

See opposite –>

Mallard with Crab Apples and Watercress

Preparation: 10 minutes
Cooking: 20 minutes, plus resting time
Serves 4

2 mallards, oven ready
75 g/2¾ oz (⅓ cup) pork lard, softened
a few sprigs of thyme
6 crab apples, cored and quartered
2 tablespoons apple syrup
2 tablespoons apple cider vinegar
a handful of watercress, picked
sea salt

If you can't source crab apples, you can use any seasonal apples. An oven-ready bird will be plucked and gutted – i.e., ready to put in the oven.

Preheat the oven to 200°C/400°F/Gas Mark 6.

Rub the mallards with the lard and season with sea salt. Place some thyme in the cavity of the birds.

Put the apples onto the base of a roasting pan and season with some salt, the apple syrup and vinegar. You're looking for a nice balance of the three elements.

Rest the mallards on top of the apples and roast in the preheated oven, basting occasionally, for 20 minutes until medium-rare or it reaches a core temperature of 58°C/136°F on a meat thermometer.

Rest the birds for 5 minutes before serving. Spoon the apples into a bowl. Carve the mallards and serve with the watercress.

Wild Game

Mallard with Roasted Orange and Juniper

Preparation: 10 minutes
Cooking: 20 minutes, plus resting time
Serves 4

2 mallards, oven ready
rapeseed (canola) oil
a few sprigs of thyme
2 oranges, each cut into six
4 tablespoons orange liqueur
100 ml/3½ fl oz (scant ½ cup) chicken
   stock (broth)
5 juniper berries
sea salt and freshly ground black pepper

Preheat the oven to 200°C/400°F/ Gas Mark 6.

Rub the mallards with oil and season with sea salt. Put some thyme and a piece of orange into the cavity of the birds.

Put all the rest of the ingredients into a roasting pan and rest the mallards on top.

Roast in the preheated oven, basting occasionally, for 20 minutes until medium-rare or the core temperature reaches 58°C/136°F on a meat thermometer.

Rest the birds for 5 minutes before serving. Carve the mallards and serve with the roast oranges and some sauce.

See opposite –>

Pheasant with Prunes and Sherry

Preparation: 15 minutes, plus 2–3 hours
soaking time
Cooking: 55 minutes
Serves 4

100 g/3½ oz (⅔ cup) prunes, diced
150 ml/5 fl oz (⅔ cup) cream sherry
2 pheasant crowns
3 tablespoons rapeseed (canola) oil
50 g/2 oz (4 tablespoons) butter
2 cloves garlic
2 sprigs of thyme
200 ml/7 fl oz (scant 1 cup) chicken
   stock (broth)
sea salt

Soak the prunes in a small bowl with the sherry for 2–3 hours.

Preheat the oven to 180°C/350°F/ Gas Mark 4.

Season the pheasant crowns with salt. Heat the oil in a frying pan (skillet) over a medium heat, add the pheasant and sear briefly all over. Add the butter, garlic and thyme and baste the crowns for about 5 minutes until they are golden brown.

Transfer to a roasting pan and roast in the preheated oven for 25 minutes until nicely browned.

Remove the pheasant from the pan and rest in a warm place. Deglaze the pan with the sherry. Simmer for about 15 minutes to reduce by half, then add the stock (broth) and prunes and reduce by half again for a further 10–15 minutes.

Carve the breasts off the pheasant and serve with the prunes and sherry.

Pheasant Wrapped in Lardo Stuffed with Sweet Chestnuts

Preparation: 20 minutes
Cooking: 50 minutes
Serves 4

100 g/3½ oz (7 tablespoons) butter
1 onion, diced
a few sprigs of thyme, leaves chopped
150 g/5 oz cooked chestnuts, crushed
50 g/2 oz (1 cup) fresh breadcrumbs
2 tablespoons finely chopped parsley
2 pheasants, oven ready
16 slices of Lardo (see page 372)
sea salt

Preheat the oven to 180°C/350°F/ Gas Mark 4.

To make the stuffing, melt the butter in a frying pan (skillet) over a medium heat. Fry the onion for about 5 minutes until soft, then season with the thyme and salt. In a large mixing bowl, combine the onion with everything else apart from the lardo and pheasants.

Stuff the pheasants with the stuffing and cover with the lardo. Roast in a roasting pan in the preheated oven for 45 minutes until cooked through.

Rest the pheasants for 5 minutes before serving.

      Wild Game

Wild Game

Partridge with Blackberry Sauce

Preparation: 15 minutes
Cooking: 55 minutes
Serves 2

2 partridges, oven ready
3 tablespoons rapeseed (canola) oil
50 g/2 oz (4 tablespoons) butter
a few sprigs of thyme
sea salt

For the blackberry sauce
1 tablespoon extra virgin rapeseed (canola) oil
1 shallot, finely diced
1 clove garlic, finely diced
100 ml/3½ fl oz (scant ½ cup) cider (hard cider)
2 juniper berries, crushed
1 teaspoon honey
300 ml/10 fl oz (1¼ cups) chicken stock (broth)
150 g/5 oz (1 cup) fresh blackberries

Preheat the oven to 180°C/350°F/ Gas Mark 4.

To cook the partridges, season the birds with sea salt. Heat the oil in a large frying pan (skillet) over a medium heat, add the partridges and brown on all sides. Allow to cool slightly and then rub with the butter. Place some thyme in the cavity of the birds.

Put the partridges into a roasting pan and roast in the preheated oven for 25 minutes. Remove from the oven and allow to rest.

Meanwhile, prepare the blackberry sauce. Heat the oil in a medium pan over a medium heat and fry the shallot and garlic for 2–3 minutes until soft. Add the cider, juniper berries and honey and simmer for about 10 minutes until reduced by half. Add the chicken stock (broth) and simmer for a further 10–15 minutes until reduced by half again. Fold in the blackberries and warm gently so as not to break up the fruit too much. Season with a little sea salt.

Serve the partridges with the blackberry sauce.

Grouse and Poteen

Preparation: 15 minutes, plus overnight chilling time
Cooking: 25 minutes
Serves 4

2 grouse, oven ready
4 tablespoons poteen
2 onions, peeled
2 cloves garlic, crushed
100 g/3½ oz (7 tablespoons) butter, melted
thyme, nicely chopped
sea salt

Poteen (or poitín) is a potent Irish spirit made from potatoes or grains. Though it was outlawed in 1661, being illegal didn't stop its production. It took more than three hundred years before poteen became legal once again in 1997. Pádraic Ó Griallais is a sixth-generation poteen producer based in Connemara and represents the future of the drink. He continues an almost 200-year-old family tradition. The distillery can trace its roots back to the mid-nineteenth century. If you can't find poteen, you could substitute with vodka or gin.

The night before, brush the grouse with the poteen and refrigerate overnight. Reserve a little for brushing the following morning.

The following day, preheat the oven to 180°C/350°F/Gas Mark 4. Put an onion and garlic clove into the cavity of each bird. Brush again with the leftover poteen.

Put the birds into a roasting pan, brush with the melted butter and season with some salt and the herbs. Put into the preheated oven and roast for 25 minutes, brushing the grouse with the melted butter every 5 minutes.

Rest the grouse for 5 minutes before serving.

Grouse with Porridge

Preparation: 15 minutes, plus overnight
standing and soaking time
Cooking: 25 minutes
Serves 4

2 grouse, oven ready
4 tablespoons whiskey
50 g/2 oz (4 tablespoons) butter, melted
a selection of herbs such as sage, rosemary
    and thyme, to stuff the birds
2 teaspoons honey, warmed
sea salt

For the porridge
200 g/7 oz (2¼ cups) rolled oats
25 g/1 oz (1¾ tablespoons) butter
1 onion, finely diced
200 ml/7 fl oz (scant 1 cup) milk
2 teaspoons apple syrup

Grouse season begins in September in Ireland. Unless you know a hunter, they are a rare bird to see on menus these days, which is a pity. Grouse bones were uncovered at Ferriter's Cove (a Mesolithic and Neolithic site).

Brush the grouse with the whiskey and allow to stand overnight. Cover the oats with 200 ml/7 fl oz (scant 1 cup) slightly salted water and leave to soak overnight.

The following morning, preheat the oven to 180°C/350°F/Gas Mark 4.

Put the birds into a roasting pan, brush with the melted butter and season with sea salt. Stuff the cavity with the herbs. Roast in the preheated oven for 15 minutes, then brush with the honey.

Return to the oven for a further 10 minutes. Remove from the oven and allow to rest.

Meanwhile, for the porridge, melt the butter in a medium pan over a medium heat and fry the onion for about 5 minutes until soft. Add the oats (they will have soaked up the water) and milk, then cook for about 5 minutes until the oats are tender. Finish with the apple syrup.

Carve the breasts and legs from the birds and serve with the porridge.

Squab with Smoked Bacon, Figs and Whiskey

Preparation: 10 minutes
Cooking: 30 minutes
Serves 4

100 ml/3½ fl oz (scant ½ cup) chicken
    stock (broth)
2 tablespoons honey
2 tablespoons apple balsamic vinegar
75 ml/2½ fl oz (⅓ cup) whiskey
4 squab, oven ready
100 g/3½ oz smoked bacon
8 figs, halved
sea salt and freshly ground black pepper

A squab is a young domestic pigeon, typically under four weeks old.

Preheat the oven to 200°C/400°F/ Gas Mark 6.

Put the chicken stock (broth), honey, vinegar and whiskey into a small pan, bring to the boil and simmer for about 10 minutes until reduced to a sauce.

Wrap the squabs in bacon and put them into a roasting pan with the figs. Pour the sauce over the birds and figs.

Roast the squab in the preheated oven for 15 minutes. Remove from the oven and allow to rest for 5 minutes before carving. Season as desired with salt and pepper.

Wild Game

Pigeon and Stout

Preparation: 15 minutes
Cooking: 1 hour
Serves 4

4 pigeons, plucked and gutted
4 tablespoons rapeseed (canola) oil
75 g/2¾ oz (5½ tablespoons) butter
a few sprigs of thyme
2 onions, chopped
2 cloves garlic, very finely chopped
250 g/9 oz mushrooms, sliced
500 ml/17 fl oz (generous 2 cups) chicken
    stock (broth)
4 tablespoons whiskey
500 ml/17 fl oz (generous 2 cups) stout
sea salt

Wood pigeon bones have been found at both Mount Sandel and Lough Boora in abundance, testifying to the importance this bird had in the diet of the first settlers nearly 10,000 years ago. There is a continued use of pigeon throughout Irish food history, from pickled pigeon in the seventeenth and eighteenth century (see below) to pigeon and stout in the nineteenth and twentieth.

Season the pigeons with sea salt. Heat 3 tablespoons of the oil in a large pan over a medium heat, add the pigeons and sear. After a few minutes, add the butter with the thyme and allow to caramelize. Baste the pigeons for a few minutes until nicely browned. Remove the pigeons from the pan and allow to rest.

Wipe the pan with some paper towels, discarding the butter and thyme. Heat the remaining oil in the pan over a medium heat and fry the onions and garlic for 3–4 minutes until translucent.

Season with sea salt, add the mushrooms and cook for 5–7 minutes until the mushrooms have a nice colour. Add the chicken stock (broth), whiskey and stout. Bring to the boil, reduce the heat and simmer for 30 minutes.

Return the pigeons to the pan, cover and simmer for a further 20 minutes until the pigeons are cooked; the core temperature of the breast meat should reach 65°C/150°F on a meat thermometer.

See opposite –>

Pickled Pigeon

Preparation: 10 minutes, plus overnight chilling time
Cooking: 30 minutes
Serves 4

8 pigeon breasts, skin removed
3 tablespoons rapeseed (canola) oil
1 onion, sliced
1 teaspoon chopped marjoram
1 teaspoon chopped winter savory or thyme
1 teaspoon chopped sage
a few black peppercorns
freshly grated nutmeg
300 ml/10 fl oz (1¼ cups) white wine
350 ml/12 fl oz (1½ cups) white wine vinegar
250 ml/8 fl oz (1 cup) chicken stock (broth)
sea salt

This recipe dates back to c.1780. Though is may seem strange to pickle birds (or other game), pickling was an important method to help preserve the meat for future use. The Spanish dish of escabeche is not entirely dissimilar – in La Mancha, they pickle squab pigeon in a similar manner.

Season the pigeon breasts with salt. Warm the oil in a large frying pan (skillet) over a medium heat and brown the breasts 2–3 minutes on each side. Remove from the pan and set aside.

Add the onion to the pan with the herbs and spices, adding a little more oil if necessary, and fry for about 5 minutes until the onion is nicely coloured.

Add the wine, vinegar and stock (broth) and bring to the boil. Return the pigeons to the pan, reduce the heat and simmer for about 15 minutes until the pigeons are cooked. They should be firm to the touch.

Allow to cool and then refrigerate. Serve the following day with some crisp salad.

Wild Game

Rabbit

'Until about ten years ago, Ireland was overrun with wild rabbits. They became a positive plague in the country, eating the vegetables in the garden and the crops in the fields. At one time they could be bought in the city shops for twelve cents apiece, while in the country they cost no more than the price of a shot-gun cartridge.'

Monica Sheridan, *The Art of Irish Cooking*, 1965

In terms of its history in Ireland, rabbit was popular as both a food and for its fur. Following on from the Romans (and their penchant for rabbits), the Normans introduced rabbits to Ireland in the late twelfth century. Rabbit meat seems to have been a food allowed during Lent, however initially they were the preserve of the rich. There are several recipes for rabbit stew from this period in English cookbooks, so we can assume that similar dishes were also made in Ireland. Rabbit bones were found at many medieval sites, from castles (Trim Castle, County Meath) to abbeys (Tintern Abbey, County Wexford), thus demonstrating their popularity as a food source. Because of the British desire for rabbit fur, rabbits became a major export from Ireland in the seventeenth century. Their meat was also exported to England and eaten in large quantities.

The Irish have mixed feelings towards the rabbit. Before the 1950s, Ireland was awash with rabbits and they were readily available as a cheap source of food. Rabbit stew was a staple of many a country house, big or small. When I was growing up, however, it was a pest for farmers. In 1954, farmers illegally infected the rabbit population with myxomatosis. By the 1960s, the disease was widespread, and the consumption of rabbits effectively ceased. Nowadays, people seem to want them as pets but not to eat them. The rise of cheap chicken also led to the decline of rabbit meat in the latter half of the twentieth century. As with all wild food, people rejected it as their wealth increased. This is unfortunate because wild rabbit is a much more ethical and sustainable choice than caged chicken. Eating it also connects you with a long tradition of its consumption.

In the restaurant, we still get a delivery of wild rabbit once a week and I always encourage people to try it, whether in a stew, a croquette or roasted whole. Rabbits are extremely lean, so they require delicate cooking and a little extra fat to stop them drying out.

Rabbit Croquettes

Preparation: 20 minutes
Cooking: 20 minutes, plus cooling time
Serves 4

50 g/2 oz (4 tablespoons) butter
50 g/2 oz (⅓ cup) plain (all-purpose) flour
500 ml/17 fl oz (generous 2 cups) milk, warmed
200 g/7 oz (1½ cups) cooked rabbit/hare meat, shredded
a pinch of ground cloves
2 tablespoons chopped parsley
rapeseed (canola) oil, for deep-frying
sea salt and freshly ground black pepper
mayonnaise, to serve

To coat the croquettes
100 g/3½ oz (¾ cup) plain (all-purpose) flour
2 eggs, beaten
100 g/3½ oz (2 cups) fresh breadcrumbs

These croquettes can also be made with cooked hare meat. I came across a recipe for hare croquettes in my grandmother's 1949 edition of Mrs Beeton's *All-About Cookery*.

Make a roux for a sauce. Heat the butter in a medium pan over a medium heat until it melts. Stir in the flour and cook for about 2 minutes to form a brown paste. Slowly add the warm milk and heat, stirring, for about 10 minutes until it thickens to a sauce.

Add the rabbit meat, ground cloves and parsley and season with salt and pepper. Allow to cool completely in the refrigerator.

Preheat the oil in a deep-fat fryer until it reaches a temperature of 180°C/350°F or until a cube of bread browns in 30 seconds.

Put the flour, eggs and bread-crumbs for the coating into three separate shallow dishes.

Form the cold rabbit mixture into small oval shapes with your hands or with two spoons (the mixture should make at least twelve). Roll the croquettes in the flour, then the egg and finally the breadcrumbs.

Fry the croquettes in the hot oil in batches for 4–6 minutes until golden brown and crispy.

Serve with mayonnaise.

See opposite –>

Wild Game

Deep-fried Rabbit Legs with Wild Garlic Mayonnaise

Preparation: 15 minutes, plus overnight
marinating time
Cooking: about 12 minutes per batch
Serves 8

8 rabbit legs
500 ml/17 fl oz (generous 2 cups) buttermilk
300 g/11 oz (2⅓ cups) plain
    (all-purpose) flour
a few sprigs of thyme and rosemary,
    leaves finely chopped
rapeseed (canola) oil, for deep-frying
sea salt

To serve
wild garlic (ramps) flowers (optional)
Wild Garlic Mayonnaise (see page 383)

Season the rabbit legs with salt
and put into a suitable container.
Cover with the buttermilk and
allow to marinate in the refrigerator
overnight.

Preheat oil in the deep-fat fryer
until the oil reaches a temperature
of 160°C/325°F.

Season the flour with the herbs
and some salt. Remove the rabbit
from the buttermilk and dredge
in the seasoned flour.

Fry the rabbit legs, in batches, in
the hot oil for 8–12 minutes until
brown and crispy.

Season again with sea salt and serve
with the Wild Garlic Mayonnaise
and some wild garlic (ramps)
flowers, if using.

See opposite –>

Rabbits Braised in the Traditional Manner

Preparation: 20 minutes, plus overnight
marinating time
Cooking: 1 hour 50 minutes
Serves 8

2 rabbits, jointed
500 ml/17 fl oz (generous 2 cups) buttermilk
a few sprigs of thyme
2 bay leaves
3 tablespoons rapeseed (canola) oil
2 onions, diced
2 cloves garlic, crushed
4 carrots, diced
50 g/2 oz (⅓ cup) plain (all-purpose) flour
250 ml/8 fl oz (1 cup) cider (hard cider)
750 ml/25 fl oz (3 cups) chicken stock (broth)
2 tablespoons chopped parsley
sea salt and freshly ground black pepper

Soak the rabbit pieces in the
buttermilk in a suitable container,
with half the thyme and 1 bay leaf
overnight in the refrigerator. This
will help tenderize it and stop it
from drying out while cooking.

The following day, pat the rabbit
dry and season with sea salt.

Heat the oil in a cast-iron pan.
Fry the rabbit pieces in batches
for about 5 minutes until nicely
browned. Set aside.

Add the onions, garlic and bay
leaf to the pan and fry for about
5 minutes until the onions are soft.

Add the carrots and the remaining
thyme and fry for about 3 minutes
until the carrots are soft. Add the
flour and cook for about 3 minutes
until no longer raw.

Return the rabbit pieces to the
pan and cover with the cider and
chicken stock (broth). Cover the
pan with a lid and simmer for about
1 hour 30 minutes until the rabbit
is tender. Ensure the rabbit pieces
are well covered during cooking
and turn them occasionally.

Season with salt and pepper before
serving and garnish with the
chopped parsley.

Wild Game

Rabbit and Potato Stew

Preparation: 20 minutes, plus overnight
marinating time
Cooking: 1 hour 30 minutes
Serves 8

2 rabbits, jointed
150 ml/5 fl oz (⅔ cup) buttermilk
4 carrots, chopped
2 onions, chopped
4 celery stalks, chopped
4 potatoes, peeled and chopped
2 small white turnips, chopped
1 bay leaf
a few sprigs of thyme
a few sprigs of parsley
sea salt and freshly ground black pepper

This is a super easy rabbit stew, just ensure you have everything chopped before you begin.

Brush the rabbit pieces with the buttermilk and leave to marinate in the refrigerator overnight.

The following day, wipe the rabbit dry.

Put the rabbit and all the vegetables and herbs into a large stockpot, add some seasoning and cover with water (for a richer stew cover with chicken stock/broth).

Bring to the boil, reduce the heat and then simmer for 1 hour 30 minutes or until the rabbit is tender.

Remove the herbs from the stew. Season as desired with salt and pepper.

Roasted Whole Rabbit with Herbs

Preparation: 5 minutes
Cooking: 25 minutes
Serves 4

1 whole rabbit, skinned and gutted
75 g/2¾ oz (⅓ cup) softened pork lard,
  for brushing
a few sprigs of rosemary and thyme,
  leaves chopped
sea salt

Serve this rabbit as you would any other roast, with vegetables such as cauliflower, carrots, peas and spinach.

Preheat the oven to 180°C/350°F/Gas Mark 4.

Brush every surface of the rabbit with the pork lard. Splay the rabbit onto a roasting pan. Season with sea salt and the herbs.

Roast in the preheated oven for 20–25 minutes or until the rabbit reaches a core temperature of 65°C/150°F on a meat thermometer.

Rest for a few minutes and then carve.

Rabbit Rillette

Preparation: 30 minutes, plus overnight
chilling time
Cooking: 1 hour 30 minutes
Serves 4

1 rabbit, cut into pieces
500 g/1 lb 2 oz pork belly, skin off and diced
4 cloves garlic, peeled
a few sprigs of thyme and rosemary
2 bay leaves
250 ml/8 fl oz (1 cup) cider (hard cider)
4 tablespoons finely chopped chives
sea salt
sourdough bread, to serve

Season the rabbit pieces and pork belly with sea salt. Put them into a large pan with the garlic, thyme, rosemary and bay leaves. Add the cider, then top up with water until covered. Bring to the boil, reduce the heat and simmer for about 1 hour 30 minutes until the rabbit and pork are tender.

Discard the herbs and strain through a sieve, reserving the liquid.

Shred the rabbit and pork, removing any bones, put into the bowl of a food processor and mix with the paddle attachment. Add just enough of the reserved liquid to make a smooth paste. Season liberally with salt and add the chopped chives.

Place the mixture into individual pots or one large terrine mould. Refrigerate overnight before serving.

See opposite –>

Wild Game

Wild Game

Hare

Hare was an important source of food for early Irish settlers. It was probably roasted over an open fire or smoked and dried for later. In Celtic mythology, the hare is associated with the supernatural. The animal's form was supposedly taken by shapeshifters – a belief demonstrated in the legend of the warrior Oisin. Folklore tells that Oisin wounded a hare in the leg, but after following the hare into a mysterious underground hall, he finds a woman on a throne bleeding from the same spot. As well as possessing possible otherworldly powers, the hare was admired for its strength, speed and agility. There is archaeological evidence to suggest that the hare was one of the most hunted animals in Celtic Britain and Ireland. Hare was also both sport and food in the medieval period and there is archaeological evidence of its consumption at many sites, from castles to urban areas. However, much of this consumption was controlled by the elite and any hare that made its way to the urban poor would have been poached. Hare at a meal then would have implied a certain status and many used this food source to showcase their standing.

Mythologically speaking, witches were said to turn into hares at night and drink milk from the cows. This was one reason, among many, that the rural poor shied away from eating hare meat. But beggars cannot be choosers and, despite the myths of people's souls being reincarnated as a hare, they were much hunted and eaten. Irish recipe books of the eighteenth and nineteenth century include recipes for hare. In the collection of recipes from Creagh Castle in County Cork, dating from 1770–1820, there is a recipe for hare with anchovy stuffing. The wild Irish mountain hare is now a protected species in Ireland.

Jugged Hare

Preparation: 15 minutes
Cooking: 2 hours 15 minutes
Serves 6

1 hare, skinned and jointed
50 g/2 oz (⅓ cup) plain (all-purpose) flour, seasoned with salt and pepper
50 g/2 oz (4 tablespoons) butter
1 onion, diced
350 ml/12 fl oz (1½ cups) cider (hard cider)
350 ml/12 fl oz (1½ cups) chicken stock (broth)
1 bouquet garni of parsley, thyme and a bay leaf
1 blade of mace
4 cloves
2 tablespoons chopped parsley

To 'jug' a hare meant stewing it slowly in liquid, such as red wine, in a pot or earthenware jug (pitcher). Traditional recipes for jugged hare often added the hare's blood at the last minute to enrich the sauce. Rabbit can also be 'jugged'.

Roll the pieces of hare in the seasoned flour.

Melt the butter in a large pan over a medium heat and fry the hare pieces, in batches, for about 5 minutes until brown. Remove the meat from the pan and allow to rest.

In the same pan, make a roux by frying the onion in the butter for about 5 minutes over a medium heat until soft and then adding the remaining flour and cooking for about 2 minutes to form a paste.

Return the hare to the pan and cover with the cider, stock (broth), bouquet garni and spices. Simmer for about 2 hours until the hare is tender.

Remove the cloves and bouquet garni and add the chopped parsley.

Hare Soup with Bacon and Cider

Preparation: 30 minutes
Cooking: 2 hours 30 minutes
Serves 6–8

1 hare, skinned and jointed
3 tablespoons rapeseed (canola) oil
50 g/2 oz (4 tablespoons) butter
1 onion, diced
1 clove garlic, very finely chopped
1 bay leaf
a few sprigs of thyme and rosemary
200 g/7 oz (3 cups prepared) mixed
    mushrooms, sliced
100 g/3½ oz smoked bacon, diced
50 g/2 oz (⅓ cup) plain (all-purpose) flour
250 ml/8 fl oz (1 cup) cider (hard cider)
2 litres/70 fl oz (8½ cups) beef stock
    (broth), warmed
sea salt and freshly ground black pepper

Hare soup was a common affair in the British Isles and many recipes abound. Some contain the blood of the hare and redcurrant jelly to finish.

Season the pieces of hare. Heat the oil in a large pan over a medium heat. Fry the hare pieces in batches for about 5 minutes until nicely coloured. Remove from the pan and set aside.

Melt the butter in the pan and add the onion, garlic, bay leaf, rosemary and thyme. Fry over a medium heat for about 5 minutes until the onion is soft. Add the mushrooms and bacon and fry for about 5 minutes until the mushrooms are soft.

Stir in the flour and cook for 2 minutes. Gradually add the cider.

Add the warm beef stock (broth) and return the hare to the pan. Simmer for about 2 hours until the hare meat is coming off the bone. Remove the hare from the pan, taking all the meat off the bones. Return the meat to the soup and discard the bones.

Game Pie

Preparation: 30 minutes
Cooking: 1 hour 30 minutes
Serves 6

about 4 tablespoons rapeseed (canola) oil
1 kg/2¼ lb mixed game meat, such as
    venison, pheasant, rabbit or hare,
    all skinned and boned
leaves from a few sprigs of rosemary,
    sage and thyme, finely chopped
60 g/2¼ oz (4½ tablespoons) butter
2 onions, sliced
1 clove garlic, peeled and crushed
125 g/4½ oz smoked streaky (regular)
    bacon, chopped
150 g/5 oz (2½ cups prepared) chestnut
    (cremini) mushrooms, sliced
60 g/2¼ oz (½ cup) plain (all-purpose) flour
450 ml/15 fl oz (scant 2 cups) chicken
    stock (broth)
250 ml/8 fl oz (1 cup) cider (hard cider)
1 bay leaf
puff pastry, to cover the pie
1 egg yolk, for glazing
sea salt

Cook the game meat in batches. Heat 2 tablespoons of the oil in a large pan over a medium heat. Season the meat with salt and the chopped herbs. Add some of the meat without crowding the pan and fry for about 5 minutes until nicely browned. Remove the meat from the pan and set aside. Repeat with the remaining meat – you may need more oil depending on how many batches you fry.

In the same pan, melt the butter over a medium heat and fry the onions, garlic, bacon and mushrooms and for about 5 minutes until soft. Stir in the flour and cook for 3–4 minutes until no longer raw. Add the stock (broth) and cider and bring to the boil. Add the meat and bay leaf. Reduce the heat and simmer for 40–50 minutes until all the meat is tender. Remove from the heat, adjust the seasoning and allow to cool slightly.

Meanwhile, preheat the oven to 170 °C/340 °F/Gas Mark 3½.

Transfer the filling to a pie dish and cover with the puff pastry. Make a steam hole in the centre and crimp the sides to be sure it's sealed. Beat the egg yolk and glaze the top of the pie. Bake in the preheated oven for about 30 minutes until the pastry is golden brown.

Notes
This pie can also be made with one type of bird such as a pigeon or snipe. Because of the size of the birds, you'll need a few of them.

The livers of the venison, hare and rabbit were also traditionally used in Irish game pies.

Boar and Pork

Boar and Pork

Pigs were the first animals to be transported to Ireland by early Neolithic farmers. These pigs would have roamed in the native woodlands eating nuts and acorns and would have been culled in the late autumn (fall) or early winter. The salting of the pork more than likely arose to preserve the pork for a later date. Wild boar, as a native species, may have existed in Ireland before its introduction, but this is hard to conclusively prove. Wild boar continued to be an important both as foodstuff and game (hunting for sport) well into the Middle Ages. Because of its ferocity when under attack, the wild boar was a potent symbol for the warrior class of people. The pig appears in many early Irish tales, particularly concerning the Fianna, bands of warriors in Irish mythology. Wild pigs in these tales are often ferocious or enchanted. Magical pigs emerge more than once in these wild tales to lure or challenge the warriors and their people. The pigs and their habitat also feature in many folk cures and proverbs, such as 'the priest's pig gets the most porridge' and 'the quiet pig eats the cabbage'.

Domestic pig farming emerged slowly and eventually replaced the pursuit of the wild boar. As food historian Regina Sexton remarks, the keeping and feeding of pigs was 'exclusively women's work, and they fattened them up on a mash of milk and corn […] improving their flesh prior to slaughter'. Even before the arrival of the potato (which increased the pig population as they loved their spuds), the pig was vital to the Irish economy. The 11th of November (the feast of St Martin) was a key date for slaughtering pigs. References to wild boars and pigs occur in other eleventh-century texts such as *The Cattle Raid of Cooley* and *The Annals of Clonmacnoise*. Many texts in the Brehon Laws concern themselves with the pig.

In his twelfth-century book *Topography of Ireland,* Gerald of Wales observed that 'in no part of the world are such vast herds of boars and wild pigs to be found'. While this is no longer the cases in terms of wild boars, the pig is still firmly entrenched in the Irish psyche. In terms of varieties, other than the wild boar, the Greyhound pig (so called because of its shape) is frequently cited. Both the Tamworth and Large White Ulster are a mixed of the Greyhound and other native English varieties. Due to our desire for leaner pigs, the Large White became extinct in the 1960s. Most Irish pigs today are of mixed breed, a fusion of European and Asian varieties, though many smaller artisan farmers are returning to heritage varieties. The difference between heritage pork varieties and their industrial equivalence is incomparable, hence the need to seek out these pigs and support their producers.

Boar's Head with Pistachios

Preparation: 20 minutes, plus overnight
chilling time
Cooking: 30 minutes
Serves 6

1 boar's head (you can use pig's head if
  you can't source boar; ask your butcher
  in advance)
650 g/1 lb 7 oz pork belly, bone in
2 cloves garlic, peeled
a few sprigs of rosemary and thyme
4 tablespoons brandy
200 g/7 oz (1 cup) shelled pistachios
25 g/1 oz (scant ½ cup prepared) flat leaf
  parsley, chopped
grated zest and juice of 2 lemons
sea salt

Food plays an important part in James Joyce's *Ulysses*, an epic of Irish modernism. This dish is mentioned in a passage in the novel, along with other foods, such as veal, widgeon, squab and venison. Published in 1922 but set in 1904, Joyce's book testifies to the rich colonial tradition that existed in Dublin at the turn of the twentieth century.

Line a 900-g/2-lb terrine mould with cling film (plastic wrap).

Put the boar's head and pork belly into a large pan with the garlic, rosemary and thyme. Bring to the boil, then reduce the heat and simmer, skimming occasionally, for about 30 minutes until the meat is soft and coming away from the bone. Remove the head and belly and set aside. Strain the liquid through a sieve and reserve 500 ml/17 fl oz (generous 2 cups) of the stock (broth).

Pick the meat off the head and belly and put into a mixing bowl with the brandy, pistachios, parsley and lemon juice and zest. Mix until thoroughly combined, adding enough of the reserved stock to make a loose mixture. Don't break the mixture up too much as you want it to be nicely textured.

Put the mixture into the lined mould and cover the top with cling film. Place a weight on top such as some cans and allow to chill overnight.

Salted Leg of Wild Boar with Honey and Juniper

Preparation: 15 minutes, plus 5 days chilling
time and overnight drying
Cooking: 4–6 hours
Serves 8–10

2 teaspoons juniper berries, toasted
1 tablespoon thyme leaves
750 g/1 lb 10 oz (2½ cups) salt
1 leg of wild boar, bone in
100 g/3½ oz (scant ⅓ cup) honey
rapeseed (canola) oil

The ingredients in this dish, and the technique of salting, are inspired by Celtic feasts.

Blend the juniper berries, thyme and the salt together in a food processor. Rub the salt mixture into the leg. Drizzle the honey over the leg.

Refrigerate for 5 days. Every day, turn the leg and rub the mixture into the leg.

On day 5, rinse the leg. Return to the refrigerator and allow to dry overnight.

On day 6, preheat the oven to 140°C/275°F/Gas Mark 1.

Score the skin of the leg and rub oil onto the skin. Slow roast in a roasting pan in the preheated oven for 4–6 hours until the meat is tender.

Boar and Pork

Pork Chops with Baked Apples

Preparation: 15 minutes
Cooking: 20 minutes
Serves 4

4 pork chops, on the bone
4 apples, whole
125 g/4½ oz (1 stick plus 1 tablespoon)
    butter, softened
175 ml/6 fl oz (¾ cup) apple sack
2 tablespoons honey
8 sage leaves
4 juniper berries, toasted and crushed
2 tablespoons rapeseed (canola) oil
Herb Vinegar (see page 352, optional)
sea salt

Apple sack is a type of Irish 'sherry' made from apples. If you can't source this, any medium sherry will do. I like to use Oloroso or Amontillado. Sherry has a great history of use in Irish food and drink culture, demonstrating our trade link with the Spanish. Highbank Orchard in County Kilkenny produce a great apple sack.

Preheat the oven to 180°C/350°F/ Gas Mark 4. Season the chops with sea salt and allow to come to room temperature.

To bake the apples, rub the apples with 50 g/2 oz (4 tablespoons) of the butter and season with sea salt. Put into a baking pan and pour in the apple sack and honey. Add four of the sage leaves and the juniper berries. Bake in the preheated oven, basting occasionally, for 20 minutes until soft but still firm.

Meanwhile, heat the oil in a large frying pan (skillet) over a medium heat. When hot, add the pork chops. Brown for 2–3 minutes on one side, then 1–2 minutes on the other side until nicely coloured, then add the remaining butter and sage. Baste for 5 minutes.

Transfer to a roasting pan and cook in the preheated oven for about 10 minutes until they reach a core temperature of 62°C/144°F on a meat thermometer. Rest for 10 minutes in a warm place.

To serve, brush the chops with a little of the sauce from the apples on both sides and season with a little Herb Vinegar (if using). Place the chops and apples on a platter.

Note
Pork goes very well with fruit. Though the Irish cherry season is short, I love to serve pork chops with a cherry sauce, made by simmering 200 g/7 oz (1½ cups) pitted cherries with 1 finely diced shallot, 150 ml/5 fl oz (⅔ cup) red wine, 50 g/2 oz (¼ cup) granulated sugar, 4 tablespoons red wine vinegar and a pinch of sea salt for about 5 minutes, or until syrupy.

See opposite –>

Pork Rib and Potato Stew

Preparation: 25 minutes
Cooking: 1 hour 30 minutes
Serves 4

2 skirts of pork ribs
50 g/2 oz (4 tablespoons) butter, melted
a few sprigs of thyme, rosemary and sage
2 tablespoons rapeseed (canola) oil
2 onions, chopped
1 clove garlic, very finely chopped
1 bay leaf
2 carrots, chopped
5 potatoes, peeled and chopped
250 ml/8 fl oz (1 cup) cider (hard cider)
2 litres/70 fl oz (8½ cups) chicken stock (broth)
sea salt and freshly ground black pepper
2 tablespoons finely chopped parsley

Preheat the oven to 180°C/350°F/ Gas Mark 4.

Brush the pork ribs with the butter and season with salt and pepper. Finely chop the leaves of the rosemary, thyme and sage and sprinkle over the ribs. Put into a roasting pan and roast in the preheated oven for 1 hour. Remove from the oven and cut into individual ribs.

Heat the oil in a large pan over a medium heat, add the onion, garlic and bay leaf and fry for about 5 minutes until translucent. Add the rest of the vegetables, cover and cook for a few minutes. Add the cider, stock (broth) and pork ribs to the stew and simmer for about 20 minutes until the potatoes are tender.

Garnish with the parsley before serving.

Boar and Pork

Boar and Pork

Pork Chops with Black Pudding, Potatoes and Goat's Yogurt

Preparation: 15 minutes
Cooking: 20 minutes, plus resting time
Serves 4

2 tablespoons rapeseed (canola) oil
4 pork chops, on the bone, at room
   temperature and seasoned
40 g/1¼ oz (2½ tablespoons) butter
8 sage leaves, thinly sliced
1 log Black Pudding (see page 245, or use
   shop-bought), sliced into rounds
   and quartered
300 g/11 oz new potatoes, cooked until tender
75 g/2¾ oz (⅓ cup) goat's yogurt
sea salt

There are many great black puddings (blood sausage) in Ireland, each with a unique taste. I like those made with fresh blood, but for some these are too irony in taste. Jack McCarthy, Inch House and Hugh Maguire are some of my favourites. Goat's yogurt cuts through the richness of the pork chop and black pudding. If you can't find goat's yogurt, use sheep or cow's.

Preheat the oven to 180 °C/350 °F/ Gas Mark 4.

Heat the oil in a large frying pan (skillet) over a medium heat and brown the chops for 2–3 minutes on one side, then 1–2 minutes on the other side until nicely coloured.

Transfer the chops to a roasting pan. Place a knob (pat) of butter and some sage on top of each chop. Roast in the preheated oven for 10–12 minutes, until the meat is firm to touch. I like to cook my pork medium and allow it to rest for 5–10 minutes.

Meanwhile, for the accompaniments, add the rest of the butter and sage to a large frying pan over a medium heat and fry the black pudding and cooked new potatoes for about 5 minutes until nice and crispy. Reduce the heat and cook for a further 5 minutes until the butter has caramelized. Remove from the heat and allow to cool slightly.

To serve, place the potatoes and black pudding in the centre of the plate and rest a pork chop on top. Serve with the yogurt.

See opposite –>

Pork Neck with Carrot Purée and Oats

Preparation: 25 minutes, plus overnight
chilling time
Cooking: 2 hours 40 minutes
Serves 4

250 g/9 oz (1¼ cups) granulated sugar
250 g/9 oz (scant 1 cup) salt
1 star anise
2 bay leaves
1 × 2.5-kg/5½-lb pork neck
pork fat or dripping, for roasting
leaves of a few sprigs of thyme, finely chopped

For the carrot purée
6 carrots, peeled
100 g/3½ oz (7 tablespoons) butter
salt

For the oats
100 g/3½ oz (generous 1 cup) rolled oats
2 tablespoons rapeseed (canola) oil
2 tablespoons honey
1 teaspoon salt

Add the sugar and salt to a large stewpot with 5 litres/175 fl oz/ 20 cups of water. Add the star anise and bay leaves and bring to the boil. Allow to cool. Add the pork neck to the brine and refrigerate for 12–24 hours.

Preheat the oven to 180 °C/350 °F/ Gas Mark 4. Remove the pork neck from the brine and dry. Rub with the dripping and thyme and put into a roasting pan. Put into the preheated oven and roast for about 2 hours 30 minutes, basting occasionally, until it reaches a core temperature of 65 °C/150 °F on a meat thermometer.

Meanwhile, make the carrot purée. In a medium pan, bring to a boil just enough salted water to cover

the carrots, then add the carrots and the butter and simmer for about 5 minutes until soft. Strain through a sieve, reserving the cooking liquid. Put the carrots into a food processor and blend to a smooth purée. Use as much of the cooking liquid as required to give a smooth consistency.

To make the oats, mix all the ingredients together in a roasting pan and put onto a low shelf in the preheated oven. Cook for 20 minutes or until the oats are golden, stirring every 3 minutes. Allow to cool.

To serve, carve the neck and serve it with the carrot purée and oats.

Boar and Pork

Pork Fillets with Sage Stuffing

Preparation: 20 minutes
Cooking: 20 minutes
Serves 4

2 pork fillets (tenderloins), trimmed of sinew
50 g/2 oz (¼ cup) pork dripping or lard
25 g/1 oz (1¾ tablespoons) butter, cubed
a few sage leaves
sea salt

For the stuffing
75 g/2¾ oz (5½ tablespoons) butter
1 onion, finely diced
75 g/2¾ oz (1⅔ cups) fresh white breadcrumbs
3 tablespoons finely chopped sage
1 egg, beaten (optional)
sea salt

Preheat the oven to 180°C/350°F/
Gas Mark 4.

To make the stuffing, melt the butter in a pan over a medium heat and add the onion. Cook for about 5 minutes until the onion is translucent. Fold in the breadcrumbs and sage. Transfer to a bowl and add enough egg to bind, if necessary. Season with salt.

Slice open the pork fillets (tenderloins) on one side and fill with the stuffing. Tie the pork fillets with some kitchen string (twine) and season with sea salt.

Heat the dripping in a large frying pan (skillet) over a medium–high heat, add the pork and fry for 2–3 minutes on each side until browned. Add the butter and sage and baste for 5 minutes.

Transfer the pork to a roasting pan and roast in the preheated oven for 7–10 minutes.

Rest for 10 minutes before carving. Garnish with edible flowers and herbs if you wish.

See opposite –>

Pork Fillets with Apricots and Sherry

Preparation: 10 minutes
Cooking: 20 minutes
Serves 4

2 pork fillets (tenderloins), trimmed of sinew
2 tablespoons rapeseed (canola) oil
50 g/2 oz (4 tablespoons) butter
a few sprigs of thyme
250 ml/8 fl oz (1 cup) dry sherry
60 g/2¼ oz (⅓ cup prepared) dried
   apricots, chopped
sea salt
parsley, to garnish

Preheat the oven to 180°C/350°F/
Gas Mark 4. Cut the pork fillets (tenderloins) in two and season.

Heat the oil in a frying pan (skillet) over a medium–high heat, add the pork and fry for 2–3 minutes on each side until browned. Add the butter and thyme and baste for 5 minutes.

Transfer the pork to a roasting pan and roast in the preheated oven for 7–10 minutes.

Meanwhile, discard the brown butter from the frying pan and add the sherry and apricots. Bring to the boil, reduce to a simmer and cook for 5–7 minutes.

Remove the fillets from the oven, transfer to the pan and turn in the sauce to coat.

Rest for 10 minutes before carving. Garnish with some parsley.

Pork Loin with Jerusalem Artichokes

Preparation: 25 minutes
Cooking: 1 hour, plus resting time
Serves 4

1 × 1.5-kg/3¼-lb boneless, rindless loin of pork
2 cloves garlic, very finely chopped
100 g/3½ oz Lardo (see page 372), sliced
2 onions, peeled and quartered
750 g/1 lb 10 oz Jerusalem artichokes
   (sunchokes), scrubbed clean
a few sprigs of thyme, finely chopped
350 ml/12 fl oz (1½ cups) cider (hard cider)
sea salt

Preheat the oven to 180°C/350°F/
Gas Mark 4.

Butterfly the pork loin to make it lay flat. Season both sides with salt. Spread the garlic over the meat, then lay the lardo on top. Tie up the loin with kitchen string (twine), ensuring the lardo is secured inside.

Put the onions and Jerusalem artichokes (sunchokes) in a large roasting pan and lay the pork loin on top. Season with the chopped thyme.

Roast in the preheated oven for about 30 minutes, pour the cider over the pork then roast for a further 30 minutes or until it reaches a core temperature of 65°C/150°F on a meat thermometer.

Rest for 10 minutes before carving.

Boar and Pork

Rolled Pork Belly with Fennel Seeds and Cider

Preparation: 20 minutes, plus marinating time
Cooking: 3 hours, plus resting time
Serves 6

rapeseed (canola) oil
1 × 3-kg/6½-lb pork belly, boned with skin on
2 onions, chopped
2 carrots, chopped
2 celery stalks, chopped
1 head of garlic, broken into cloves
500 ml/17 fl oz (generous 2 cups) cider (hard cider)

For the marinade
4 bay leaves
2 tablespoons fennel seeds
a few sprigs of rosemary and thyme
sea salt and freshly ground black pepper

I often serve this with a fresh fennel salad.

Make the marinade. Put the bay leaves, fennel seeds, rosemary, thyme, salt and pepper into a food processor and blend to a powder.

Rub some oil into the flesh of the pork belly and season with the powder. Marinate for a few hours.

Preheat the oven to 160 °C/325 °F/ Gas Mark 3.

Tie the belly into a cylinder with the aid of some kitchen string (twine).

Put the vegetables and garlic into a roasting pan and place the pork on top. Pour the cider over the vegetables. Roast in the preheated oven for 2–3 hours until the pork is tender. Keep an eye on the level of liquid around the vegetables. If it starts to evaporate too quickly, top up with some chicken stock (broth) or water.

Allow the belly to rest for 15 minutes before carving.

See opposite –>

Pork Belly with Apple and Clams

Preparation: 15 minutes
Cooking: 3 hours 20 minutes, plus resting time
Serves 4

1 × 1-kg/2¼-lb pork belly, skin and bones removed
about 3 tablespoons rapeseed (canola) oil
leaves of a few sprigs of rosemary and thyme, finely chopped
4 baby fennel (or one large fennel, cored and cut into four)
1 apple, cored and cut into six
25 clams
sea salt
crisp green salad, to serve

For the sauce
200 ml/7 fl oz (scant 1 cup) apple juice
100 ml/3½ fl oz (scant ½ cup) double (heavy) cream

Preheat the oven to 160 °C/325 °F/ Gas Mark 3.

Rub the pork belly with some oil and season with sea salt. Put it into a roasting pan and sprinkle the herbs over the belly. Roast in the preheated oven for 2–3 hours. Check the belly in the last hour of cooking. When it is cooked, a knife will pass easily through it. Remove the belly from the oven and allow to cool. Keep the oven on.

Meanwhile, warm 1 tablespoon of the oil in a large frying pan (skillet) over a medium heat and fry the fennel for about 5 minutes until coloured. Remove and set aside. In the same pan, warm another tablespoon of oil and fry the apple wedges for a few minutes until coloured.

Make the sauce. Pour the apple juice and cream into a small pan and bring to the boil. Reduce the heat and simmer for 3 minutes. Season to taste.

Put the apple and fennel into a large casserole dish (Dutch oven). Season with a little salt. Cut the pork belly into 3–4 slices. Place the pork belly on top of the apple and fennel. Pour the sauce over the fennel and apple and put into the oven for 10 minutes.

Remove from the oven and place the clams around the pork belly. Return to the oven, cover and bake for about 10 minutes until all the clams have opened. Discard any that have not opened.

Serve immediately with a crisp green salad.

Boar and Pork

Pork Rib Roast with Mustard Potatoes

Preparation: 25 minutes
Cooking: 1 hour, plus resting time
Serves 4

1 × 1.5-kg/3¼-lb pork loin, bone in, skin on
rapeseed (canola) oil, for rubbing
a few sprigs of thyme, rosemary and sage,
  finely chopped
5 shallots, peeled and halved
1 leek, sliced
2 cloves garlic, crushed
250 ml/8 fl oz (1 cup) chicken stock (broth)
sea salt

For the potatoes
1 kg/2¼ lb (9 medium) potatoes, unpeeled
100 ml/3½ fl oz (scant ½ cup) extra virgin
  rapeseed (canola) oil
2 teaspoons wholegrain mustard

Preheat the oven to 160°C/325°F/ Gas Mark 3.

Score the skin of the pork loin and rub the entire loin with oil. Put into a roasting pan, season with salt and sprinkle the herbs all over. Add the vegetables and garlic to the pan and cover with the chicken stock (broth).

For the potatoes, put all the ingredients into a separate roasting pan and mix thoroughly.

Put both roasting pans into the preheated oven and roast for about 1 hour, basting the pork occasionally, until the potatoes are crispy and the pork reaches a core temperature of 65°C/150°F on a meat thermometer.

Allow the pork to rest for 10 minutes before serving with the potatoes.

Boiled Pig's Trotters

Preparation: 5 minutes
Cooking: 3 hours
Serves 4

4 pig's trotters (feet) from the hind legs
1 onion
1 carrot
1 bay leaf
6 black peppercorns
a few sprigs of thyme
a small bunch of parsley, reserving some
  for garnish
sea salt
cooked potatoes and cabbage, to serve

In Ireland, pig's trotters are called crubeens. Make sure you buy the feet from the hind legs, because there isn't much meat on the front feet. Pig's trotters were once served in many public houses. Butchers will often brine the pig's trotters, which will give them a pink hue when cooked. They were usually eaten with fingers and washed down with beer or stout. Be prepared for sticky fingers if you want this Irish experience!

Put all the ingredients into a large pan and cover with water. Bring to the boil over a medium heat and simmer for 2–3 hours or until the pig's trotters (feet) are tender.

Strain and serve with some potatoes and cabbage and garnish with parsley.

See opposite –>

Stuffed Pig's Trotters

Preparation: 20 minutes
Cooking: 2 hours, plus overnight setting time
Serves 4

2 pig's trotters (feet) from the hind legs
1 ham hock
2 carrots
1 onion
1 lemon, halved
a small bunch of parsley
a few black peppercorns

Put all the ingredients into a large pan and cover with water. Bring to the boil, then simmer for 2–3 hours until the pig's trotters (feet) and ham hock are tender. Strain and discard everything except the pig's trotters and ham hock.

Pick the meat from both and discard any bone or sinew. Reserve the skin of the feet and hock.

Place a large piece of cling film (plastic wrap) on a clean surface. Lay the skin on the cling film and top with the meat. Roll tightly, ensuring the skin covers the meat. Set in the refrigerator for about 4 hours, or overnight if possible.

They can be eaten cold or pan-fried in a little oil. Serve with pickles or greens to cut through the richness.

Boar and Pork

Boar and Pork

Brawn

Preparation: 30 minutes
Cooking: 3 hours 20 minutes, plus overnight
chilling time
Serves 6

1 pickled pig's head (or brined pig's head,
  ask your butcher)
1 pig's trotter (foot)
1 onion
1 bay leaf
6 black peppercorns
a few sprigs of thyme
a few cloves
1 blade of mace
a handful of parsley, finely chopped
freshly ground black pepper

<u>To serve</u>
watercress
Rhubarb Compote (see page 44)

Brawn is a pressed terrine of brined (pickled) pig's head. If you want a pig's head, you'll have to ask your butcher in advance. This recipe can also be made with ham hocks or a mixture of shoulder and hocks. Make sure the head has been brined, as otherwise it will not have as much flavour.

Put all the ingredients except the parsley into a large pan and cover with water. Bring to the boil over a high heat, the reduce the heat and simmer for 2–3 hours or until the pig's head is tender. Strain the stock (broth) into another pan. Reserve the pig's head and discard the other ingredients. Heat the stock over a medium heat and simmer for 15–20 minutes until reduced by half.

Meanwhile, when the head is cool enough to handle, shred the meat and put it into a bowl. Add the chopped parsley and black pepper. Set aside the ears.

Add enough of the stock to the bowl to moisten the mixture.

The stock should be around the same level as the meat and when you press your hand into the mix, stock should come up from the edges. If there isn't enough stock, the brawn will be too dry.

Slice the ears and fold them into the mixture. Place the mixture into a suitable container lined with cling film (plastic wrap), weigh it down with two cans and press overnight.

The following day, unwrap the brawn and slice. Serve with watercress and compote, or pickles.

See opposite –>

Pig's Cheeks with Girolles

Preparation: 15 minutes
Cooking: 3 hours 10 minutes, plus cooling time
Serves 4

4 pig's cheeks, sinew removed
1 onion, chopped
1 carrot, chopped
1 leek, chopped
1 clove garlic
a little thyme
50 g/2 oz (4 tablespoons) butter
2 teaspoons honey
4 tablespoons whiskey
1 tablespoon duck fat
100 g/3½ oz girolles
sea salt

<u>To garnish</u>
hazelnuts, crushed
chopped parsley

Preheat the oven to 160°C/325°F/ Gas Mark 3.

To cook the cheeks, put the 4 cheeks into a casserole dish (Dutch oven). Add the chopped vegetables, garlic and thyme. Season with sea salt. Cover with water and cover with a lid.

Bake in the preheated oven for 2–3 hours, or until the cheeks are tender. Remove from the oven and leave to cool. Remove the cheeks from the stock (broth). Strain the stock and reserve the liquid.

Melt the butter in a frying pan (skillet) and add the cheeks. Fry gently over a medium heat for 2–3 minutes one side until brown.

Add the honey, whiskey and a little reserved pork stock. Baste continually for a further 2–3 minutes until the pork cheeks are nice and caramelized.

Heat the duck fat in a small pan over a medium heat and fry the girolles for 2–3 minutes until soft. Season to taste.

To serve, place the pig cheeks on warm plates and lay some girolles beside each cheek. Spoon a little of the pan juices over the cheeks. Garnish with some crushed hazelnuts and chopped parsley.

Boar and Pork

Ham, Bacon and Sausages

Where would Ireland be without its ham, bacon and sausages? Salted pork is mentioned as far back as the ninth century in *Scéla Mucce Meic Dathó* (*The Story of Mac Dathó's Pig*). In the Brehon Laws, pigs are valued as much as sheep and rent could be paid to a lord with a flitch of bacon. Until the modern bacon industry, most households killed their own pigs, salted the pork to produce their own bacon and used the intestines as casings for their own sausages. As Bríd Mahon observes, though the men were responsible for killing the pig, the women did the smoking and curing. The modern bacon industry began in the nineteenth century with towns such as Limerick and Waterford producing vast quantities of bacon for the domestic and international markets. Though bacon and cabbage is probably not at the forefront of everyone's mind in Ireland nowadays, it still clings symbolically to the outsider's idea of Irish food.

The word 'sausage' derives from the Latin *salus*, which means salted. At the outset it may have referred to any salted meat. The tradition of sausage-making in Europe goes back at least as far as the Greeks and Romans. Many European countries have their own traditions of salted, smoked or dried sausages, all techniques that preserved the meat. Nowadays, thanks to modern refrigeration, flavour is the driving force behind the making of sausages. However, many traditional sausage makers remain in Ireland, producing handmade sausages with only salt as a preserving agent. Hugh McGuire is one such award-winning butcher. When I had the pleasure of making sausages in his company, he demonstrated that all that was required was good-quality pork (he used the belly of a Durac pig), sea salt, herbs and spices. All Irish sausages are spiced in some capacity. This is another nod to our colonial past and our fascination with spices such as mace, nutmeg, allspice and cinnamon.

Limerick Ham

Preparation and cooking: 2 hours 30 minutes
Serves 8

1 × 3-kg/6½-lb uncooked smoked ham
500 ml/18 fl oz (generous 2 cups) cider
   (hard cider)
2 tablespoons juniper berries
1 bay leaf
1 onion, peeled and left whole

For the glaze
150 g/5 oz (⅔ cup) brown sugar
150 ml/5 fl oz (⅔ cup) gin
100 g/3½ oz (¾ cup) English mustard

Limerick ham (*liamhás Luimnigh*) is cured and smoked over juniper wood, then cooked in cider and finally roasted to crisp the fat. The residual sugar in the cider helps to caramelize the fat and lend the ham a unique apple sweetness. Several modern recipes use gin to imbue the ham with a gin flavour. Limerick has long been known as the home of ham and was recently christened 'Pig town' to celebrate its past legacy of producing ham of international repute.

Put the ham in a large pan with the rest of the ingredients and cover with water. Bring to the boil, then reduce the heat and simmer for 1 hour 30 minutes.

Remove from the pan and retain 100 ml/3½ fl oz (scant ½ cup) of the cooking liquid. Once cool enough to handle, remove the skin from the ham and score the fat.

Preheat the oven to 180°C/350°F/Gas Mark 4.

Place the reserved ham liquid in a medium pan with the rest of the glaze ingredients. Bring to the boil, then reduce the heat and simmer for 10 minutes to create a glaze.

Put the ham in a roasting pan and glaze with half the glaze. Transfer to the preheated oven and roast for 45 minutes, brushing with more of the glaze every 10 minutes. Turn the oven up to 220°C/425°F/Gas Mark 7 for the last 5 minutes for a crispy and coloured skin.

Roast Ham on the Bone with Madeira Sauce

Preparation: 15 minutes
Cooking: 3 hours 10 minutes
Serves 12

1 × 4-kg/8¾-lb unsmoked, uncooked ham, knuckle in
150 g/5 oz (scant ½ cup) honey
250 ml/8 fl oz (1 cup) Madeira
a few cloves

Put the ham in a large pan of cold water, bring to the boil, then reduce the heat and simmer for 2 hours. Remove the ham from the liquid and place on a wire rack. Reserve the liquid.

Preheat the oven to 180°C/350°F/ Gas Mark 4. Peel the skin off the ham and score the fat. Put into a roasting pan.

Put the honey, Madeira and 100 ml/ 3½ fl oz (scant ½ cup) of the reserved pork stock (broth) into a small pan, bring to the boil and simmer briefly to dissolve.

Dot the fat on the ham with cloves. Spread the glaze over the ham and bake for 1 hour, glazing it every 10–15 minutes.

Ham Cooked in Stout and Hay

Preparation: 15 minutes
Cooking: 3 hours 45 minutes
Serves 18

a handful of hay
1 × 4-kg/8¾-lb unsmoked, uncooked ham
150 g/5 oz (¾ cup firmly packed) soft brown sugar
1.5 litres/50 fl oz (6¼ cups) stout

Place the hay into the bottom of a large pan. Lay the ham on top of the hay and add the sugar and stout. Top with enough water to cover. Bring to the boil over a high heat and then reduce to a simmer and cook for 3 hours (45 minutes per kg/20 minutes per lb) or until the ham is tender.

Preheat the oven to 200°C/400°F/ Gas Mark 6. Remove the ham from the pan and strain the sauce through a sieve.

Return the sauce to the pan over a medium–low heat and simmer gently for 45 minutes until reduced to a loose glaze.

Put the ham into a roasting pan, glaze with the sauce, and bake in the preheated oven for about 15 minutes until caramelized.

Roasted Ham Hock with Parsley and Hazelnut Sauce

Preparation: 25 minutes
Cooking: 2 hours 15 minutes
Serves 2

1 ham hock (hock end of a half ham)
1 carrot, chopped
1 onion, halved
1 clove garlic
a few sage leaves
4 tablespoons apple syrup (or maple syrup or honey)

For the parsley and hazelnut sauce
100 g/3½ oz (7 cups) parsley
25 g/1 oz (3 tablespoons) hazelnuts, roasted
200 ml/7 fl oz (scant 1 cup) extra virgin rapeseed (canola) oil
apple balsamic vinegar, to taste
sea salt

Put the ham, carrot, onion, garlic and sage into a large pan and cover with water. Bring to the boil and then reduce to a simmer and cook for about 2 hours, or until you can easily pierce the hock with a knife. Remove the ham from the liquid and transfer to a roasting pan.

Preheat the oven to 180°C/350°F/ Gas Mark 4. Brush the ham with the apple syrup.

Roast in the preheated oven for about 15 minutes until the skin caramelizes.

Meanwhile, to make the sauce, blend the parsley with the hazelnuts in a food processor. Gradually add the oil to form an emulsion. Season to taste with the vinegar and salt.

Pour the sauce into a bowl and serve the roasted hock on a separate serving dish.

Boar and Pork

Bacon and Cabbage
with Parsley Sauce

Preparation: 25 minutes
Cooking: 2 hours 15 minutes
Serves 4

1 onion, peeled
a few whole cloves
1 × 1.5-kg/3¼-lb piece of bacon loin
   (shoulder butt or loin of pork), skin on
Parsley Sauce (see page 380), to serve

To crumb the bacon
25 g/1 oz (2 tablespoons) granulated sugar
50 g/2 oz (1 cup) fresh breadcrumbs
thyme leaves

For the cabbage
1 white (green) cabbage, core removed
   and thinly sliced
75 g/2¾ oz (5½ tablespoons) butter
250 ml/8 fl oz (1 cup) reserved bacon
   stock (broth)
freshly ground black pepper
3 tablespoons chopped parsley

This is a very famous Irish dish, and it was also the inspiration for the corned beef and cabbage so popular in the United States on St Patrick's Day, with the salted pork being replaced by salted beef. This isn't eaten together so much in Ireland, but we do eat corned beef, for which there is a recipe on page 370.

Stud the onion with cloves and put into a large pan with the bacon, cover with water and bring to the boil over a high heat. Reduce the heat and simmer gently for 1 hour to 1 hour 30 minutes, topping up with water to cover if needed. Strain through a sieve and reserve 250 ml/8 fl oz (1 cup) of the water. Pat the bacon dry with paper towels and remove the skin. Discard the onion.

Preheat the oven to 200°C/400°F/ Gas Mark 6.

Combine the sugar, breadcrumbs and thyme and pat evenly all over the bacon. Put into a roasting pan and bake in the preheated oven for 30–40 minutes until the top has caramelized.

Meanwhile, put the cabbage into a large pan with the reserved water and the butter. Simmer over a medium heat for 10 minutes until soft. Season with black pepper and add the chopped parsley.

Carve the bacon and serve with the cabbage and Parsley Sauce.

See opposite –>

Split Pea and Ham Hock Soup

Preparation: 30 minutes, plus overnight soaking time
Cooking: 3 hours 40 minutes
Serves 4

For the ham hock
1 ham hock (hock end of a half ham)
1 carrot, chopped
1 onion, diced
3 celery stalks, chopped

For the soup
50 g/2 oz (4 tablespoons) butter
750 g/1 lb 10 oz (3¾ cups) green split peas
   (soaked in cold water overnight)
1 onion, diced
a handful of parsley
a small handful of mint leaves

To garnish
vetch flowers and shoots (or pea flowers
   and shoots)
extra virgin rapeseed (canola) oil

Preheat the oven to 160°C/325°F/ Gas Mark 3.

Put the ham hock into a deep roasting pan. Put the carrot, onion and celery in among the ham and cover with water. Cover the dish with a lid or aluminium foil and bake in the preheated oven for 3 hours or until the meat is falling off the bone.

When the ham hock is cooked, remove it from the pan. Strain the stock (broth) and reserve the liquid. Shred the ham from the bone and reserve.

For the soup, melt the butter in a medium pan over a medium heat, add the onion and fry for about 5 minutes until soft.

Strain the peas of their soaking water and add to the onion. Fry briefly, then add the reserved hock stock. Simmer for about 40 minutes until the peas are soft.

When the split peas for the soup are soft, remove the pan from the heat and add the herbs. Blend with an immersion blender until smooth and strain through a fine sieve if required.

Place some shredded ham hock in the centre of four warmed bowls. Pour the soup around the meat. Garnish with some vetch flowers and shoots. Dress with a little oil.

Boar and Pork

Ham Hock Terrine

Preparation: 30 minutes
Cooking: 2 hours, plus chilling time
Serves 6

2 ham hocks (hock ends of 2 half hams)
1 onion, halved
2 carrots
2 bay leaves
2 sprigs of rosemary and thyme
500 ml/17 fl oz (generous 2 cups) cider
  (hard cider)
chopped herbs, such as chive, chervil,
  parsley, fennel

To serve
Pickled Cucumbers (see page 357)
strong Irish cheddar such as Mount Callan
  Cheddar (County Clare)

Put the ham hocks into a large pan with the halved onion, the carrots (whole), the bay leaves, rosemary and thyme. Add the cider and enough water to cover and bring to the boil over a high heat, then reduce the heat and simmer for about 2 hours, or until you can pass a knife through the hocks with ease.

Remove the ham hocks from the pan and set aside. Strain the cooking liquid through a fine sieve and pour 250 ml/8 fl oz (1 cup) of it into a small pan (the rest could be saved and used as a soup or a stew base.)

Remove the ham from the bones and flake into a large bowl. Mix the meat with the chopped herbs, then add the reserved liquid.

Line a 450 g/1 lb terrine mould with a large piece of cling film (plastic wrap). Add the ham mix to the mould. Alternatively, you can roll the terrine into a cylindrical shape with the aid of some cling film.

Fold the cling film over the terrine and place two cans on top to weigh it down. Refrigerate for at least 2 hours, or until set.

To serve, remove the cling film from the terrine and cut the terrine into slices. Place onto serving plates with the Pickled Cucumbers (drained of their vinegar) and some strong Irish cheddar.

Making Your Own Sausages

Preparation: 45 minutes, plus overnight resting
Serves 8

500 g/1 lb 2 oz pork shoulder (shoulder butt)
500 g/1 lb 2 oz pork belly, cut into
  bite-sized pieces
100 g/3½ oz (2 cups) fresh breadcrumbs
4 cloves garlic, very finely chopped
1 tablespoon finely chopped thyme
1 tablespoon finely chopped sage
1 tablespoon finely chopped rosemary
1 tablespoon black pepper
1 tablespoon cider (hard cider)
1 tablespoon apple cider vinegar
1 tablespoon sea salt
natural hog casings, soaked in cold water

Sausage making at home is not as difficult as it sounds. All you need is a little equipment. While you can buy pork mince (ground pork) from your butcher and flavour it yourself, I prefer to grind my own meat because you can choose your own texture. You can buy tabletop meat grinders or ones that attach to your mixer. The latter may include a stuffing attachment. Natural or synthetic casings can be purchased online or you can ask your local butcher. Make sure there is enough fat on your meat before you grind it because it will help keep your sausages moist while cooking. Finally, keep all your ingredients cold during the process of making the sausages. Feel free to change any of the seasonings: from allspice to nutmeg and cinnamon, sausages in Ireland comes in all tastes and sizes. Breadcrumbs are optional, especially if you want your sausages to be gluten free.

Mince (grind) the pork shoulder and pork belly through a meat grinder.

Put the minced (ground) meat into a large mixing bowl with the rest of the ingredients (except the casings) and combine. Mince everything once more.

Fit the sausage stuffing attachment onto a mixer and thread the casing over it. Alternatively, fit the casing over a wide nozzle (tip) attached

to a piping (pastry) bag. Tie the sausage casing at the end.

Feed the mince down into the attachment or piping bag, holding the sausage casings as they begin to fill with sausage meat. When all the meat has passed through, tie the casing on the other end.

Twist the sausages into individual lengths and rest at least overnight before frying. The dryer the sausages, the better they will fry.

Boar and Pork

Black Pudding

Preparation: 30 minutes, plus overnight soaking time
Cooking: 30 minutes–1 hour, depending on the method
Makes about 1.5 kg/3¼ lb

450 g/1 lb (2¼ cups) pork fat, diced
200 g/7 oz (1¼ cups prepared) onions, finely diced
1 litre/34 fl oz (4¼ cups) pig's blood, strained through a sieve
250 ml/8 fl oz (1 cup) milk
350 g/12 oz (generous 2 cups) pinhead (steel-cut) oats, soaked in water overnight
1 teaspoon ground allspice
freshly grated nutmeg, to taste
1 teaspoon white pepper
1 tablespoon sea salt
natural ox casing, soaked in cold water

Black pudding (blood sausage) is a sausage made from pig's blood with pork fat, spices and oats, hence the name blood sausage used in the United States. There are many different regional recipes. Nowadays, most black pudding is made from dried pig's blood. For me, it doesn't have the same texture or flavour but unfortunately most butchers have made the switch. Inch House in County Mayo still make a wonderful black pudding with fresh blood as do McCarthy's of Kanturk (County Cork) and Hugh Maguire (County Meath). If you don't want to pipe the mixture into ox/sausage casings, you can bake the mixture in a loaf pan. This recipe is adapted from Florence Irwin's *The Cookin' Woman: Irish Country Recipes* (1949). Feel free to change the spices and herbs. You can add anything from cumin and ground coriander to parsley, thyme and marjoram. Barley can be used instead of oats, but cook it before adding to the blood mixture.

Heat the pork fat in a medium pan over a low heat, add the onions and fry for about 5 minutes until the onions are soft.

Put all the ingredients except the casing into a large mixing bowl and mix together.

If piping into the casing, use a funnel to help you pipe the mixture in. Don't forget to tie one end of the casing before filling! Pipe the mixture into the casing until you have a nice round cylinder. Tie the end of the casing when you're done.

Bring a large pan of salted water to the boil, reduce to a simmer, add the black pudding and poach for 25 minutes until firm.

Alternatively, preheat the oven to 160°C/325°F/Gas Mark 3. Add the mixture to two non-reactive 450-g/1-lb loaf pans and cover with aluminium foil. Bake for about 1 hour in the preheated oven until firm.

Cool before slicing. The pudding can be grilled (broiled) or fried to make it crispy.

See image on page 247.

White Pudding

Preparation: 15 minutes, plus overnight soaking time
Cooking: 25 minutes
Serves 4

450 g/1 lb pork belly
250 g/9 oz (1½ cups) pinhead (steel-cut) oats, soaked in water overnight
2 onions
50 g/2 oz (1 cup) fresh breadcrumbs
1 tablespoon sea salt
1 teaspoon ground white pepper
1 teaspoon ground mace
1 teaspoon ground nutmeg
1 teaspoon ground allspice
natural sausage casing, soaked in water

White pudding is similar to black pudding but does not contain any blood. It originated in the Middle Ages and there are many extant recipes from the sixteenth to the eighteenth centuries containing a variety of fillings, from almonds to rice and eggs. Most Irish white pudding contains oats, lard and onions with various spices. Like the black pudding, it can be made either as a sausage or in a loaf form. If using pork belly, make sure there is a good meat-to-fat ratio. I love fried white pudding for breakfast with poached eggs and toast

Mince (grind) the pork belly and then the onion with the fine blade of the mincer (grinder).

Put the meat into a large mixing bowl and mix with the rest of the ingredients (except the casing). Fill the sausage casing with the mixture.

Bring a large pan of salted water to the boil over a high heat, reduce to a simmer and poach the sausage for 25 minutes until firm.

Cool before slicing and grilling (broiling).

See image on page 247.

Drisheen

Preparation: 25 minutes, plus standing time
Cooking: 1 hour
Serves 6–8

1 litre/34 fl oz (4¼ cups) sheep's blood,
    strained
500 ml/17 fl oz (generous 2 cups) double
    (heavy) cream
500 ml/17 fl oz (generous 2 cups) milk
300 ml/10 fl oz (1¼ cups) apple cider vinegar
150 ml/5 fl oz (⅔ cup) water
450 g/1 lb (2¼ cups) rendered mutton fat
    or butter
350 g/12 oz (3½ cups) dry breadcrumbs
2 tablespoons sea salt
thyme or tansy

Drisheen is a blood sausage that hails from Cork and is made with sheep's blood. Less popular nowadays, drisheen was fashionable in the nineteenth and twentieth centuries. Many variations exist across Cork. Several are not for the faint hearted! The sausage can be flavoured with herbs such as tansy. I have added cream along with the milk, and cider vinegar for acidity. Traditionally, the recipe was made with milk but without vinegar. In this recipe, the drisheen is made in a cake pan (as opposed to using the main intestine of a sheep as the sausage casing). Slices of drisheen can be fried in a litter butter and served with eggs and bread.

Grease a 25-cm/10-inch-diameter cake pan and set aside.

Mix all the ingredients in a large mixing bowl and allow to stand at room temperature for 1 hour.

Pour all of the ingredients into a saucepan and simmer for 45 minutes–1 hour.

Purée with an immersion blender. Strain the mixture though a fine sieve and pour into the greased cake pan.

Allow to cool before serving.

The Full Irish

Preparation: 5 minutes
Cooking: 25 minutes
Serves 4

5 tablespoons rapeseed (canola) oil
8 Sausages (see page 244)
75 g/2¾ oz (5½ tablespoons) butter
3 sprigs of thyme
8 rashers (slices) back bacon
4 slices Black Pudding (see page 245)
4 slices White Pudding (see page 245)
8 eggs

The full Irish is a breakfast dish that consists of eggs, sausages, bacon and black pudding (blood sausage). Up in Ulster (Northern Ireland), it is served with a soda farl or potato bread. Some versions contain white pudding (see page 245), which I think is necessary! Grilled (broiled) tomatoes are also sometimes included, which I like in the summer. Perhaps the biggest difficulty when cooking a full Irish for a number of people is the order to cook the items in. I find you need an oven and a separate grill (broiler). Cooking a nice full Irish is as difficult as preparing a beautiful dinner, so great care should be taken with the ingredients.

Preheat the oven to 65°C/150°F/ Gas Mark ¼.

Warm 2 tablespoons of the oil in a large frying pan (skillet) over a medium heat. Fry the sausages, turning them occasionally, for about 10 minutes, until beginning to brown, add a knob (pat) of the butter and the thyme and fry for a further few minutes. Transfer the sausages to the oven to keep warm.

Meanwhile, grill (broil) the bacon for 7–10 minutes until crispy. Cook on one side only. Transfer into the warm oven.

Wipe the frying pan clean and add a tablespoon of the oil. Fry the puddings for 3–4 minutes on one side only until crispy. Transfer to the warm oven.

Divide the remaining oil and butter between two separate clean frying pans over a low heat. Crack four eggs into each pan and fry gently for about 3 minutes. The butter should not colour at all. If you want to cook the yolks a little more, cover the pans for a few minutes. If you only have one frying pan, fry the eggs in batches and place in the warm oven.

Serve on four warmed plates.

See opposite –>

Boar and Pork

Coddle

Preparation: 20 minutes
Cooking: 1 hour
Serves 8

2 tablespoons rapeseed (canola) oil,
 plus extra if needed
500 g/1 lb 2 oz sausages, cut into pieces
 if preferred
500 g/1 lb 2 oz streaky (regular) bacon,
 cut into pieces
500 g/1 lb 2 oz (4⅓ cups prepared)
 onions, sliced
2 tablespoons chopped thyme
2 bay leaves
1 litre/34 fl oz (4¼ cups) chicken
 stock (broth)
1 kg/2¼ lb (9 medium) potatoes, peeled
 and cut into chunks
4 tablespoons chopped parsley
freshly ground black pepper

Coddle, or Dublin coddle to be more precise, is a dish made up of leftover sausages and bacon. Traditionally, the sausages and bacon were cut up and combined with onions and potatoes and left to stew in a light broth. Though often unappetizing to look at, the dish was made famous by several Irish writers, from Jonathan Swift to James Joyce and Seán O'Casey. Modern versions include barley and carrots. It is essentially a dish that grew out of poverty and famine and then migrated into the working-class areas of Dublin at the beginning of the twentieth century to become a dish of central importance to the people who lived there. Often it contained a drop of Guinness (or it was eaten with plenty of pints and soda bread). It is said that the housewives would prepare the coddle during the day and it would sit on the stove until the men returned home from the pub. The word itself is derived from the verb 'to coddle' or 'to cook' (from French *caulder*). With its associations of poverty, it is surprising to find 'authentic' recipes, especially given the status of the dish as being made with whatever leftovers were to hand (as in pig's trotters/feet, pork ribs, etc.). Some associate it with the Catholic Church's insistence of abstaining from meat on a Friday. Coddle was a way of using up the bacon and sausages on a Thursday. In this recipe, I fry the ingredients before covering them with the stock, but traditionally they were just layered and simmered until cooked.

Warm the oil in a large pan over a medium heat. Add the sausages and bacon and fry for about 10 minutes until they have a nice colour. Remove the meat from the pan and set aside.

Add the sliced onions to the pan and a little more oil if necessary. Reduce the heat and fry for about 10 minutes so that the onions caramelize slowly.

When the onions have a nice colour, return the sausages and bacon to the pan and add the thyme and bay leaves. Cover with the chicken stock (broth) and return to the boil. Reduce the heat to a simmer and add the potatoes. Cook for about 30 minutes.

Add the chopped parsley and plenty of black pepper and serve.

See opposite –>

Stout-battered Sausages

Preparation: 20 minutes
Cooking: 5 minutes
Serves 4

8 sausages
rapeseed (canola) oil, for deep-frying

For the batter
300 ml/10 fl oz (1¼ cups) beer or stout
150 g/5 oz (1¼ cups) plain (all-purpose)
 flour, plus a little extra for dusting
¾ teaspoon fast action dried (active dry) yeast
sea salt

Most battered sausages you get in Ireland will be made with plain batter, but it's nice to use some type of alcohol such as beer, stout or cider for additional flavour.

To make the batter, combine all the ingredients in a bowl and allow to stand for about 15 minutes.

Heat the oil in a deep-fat fryer until the temperature reaches 180°C/350°F, or until a cube of bread browns in 30 seconds.

Dust the sausages in flour and then dip into the batter.

Deep-fry the sausages in the hot oil for 3–4 minutes until golden brown and cooked through.

Boar and Pork

Toad in the Hole with Stout and Onion Gravy

Preparation: 10 minutes
Cooking: 45 minutes
Serves 4–6

8 pork sausages, pricked with a fork
a few sprigs of thyme
rapeseed (canola) oil

For the batter
200 g/7 oz self-raising flour (1⅔ cups plain/
   all-purpose flour mixed with 1¾ teaspoons
   baking powder)
4 eggs
400 ml/14 fl oz (1⅔ cups) milk
sea salt and freshly ground black pepper

For the stout and onion gravy
25 g/1 oz (1¾ tablespoons) butter
1 onion, thinly sliced
1 bay leaf
120 ml/4 fl oz (½ cup) stout
25 g/1 oz (3½ tablespoons) plain
   (all-purpose) flour
500 ml/17 fl oz (generous 2 cups) beef
   stock (broth)
sea salt and freshly ground black pepper

Toad in the hole is a dish made by cooking sausages in Yorkshire pudding batter (a batter pudding commonly served with roast meats). It originally came about as a way to make a small amount of meat stretch further. Though it is often associated more with England and Scotland than Ireland, my mother used to make a curious version of it in the 1980s, with sausages and mashed potatoes. Gravy for my mum was always made with OXO or Bisto granules, but I include a quick beef gravy recipe here.

Preheat the oven to 180°C/350°F/ Gas Mark 4.

Put the sausages and thyme into a deep roasting pan or baking dish, toss with a little oil and roast in the oven for about 15 minutes until beginning to brown.

Meanwhile, whisk the batter ingredients together in a medium mixing bowl until smooth.

Remove the pan from the oven and pour the batter around the sausages. Return to the oven for 30 minutes until the batter has a nice colour and is well risen.

Meanwhile, to make the onion gravy, melt the butter in a medium pan over a medium heat and fry the onion for about 10 minutes until caramelized. Add the bay leaf and the stout and bring to the boil. Whisk in the flour and then add the beef stock (broth). Simmer for 10–15 minutes until the gravy thickens. Season to taste with salt and pepper.

See opposite –>

Sausages and Lentils

Preparation: 10 minutes
Cooking: 25 minutes
Serves 4

3 tablespoons rapeseed (canola) oil
1 onion, finely diced
2 cloves garlic, crushed
1 teaspoon fennel seeds
1 teaspoon coriander seeds
freshly grated nutmeg, to taste
a pinch of ground cloves
1 bay leaf
350 g/12 oz (scant 2 cups) green lentils
1 litre/34 fl oz (4¼ cups) chicken stock (broth)
8 sausages (about 450 g/1 lb)
1 tablespoon chopped parsley, to garnish
sea salt

Heat 1 tablespoon of the oil in a large pan over a medium heat. Add the onion, garlic, spices and bay leaf. Cook for about 5 minutes until the onions are soft and trans-lucent. Add the lentils and coat with the onion and spices. Then add the chicken stock (broth) and simmer for 15–20 minutes until the lentils are cooked.

Meanwhile, heat the remaining oil in a large frying pan over a medium heat, add the sausages and fry for 10–15 minutes, depending on their size, until nicely browned.

To serve, ladle the lentils into four warmed bowls and place two sausages on top. Garnish with some fresh parsley.

Boar and Pork

Lamb, Mutton and Goat

Lamb, Mutton and Goat

'Lamb and fattened young wethers were considered a delicacy from early medieval times, and were demanded as food rents by the aristocratic classes. Sometimes, if a young animal died though misadventure, then lamb featured as an unexpected treat on the plates of the small to middling farmer.'

Regina Sexton, *A Little History of Irish Food*, 1998

Two things about lamb dominate the Irish food story. One of the most iconic dishes attributed to Irish food culture is their lamb stew. It is the cause of many debates and controversies. Does one add potatoes or barley? Carrots and onions? Lamb stew is perhaps the only food the Irish fight about. Of course, authenticity is a fluid idea that shifts and changes with time and place. The are many regional variations of lamb stew and in truth it was probably a case of what was to hand. The other issue about lamb is highlighted in a question asked by visiting Americans travelling through Connemara. Why are there so many sheep on the road and none on the menu? We have perhaps let our lambs down in the way we let down our seafood. This could well be tied to historical reasons, because sheep were generally kept for their wool and milk. Only older sheep (mutton) ended up on the dinner table (unless a young lamb went astray).

There are almost as many sheep in Ireland as there are people. Sheep have been farmed in Ireland since the Neolithic period. From about six thousand years ago, farmers kept sheep for their meat, wool and milk. Sheep's wool was popular for clothes, blankets, floor rugs and stuffed into pillows and bedding. Sheepskin could be used to produce parchment for writing. Most rearing of sheep was concentrated on the hill areas due to the unsuitability of this land for anything else. Hence the continued tradition of wonderful Irish mountain lamb, particularly in the west of the country in places such as Connemara and Achill. During the Middle Ages, sheep farming was spread across the country. Like cattle, sheep were important for the Celtic tribes of Ireland and were also used as currency to trade between tribes. Around the same time, in Roman-occupied Winchester, England, a large wool factory was founded. This may have contributed to the value of sheep farming in Ireland, as trade is known to have existed between Ireland and England at the time. By AD 1000, England was one of the biggest lamb producers in Europe. The tradition of only eating mutton continued into the Middle Ages, which is evident in the Brehon Laws. Most sheep during this early part of Irish history were black or dark coloured with shorter, curlier coats. White sheep were valued more, because their wool was easier to shear. There are many varieties of sheep in Ireland, from the Blackface to the Charollais. However, it is claimed that the only native breed still in existence is the Galway sheep. They are a large white-faced sheep, with a characteristic bob of wool on the head and wool on the legs. In his recipe book *Ouverture de cuisine* (1604), the French chef, Lancelot de Casteau, included a recipe for 'A leg of mutton roasted in the Irish style': what the inclusion of this recipe shows is that Irish traditions often made their way to France (even if the French ended up codifying them).

Though sheep's milk has not been as popular in Ireland as cow's milk (or goat's milk), cheese and yogurt made from the milk is beautiful and delicate in flavour. Shepherd's Store and Cáis na Tíre are wonderful examples of Irish sheep's cheese being made in Ireland. Velvet Cloud sheep's yogurt, produced in County Mayo, is probably the finest yogurt I have ever tasted. Mild and delicately acidic, it's beautiful with lamb and summer vegetables, such as courgettes and tomatoes.

Outside the classic pairing of mint, shellfish and seaweed pair well with lamb, especially coastal lamb that feed off the sea plants and breed in the salted air. I love to wrap a leg of lamb in fresh kelp. Clams, mussels, samphire (sea beans) and sea lettuce all work well with lamb. A recent tradition of cured lamb has emerged in the last decade, too. McGeough's in Oughterard, County Galway make a wonderful air-dried lamb.

Lamb, Mutton and Goat

Lamb Croquettes with Onion Jam

Preparation: 45 minutes, plus chilling time
Cooking: 3 hours 25 minutes
Serves 8

1 × 2-kg/4½-lb lamb shoulder, on the bone
2 carrots
2 leeks
2 celery stalks
1 bay leaf
2 cloves garlic
25 g/1 oz parsley
sea salt

For the onion jam
6 onions, sliced
150 ml/5 fl oz (⅔ cup) cider vinegar
75 g/2¾ oz caster (superfine) sugar
2 tablespoons finely chopped thyme
sea salt, to taste

For the croquettes
rapeseed (canola) oil, for deep-frying
150 g/5 oz plain (all-purpose) flour
150 ml/5 fl oz (⅔ cup) buttermilk
150 g/5 oz (1½ cups) dry breadcrumbs

Preheat the oven to 160°C/325°F/Gas Mark 3.

Season the lamb shoulder and put into a deep casserole dish (Dutch oven). Lay the vegetables, bay leaf and garlic around the lamb and cover with water. Cover and bake in the preheated oven for 3 hours.

Meanwhile, to make the onion jam, put all the ingredients (except the salt) into a medium pan and simmer over a low heat for about 45 minutes until a jam consistency. With an immersion blender, blend into a fine purée and push through a fine sieve. Season to taste.

When the lamb is cooked, strain the stock through a sieve into a medium pan. Bring to the boil, then reduce the heat and simmer for about 15 minutes until reduced by half. Discard the vegetables. Pick the lamb meat from the bone. Season with sea salt.

Add the parsley and enough of the reduced liquid to make a sticky mass. Roll into cylinders with the aid of cling film (plastic wrap) and chill for at least 1 hour until firm.

To make the croquettes, preheat the oil in a deep-fat fryer until the temperature of the oil reaches 180°C/350°F or a cube of bread browns in 30 seconds. Unwrap and slice the lamb cylinder into rounds. Put the flour, buttermilk and breadcrumbs into separate bowls.

Dredge the lamb rounds in the flour and then dip in the buttermilk. Finally, gently coat them in the breadcrumbs. Deep-fry in the hot oil, in batches, for 2–3 minutes until golden brown. Allow the oil to return to temperature before frying another batch.

Serve with the onion jam.

Lamb Gigot Chops with New Season Peas

Preparation: 5 minutes
Cooking: 15 minutes
Serves 4

4 lamb gigot chops (lamb leg steaks, bone in)
2 tablespoons rapeseed (canola) oil
50 g/2 oz (3½ tablespoons) butter
1 clove garlic
1 sprig of rosemary
sea salt

For the peas
1 kg/2¼ lb (2 cups shelled) peas, in their pods
50 g/2 oz (3½ tablespoons) butter
a few sprigs of mint

First pod (shell) all the peas. Bring a medium pan of salted water to the boil over a high heat, add the peas and blanch for about 2 minutes. Drain and transfer to a bowl with the butter and mint and season with salt.

To cook the chops, season them with sea salt. Heat the oil in a frying pan (skillet) over a medium heat.

When hot, add the chops and fry for 3–4 minutes on each side until nicely browned. Add the butter, garlic clove and sprig of rosemary. Baste with the foaming butter for 1–2 minutes. Remove from the heat and allow to rest for 5 minutes.

Serve the chops with the peas.

Lamb, Mutton and Goat

Lamb Fillets with Samphire and Cockles

Preparation: 10 minutes
Cooking: 15 minutes, plus resting time
Serves 4

4 × 140-g/5-oz lamb fillets (tenderloins),
   trimmed of sinew
2 tablespoons rapeseed (canola) oil
75 g/2¾ oz (5½ tablespoons) butter
a few sprigs of thyme
100 g/3½ oz (⅔ cup) samphire (sea beans)
sea salt

For the sauce
330 ml/11 fl oz (1¼ cups) cider (hard cider)
1 onion, chopped
1 clove garlic, crushed
a few sprigs of thyme
250 g/9 oz cockles
200 g/7 oz (1¾ sticks) cold butter, cubed
apple cider vinegar, to taste

Lamb, shellfish and sea herbs work really well together. You can also try lamb fillets with mussels or clams and dillisk (dulse), cooked in the same manner as this recipe.

To make the sauce, pour the cider into a large pan and add the onion, garlic and thyme. Bring to the boil over a medium heat. Add the cockles, cover and steam for 90 seconds.

Remove the cockles from the pan. Take the meat from their shells and discard the shells. Discard any that are unopened. Strain the liquid through a sieve into the pan and return to the boil. Whisk in the cold butter to form an emulsion. This can also be done with an immersion blender for a smoother result. Season with a little vinegar and sea salt.

To cook the lamb, season the fillets (tenderloins) with sea salt. Heat the oil in a large frying pan

(skillet) and sear the fillets for about 30 seconds each on all sides. Add the butter and thyme. When the butter begins to foam, baste the lamb for about 3 minutes. Transfer to a wire rack and allow to rest for about 5 minutes.

To serve, bring a small pan of water to the boil over a high heat and blanch the samphire (sea beans) for 15 seconds. Drain and season with sea salt. Warm the sauce, blending again if necessary, and add the cockles. Spoon some cockles and sauce onto each plate. Carve each lamb fillet into two and rest on top of the cockles. Garnish with the samphire.

See opposite –>

Lamb Shin and Blackened Leeks

Preparation: 30 minutes
Cooking: 3 hours 15 minutes
Serves 4

4 lamb shins
2 carrots, roughly chopped
1 onion, roughly chopped
a few sage leaves
1 litre/34 fl oz (4¼ cups) cider (hard cider)
sea salt

For the leeks
4 large leeks
extra virgin rapeseed (canola) oil

Preheat the oven to 160°C/325°F/Gas Mark 3.

Season the lamb shins with sea salt. Put them into a large ovenproof dish with the vegetables and sage leaves. Pour the cider over the shins. Pour in just enough water until the shins are covered. Cover the dish with a lid and bake in the preheated oven for 2–3 hours until the meat is tender.

Meanwhile, cook the leeks. Heat a flat cast-iron grill (griddle) pan over a medium–high heat, and when hot add the leeks and dry-fry for 5–7 minutes, until blackened, turning them to colour evenly. By this stage the inside should be soft. Peel off the outer black layer. Cut the leeks into strips lengthwise.

Remove the lamb from the oven and transfer the shins to a roasting pan, reserving the liquid. Increase the oven temperature to 200°C/400°F/Gas Mark 6.

Roast the lamb shins in the hot oven for about 15 minutes until the flesh starts to caramelize.

Meanwhile, strain the stock (broth) through a sieve. Pour the broth into a medium saucepan over a high heat and simmer for about 15 minutes or until the liquid has been reduced by half.

To serve, warm the leeks in a little water and oil. Glaze the lamb shin with the sauce and place the leeks on top.

　Lamb, Mutton and Goat

Lamb, Mutton and Goat

Lamb Shanks with Red Wine and Rosemary

Preparation: 15 minutes
Cooking: 3 hours 30 minutes
Serves 6

6 lamb shanks
3 tablespoons rapeseed (canola) oil,
    plus extra for brushing
2 tablespoons finely chopped rosemary
2 onions, chopped
2 carrots, chopped
2 leeks, chopped
500 ml/17 fl oz (generous 2 cups) red wine
500 ml/17 fl oz (generous 2 cups) lamb
    stock (broth)
1 bay leaf
sea salt

Preheat the oven to 160°C/325°F/
Gas Mark 3. Brush the lamb shanks
with oil and season them with salt
and rosemary.

Heat the oil in a large flameproof
casserole dish (Dutch oven) over
a medium heat, add the shanks
and fry for 5–10 minutes until
nicely coloured all over. Remove
the shanks from the dish, add the
vegetables and fry for 5–7 minutes
until soft and nicely coloured.

Add the red wine and bring to
the boil over a medium–high heat,
then add the stock (broth) and
the bay leaf. Return the shanks
to the dish and cover with a lid
or aluminium foil.

Transfer to the preheated oven
and bake for 3 hours until the meat
is tender.

Rack of Lamb with Hazelnut Crumb and Mushrooms

Preparation: 15 minutes
Cooking: 20 minutes, plus resting time
Serves 4

4 × 4-bone racks of lamb, French trimmed
2 tablespoons rapeseed (canola) oil
sea salt

For the hazelnut crumb
75 g/2¾ oz (1⅔ cups) fresh breadcrumbs
75 g/2¾ oz (½ cup) hazelnuts, blended to
    a coarse powder
3½ tablespoons rapeseed (canola) oil
1 clove garlic, very finely chopped
1 teaspoon chopped thyme
1 teaspoon chopped rosemary
1 teaspoon chopped parsley

For the mushrooms
1 tablespoon rapeseed (canola) oil
150 g/5 oz mixed mushrooms, wild if possible
25 g/1 oz (1¾ tablespoons) butter
1 teaspoon finely chopped sage

A French-trimmed rack of lamb has a layer of fat removed and the sinew
removed to expose the rib bones. You can ask your butcher to do this for
you or buy it already trimmed.

Preheat the oven to 180°C/350°F/
Gas Mark 4.

Season the racks of lamb with sea
salt. Heat the oil in a large pan over
a high heat and sear two of the
racks for about 1 minute on each
side until browned. Repeat with
the remaining two racks. Put the
four racks into a roasting pan.

Mix all the ingredients for the
hazelnut crumb together in a
medium mixing bowl. Place some
of the crumb mix on the top of
each rack. Roast the lamb in the
preheated oven for 10–12 minutes.
Allow the lamb to rest for about
5 minutes.

Meanwhile, to cook the mushrooms,
heat the oil in a medium pan over
a medium heat. Add the mushrooms.
After a minute, add the butter and
sage, allow to foam and fry, stirring
occasionally to ensure they cook
evenly, for about 5 minutes until
tender. Season with sea salt.

Cut the lamb into cutlets and serve
with the mushrooms.

Leg of Lamb Baked in Hay

Preparation: 15 minutes
Cooking: 2 hours 10 minutes, plus resting time
Serves 8

200 g/7 oz hay
1 × 2-kg/4½-lb of lamb
rapeseed (canola) oil
a handful of thyme, leaves chopped
a few sprigs of fresh heather
sea salt

From the Bronze Age to the Normans, hay has been used in Irish cooking. Early settlers wrapped meats in hay before cooking them in a *fulacht fiadh* cooking pit. The Normans boiled their meat in hay and water. The tannic quality in hay not only added an earthy flavour but helped preserve the meat for longer. You can also use this method to cook a leg of goat.

Preheat the oven to 160°C/325°F/ Gas Mark 3.

Put half the hay in the bottom of a suitable roasting pan. Put the hay into the preheated oven and bake for 10 minutes, then remove.

Rub the leg of lamb with oil and season with salt and the thyme. Put the lamb on top of the hay. Sprinkle the heather over the hay.

Roast in the preheated oven for 1 hour 30 minutes–2 hours, then remove and rest for 10 minutes.

Boiled Leg of Lamb with Barley

Preparation: 15 minutes
Cooking: 2 hours
Serves 8

1 × 2-kg/4½-lb leg of lamb
1 bay leaf
a little parsley, plus extra chopped to garnish
a little thyme
300 g/11 oz (1½ cups) barley
2 carrots, sliced
2 leeks, sliced
2 onions, sliced
2 celery stalks, sliced
3 cloves garlic, whole
sea salt

Put the lamb into a large stewpot and cover with water. Season with salt and add the bay leaf, parsley and thyme. Bring to the boil over a high heat and then reduce to a simmer for 1 hour.

Add the barley and all the vegetables. Cook for a further hour over a low heat.

When the lamb is tender, remove from the pot and slice the meat off the bone. Discard the bay leaf.

Place the sliced meat into bowls and pour over the barley and vegetable broth. Finish with a little chopped parsley.

Leg of Lamb with Seaweed

Preparation: 20 minutes
Cooking: 1 hour 50 minutes, plus resting time
Serves 8

1 × 2-kg/4½-lb leg of lamb
light rapeseed (canola) oil
2 teaspoons milled nori
a small handful of thyme tips
2 onions, roughly chopped
2 leeks, roughly chopped
15 g/½ oz (3 tablespoons) dried kelp
1 litre/34 fl oz (4¼ cups) chicken or vegetable stock (broth)
sea salt

Preheat the oven to 160°C/325°F/ Gas Mark 3.

Rub the lamb leg with oil and season with salt. Sprinkle with the milled nori and thyme tips.

Put the onions, leeks and dried kelp into a large roasting pan. Place the lamb on top and roast in the preheated oven for 1 hour. After an hour, pour the stock (broth) around the lamb.

Cook for a further 30–45 minutes. After 1 hour 30 minutes, the lamb should be rare to medium rare (58°C/135°F) on a meat thermometer.

Remove the lamb from the oven and leave to rest for 15 minutes. Strain the liquid from the roasting pan into a saucepan, bring to the boil, and strain through a fine sieve.

Carve the lamb and serve with the light broth in warm bowls.

Lamb, Mutton and Goat

Boned Leg of Lamb with Mint Sauce

Preparation: 20 minutes
Cooking: 3 hours, plus resting time
Serves 8

1 × 2-kg/4½-lb leg of lamb, boned and rolled
rapeseed (canola) oil, for rubbing
1 teaspoon finely chopped thyme
1 teaspoon finely chopped sage
1 teaspoon finely chopped rosemary
1 onion, halved but unpeeled
1 head of garlic, halved
sea salt

For the mint sauce
1 tablespoon caster (superfine) sugar
2 tablespoons white wine vinegar
sea salt
a large handful of mint, stems removed,

Preheat the oven to 160°C/325°F/ Gas Mark 3.

Rub the lamb with oil and season with sea salt. Sprinkle the herbs all over the top and sides of the lamb. Put the lamb into a roasting pan with the onion and garlic and pour in 500 ml/17 fl oz (generous 2 cups) of water around the lamb. It will keep the lamb moist during cooking.

Place the lamb in the preheated oven and roast for 2–3 hours, depending on the size of the joint (roast), until it reaches a core temperature of 58°C/136°F on a meat thermometer.

Remove from the oven and rest for about 10 minutes before carving.

While the lamb is resting, make the mint sauce. Put the sugar, vinegar and salt into a heatproof bowl and cover with about 100 ml/3½ fl oz (scant ½ cup) of boiling water. Stir until the sugar dissolves, then add the mint leaves. Carve the lamb and serve with the mint sauce and roasted garlic.

See opposite –>

Braised Lamb Shoulder

Preparation: 25 minutes
Cooking: 3 hours 30 minutes
Serves 6

1 lamb shoulder, boned and rolled
50 g/2 oz (3½ tablespoons) butter
2 cloves garlic
a selection of herbs such as sage, rosemary and thyme
500 ml/17 fl oz (generous 2 cups) cider (hard cider)
2 carrots, chopped
2 onions, chopped
2 leeks, chopped
2 litres/70 fl oz (8½ cups) beef stock (broth)
sea salt

Preheat the oven to 160°C/325°F/ Gas Mark 3.

Season the lamb shoulder with sea salt. Melt the butter with the garlic cloves and the herbs in a large sauté pan over a medium heat. When the butter begins to sizzle, add the seasoned lamb shoulder. Roll the shoulder in the butter for about 10 minutes until it is nicely caramelized.

Transfer the lamb to a large oven-proof dish and discard the butter.

Deglaze the pan with the cider and simmer for about 15 minutes until reduced by half. Pour the reduced cider over the lamb.

Place the vegetables in and around the lamb and cover with the beef stock (broth). Cover the dish and bake in the preheated oven for 2–3 hours or until the lamb is tender.

Lamb, Mutton and Goat

Lamb, Mutton and Goat

Lamb Hotpot

Preparation: 30 minutes
Cooking: 1 hour 10 minutes
Serves 6–8

750 g/1 lb 10 oz lb lamb shoulder, diced
50 g/2 oz (¼ cup) beef dripping
3 onions, sliced
2 tablespoons finely chopped thyme
2 tablespoons plain (all-purpose) flour
750 ml/25 fl oz (3 cups) lamb stock
 (broth), warmed
750 g/1 lb 10 oz lb (7 medium) potatoes,
 peeled and thinly sliced
50 g/2 oz (3½ tablespoons) butter, melted
sea salt and freshly ground black pepper

Hotpot is a potato-topped lamb or mutton stew that was originally created in Lancashire, in the north-west of England. Darina Allen's version in her *Irish Traditional Cooking* (1995) includes lamb kidneys and is made with bone-in shoulder chops. In essence, hotpot is similar to Irish stew in that it was a peasant dish of the north of England that migrated to different parts of the British Isles. Different versions include oysters, carrots and turnips, bacon and cheese and a pastry topping.

Preheat the oven to 180°C/350°F/Gas Mark 4.

Season the lamb with black pepper and salt. Heat the beef dripping in a cast iron pot over a medium heat, add the lamb and fry, in batches, for 5–10 until nicely browned. Remove and reserve in a warm place.

Add the onions and half the thyme to the pot and cook for about 5 minutes until soft and translucent. To make a roux, add the flour and cook for 2 minutes to form a loose paste. Gradually pour in the warm lamb stock (broth) and stir until the roux has dissolved.

Return the browned lamb to the pot. Place the potato slices on top in a circular pattern. Brush with the melted butter and season with sea salt, black pepper and the remaining thyme.

Cover and bake in the preheated oven for 45 minutes. Remove the lid during the last 15 minutes to allow the potatoes to brown.

See opposite –>

Lamb Stew with Carrots

Preparation: 15 minutes
Cooking: 1 hour 40 minutes
Serves 4

1.5 kg/3¼ lb bone-in lamb or mutton neck
 or shoulder chops
25 g/1 oz (2 tablespoons) butter
a few sprigs of rosemary and thyme,
 leaves chopped
4 onions, quartered
4 carrots, quartered
1 litre/34 fl oz (4¼ cups) lamb or beef
 stock (broth)
6 potatoes, quartered
sea salt
parsley, chopped, to garnish

In her book, *Irish Traditional Cooking*, Darina Allen includes a recipe for 'Irish Stew Pie'. Her recipe is based on the manuscript cookbook of Annie Kiely of Blackpool in Cork. The pie is topped with pastry.

Season the chops with sea salt.

Melt the butter in a large pan over a medium heat and fry the chops, in batches, for 1–2 minutes on each side until nicely browned. Set the chops aside and season with the chopped herbs.

Add the onions and carrots to the pan and fry for 5–10 minutes until soft. Return the chops to the pan and add the stock (broth).

Cover and simmer for 1 hour. Add the potatoes and simmer for a further 30 minutes until the meat is tender. You can remove the meat from the bones before serving if desired. Check the seasoning and adjust as necessary.

Serve in bowls and garnish with some chopped parsley.

Lamb, Mutton and Goat

Traditional Lamb Stew

Preparation: 10 minutes
Cooking: 2 hours
Serves 4

1–1.5 kg/2¼–3¼ lb lamb neck (shoulder),
    on the bone
4 onions, sliced
a few sprigs of thyme
10–12 potatoes, peeled and halved
sea salt
chopped parsley, to garnish (optional)

Lamb stew, or Irish stew as it has come to be called around the world, is probably one of the best-known dishes that people associate with Ireland. Surprisingly then, many argue over the exact ingredients that go into its making. Carrots appear in several recipes, but for the purists, these are a firm no. Though Myrtle Allen, the grande dame of Irish cooking, included carrots in her recipe in her *Ballymaloe Cookbook* (1977). As Florence Irwin, another great Irish food writer, observes, lamb stew originated in the 'Irish cabin'. If a sheep was killed at the landlord's house, the off-cuts (neck or scrag-end and ribs) would come down to the tenants and would be put into a pot with whatever was to hand, i.e. potatoes, onions and possibly carrots. Many 'national' dishes began their lives this way, before being codified into a recipe book. In one of her recipes for 'Irish stew' from her book *The Cookin' Woman* (1949) Irwin includes a pig's kidney and pork ribs. Lamb was often scarce and mutton (older sheep) was all that people got because sheep were prized for their wool. In her book *The Farm by Lough Gur: the story of Mary Fogarty* (1937), Mary Carbery recounts the story of Sissy (Mary) O'Brien and farming in post-famine Munster (County Limerick). For Sissy, unless a sheep died by accident or became very old, they rarely ate lamb.

Put all the ingredients except the potatoes into a large pan and cover with water. Bring to the boil, then reduce the heat and simmer for 1 hour 30 minutes.

Add the potatoes and cook for a further 30 minutes, or until the meat falls from the bone. Season to taste.

See opposite –>

Sheep's Head Cooked in Ale

Preparation: 45 minutes, plus overnight
soaking time
Cooking: 2 hours
Serves 4

1 sheep's head
2 onions, diced
2 leeks, chopped
2 carrots, diced
1 litre/34 fl oz (4¼ cups) ale
25 g/1 oz (2 cups loosely packed) parsley,
    and a little extra for garnish
sea salt

Seldom, if ever, used today, a recipe for sheep's head is included in *All in the Cooking* (1946). In author Josephine B. Marnell's version, the sheep's head is served with parsley sauce, rolls of bacon and lemon slices. The cheek meat is similar to pork cheeks, if not a little more tender.

Soak the sheep's head in a large bowl filled with salted water overnight. Remove the following morning and rinse under cold running water for 15 minutes.

Put the head into a large stewpot and cover with water. Bring to the boil over a high heat, skim away all the scum, then reduce the heat and simmer for 1 hour.

Put all the vegetables and ale into a separate large stewpot. Transfer the head to the new pot and cover with fresh water.

Add the parsley. Bring to the boil then reduce the heat and simmer for a further 1 hour.

Remove the head from the pot and take the tongue, jowl and cheek meat from the head. Flake the meat (skinning the tongue) and return to the broth. Season to taste with sea salt. Serve with some chopped parsley.

Lamb, Mutton and Goat

My Mum's Shepherd's Pie

Preparation: 25 minutes
Cooking: 1 hour 20 minutes
Serves 4

1 tablespoon rapeseed (canola) oil
1 onion, chopped
4 cloves garlic, very finely chopped
1 kg/2¼ lb (ground) lamb mince
2 teaspoons chopped thyme
2 teaspoons chopped rosemary
2 bay leaves
500 ml/17 fl oz (generous 2 cups) lamb
  stock (broth)
200 g/7 oz (1¼ cups) peas, fresh or frozen
sea salt

For the mashed potato topping
750 g/1 lb 10 oz (7 medium) potatoes, peeled
100 ml/3½ fl oz (scant ½ cup) milk
100 g/3½ oz (7 tablespoons) butter

Shepherd's pie was a regular dish of my youth. Though this recipe is not the exact one my mother made, it evokes her memory. I think she may have added sweetcorn to the dish, or maybe it was peas. The term Shepherd's pie did not appear in print until 1854 and initially it also referred to cottage pie (a similar dish made with minced/ground beef). In early cookbooks, the pie was made with leftover meat.

For the lamb, heat the oil in a large sauté pan over a medium heat and fry the onion and the garlic for about 5 minutes until the onion is soft and translucent. Add the lamb and herbs and fry for about 5 minutes until the meat is nicely coloured. Add the stock (broth), bring to the boil, then reduce the heat and simmer for about 40 minutes until most of the liquid has evaporated.

Meanwhile, preheat the oven to 180°C/350°F/Gas Mark 4.

Make the mashed potato topping. Put the potatoes into a large pan of salted water, bring to the boil and simmer for about 20 minutes until tender. Strain and mash with the milk and butter. Season to taste with salt.

Pour the lamb mixture into an ovenproof dish. Mix in the peas. Pipe or scoop the mashed potato on top of the lamb, covering it completely. Bake in the preheated oven for 25 minutes until the topping is a golden colour.

See opposite –>

Lamb's Tongue and Lentils

Preparation: 20 minutes, plus overnight
soaking time
Cooking: 2 hours 30 minutes
Serves 4

250 g/9 oz (2 cups) salt
4 lamb's tongues
1 bay leaf
a little thyme
1 tablespoon rapeseed (canola) oil
1 onion, diced
1 carrot, diced
1 celery stalk, diced
500 g/1 lb 2 oz (2½ cups) green lentils
sea salt
chopped parsley, to garnish

Lentils, and other pulses, have been part of the Irish diet for centuries. Originally grown as fodder for animals, they became part of the diet of the rural poor. It seems the Normans brought lentils to Ireland, but they could have arrived earlier with the Vikings or early Christian settlers. Indeed, Neolithic pottery displays evidence of some type of legumes so the lentil may have got here earlier. Irish author James Joyce's *Finnegans Wake* (1939) includes a mention of lentils.

Make a 5 per cent brine solution by adding the salt to 5 litres/ 170 fl oz (21 cups) of water. Put the lamb's tongues into a bowl, pour in enough of the brine solution to cover the tongues and soak overnight.

The next day, place the lamb's tongues into a large pan of water with the bay leaf and thyme. Bring to the boil, reduce the heat and simmer for 2 hours or until the tongues are tender.

Strain and reserve the water. Peel the tongues, nestle into a suitable dish and top with a plate and

weights. Press the tongues for 6 hours, or preferably overnight.

Heat the oil in a medium pan over a medium heat and fry the onion for about 5 minutes until soft and translucent. Add the other vegetables and fry for a few minutes to soften, then add the lentils and cover with the reserved tongue stock (broth). Simmer for 15–20 minutes until the lentils are tender. Season as desired.

Carve the lamb's tongues into pieces and serve over the lentils. Garnish with the parsley.

Lamb, Mutton and Goat

Lamb's Liver with Bacon and Watercress

Preparation and cooking: 15 minutes
Serves 4

1 tablespoon rapeseed (canola) oil
100 g/3½ oz streaky (regular) bacon, diced
250 g/9 oz lamb's liver, sliced into strips
plain (all-purpose) flour, for dusting
30 g/1 oz (2 tablespoons) butter
sea salt and freshly ground black pepper
50 g/2 oz (2 cups) watercress, to serve

Heat the oil in a frying pan (skillet) over a medium heat, add the bacon and fry for 2–3 minutes until crispy.

Dredge the liver in the flour and season with salt and pepper.

Heat the butter in a separate frying pan (skillet) over a medium heat until foaming. Add the liver and fry for 2–3 minutes on each side until nice and browned.

Serve the liver with the crispy bacon and some watercress.

Lamb Sweetbreads with Lemon

Preparation: 15 minutes, plus overnight soaking time
Cooking: 5 minutes
Serves 4

450 g/1 lb lamb sweetbreads
plain (all-purpose) flour, for dusting
15 g/½ oz (1 tablespoon) butter
1 tablespoon rapeseed (canola) oil
sea salt
lemon wedges, to serve

Put the sweetbreads into a bowl of cold water and soak overnight in the refrigerator. Strain and clean, removing the gristle and membrane.

Dry the sweetbreads and dust in the flour. Season with some salt. Heat the oil and butter in a frying pan (skillet) over a medium heat and fry the sweetbreads for about 2 minutes on each side until nicely browned.

Dry on some paper towels and serve with lemon wedges.

Mutton Broth

Preparation: 15 minutes, plus soaking time
Cooking: 2 hours 20 minutes
Serves 4

1 × 1-kg/2¼-lb mutton shoulder or leg, on the bone
rapeseed (canola)oil, for rubbing
leaves of a few sprigs of rosemary and thyme, finely chopped
2 leeks, sliced
2 carrots, diced
1 turnip, diced
4 celery stalks, diced
2 bay leaves
3 litres/105 fl oz (12½ cups) lamb or chicken stock (broth)
200 g/7 oz (1 cup) split peas, soaked overnight
250 g/9 oz (1¼ cups) pearl barley
sea salt
chopped parsley, to garnish

Broths were part and parcel of Irish country cooking in the eighteenth and nineteenth centuries. Though often made with bacon or beef, mutton or even sheep's head would be used too. Braised together with vegetables such as leeks, carrots and turnip, they provided sustenance to many farmers and working men.

Preheat the oven to 200°C/400°F/ Gas Mark 6.

Rub the mutton with a little oil and season with the rosemary and thyme and some sea salt. Put the shoulder in a roasting pan and brown in the oven for 20 minutes.

Remove the mutton from the oven and put it in a large pan with all the vegetables and the bay leaves. Cover with the stock (broth). Bring to the boil over a high heat, then reduce the heat and simmer for 1 hour. Skim the excess fat off the surface.

Add the peas and barley and cook over a low heat for a further 1 hour.

To serve, remove the meat from the broth and flake from the bone. Season and place in bowls. Pour the broth over the meat and garnish with the parsley.

See opposite –>

Lamb, Mutton and Goat

Lamb, Mutton and Goat

Dingle Pies

Preparation: 30 minutes, plus chilling time
Cooking: 1 hour 45 minutes
Serves 4

For the pastry

200 g/7 oz (1⅔ cups) plain (all-purpose)
   flour, sifted, plus extra for dusting
100 g/3½ oz (7 tablespoons) cold butter, cubed
2 eggs, beaten, one for brushing
½ teaspoon sea salt

For the filling

50 g/2 oz (3½ tablespoons) butter
1 onion, diced
leaves of a few sprigs of thyme, sage and
   rosemary, finely chopped
500 g/1 lb 2 oz mutton, diced
50 g/2 oz (⅓ cup) plain (all-purpose) flour
450 ml/15 fl oz (scant 2 cups) lamb stock (broth)
sea salt

Dingle or 'Kerry' pies are savoury mutton pies, a specialty of the Dingle Peninsula and the surrounding region in County Kerry, and are probably the most famous pie in Ireland, but many regions have their own pie, from Donegal to Dublin. Dingle pies are a feature of the centuries-old Puck Fair held every August. According to Darina Allen, they were traditionally cooked in a bastible, a type of flat-based iron pot, then reheated in mutton broth. In *The Country Cooking of Ireland* (2009), food writer Colman Andrews wrote, 'They were a popular food in general at public celebrations and on market days in the area and were also taken up into the hills as lunch for local shepherds.' The pastry was originally made with mutton fat. Pies appear many times in recipe collections of the Protestant landed aristocracy (for example, Jane Bury's recipe book from the eighteenth century). Pies may have infiltrated into the Irish diet in this manner.

To make the pastry, combine the flour and salt in a mixing bowl. Rub in the butter and then add one egg. Use a tablespoon or two of ice-cold water to bring the dough together, if required. Wrap in cling film (plastic wrap) and refrigerate for at least 1 hour. When ready, roll out the dough on a lightly floured work surface and cut into 4 rounds with a 10-cm/4-inch-diameter pastry cutter and 4 rounds with a 14-cm/5½-inch circular pastry cutter.

Meanwhile, make the filling. Melt the butter in a large pan and fry the onion with the herbs for about 5 minutes until the onion is soft and translucent. Add the mutton to the pan and brown all over. When nicely coloured, add the flour and cook for 2 minutes to make a paste.

Add the lamb stock (broth), reduce the heat and simmer for 1–1½ hours until the mutton is extremely tender. Remove from the heat and allow to cool.

Preheat the oven to 180°C/350°F/Gas Mark 4.

Place a quarter of the mutton mixture into the middle of the 4 larger pastry rounds. Brush the sides with a little water and cover with the remaining four lids. Make a small circular hole in the centre of each pie. Brush each pie with the remaining egg and crimp the edges with a fork.

Bake in the preheated oven for 30 minutes or until the filling is hot and the pastry tops are a golden brown.

See opposite –>

Lamb, Mutton and Goat

Mutton Curry with Cider

Preparation: 15 minutes, plus overnight
marinating time
Cooking: 30 minutes
Serves 4

1 tablespoon good-quality curry powder
a few sprigs of thyme
75 ml/2½ fl oz (⅓ cup) rapeseed (canola) oil
750 g/1 lb 10 oz mutton chops
sea salt

For the curry sauce
50 g/2 oz (3½ tablespoons) butter
2 onions, sliced
2 cloves garlic, crushed
2 tablespoons good-quality curry powder
1 bay leaf
250 ml/8 fl oz (1 cup) cider (hard cider)
250 ml/8 fl oz (1 cup) double (heavy) cream
2 tablespoons chopped coriander (cilantro)
50 g/2 oz (½ cup) flaked (sliced) almonds,
   lightly toasted
75 g/2¾ oz (⅓ cup) sheep's yogurt

The Irish, as the British, developed a taste for curry due to the many Irishmen who served in the British Army in India in the days of the Raj. Curry recipes abound in most Irish cookbooks of the twentieth century. Almonds, though not grown here, have long been used in Irish cooking.

To prepare the mutton chops, mix the curry powder and thyme with the oil, reserving 1 tablespoon for frying. Rub the mixture over the chops and marinate them overnight in the refrigerator.

To make the sauce, melt the butter in a medium pan over a medium heat. When lightly bubbling, add the onions and garlic. Season with a little sea salt and fry for about 5 minutes until the onions are soft. Add the curry powder and bay leaf. After a minute, add the cider and simmer for about 10 minutes until reduced by half. Add the cream and simmer again for about 10 minutes until reduced by half.

Meanwhile, season the chops with salt. Heat the remaining oil in a large frying pan (skillet) over a medium–high heat and fry the chops for 3–4 minutes on each side to how you like them.

Remove the sauce from the heat and add the coriander (cilantro) and toasted almonds. Stir in the yogurt and serve with the chops.

Mutton and Laverbread with Cockles

Preparation: 15 minutes
Cooking: 3 hours 25 minutes, plus resting time
Serves 4

For the mutton
4 mutton chops, from the shoulder or leg
1 tablespoon rapeseed (canola) oil
50 g/2 oz (3½ tablespoons) butter
1 clove garlic, crushed
a few sprigs of thyme
sea salt and freshly ground black pepper

For the laverbread
600 g/1 lb 5 oz fresh nori
50 g/2 oz (4 tablespoons) butter
30 ml/1 fl oz (2 tablespoons) apple cider vinegar
300 g/11 oz (3½ cups) rolled oats
rapeseed (canola) oil, for frying

For the cockles
1 leek, diced
a few sprigs of thyme
250 ml/8 fl oz (1 cup) white wine
500 g/1 lb 2 oz cockles

Laverbread is more of a cake than a bread and is made by combining cooked nori seaweed with rolled oats. The tradition of laverbread extends from Sligo, in the west of Ireland, to Wales and parts of England.

To make the laverbread, put the seaweed into a large pan over a low heat and cook for a few hours until the mixture resembles a dark pulp. Season with butter, salt and vinegar.

Weigh the seaweed and mix with the same volume of oats. Shape the mixture into patties. Heat some oil in a frying pan (skillet) over a medium heat and fry the mixture on both sides for 3–4 minutes until nicely browned. Keep warm

To cook the cockles, put the leek, thyme and white wine into a large pan and bring to the boil.

Add the cockles, cover and steam for 1–2 minutes until all the cockles open.

To cook the mutton, season the chops with salt and pepper. Heat the oil in a frying pan over a medium–high heat. When hot, add the chops and brown for about 4 minutes on each side until nicely coloured. Add the butter, garlic and thyme and baste for a few minutes over a low heat. Rest for 5 minutes before serving with the cockles and laverbread.

Lamb, Mutton and Goat

Goat

I do wonder why we don't have a history of eating goat meat in Ireland. Though goat's milk plays a central role in the production of some of our best farmhouse cheeses, goat meat is nowhere to be found. That is, until recently. New goat farmers are popping up all over the country, from Galway to Westmeath. Can goat meat save us? Several recent articles suggest goat is the new lamb, and its consumption is more sustainable than any other meat. This is because we all eat goat's cheese. And what do you think happens to all the males? If you eat goat's cheese, you should, according to food writer Felicity Cloake writing in the British newspaper the *Guardian*, eat goat's meat. It's an ethical responsibility. But this returns me to my initial thought: why didn't we farm goat for meat in Ireland? Of course, there is the possibility that we did. Sheep and goat bones are difficult to distinguish between, so early archaeology of Ireland acknowledges we may have eaten goats (as well as drunk their milk). Goats were the first domesticated meat and I can't imagine Neolithic farmers only milking their goats. Is it about religion? European Christian folklore associates goats with Satan. Indeed, during the Middle Ages, it was believed that goats whispered unseemly things into the ears of saints. The brats! It was Arab merchants who brought goat to Spain along with spices, citrus fruits and nuts. Did Catholicism corner the lamb market in the same way Arab Muslims celebrated the cooking of goat meat? Does this explain it? Whatever the history, superstitions and cultural habits, we have a chance now to turn things around and embrace goat's meat. Anything you do with lamb, you can do with goat: stew, fry, braise, roast and curry. I like it with seaweed!

Goat Loin with Sage and Bay Leaves

Preparation and cooking: 15 minutes
Serves 4

1 × 400–500-g/14-oz–1-lb 2-oz medium goat loin, trimmed
2 tablespoons rapeseed (canola) oil
30 g/1 oz (2 tablespoons) butter
5 sage leaves
2 bay leaves
sea salt

If you prefer your meat cooked longer than medium-rare, preheat the oven to 180°C/350°F/ Gas Mark 4.

Season the goat loin with salt. Heat the oil in a frying pan (skillet) over a medium heat and sear the loin briefly on both sides. Add the butter and allow to foam. Add the herbs and baste the loin for 3–4 minutes until cooked to your liking. Transfer to the preheated oven for 5–10 minutes if you want to cook it beyond medium-rare.

Allow the loin to rest for 5 minutes before carving.

Note
I like to serve some wakame seaweed with this dish. If using dried wakame, soak it in cold water for an hour before serving. Roughly chop and season with oil, salt and vinegar.

Beef

Beef

'We return'd before the
heate of the day to our
greate cabbin, where we
had dinner, no less than
a whole beef, boyl'd and
roasted.'

John Dunton, *Teague Land: or A Merry Ramble
to the Wild Irish*, 1698

From the first auroch in Kerry to the establishment of Ireland as a breeding
ground for beef for the British Empire, the island of Ireland has had a long-
standing relationship with the cow. Ireland is home to many indigenous
breeds of cattle, such as the Dexter, Moiled and Kerry Blue. Cows more than
likely were transported to Ireland by boat around 5,000 BC. Though there
are several earlier remains in Kerry, the wholesale introduction of cattle
does not seem to have occurred until the early Neolithic period, when
farming was beginning to establish itself among the many communities
that occupied Ireland, and the people began to turn away from the sea as
a source of food. Cattle grew in such esteem, that by the introduction of
the Celtic people, it was almost a totem in society. By the eighth century,
cattle functioned as currency and was a signifier of wealth. Because of
this, cattle raids take place in much early Irish literature, such as *The
Cattle Raid of Cooley* (written around the twelfth century, but probably
from an older oral tradition) and in *The Annals of Ulster* (431–1540).
Due to the high status of the cow, dairy consumption took precedence
over the eating of beef. The size of one's herd was an indication of power;
therefore, numbers mattered. Yet, beef was eaten, but more than likely
only the wealthy got to enjoy the delights that we now take for granted.
It certainly played a part in feasts. Many recipes for cows (and their heads!)
can be found in surviving manuscripts.

From the 1600s, Ireland was effectively a grazing pasture for rearing cattle
for England. Live cattle were continually exported abroad. This pattern
continued in the nineteenth century, with landlords evicting people to
use the land for cattle. The Shorthorn (a dual-purpose cow, used both
for milk and beef) was the dominant breed. Despite the famine, large
amounts of meat went into the production of salted beef (corned beef)
in Cork and was then exported. Sadly, Ireland was used to feed the world
while its indigenous people starved. It is somewhat ironic, therefore, that
we seem so tied to beef production in the present day. Beef today is still
our biggest export.

In an age of homogeneity, we would do well to look to heritage breeds of
cattle, to dual-purpose cows and to eating less beef. Since our diet turned
inwards in the Neolithic period, away from the sea and towards the land –
as I have intimated elsewhere in the book – we have forgotten much,
creating a veritable monoculture based around beef. Better balance is
needed to re-evaluate our relationship to the sacred and commodious
cow. I love Irish beef, but only in moderation. There are many more
products that make up Irish food culture. All beef is aged when you
purchase it. The common duration is twenty-one days. Yet, some beef is
now aged for a much shorter period. I prefer between twenty-eight and
thirty-five days. We had a butcher age beef for sixty-five days before
use and I loved the results. My friend Matt Orlando has aged beef in his
restaurant AMASS for a whole year! There is still plenty more to discover
about maturing beef in Ireland.

Whipped Bone Marrow on Rye Sourdough

Preparation: 10 minutes, plus chilling time
Cooking: 20 minutes
Serves 4

2 canoe-cut marrow bones
1 tablespoon chopped tarragon
tarragon vinegar (see Herb or Fruit Vinegar, page 352), to taste (optional)
sea salt
a few slices of rye sourdough bread, to serve

Preheat the oven to 180°C/350°F/ Gas Mark 4.

Put the bones into a roasting pan and roast in the preheated oven for 20 minutes.

When the bones have cooled enough to handle, scoop the marrow out into a bowl. Refrigerate the marrow to cool.

When the marrow has cooled, whip it until it is fluffy, using a whisk or immersion blender. It will look like whipped butter. Fold in the tarragon and season with salt and vinegar (if using).

Toast the sourdough bread and spread the bone marrow butter over the toast.

Beef and Whiskey Tea

Preparation: 10 minutes
Cooking: 3 hours
Serves 8

450 g/1 lb beef shoulder, diced
3½ tablespoons whiskey
sea salt, to taste

Though beef 'tea' was often seen as a drink for the sick, it was also a way of extending the meat to feed the most amount possible. If you omit the whiskey, beef tea could also be made with the addition of herbs or onions. The beef can be used for another dish, such as a pie or to make croquettes.

Season the meat with salt. Put the meat into a large pan with 2 litres/70 fl oz (8½ cups) of water and simmer for about 2–3 hours.

Strain and add the whiskey. Keep warm, or cool and refrigerate until needed.

Beef Cooked Over a Turf Fire

Preparation: 10 minutes
Cooking: 45 minutes, plus resting time
Serves 6

1 × 1.5-kg/3¼-lb beef striploin (sirloin)
75 g/2¾ oz (5½ tablespoons) beef dripping
leaves of a few sprigs of thyme, rosemary and sage, finely chopped
sea salt

Cooking beef over the turf fire was quite common before the advent of electric and gas cookers (ovens). The technique is similar to cooking over charcoal or an open fire, but the turf lends a smoky character to the beef. As food writer Monica Sheridan writes, 'The smoke goes up the chimney and the steak is just as nice as if one had the most elaborate barbecue.'

Brush the striploin with the beef dripping, cover with the herbs and season with salt.

Put onto a wire rack over a turf fire and cook for about 45 minutes until it reaches a core temperature of 55°C/130°F on a meat thermometer. Turn the beef continually to ensure an even cooking and keep

brushing it with the fat. Ensure the fire is not too hot as this will scorch the outside of the beef.

Remove from the fire and allow to rest in a warm place for 15 minutes before carving.

Steak and Kidney Pie

Preparation: 40 minutes, plus chilling time
Cooking: 55 minutes
Serves 6–8

<u>For the pastry</u>
500 g/1 lb 2 oz (4 cups) plain (all-purpose)
   flour, sifted, plus extra for dusting
1 teaspoon sea salt
250 g/9 oz (2¼ sticks) cold butter, cubed
2 egg yolks, whisked

<u>For the filling</u>
3 tablespoons rapeseed (canola) oil
1 onion, diced
200 g/7 oz mushrooms (I prefer to use
   a mixture of wild and cultivated)
400 g/14 oz beef kidneys, cut into
   smaller pieces
2 tablespoons finely chopped thyme
1 kg/2¼ lb beef rump (sirloin), diced
75 g/2¾ oz (⅔ cup) plain (all-purpose) flour
75 g/2¾ oz (5½ tablespoons) butter
550 ml/18 fl oz (2½ cups) beef stock (broth)
sea salt

<u>To glaze the pastry</u>
1 egg yolk, beaten with a pinch of salt and sugar

The Irish love of pies emerges out of our continual interaction with British food culture, which itself drew widely from other European influences. Steak and kidney pie was popular in the nineteenth century to the early part of twentieth century. It can still be found in a few Dublin restaurants.

To make the pastry, put the flour, salt and butter into a bowl and rub together until the mixture resembles breadcrumbs. Add the egg yolks and just enough ice-cold water to bring the dough together. Wrap the dough in cling film (plastic wrap) and refrigerate for 1 hour, or longer.

For the filling, heat 1 tablespoon of the oil in a medium pan over a medium heat and fry the onion for about 5 minutes until soft. Remove from the pan and set aside. Heat another tablespoon of the oil and fry the mushrooms for about 5 minutes until tender, then remove from the pan. Heat the third tablespoon of oil in the pan, season the kidney pieces with sea salt and thyme, cook briefly in the pan and then strain through a sieve to remove the additional fat.

Toss the beef in the flour. Melt the butter in a large pan over a medium heat and fry the beef for about 5 minutes until browned all over.

Remove from the pan and add the remaining flour. Cook for about 2 minutes to form a paste. Gradually add the beef stock (broth) and then bring to the boil. Blend to remove any lumps and cool. Return the beef to the sauce along with the mushrooms, onion, and kidney and set aside to cool for 30 minutes.

Meanwhile, preheat the oven to 180°C/350°F/Gas Mark 4 and grease a pie dish or pan.

On a floured surface, roll out two pastry circles, one slightly larger. Use this larger one to line the base and sides of the greased dish. Spoon the beef mixture into the dish. Wet the edges of the pastry and place the smaller circle on top for the lid, pinching the edges to seal. Brush with the egg yolk.

Bake in the preheated oven for 30 minutes or until the pastry is golden brown.

See opposite –>

Beef Shin and Barley Broth

Preparation: 10 minutes
Cooking: 4 hours 20 minutes
Serves 6

1 × 2.5-kg/5½-lb beef shin (I use Dexter beef)
rapeseed (canola) oil
100 g/3½ oz (7 tablespoons) butter
a few sprigs each of rosemary and thyme
500 ml/17 fl oz (generous 2 cups) cider
   (hard cider)
20 g/¾ oz dried kelp flakes
4 leeks, cut into chunks
4 carrots, cut into chunks
4 white turnips, quartered
1 head of garlic, whole
3 litres/105 fl oz (12½ cups) veal stock (broth)
200 g/7 oz (1 cup) barley
sea salt

This is a version of a classic Irish broth with beef and barley. For a little twist, I add some kelp to give it an additional umami flavour.

Rub the shin with oil and season with salt. Heat a large frying pan (skillet) over a medium heat and brown the shin all over. Add the butter, rosemary and thyme. Baste the shin continually until golden brown, about 5 minutes. Transfer to a flame-proof casserole dish (Dutch oven).

Discard the fat from the pan and deglaze with the cider. Add the kelp flakes and simmer for 45 minutes. Do not boil.

Preheat the oven to 160°C/325°F/Gas Mark 3.

Pour the cider over the beef and arrange the vegetables, garlic and kelp around it. Pour over the stock (broth) and cover with a lid.

Place in the preheated oven and cook for 2 hours 30 minutes. Add the barley and cook for a further hour or until the shin meat is falling off the bone.

Beef

Beef

Beef with Wild Leeks and Walnuts

Preparation: 20 minutes, plus chilling time
Cooking: 15 minutes, plus cooling time
Serves 4

500 g/1 lb 2 oz beef fillet (tenderloin),
   trimmed of all fat and sinew
1 teaspoon honey
100 ml/3½ fl oz (scant ½ cup) apple
   cider vinegar
1 sprig of thyme
50 g/2 oz (½ cup) walnuts, roughly chopped
100 ml/3½ fl oz (scant ½ cup) extra virgin
   rapeseed (canola) oil
8 wild leeks (or you can use spring onions/
   scallions instead)
1 apple
celery cress, to garnish
sea salt

Wrap the beef fillet (tenderloin) in cling film (plastic wrap) and freeze for 2 hours. This will help you to cut the slices as thin as possible.

To make a dressing, pour the honey and the vinegar into a small pan and bring to the boil over a low heat. Add the thyme and the walnuts and simmer for about 10 minutes until reduced by half. Remove from the heat and allow to cool. Discard the sprig of thyme.

Whisk the vinegar and walnut mixture with 75 ml/2½ fl oz (⅓ cup) of the oil to form a dressing. Season to taste.

Heat a griddle (grill) pan until extremely hot. Char the leeks on both sides. Remove from the pan and season with a little oil and salt. Cut each leek into two.

Remove the beef from the freezer and slice as thinly as possible. Slice the apple thinly on a mandoline and cut into matchsticks. Arrange four to six slices of beef on each plate. Lay two leeks over the beef. Dress the plate with the walnut dressing. Garnish with the apple matchsticks, some celery cress and a little sea salt.

Steak with Mushrooms and Cider

Preparation: 10 minutes
Cooking: 25 minutes, plus resting time
Serves 2

2 × 280-g/10-oz steaks
2 tablespoons rapeseed (canola) oil
35 g/1¼ oz (2½ tablespoons) butter
150 g/5 oz wild mushrooms
dried ceps (porcini), blended into a fine
   powder, to serve (optional)

For the sauce
100 ml/3½ fl oz (scant ½ cup) cider
   (hard cider)
100 ml/3½ fl oz (scant ½ cup) apple juice
100 ml/3½ fl oz (scant ½ cup) double
   (heavy) cream
50 g/2 oz (4 tablespoons) butter
1 tablespoon apple balsamic vinegar

Allow the meat to come to room temperature. If you prefer your steaks well done and they are large, preheat the oven to 160°C/325°F/ Gas Mark 3.

To make the sauce, pour the cider and apple juice into a small pan over a medium heat and simmer for about 10 minutes until reduced by half. Add the cream and bring to the boil. Reduce a little, then whisk in the butter. Season with some salt and the apple balsamic vinegar.

Season the steaks with salt and heat 1 tablespoon of the oil in a frying pan (skillet) over a medium–high heat. When the oil is hot, add the steaks. Brown on all sides, then reduce the heat to medium–low, add the butter and baste the steaks for 3–8 minutes, depending on the thickness of the steaks and how well done you prefer them. Keep covering the steaks in the butter to give it a nice caramel flavour and

keep it moist. Ensure that the heat is not too high as this will cause the outside to become tough before the inside is warm. If the steaks are large, you may want to put them into the preheated oven for a few minutes to ensure a proper cooking temperature. Remove the steaks from the pan and allow to rest for 5 minutes in a warm place.

Put the pan back over a medium heat, heat the rest of the oil in the pan, then add the mushrooms and some salt and fry for about 5 minutes until the mushrooms are tender.

To plate, slice each steak into three pieces and place on the plates. Rest some mushrooms beside the meat. Blend the sauce with an immersion blender. Spoon over some sauce. Sprinkle the dried cep powder over the steaks, if using.

Beef

T-bone Steak with Bone Marrow Butter and Bone Broth

Preparation: 30 minutes
Cooking: 5 hours 30 minutes, plus overnight chilling time
Serves 4

2 × 400-g/14-oz T-bone steaks
rapeseed (canola) oil
50 g/2 oz (4 tablespoons) butter
a few sprigs of rosemary
sea salt

For the bone marrow butter
2 kg/4½ lb beef leg bones, cut into 4-cm/ 1½-inch pieces
450 g/1 lb (4 sticks) butter, room temperature
sea salt

For the bone broth
4 chicken's feet or 8 chicken wings
1 tablespoon rapeseed (canola) oil
2 kg/4½ lb beef bones
1 onion, chopped
2 carrots, chopped
2 celery stalks
3½ tablespoons apple cider vinegar
a pinch of dried woodruff (optional)
1 bunch of mixed herbs (parsley, fennel, dill, chervil)
2 cloves garlic
sea salt

Bone broths are a great way of rejuvenating the body. In this recipe, the leg bone is roasted, the marrow removed and the bones used for the broth. Sirloin (strip steak), fillet (tenderloin) or rib-eye steak will also work well.

Preheat the oven to 220°C/425°F/ Gas Mark 7.

To make the bone marrow butter, put the bones into a roasting pan and bake in the preheated oven for 45 minutes. Remove from the heat and scoop out the marrow as soon as they are cool enough to handle.

Put the marrow and the butter into a mixer and blend together until smooth. Season to taste. Roll the butter into cylinders with cling film (plastic wrap). Refrigerate.

To make the bone broth, roast the chicken feet/wings with the oil in a roasting pan in the preheated oven for 25 minutes until crispy. Roast the bones in a separate pan.

Put the feet/wings and bones in a large stewpot over a high heat with the vegetables, the vinegar and the woodruff, if using. Add enough water to cover and bring to the boil. Reduce the heat and simmer

for 3–4 hours, skimming the top regularly. In the last 30 minutes, add the herbs and garlic. Remove from the heat, strain and season. Allow the broth to cool (ideally overnight), then skim off any fat on the top. Check the seasoning.

To cook the steaks, preheat the oven to 100°C/210°F/Gas Mark ¼. Season both sides of the steaks with oil and sea salt, and let come to room temperature.

Heat the oil in a pan over a medium heat and add the steaks. Cook for 4 minutes on each side. When you turn the steaks the first time, add the rosemary to the pan. When the steak is nicely caramelized, add the butter and allow to foam. Baste the steak for 3–5 minutes. Rest in the preheated oven for 10 minutes.

To serve, slice the steak, place a piece of bone marrow butter on top of the steaks and serve the broth on the side to dip into.

Calf's Liver with Whiskey Sauce

Preparation: 5 minutes
Cooking: 20 minutes
Serves 4

450 g/1 lb calf's liver, sliced
plain (all-purpose) flour, for dusting, seasoned
1 tablespoon rapeseed (canola) oil
50 g/2 oz (4 tablespoons) butter
a little thyme

For the whiskey sauce
75 ml/2½ fl oz (⅓ cup) whiskey
1 shallot, diced
a few sprigs of thyme
500 ml/17 fl oz (generous 2 cups) beef stock (broth)
75 ml/2½ fl oz (⅓ cup) double (heavy) cream
sea salt

To make the sauce, pour the whiskey into a medium pan over a medium heat and add the shallot and thyme. Bring to the boil and then ignite. When the flame has died off, add the beef stock (broth). Simmer for 10–15 minutes until the stock is reduced by half and then strain into another pan. Add the cream and bring to the boil. Season to taste.

Meanwhile, fry the liver. Dredge the liver slices in the seasoned flour. Heat the oil in a frying pan (skillet) over a medium heat. When hot, add the liver and fry for 1–2 minutes on each side, then add the butter and thyme. Baste for 2 minutes.

Serve the liver with the sauce.

Beef Ribs in Stout

Preparation: 15 minutes
Cooking: 4 hours 30 minutes
Serves 6

1 rack of beef back ribs, cut into
    individual pieces
rapeseed (canola) oil
2 onions, chopped
2 leeks, chopped
2 carrots, chopped
1 head of garlic, halved
a few sage leaves
a few sprigs of thyme and rosemary
1 bay leaf
1 litre/34 fl oz (4¼ cups) stout
1 litre/34 fl oz (4¼ cups) beef stock (broth)
sea salt

Preheat the oven to 200°C/400°F/
Gas Mark 6.

Rub the ribs with oil and season
with sea salt. Roast in the preheated oven in a roasting pan
for 30 minutes until brown.
Reduce the oven temperature
to 160°C/325°F/Gas Mark 3.

Place the vegetables and herbs in
an ovenproof dish large enough to
accommodate the ribs. Lay the ribs
on top of the vegetables and pour
over the stout and stock (broth).

Cover and braise in the preheated
oven for 3–4 hours or until the ribs
are tender.

See opposite –>

Beef and Stout Stew

Preparation: 20 minutes, plus overnight
marinating time
Cooking: 3 hours 15 minutes
Serves 8

1 kg/2¼ lb braising beef (chuck shoulder
    steak), cut into cubes
750 ml/25 fl oz (3 cups) stout
1 bay leaf
leaves of a few sprigs of thyme, chopped
2 tablespoons rapeseed (canola) oil
2 onions, chopped
2 leeks, roughly chopped
4 carrots, roughly chopped
4 cloves garlic, very finely chopped
750 ml/25 fl oz (3 cups) veal or beef
    stock (broth)
sea salt

This was traditionally made with Guinness, but there are now many
alternative stouts being produced around the country (and the world!).
I like to use Galway Hooker stout (named after the traditional sailing
boat). It is brewed in Oranmore, County Galway. You can also make
this stew with oxtail.

Marinate the beef in the stout, bay
leaf and thyme overnight in the
refrigerator.

The following day, strain and
reserve the liquid.

Heat the oil in a large pan over
a medium heat. Add the onions,
leeks, carrots and garlic and fry
for about 10 minutes until nicely
browned. Add the beef and sear,
in batches if necessary, for about
5 minutes until browned all over.

Add the reserved stout and the
stock (broth), increase the heat
to high to bring to a boil and then
reduce the heat and simmer for
3 hours or until the meat is tender.
Season to taste before serving.

Note
Suet dumplings are a nice addition
to beef stew. Combine 300 g/11 oz
flour with 150 g/5 oz suet with
some chopped herbs and salt. Add
enough water to form a dough.
Shape into dumplings. Simmer for
15 minutes, then add to the stew
at the end.

Beef

Rib Roast, Duck Fat Potatoes and Beer-pickled Onions

Preparation: 15 minutes
Cooking: 1 hour 15 minutes, plus resting time
Serves 4

1 × 4-bone rib roast
2 tablespoons rapeseed (canola) oil
750 g/1 lb 10 oz (7–8 medium) potatoes, peeled
100 g/3½ oz (½ cup) duck fat
100 g/3½ oz (7 tablespoons) butter
a small handful of rosemary and thyme
sea salt

For the onions
200 ml/7 fl oz (scant 1 cup) beer (I use Galway Hooker)
200 ml/7 fl oz (scant 1 cup) malt vinegar
50 g/2 oz (¼ cup) caster (superfine) sugar
1½ teaspoons salt
1 teaspoon juniper berries
1 bay leaf
350 g/12 oz pearl onions, peeled

Preheat the oven to 160°C/325°F/Gas Mark 3.

For the onions, pour the beer and vinegar into a medium pan over a high heat and bring to the boil. Add the sugar, salt, juniper berries and bay leaf. When the sugar has dissolved, add the onions and simmer for 4 minutes. Remove from the heat and set aside.

Season the beef with sea salt. Heat the oil in a large frying pan (skillet) over a medium heat. Add the beef and sear for about 5 minutes until browned all over and transfer to a roasting pan. Place the potatoes in beside the beef and dress with the duck fat. Lay the herbs around the beef.

Roast the meat in the preheated oven for about 1 hour. Remove the ribs from the oven and baste with the duck fat. Check the internal temperature of the meat (you're looking for about 60°C/140°F on a meat thermometer for medium). If you want to cook it more, return to the oven. Allow the meat to rest for at least 15 minutes.

To serve, warm up the onions. Carve the beef and serve alongside the potatoes.

Roast Beef with Mustard

Preparation: 15 minutes
Cooking: 50 minutes, plus resting time
Serves 10

50 g/2 oz (¼ cup) beef dripping
1 tablespoon English mustard
1 × 2-kg/4½-lb sirloin (short loin), neatly trimmed
4 onions, halved
4 carrots, halved
350 ml/12 fl oz (1½ cups) beef stock (broth)
sea salt
boiled potatoes, to serve

Preheat the oven to 180°C/350°F/Gas Mark 4.

Melt the beef dripping in a small pan over a medium–low heat and mix in the mustard. With the aid of a pastry brush, smear the beef with the mustard and season with sea salt.

Put the onions and carrots into a roasting pan and lay the beef on top of the vegetables. Pour the beef stock (broth) around the meat.

Put into the preheated oven and roast, basting occasionally, for 45 minutes until it reaches a core temperature of 55°C/130°F on a meat thermometer. Remove from the oven and allow to rest for 5–10 minutes.

Carve and serve with boiled potatoes.

Pot-roasted Beef with Stout and Mustard

Preparation: 20 minutes
Cooking: 3 hours 30 minutes
Serves 6

1 × 1.5-kg/3¼-lb beef brisket, rolled and tied
2 tablespoons rapeseed (canola) oil, plus extra for oiling
50 g/2 oz (4 tablespoons) butter
4 onions, quartered
2 tablespoons wholegrain mustard
3 sprigs of thyme
1 large bay leaf
1 tablespoon soft brown sugar
4 juniper berries
50 g/2 oz (⅓ cup) plain (all-purpose) flour
250 ml/8 fl oz (1 cup) stout
4 large carrots, cut into chunks
6 celery stalks, chopped
750 ml/25 fl oz (3 cups) beef stock (broth)
sea salt and freshly ground black pepper

Preheat the oven to 160°C/325°F/ Gas Mark 3. Rub the brisket with oil and season with salt and pepper.

Heat the oil a large flameproof casserole dish (Dutch oven) over a medium heat and sear the beef for about 5 minutes until beautifully browned on all sides. Remove the beef from the dish and set aside. Discard the excess fat in the dish.

Melt the butter in the casserole and add the onions. Cook for 5 minutes and then add the mustard, herbs, sugar and juniper berries.

Scrape the bottom of the dish to ensure you release the residual flavour of the beef. Add the flour and cook, stirring, for 2 minutes to form a paste. Add the stout and bring to the boil, then add the rest of the vegetables followed by the beef stock (broth).

Return the brisket to the dish and submerge into the liquid. Cover with the lid or aluminium foil and cook in the preheated oven, turning once, for about 3 hours until extremely tender.

Stuffed Beef Heart with Chestnuts and Prunes

Preparation: 20 minutes
Cooking: 1 hour 40 minutes
Serves 2

1 large beef heart
1 tablespoon rapeseed (canola) oil, plus extra for oiling
1 onion, finely chopped
1 bay leaf
2 cloves garlic, very finely chopped
1 teaspoon caraway seeds
75 ml/2½ fl oz (⅓ cup) dry sherry
200 g/7 oz (1⅓ cups) cooked chestnuts
75 g/2¾ oz (⅓ cup) prunes, soaked and chopped
100 g/3½ oz (2 cups) fresh breadcrumbs
sea salt

Preheat the oven to 160°C/325°F/ Gas Mark 3.

Trim the hard fat from the outside of the beef heart. Cut the middle out and remove the arteries, blood vessels and any other gristle.

To make the stuffing, heat the oil in a frying pan over a medium heat and fry the onion and the bay leaf for a few minutes, then add the garlic and the caraway seeds and cook for a few minutes more.

When the onions are translucent, about 5 minutes in total, add the sherry with the chestnuts and prunes. Cook for 5 minutes to burn off the alcohol and then add the breadcrumbs. Remove the stuffing from the pan and season with salt.

Stuff the hollow centre of the heart and put the heart into a roasting pan. Oil the outside of the heart and season with sea salt. Bake in the preheated oven for 1 hour 30 minutes. Baste the heart with more sherry during cooking if desired.

Beef

Beef Cheeks with Barley and Onions

Preparation: 25 minutes
Cooking: 3 hours 20 minutes
Serves 4

For the beef cheeks
4 beef cheeks, cap removed and trimmed
  of sinew
2 tablespoons rapeseed (canola) oil
4 carrots, chopped
2 onions, quartered
2 cloves garlic
50 g/2 oz (4 tablespoons) butter
a few sprigs of rosemary and thyme
450 ml/15 fl oz (scant 2 cups) stout
450 ml/15 fl oz (scant 2 cups) beef stock (broth)
sea salt

For the barley and onions
300 g/11 oz (2½ cups) barley
2 onions, halved, skin on
50 g/2 oz (4 tablespoons) butter, cubed

Preheat the oven to 160°C/325°F/ Gas Mark 3.

To braise the beef cheeks, season the cheeks with sea salt. Heat the oil in a large frying pan (skillet), add the cheeks and fry for 1–2 minutes on each side until nicely browned. Add the carrots, onions and garlic. After a minute, add the butter and herbs and baste for 2–3 minutes until the vegetables are caramelized.

Transfer to an ovenproof dish and discard any excess fat. Pour the stout and stock (broth) over the cheeks until completely submerged. Cover the dish with a lid or aluminium foil and put into the preheated oven for 3 hours.

Meanwhile, simmer the barley in a large pan of water over a low heat for 40 minutes until tender. Strain and reserve.

Strain the sauce from the cheeks and carrots and keep them warm. Allow the fat to settle and skim

it off the top. Heat the sauce in a pan over a high heat for about 15 minutes until reduced by half.

Put the onions in a dry pan over a medium–low heat and cook for 18–20 minutes until soft to touch and the edges are blackened. Peel into individual pieces, keeping the lobes intact. Remove any large charred pieces.

When ready to serve, melt the butter in the barley and season with sea salt to taste. Spoon the barley over the plates and add the charred onions. Slice the beef cheeks and lay near the onions. Finish with some sauce.

Note
The cheeks can also be cooked in a lower oven, at 120°C/250°F/ Gas Mark ½, for 5 hours for a more tender meat.

See opposite –>

Spiced Ox Tongue

Preparation: 20 minutes, plus at least
1 week marinating time
Cooking: 4 hours
Serves 6

1 ox tongue
1 onion, halved
2 carrots, sliced
a few sprigs of thyme
a few green peppercorns

For the spice mixture
250 g/9 oz (generous ¾ cup) salt
100 g/3½ oz (½ cup firmly packed)
  soft brown sugar
1 teaspoon ground allspice
½ teaspoon ground nutmeg
½ teaspoon crushed cloves
1 teaspoon thyme, finely chopped
1 teaspoon black peppercorns
2 bay leaves

Put all the ingredients for the spice mixture into a food processor and blend until thoroughly combined.

Place the tongue in a non-reactive container and cover with the spice mix, rubbing it into all sides. Leave the tongue for at least a week, turning it every day.

When ready to cook, place the tongue in a large pan of cold water with the other ingredients and cover. Bring to the boil, reduce the heat and simmer for 3–4 hours until the tongue is tender and the skin is blistered. Lift out of the liquid and leave to cool, then peel off the skin. Serve either warm or cold.

Beef

Beef

Veal Shanks with Onion Salad

Preparation: 30 minutes, plus overnight
chilling and resting time
Cooking: 2 hours 15 minutes
Serves 4

2 veal shanks
1 calf's foot
1 onion, chopped
1 leek, chopped
1 carrot, chopped
bouquet garni of a small handful of thyme,
    sage and rosemary
2 tablespoons plus 1 teaspoon honey
apple cider vinegar, to taste
a handful of chopped parsley
sea salt

For the onion salad
4 red onions, sliced
2 tablespoons honey
5 teaspoons apple cider vinegar
100 ml/3½ fl oz (scant ½ cup) extra virgin
    rapeseed (canola) oil
25 g/1 oz (⅓ cup prepared) parsley, chopped

Veal is meat from a young calf, usually up to 20 weeks old. It is typically the meat from a male dairy calf that will not be used for breeding. Though many disagree with the production of veal, it is a by-product of the dairy industry and therefore should be used. Bad practices or living conditions for the animals have contributed to the negative perception of veal. There are a number of veal farmers in Ireland. Kilkenny Rose Veal are one such producer who are leading the way in producing ethically minded veal that takes the welfare of the animal into consideration. Their animals are reared for 38 weeks in spacious conditions with plenty of natural light.

Add the veal shanks and calf's foot to a large stewpot over a high heat along with the vegetables and bouquet garni. Pour in enough water to cover everything and bring to the boil. Reduce the heat and simmer for about 2 hours until the meat is tender and coming away from the bone.

Strain and reserve the liquid. Discard the vegetables, herbs and calf's foot. Remove the meat from the veal shanks and put into a bowl.

Pour 500 ml/17 fl oz (generous 2 cups) of the broth into a small pan and simmer for about

15 minutes until reduced by half and add to the meat mixture. Add the honey, vinegar and parsley and season. Using a piece of muslin (cheesecloth) or cling film (plastic wrap), roll the mixture into a cylinder and refrigerate overnight until set.

To make the onion salad, lightly salt the onion slices and leave to rest for 15 minutes. Strain and rinse lightly. Mix the honey, vinegar and oil together. Combine the onions with the dressing and the parsley.

Cut the meat into slices and serve with the onion salad.

Veal Chops with Caper Sauce

Preparation: 15 minutes, plus marinating time
Cooking: 20 minutes
Serves 4

2 cloves garlic
4 canned anchovies
100 ml/3½ fl oz (scant ½ cup) extra virgin
    rapeseed (canola) oil
4 × 250-g/9-oz veal chops
a few sprigs of thyme
a few sage leaves
sea salt and freshly ground black pepper

For the caper sauce
1 shallot, finely diced
2 tablespoons capers, chopped
a sprig of thyme
250 ml/8 fl oz (1 cup) white wine
150 ml/5 fl oz (⅔ cup) double (heavy) cream
50 g/2 oz (4 tablespoons) butter, cubed
1 tablespoon chopped parsley

Though regular capers are used in this recipe, you can use wild garlic, nasturtium or elderberry capers if you have them preserved. Using anchovies to add flavour to meat (and fish) was a common practice in seventeenth- and eighteenth-century Ireland and features in many recipe collections from that period, as Regina Sexton has observed in her paper 'Food and Culinary Cultures in Pre-Famine Ireland' (2015).

To make a marinade, blend the garlic and anchovies with the oil. Spread over the veal chops with the herbs and marinate for 2–3 hours.

Preheat the grill (broiler).

To make the sauce, put the shallot, capers and thyme into a medium pan over a high heat along with the wine, bring to the boil, then reduce the heat and simmer for about 10 minutes until reduced by half.

Add the cream and reduce by half again. Remove the thyme. Melt in the butter and fold in the chopped parsley. Remove from the heat

Meanwhile, shake off the herbs from the veal chops, put them under the hot grill (broiler) and cook for about 6 minutes on each side until nicely browned. Season to taste with salt and pepper. Serve the chops with the caper sauce.

Curried Veal

Preparation: 20 minutes, plus overnight chilling time
Cooking: 2 hours
Serves 6

1 kg/2¼ lb veal shoulder, diced
50 g/2 oz (⅓ cup) plain (all-purpose) flour
1 teaspoon ground ginger
1 teaspoon ground turmeric
2 tablespoons curry powder
3 tablespoons rapeseed (canola) oil
6 onions, sliced
3 cloves garlic
600 ml/20 fl oz (2½ cups) chicken stock (broth)
2 tablespoons soft brown sugar
50 g/2 oz (⅓ cup) whole almonds
50 g/2 oz (⅓ cup) raisins
200 ml/7 fl oz (scant 1 cup) double (heavy) cream
1 apple, cubed
50 g/2 oz (2 cups) baby spinach
sea salt

Monica Sheridan includes a curried veal recipe in her book *Full and Plenty* (1965). Her serving suggestion is 'chutney, mustard [and] pickles'. This is my version of a veal curry.

The night before, mix the veal with the flour, ginger, turmeric and curry powder and refrigerate.

On the day, heat 1 tablespoon of the oil in a large pan over a medium heat and fry the onions and garlic for 5 minutes until translucent and soft. Remove the onions from the pan and set aside.

Heat another tablespoon of oil the in the pan, add half the veal and fry for about 5 minutes until nicely browned all over. Remove from the pan and set aside. Repeat with the remaining oil and veal. When all the veal is browned, return the onions and garlic to the pan along with the first batch of veal. Add the chicken stock (broth), brown sugar, almonds and raisins and simmer for about 1 hour to 1 hour 30 minutes until the veal is tender.

Add the cream and heat until warmed through. Just before serving, add the apple and spinach and heat for a couple of minutes until the spinach wilts.

Veal and Blue Cheese Pie

Preparation: 40 minutes, plus chilling time
Cooking: 2 hours 40 minutes
Serves 8

For the pastry
200 g/7 oz (1⅔ cups) plain (all-purpose) flour, sifted
½ teaspoon sea salt
100 g/3½ oz (7 tablespoons) cold butter, cubed
2 egg yolks, beaten separately, one for brushing

For the filling
50 g/2 oz (4 tablespoons) butter, and a little extra for greasing
1 onion, diced
550 g/1¼ lb veal shoulder, diced
1 tablespoon chopped thyme
1 tablespoon chopped oregano
50 g/2 oz (⅓ cup) plain (all-purpose) flour
200 ml/7 fl oz (scant 1 cup) white wine
300 ml/10 fl oz (1¼ cups) chicken stock (broth)
200 g/7 oz Irish blue cheese (such as Cashel, Young Buck or Kearney)
sea salt

Ireland has a fantastic tradition of blue cheese, going back to the 1970s. Some of my favourites are Cashel Blue, Kearney Blue, Wicklow Blue Brie and Young Buck.

To make the pastry, combine the flour and salt in a bowl. Rub in the butter until the mixture resembles breadcrumbs and then add one egg yolk. Use just enough ice-cold water to bring the ingredients together to form a dough. Wrap in cling film (plastic wrap) and refrigerate for at least 1 hour.

Meanwhile, make the filling. Melt the butter in a large pan over a medium heat and fry the onion for about 5 minutes until soft and translucent. Add the veal and herbs to the pan and fry for about 5 minutes until browned all over. Add the flour and cook, stirring, for 2 minutes to make a paste. Then add the white wine and chicken stock (broth). Reduce the heat and cook for 1 hour 30 minutes–2 hours until the veal is extremely tender.

Remove from the heat and fold in the cheese. Allow to cool.

Preheat the oven to 180°C/350°F/ Gas Mark 4 and grease a 20–25 cm/ 8–10 inch pie dish.

Roll out the dough and cut into two large rounds. Line the dish with one of the pastry rounds. Put the cooled veal mixture into the pie dish. Brush the sides with a little water and cover with the remaining pastry round. Make a small circular hole in the centre of the pie. Brush the pie with the remaining egg yolk and crimp the edges with a fork.

Bake in the preheated oven for 30 minutes or until the filling is hot and the pastry top is a golden brown.

Beef

Breads, Scones and Crackers

Breads, Scones and Crackers

Ireland has a long history of baking. According to food historian Regina Sexton, 'no matter how hard you try, you can't but fall victim to Ireland's impressive bread tradition'. As early as the seventh to eighth century, we can find important references to bread making and bread-making skills – in particular, to passing these skills on to the next generation. We would do well to take a leaf out of this book, *Cáin Iarraith* (The Law of the Fosterage Fee). Foster parents were obliged by laws to pass on the traditions of baking to the young girls in their household. But what about the earlier tradition, before the written word? Grains arrived in Ireland with Neolithic farmers: emmer, barley, wheat and oats all became a staple part of the diet from around 3,000 BC onwards. Legend tells us that a woman invented sourdough when she left a little of the remaining dough in her bowl and mixed fresh dough with it. Barm liquid (liquid obtained from beer making) was also used to get the bread to rise. Two other interesting methods that Bríd Mahon writes of were the use of sowans (fermented juice of oat husks) and sour potato water. The recent rise of fermented potato bread in Ireland, for example that made by Ciaran Sweeney at Forest & Marcy, appears to have truly ancient Irish origins.

It would be wrong to see bread as a staple product of Irish cooking over time, in the sense that every invading group modified the existing bread. Furthermore, because of the weather, wheat was difficult to grow in Ireland. In one sense, this is why our own bread tradition comes and goes over the centuries. Barley bread in the Middle Ages must have taken the teeth out of the monks who consumed it. One traveller to Ireland in the eighteenth century noted that bread from the south was usually made with oats, but in the Midlands, it would be made with rye and wheat. While barley bread was associated with the fasting monks of the seventh and eighth centuries, soft wheaten cakes came with the Normans, who loved their feasts and always included luxurious spiced breads. In truth, the oven arrived with the Normans and they did much to change the nature of bread making in Ireland. It became more refined (if only for the aristocratic classes). Bakeries, or bakehouses (with ovens) became a feature of Irish towns following the Norman invasion. The spices and dried fruits that continue to appear in Irish cooking all stem from the arrival of the Normans. Though for most, the bread would remain a simple affair, cooked on a griddle pan – a large flat grill pan – over an open fire. In this sense we have two bread traditions in Ireland, one for the rich and one for the poor, until at least the rise of the middle classes in the nineteenth century. Most people today associate soda bread with Ireland, but its tradition is recent, in that bicarbonate of soda (baking soda) was only invented in the nineteenth century. Though soda bread has ruled the roost in terms of Irish bread for the past two hundred years, sourdough has made a welcome return.

The future is bright for Irish bread making with many new bakeries opening all around the country. Bread Nation, run by baker Eoin Cluskey, is one such bakery which is returning heritage and craft to baking. As well as bakeries, producers are also planting different varieties of grain and wheat in order to reclaim a little of our bread heritage. Little Mill (County Kilkenny) is the only stone-ground commercial mill in Ireland producing wholemeal flour from specifically Irish wheat.

Soda Farls

Preparation: 15 minutes
Cooking: 10 minutes
Serves 4

350 g/12 oz (2¾ cups) plain (all-purpose) flour
1 teaspoon bicarbonate of soda (baking soda)
sea salt
50 g/2 oz (4 tablespoons) cold butter, cubed,
   plus extra for frying and to serve
200 ml/7 fl oz (scant 1 cup) buttermilk

Like their potato partner (see page 84), soda farls were shaped in a round loaf, cut into four and cooked on a griddle (grill) pan over the fire. Add apple treacle (molasses) to make a sweet version. Farls were traditionally fried in pork fat to accompany a fry-up breakfast, particularly in Ulster.

Sift the flour and bicarbonate of soda (baking soda) together into a mixing bowl and add the salt. Rub the butter into the flour until the mixture resembles breadcrumbs.

Make a well in the centre of the flour and gradually add the buttermilk until you have a dough. Shape the dough into a round loaf and cut into four.

Fry the bread in butter on a flat grill (griddle) pan over a medium–low heat for 5–10 minutes until firm to the touch. Serve with more butter.

Wholemeal Fadge

Preparation: 20 minutes
Cooking: 25 minutes
Makes 2 loaves

300 g/11 oz (2½ cups) wholemeal
   (whole-wheat) flour
300 g/11 oz (2⅓ cups) plain
   (all-purpose) flour
1 teaspoon bicarbonate of soda (baking soda)
1 teaspoon sea salt
50 g/2 oz (¼ cup) pork lard
275 ml/9 fl oz (generous 1 cup) buttermilk

A fadge is another name for a farl. Often, they would be made without any raising (leavening) agent or with fillers such as potatoes and apples.

Preheat the oven to 180°C/350°F/ Gas Mark 4. Line a baking sheet with baking (parchment) paper.

Sift the flours and bicarbonate of soda (baking soda) into a large mixing bowl and combine with the salt. Rub the lard into them until the mixture resembles breadcrumbs.

Add the buttermilk and combine to form a dough.

Shape into two rounds, transfer to the lined baking sheet and bake in the preheated oven for 25 minutes until firm to the touch.

White Soda Bread

Preparation: 15 minutes
Cooking: 1 hour
Makes 1 loaf

700 g/1 lb 9 oz (5 cups) strong white bread
   flour, plus extra for dusting
1 teaspoon bicarbonate of soda (baking soda)
2 teaspoons sea salt
325 ml/11 fl oz (1⅓ cups) buttermilk,
   plus a little extra for brushing

This is a basic recipe for white soda bread. The dough can be enriched with the addition of an egg or 50 g/2 oz (4 tablespoons) of butter. You can also add different dry ingredients to the dough such as raisins or other dried fruit. Don't over-knead the bread because this will make it dense.

Preheat the oven to 180°C/350°F/ Gas Mark 4. Line a baking sheet with baking (parchment) paper.

Sift the flour, bicarbonate of soda (baking soda) and salt into a large mixing bowl. Make a well in the centre and add the buttermilk. Gently combine to form a dough.

Turn the dough out onto a lightly floured surface and shape into a round. Transfer to the lined baking sheet, score the bread with a deep cross, brush with a little buttermilk and bake for 1 hour until the bottom sounds hollow when tapped, or the core temperature is greater than 85°C/185°F on a meat thermometer.

Breads, Scones and Crackers

Brown Soda Bread with Stout and Treacle

Preparation: 20 minutes
Cooking: 1 hour 45 minutes
Makes 2 loaves

rapeseed (canola) oil, for greasing
800 g/1¾ lb (5¾ cups) strong brown (whole-wheat) bread flour
200 g/7 oz (1½ cups) strong white bread flour
1 tablespoon bicarbonate of soda (baking soda)
20 g/¾ oz (4 teaspoons) sea salt
3 handfuls of (about 1½ cups) mixed seeds (such as pumpkin seeds, sunflower seeds and linseeds/flaxseed)
200 g/7 oz (⅔ cup) treacle (molasses)
2 eggs
850 ml/30 fl oz (3½ cups) buttermilk
200 ml/7 fl oz (scant 1 cup) stout
50 g/2 oz (⅓ cup) pinhead (steel-cut) oats, for the topping

Bicarbonate of soda (baking soda) helped to feed bread to a generation of soldiers at war in Europe and afar. It is the bread we are most familiar with in Ireland. Many say this was because of the coarse flour in Ireland. Bicarbonate of soda suited it better than yeast. My own grandmother would make similar bread every second or third day. It is a tradition worth continuing. This is the brown (wheat) bread we make every day at our restaurant Aniar.

Preheat the oven to 130°C/265°F/ Gas Mark ¾. Grease two 23 × 13 × 7-cm/9 × 5 × 3-inch loaf pans.

Stir all the dry ingredients together in a large mixing bowl. Add the treacle (molasses), eggs and buttermilk and combine, then add enough stout until you achieve a wet dough.

Pour the dough into the two prepared loaf pans, sprinkle the oats on top and bake in the preheated oven for 1 hour 30 to 1 hour 45 minutes, until the loaves sound hollow when the bottoms are tapped or the core temperature is greater than 85°C/185°F on a meat thermometer.

See opposite –>

Spotted Dog

Preparation: 15 minutes
Cooking: 45 minutes
Makes 1 loaf

500 g/1 lb 2 oz (3⅔ cups) strong white bread flour, plus extra for dusting
1 teaspoon bicarbonate of soda (baking soda)
1 teaspoon sea salt
50 g/2 oz (¼ cup) caster (superfine) sugar
200 ml/7 fl oz (scant 1 cup) buttermilk
1 egg
100 g/3½ oz (⅔ cup) raisins

Spotted dog is essentially a richer soda bread made with the addition of dried fruits, sugar and eggs.

Preheat the oven to 160°C/325°F/ Gas Mark 3. Line a baking sheet with baking (parchment) paper.

Sift the flour with the bicarbonate of soda (baking soda) and salt into a mixing bowl. Add the sugar.

Mix the buttermilk and egg together in a jug (pitcher) or small bowl.

Pour into the flour mixture and bring the dough together. Add the raisins and combine gently.

Turn the dough out onto a lightly floured surface and shape into a loaf. Transfer to the lined baking sheet, cut a cross into the bread and bake in the preheated oven for 45 minutes.

Breads, Scones and Crackers

Breads, Scones and Crackers

Potato Bread

Preparation: 40 minutes, plus overnight fermenting and rising times
Cooking: 30 minutes
Makes 2 loaves

For the starter
225 g/8 oz (2¼ cups) rye flour
2 g (⅝ teaspoon) fresh yeast or ¼ teaspoon fast action dried (active dry) yeast

For the dough
400 g/14 oz (about 4) potatoes, cooked and mashed
400 g/14 oz (3⅓ cups) plain (all-purpose) flour, plus extra for dusting
20 g/¾ oz (1 tablespoon) salt
15 g/½ oz (4¾ teaspoons) fresh yeast or 2¾ teaspoons fast action dried (active dry) yeast
fermented (cultured) butter, to serve

To make the starter, add the rye flour and yeast to a mixing bowl with 200 ml/7 fl oz (scant 1 cup) of warm water and stir together. Cover and leave to ferment overnight in a cool place.

The following morning, to make the dough, combine the potatoes, flour and salt in a mixing bowl. Add the yeast to 400 ml/14 fl oz (1⅔ cups) warm water and mix. Add the starter to the dough, then gradually add the yeast mixture and mix to form a smooth dough

Turn out onto a well-floured work surface and knead for 10 minutes. Transfer the dough to a floured mixing bowl and cover with cling film (plastic wrap). Leave to rest for 45 minutes in a warm place.

Knock back (punch down) the dough and fold it over itself four times. Shape into two large circular loaves and transfer to two baking sheets lined with parchment paper. Place a dish towel over each loaf and leave to rise for 30 minutes until doubled in size.

Preheat the oven to 220°C/425°F/Gas Mark 7.

Put the loaves into the preheated oven and bake for 15 minutes. Reduce the oven temperature to 180°C/350°F/Gas Mark 4 and cook for a further 10–15 minutes, or until cooked through. Remove from the oven and allow to cool on a wire rack.

Serve with some fermented butter.

Griddle Potato Bread

Preparation and cooking: 20 minutes
Serves 4

500 g/1 lb 2 oz (2 cups prepared) cooked potatoes, mashed
50 g/2 oz (4 tablespoons) butter, plus extra for frying
150 g/5 oz (1¼ cups) plain (all-purpose) flour
sea salt

Potato bread was traditionally made by combining flour with leftover potatoes and salt. These were cooked on a flat grill (griddle) until both sides were browned.

Combine the potatoes with the butter and fold in the flour. Season with sea salt. Shape into four.

Melt some butter in a frying pan (skillet) over a medium heat and fry for about 5 minutes on each side until golden brown.

See opposite –>

Fried Bread

I don't know if people eat fried bread anymore but it was a staple of my childhood. It's simply bread fried in beef dripping or lard. My mother would have it with her breakfast on the weekend. In her book *The Cookin' Woman* (1949), Florence Irwin includes a good observation in favour of fried bread, 'Wheaten or soda bread fried in the pan almost go with bacon and eggs without saying.' For Irwin, after the eggs and bacon are cooked, a little extra dripping could be added to the pan. Perhaps it is the modern toaster that brought an end to this great tradition, or perhaps it was our unfounded fear of frying with animal fats. The next time you're having a fry up for breakfast with bacon and eggs, why not indulge?

Breads, Scones and Crackers

Breads, Scones and Crackers

Our Sourdough

Preparation: 45 minutes, plus rising and proving times
Cooking: 25 minutes
Makes 3 loaves

rapeseed (canola) oil, for greasing
450 g/1 lb (1¾ cups) sourdough starter
1 kg/2¼ lb (7¾ cups) strong white bread flour, plus extra for dusting
15 g/½ oz (2½ teaspoons) salt

This is the sourdough recipe that we have made every day for many years in our restaurant Aniar. Cultivating a good starter is paramount for making sourdough. Though it's easy, it does take practice.

Grease a large mixing bowl with a little oil. Combine the starter and 720 ml/24 fl oz (3 cups) of water in a large mixing bowl. Add the flour and salt and continue to mix until thoroughly combined. Put the dough into the oiled bowl and leave at room temperature for 4–6 hours.

Lightly dust three sourdough baskets with flour. Divide the dough into three balls and knead again using the folding technique, folding the dough over and into itself several times. Shape each ball into a loaf and place into a floured sourdough basket. Cover with a dish towel and allow to prove (rise) for a further 4–6 hours or until doubled in size. Alternatively, you can refrigerate overnight.

Preheat the oven to 240°C/475°F/ Gas Mark 9.

Bake the loaves in the preheated oven for 10 minutes and then reduce the oven temperature to 200°C/400°F/Gas Mark 6 and bake for a further 15 minutes. Remove from the oven and allow to cool on a wire rack.

See opposite –>

Stout and Treacle Bread

Preparation: 20 minutes
Cooking: 45 minutes
Makes 1 loaf

rapeseed (canola) oil, for greasing
400 g/14 oz (3⅓ cups) wholemeal (whole-wheat) flour
100 g/3½ oz (¾ cup plus 1 tablespoon) plain (all-purpose) flour
1 teaspoon bicarbonate of soda (baking soda)
1 teaspoon salt
75 g/2¾ oz (¼ cup) treacle (molasses)
150 ml/5 fl oz (⅔ cup) stout
300 ml/10 fl oz (1¼ cups) buttermilk
25 g/1 oz (2½ tablespoons) pinhead (steel-cut) oats

Preheat the oven to 150°C/300°F/ Gas Mark 2. Grease a 23 × 13 × 7-cm/ 9 × 5 × 3-inch loaf pan with a little oil.

Sift the flours with the bicarbonate of soda (baking soda) into a large mixing bowl and combine with the salt.

Blend the treacle with the stout in a small mixing bowl, then blend in the buttermilk.

Gently combine the wet mixture with the dry ingredients.

Pour the mixture into the prepared pan and bake in the preheated oven for 45 minutes until nicely browned.

Breads, Scones and Crackers

Rye and Barley Bread

Preparation: 30 minutes, plus resting and proving times
Cooking: 15 minutes
Makes 1 loaf

10 g/¼ oz (1 teaspoon) packed fresh yeast (or if not available, 2.7 g/generous ¾ teaspoon fast action dried (active dry) yeast)
350 ml/12 fl oz (1½ cups) tepid water
300 g/11 oz (2 cups plus 3 tablespoons) strong white bread flour, plus extra for dusting
100 g/3½ oz (1 cup) rye flour
100 g/3½ oz (⅔ cup) barley flour
10 g/¼ oz (2 teaspoons) sea salt

Grains such as barley are now mostly used for feeding cattle and in the beer-making industry. This is a pity. It can be quite coarse as a flour, however this did not stop Irish people making bread with it. Rye and spelt grow particularly well in Ireland. There are many references to rye throughout the history of Irish food, from bread to porridge.

Combine the yeast with the tepid water in a bowl, mix together until the yeast dissolves and allow to rest in a warm place for 10 minutes.

Sift the flours and salt into a large mixing bowl and combine. Pour in the yeast liquid and combine with the flour until a dough forms.

Turn out the dough onto a lightly floured surface and knead for 10 minutes until smooth.

Put the dough into a floured bowl, cover with a dish towel and leave to rise in a warm place for 30–45 minutes, or until doubled in size.

Flatten the dough and fold it over itself a few times. Shape into a circular loaf and score the top.

Cover with oiled cling film (plastic wrap) and place in a warm place and allow to prove (rise) until it has doubled in size.

Preheat the oven to 200°C/400°F/ Gas Mark 6. Line a baking sheet with baking (parchment) paper.

Transfer the dough to the lined baking sheet and bake in the pre-heated oven for 15 minutes until it sounds hollow when tapped on the bottom. Cool on a wire rack.

Yellow Bread

Preparation: 15 minutes
Cooking: 45 minutes
Makes 1 loaf

300 g/11 oz (2 cups plus 3 tablespoons) strong white bread flour, plus extra for dusting
1 teaspoon bicarbonate of soda (baking soda)
1 teaspoon sea salt
200 g/7 oz (1½ cups) cornmeal or polenta
225 ml/7½ fl oz (scant 1 cup) buttermilk

Yellow bread is made with cornmeal. Cornmeal arrived in Ireland during the famine, to relieve the starving population. Maura Laverty, the wonderful Irish novelist and food writer, writes of her grandmother making corn cakes in the ashes of the fire in 1920. The scene that she paints in her novel *Never No More* (1942) speaks much of the ways in which bread was cooked over a traditional open hearth.

Preheat the oven to 160°C/325°F/ Gas Mark 3. Line a baking sheet with baking (parchment) paper.

Sift the white flour, bicarbonate of soda (baking soda) and salt together into a large mixing bowl and mix in the polenta (cornmeal). Gradually, add in the buttermilk to form a dough.

Turn the dough out onto a lightly floured surface and shape into a loaf. Transfer to the lined baking sheet, cut a cross in the bread and bake in the preheated oven for 45 minutes until firm to the touch.

Breads, Scones and Crackers

Waterford Blaa

Preparation: 20 minutes, plus resting and
proving time
Cooking: 15 minutes
Makes 12 rolls

20 g/¾ oz (2 tablespoons) fresh yeast
    or 8 g (2½ teaspoons) fast action dried
    (active dry) yeast
1 teaspoon sugar
750 g/1 lb 10 oz (5⅓ cups) strong white bread
    flour, plus extra for dusting
2 teaspoons salt

The Waterford blaa is another tale of Irish food migration. When the French Huguenots fled France because of persecution in the seventeenth century they settled in Waterford. It is said that they introduced the method for making this bread roll. A poem written in the 1950s by Eddie Wymberry celebrates the bread:

A Blaa with two a's is made with fresh dough
About the size of a saucer, that's the right size you know:
But where did they come from, did they happen by chance
No, the Huguenots brought them from France

The roll now has protected European status (PGI). Walsh's bakery is one bakery that is continuing the tradition of making the bread and now supplies them nationwide. They are popular at breakfast and can be filled with grilled bacon, steak, potatoes, dillisk or relish (not all at once!).

In a small bowl, mix together the yeast and sugar. Add 350 ml/ 12 fl oz (1½ cups) warm water and mix again. Leave in a warm place for 15 minutes.

Put the flour in a large bowl, add the salt and stir together until the salt is dispersed through the flour. Gradually add the water to the flour, mixing with your hand until a rough dough forms (this can be done in a machine if desired).

Tip the dough onto a lightly floured surface and knead for 10 minutes, until smooth and elastic.

Transfer the dough to a lightly oiled bowl, cover with a dish towel and leave to rest for 30 minutes in a warm place.

After 30 minutes, remove the dough from the bowl and knock back. Shape the dough, transfer to a baking pan and allow to rise again for another 30 minutes.

Preheat the oven to 200°C/400°F/ Gas Mark 6.

Divide the dough into 12 pieces and shape into balls on the baking pan. Flatten the top slightly and dust with flour. Allow to rise again for another 25 minutes then bake in the preheated oven for 12–15 minutes, until very lightly browned.

Breads, Scones and Crackers

Batch Bread

Preparation: 30 minutes, plus resting and proving times
Cooking: 25 minutes
Makes 4 loaves

10 g/¼ oz (3¼ teaspoons) fast action dried (active dry) yeast
500 ml/17 fl oz (generous 2 cups) tepid water
750 g/1 lb 10 oz (5½ cups) strong white bread flour, plus extra for dusting
15 g/½ oz (2½ teaspoons) fine salt
50 g/2 oz (¼ cup) lard
rapeseed (canola) oil, for greasing

A batch loaf is a traditional Irish tall loaf of bread with a dark crust on the top and the bottom of the bread. There is no crust on the sides because the unbaked loaves are place side by side together in batches when rising. The loaves are baked together and then torn into individual loaves once baked. My mother fried her batch bread in dripping. You can still buy batch bread in many bakeries around Ireland. It's great for sandwiches.

Combine the yeast with the water in a bowl, mix together until the yeast dissolves and put in a warm place for 10 minutes.

Put the flour, salt and lard into a stand mixer and mix for 2 minutes. On a slow speed and using the dough hook, gradually add the yeast liquid to form a dough. Mix for 10 minutes until the dough is smooth.

Transfer to a floured bowl, cover with a dish towel and allow to rest in a warm place for an hour until the dough has doubled in size.

Grease a baking pan with a little oil. Shape the dough into four even loaves and place in the oiled pan. Cover with a dish towel and allow to prove (rise) in a warm place until doubled in volume, about 45 minutes.

Preheat the oven to 240°C/475°F/Gas Mark 9.

Put the bread into the preheated oven and bake for 25 minutes or until crusty and brown. Leave to cool in the pan for 10 minutes before transferring to a wire cooling rack to cool completely.

See opposite –>

Oaten Bread

Preparation: 20 minutes
Cooking: 45 minutes
Makes 1 loaf

rapeseed (canola) oil, for greasing
450 g/1 lb (5 cups) rolled oats
1 teaspoon bicarbonate of soda (baking soda), sifted
1 teaspoon sea salt
1 tablespoon sunflower seeds
1 tablespoon pumpkin seeds
1 tablespoon linseeds (flaxseed)
550 g/1¼ lb (2¼ cups) plain yogurt
1 egg, beaten
3½ tablespoons buttermilk

In 1790, a French traveller observed that oat bread was made predominantly in the south of Ireland. Nowadays, yogurt and seeds are popular additions to the bread, both for taste and texture. The yogurt helps keep the bread moist. If you want, sprinkle additional seeds on top of the bread. Though oat bread is denser than soda bread, it is a nutritious alternative. Feel free to change the seeds or add nuts.

Preheat the oven to 160°C/325°F/Gas Mark 3. Grease a 23 × 13 × 7-cm/9 × 5 × 3-inch loaf pan with a drizzle of oil.

Combine all the dry ingredients in a large mixing bowl and mix together thoroughly.

Mix the wet ingredients together in a jug (pitcher) or small bowl, then fold the wet ingredients into the dry mix to make a wet batter.

Spoon the batter into the prepared loaf pan and bake in the preheated oven for 45 minutes until the loaf sounds hollow when the top is tapped. Leave to cool in the pan for 10 minutes before transferring to a wire cooling rack to cool completely.

Breads, Scones and Crackers

Breads, Scones and Crackers

Scones

Preparation: 20 minutes
Cooking: 12 minutes
Makes 12–16

500 g/1 lb 2 oz plain (all-purpose) flour,
    plus extra for dusting
1 teaspoon baking powder
1 teaspoon sea salt
125 g/4½ oz (1 stick plus 1 tablespoon)
    butter, cubed
160 ml/5½ fl oz (⅔ cup) milk
4 eggs, plus extra for the egg wash

Scones and American biscuits have the same ancestry. In Ireland, butter is now used instead of lard, but lard will give a more intense flavour. My mother still bakes scones every second day.

Preheat the oven to 180°C/350°F/ Gas Mark 4. Line a baking sheet with baking (parchment) paper.

Sift the dry ingredients into a large mixing bowl. Rub in the butter with your fingertips until the mixture resembles fine breadcrumbs.

Combine the milk and eggs in a jug (pitcher). Make a well in the centre of the dry ingredients and gradually pour in the wet mixture. Combine to form a dough.

Turn the dough out onto a lightly floured surface and roll out. Cut out 12–16 rounds with a cookie cutter (I use between 6–8 cm/ 2½–3 inch) and place them on the baking sheet.

Brush the tops with a little egg wash and bake in the preheated oven for 10–12 minutes until they sound hollow when tapped.

See opposite –>

Scones with Raisins

Follow the above recipe but add 75 g/2¾ oz (½ cup) raisins with the dry ingredients. You can add other dried fruit depending on your preference.

Treacle Scones

Add 2 tablespoons of treacle (molasses) to your scone mixture with the milk and eggs. You may want to adjust the buttermilk content.

Brown Scones

Preparation: 20 minutes
Cooking: 15 minutes
Makes 12–16

400 g/14 oz (3⅓ cups) wholemeal
    (whole-wheat) flour
100 g/3½ oz (¾ cup) plain (all-purpose)
    flour, plus extra for dusting
1½ teaspoons baking powder
1 teaspoon sea salt
125 g/4½ oz (1 stick plus 1 tablespoon) butter
160 ml/5½ fl oz (⅔ cup) milk
4 eggs, plus extra for the egg wash

Preheat the oven to 180°C/350°F/ Gas Mark 4. Line a baking sheet with baking (parchment) paper.

Sift all the dry ingredients into a large mixing bowl. Cube the butter and rub in with your fingertips until the mixture resembles fine breadcrumbs.

Combine the milk and eggs in a jug (pitcher) or small bowl. Make a well in the centre of the dry

ingredients and gradually pour in the wet mixture, combining to form a dough.

Turn the dough out onto a lightly floured surface and roll out with a rolling pin. Cut out 12–16 scones with a cookie cutter and place them on the baking sheet.

Brush the tops with a little egg wash and bake in the preheated oven for 10–12 minutes.

Breads, Scones and Crackers

Griddle Scones

Preparation: 20 minutes
Cooking: 10 minutes
Makes 12–16

450 g/1 lb (3⅔ cups) plain (all-purpose) flour
1 teaspoon bicarbonate of soda (baking soda)
1 teaspoon cream of tartar
1 teaspoon salt
50 g/2 oz (¼ cup) lard (or butter), cubed
250 ml/8 fl oz (1 cup) buttermilk
butter or rapeseed (canola) oil, for frying

Before the introduction of the oven into the domestic household, scones were cooked on a 'griddle' over the open fire, a type of large, flat cast-iron plate. In Ireland this plate is called a griddle, as it is in the United States. In Scotland it is known as a girdle and the Welsh call it a bake stone. You can still bake scones in this way if you have a heavy-based frying pan (skillet). According to Darina Allen, these scones were sold at country markets, fairs and on the streets of Dublin. She suggests smearing small griddle cakes (*gátarí*) with molasses and serving them warm.

Sift the flour, bicarbonate of soda (baking soda), cream of tartar and salt into a large mixing bowl. Rub in the lard or butter using your fingertips until the mixture resembles breadcrumbs.

Gradually add the buttermilk, taking care not to over knead. Shape the mixture and cut into 12–16 small rounds.

Lightly oil a large flat grill, or griddle, pan and heat it over a medium heat. Add the scones and fry in batches for about 5 minutes on each side until golden brown. Allow to cool and serve.

Griddle Scones with Treacle

Use the above recipe and fold some treacle (molasses) into the scone mixture before frying. You may want to reduce the amount of buttermilk used to achieve the right consistency.

Buttermilk Scones

Preparation: 20 minutes
Cooking: 12 minutes
Makes 12–16

475 g/1 lb 1 oz (3¾ cups) plain (all-purpose) flour, plus extra for dusting
1 teaspoon bicarbonate of soda (baking soda)
1 teaspoon sea salt
50 g/2 oz caster (superfine) sugar
115 g/4 oz (1 stick) butter, cubed
160 ml/5½ fl oz (⅔ cup) buttermilk
4 eggs, beaten, plus extra for the egg wash

Preheat the oven to 180°C/350°F/Gas Mark 4. Line a baking sheet with baking (parchment) paper.

Sift all the dry ingredients into a large mixing bowl. Rub in the butter with your fingertips until the mixture resembles fine breadcrumbs.

Mix the buttermilk and eggs together in a jug (pitcher) or bowl, add to the dry ingredients and combine just enough to form a dough. Try to keep as much air in the mixture as possible.

Turn the dough out onto a floured surface and roll out with a rolling pin. Cut out 12–16 rounds with a cookie cutter (whichever size you like, I use between 6–8 cm/2½–3 inch) and place them on the lined baking sheet.

Brush the tops with a little egg wash and sprinkle with a little sugar. Bake in the preheated oven for 10–12 minutes until they sound hollow when tapped. Cool on a wire rack.

Cheese Scones

Preparation: 20 minutes
Cooking: 12 minutes
Makes 12–16

500 g/1 lb 2 oz (4 cups) plain (all-purpose) flour, plus extra for dusting
1 teaspoon baking powder
1 teaspoon sea salt
125 g/4½ oz (1 stick plus 1 tablespoon) butter, cubed
200 g/7 oz good-quality cheddar cheese, grated
175 ml/6 fl oz (¾ cup) milk
4 eggs, plus extra for the egg wash

These are the cheese scones we make every day in our café and wine bar in Galway.

Preheat the oven to 180°C/350°F/ Gas Mark 4. Line a baking sheet with baking (parchment) paper.

Sift all the dry ingredients into a large mixing bowl. Rub in the butter with your fingertips until the mixture resembles fine breadcrumbs, then add the cheese and stir together.

Mix the milk and eggs together in a jug (pitcher) or bowl and add to the dry ingredients. Combine until just forming a dough. Try to keep as much air in the mixture as possible.

Turn the dough out onto a floured surface and roll out with a rolling pin. Cut out 12–16 rounds with a cookie cutter (whichever size you like, I use between 6–8 cm/2½ – 3 inch) and place them on the lined baking sheet.

Brush the tops with a little egg wash and bake in the preheated oven for 10–12 minutes until they sound hollow when tapped. Cool on a wire rack.

Potato and Caraway Seed Scones

Preparation: 20 minutes
Cooking: 15 minutes
Makes 12–16

480 g/1 lb 1 oz (3¾ cups plus 1½ tablespoons) plain (all-purpose) flour, sifted, plus extra for dusting
240 g/8½ oz (generous 1 cup prepared) potatoes, cooked and mashed
120 ml/4 fl oz (½ cup) milk
15 g/½ oz (1 tablespoon) butter, softened
1 teaspoon sea salt
1 teaspoon caraway seeds
clotted cream, to serve

In my mother's recipe, she added sugar and grated apple. Caraway seeds were a popular seed to add to cakes and bread in Ireland.

Preheat the oven to 200°C/400°F/ Gas Mark 6. Line a baking sheet with baking (parchment) paper.

Combine all the ingredients in a large mixing bowl to form a soft dough.

Turn out the dough onto a lightly floured surface and using a rolling pin roll out to a thickness of

2 cm/¾ inch. Cut into 12–16 rounds with a cookie cutter (whichever size you like, I use between 6–8 cm/ 2½ –3 inch) and place on the lined baking sheet.

Bake the scones in the preheated oven for 12–15 minutes until golden brown. Cool on a wire rack before serving with some clotted cream.

Breads, Scones and Crackers

Sweet Saffron Buns

Preparation: 30 minutes, plus resting and
proving times
Cooking: 15 minutes
Makes 12

10 g/¼ oz (1 teaspoon) packed fresh yeast
  (or if not available, 2.7 g/generous
  ¾ teaspoon fast action dried/active
  dry yeast)
a few saffron strands
250 ml/8 fl oz (1 cup) water, tepid
500 g/1 lb 2 oz (4 cups) plain (all-purpose)
  flour, plus extra for dusting
50 g/2 oz (¼ cup) caster (superfine) sugar
1 teaspoon sea salt
2 eggs, beaten
rapeseed (canola) oil, for greasing
1 egg yolk, beaten with a little salt and
  a pinch of sugar

Saffron was used as a dye by the Celts of Northern Europe from at least as far back as the time of Christ. The great Irish mantle was a type of loose knee-length tunic (*léine croich*) that was normally saffron coloured. Spencer, a writer and poet of the sixteenth century, describes the great Irish mantle as, 'their house, their tent, their couch, their target [shield]'. From about the seventeenth century, the gentry in Ireland stopped wearing tunics and started imitating English dress, except in the west and north-west. However, there was a revival in the eighteenth century, which kept the wearing of the saffron mantle alive. The first reference I could find to saffron in Irish food dates to the late nineteenth century. Saffron buns were popular in Dublin around this time.

Put the yeast, saffron and tepid water into a bowl and mix together to dissolve. Rest for 10 minutes.

Sift the flour, sugar and salt into a large mixing bowl and divide half into a separate mixing bowl.

Combine the yeast and saffron mixture with half the flour until smooth. Cover with a damp cloth and allow to prove (rise) for 30 minutes at room temperature.

Add the whole eggs to the remaining flour and mix until thoroughly combined. Mix the two flour mixtures together and knead for 3–5 minutes until the dough is smooth. Return to the

bowl, cover and leave to prove until doubled in volume, about 45 minutes.

Grease a baking sheet with oil. Turn the dough out onto a lightly floured surface and divide into twelve. Shape into buns, place on the baking sheet, cover and allow to prove until doubled in volume.

Preheat the oven to 200 °C/400 °F/ Gas Mark 6.

Brush the buns with the egg yolk and bake for 10 minutes. Reduce the oven temperature to 180 °C/350 °F/Gas Mark 4 and bake for a further 5 minutes until nicely browned. Cool on a wire rack.

Pancakes

Preparation: 10 minutes, plus 2 hours
chilling time
Cooking: 15–25 minutes
Makes 12

150 g/5 oz (1¼ cups) plain (all-purpose) flour
1 egg, plus 1 egg yolk
300 ml/10 fl oz (1¼ cups) milk
25 g/1 oz (1¾ tablespoons) butter, melted
rapeseed (canola) oil, for frying
sea salt
icing (confectioners') sugar, lemon juice
  or jam (jelly), to serve

Growing up, we always ate pancakes on Shrove Tuesday (or what we called Pancake Tuesday), usually with lemon or jam (jelly). Because a lot of cooking in Ireland was done over an open fire, many different types of pancake recipes exist, from different types of flour to potatoes, buttermilk and eggs. Though less common now, there are older recipes that include alcohol and spices. In *Irish Traditional Cooking* (1995), Darina Allen mentions a recipe from 1717 for pancakes that includes ginger and brandy. My own children love pancakes, so the tradition continues.

Sift the flour and a pinch of salt into a bowl.

Whisk the eggs together in a jug (pitcher) or bowl and add the milk.

Whisk the wet ingredients into the flour, followed by the melted butter. Allow to rest in the refrigerator for 2 hours.

When ready to fry, grease a suitable frying pan (skillet) with oil, place over a medium heat and add 1–2 ladles of the mixture to the pan, depending on the size of the pan. Fry for about 1 minute on each side until golden. Stack the pancakes on top of each other. Repeat until all the batter is used. Serve with sugar, lemon juice or jam (jelly).

Breads, Scones and Crackers

Oat Biscuits

Preparation: 20 minutes, plus chilling time
Cooking: 12 minutes
Makes 12–15

175 g/6 oz (1½ cups) wholemeal
   (whole-wheat) flour, plus extra for dusting
2 teaspoons baking powder
50 g/2 oz (⅓ cup) pinhead (steel-cut) oats
2 tablespoons honey
½ teaspoon salt
100 g/3½ oz (7 tablespoons) cold butter, diced
3½ tablespoons buttermilk
100 g/3½ oz Durrus cheese, to serve

I like to serve these biscuits with Durrus cheese, a soft washed-rind cow's milk cheese made by Jeffa Gill in County Cork. It is one of the oldest farmhouse cheeses in Ireland and is still made by hand.

In a large mixing bowl, combine the flour, baking powder, oats, honey and salt. Rub the diced butter into the flour mix until thoroughly combined. Gradually add the buttermilk until a dough forms. Wrap in cling film (plastic wrap) and refrigerate for 30 minutes.

Preheat the oven to 180°C/350°F/Gas Mark 4. Line a baking sheet with baking (parchment) paper.

On a lightly floured surface, roll out the dough. Cut 12–15 biscuits with a 7.5-cm/3-inch-diameter circular cutter and place the rounds on the baking sheet. Bake in the preheated oven for 10–12 minutes until golden brown.

Allow to cool and serve with wedges of the Durrus cheese.

Linseed Crackers

Preparation: 10 minutes, plus 4 hours
softening time
Cooking: 25 minutes
Serves 8

300 g/11 oz brown linseeds (flaxseed)
½ teaspoon sea salt

Linseeds (flaxseed) have a wide variety of uses, from oil production to edible seeds, flour and fodder for livestock; though it was mostly used to produce linen in Northern Ireland in the eighteenth and nineteenth centuries. Linseed flourished in Northern Europe after being introduced by the Romans. However, there is evidence of linseed production going back to Neolithic times in Europe, and early Irish farmers may have sown linseeds for clothing and food.

Mix the linseeds (flaxseed) with 150 ml/5 fl oz (⅔ cup) of water and the salt in a large mixing bowl and allow to soften for 4 hours.

Preheat the oven to 140°C/275°F/Gas Mark 1. Line a baking sheet with baking (parchment) paper.

Spread the mixture as thinly as possible on the baking paper and bake in the preheated oven for 25 minutes until crisp. Cool the cracker and then break into pieces. Store in an airtight container at room temperature.

Rye and Seaweed Crackers

Preparation: 20 minutes, plus chilling time
Cooking: 40 minutes
Makes about 24

250 g/9 oz (2 cups) plain (all-purpose) flour
150 g/5 oz (1½ cups) rye flour
8 g/¼ oz (2¼ teaspoons) fast action dried
   (active dry) yeast
2 teaspoons milled seaweed, any kind
2 teaspoons salt

These crackers are ideal for serving with cheese.

Combine the ingredients in a bowl with enough cold water to make a soft dough, which should not be sticky. Refrigerate for 3–4 hours.

Preheat the oven to 180°C/350°F/Gas Mark 4 and line a baking sheet with baking (parchment) paper.

Divide the dough into four. On a lightly floured surface, roll out each portion as flat as possible. Cut into strips or circles and bake each batch on the baking sheet in the preheated oven for 5–10 minutes until crispy. Store in an airtight container at room temperature.

Cakes, Pastries, Biscuits and Desserts

Cakes, Pastries, Biscuits and Desserts

'A fine summer evening, music to lift your heart, the dancers gathering at the crossroads and on top of a dash-churn a fine cake, decorated with wild flowers, ringed around whatever fruit was in season.'

Bríd Mahon, *Land of Milk and Honey*, 1991.

As with bread, Ireland has a rich tradition of sweet baking, especially in the home, with apples, blackberries, gooseberries and rhubarb all finding their way into cakes, pastries and other sweet treats. Baking in Ireland was once hyper-seasonal, with the fruit that was to hand influencing the dessert. Cakes, buns and pastries served with summer and autumn (fall) fruit and whipped cream: these are the memories of my grandmother's generation. Her sister's fruit crumble and carrot cake. Then there was my mum's baking: scones, buns and other assorted sweet things. But this was just one aspect of the tradition. With their penchant for spice, the Anglo-Normans created a more worldly dimension to the simple apple pie. Spices such as cinnamon, nutmeg and allspice were all used to create a more sophisticated sense to baking sweet things, if you could afford them. For the well-off, land-owning gentry, desserts with a global flavour were not a problem. In the collection of recipes (1810) by Mrs A. W. Baker from Kilkenny, we find plum cake, seed cake and cheesecake. However, for the poorer peasant class, a simple apple pie made with apple, flour and white sugar would have to suffice. Of course, this has all changed today, but its legacy remains. Cake shops abounded in every town when I was growing up. I used to love going to the Elite coffee shop in Maynooth for a custard slice or an éclair. While these cakes have their origin elsewhere, they are firmly part of the Irish baking tradition. It seems, more so than in Irish savoury dishes, that Irish cakes and desserts demonstrate the outward-looking nature of the Irish people. Perhaps it is the weather that causes us to go in search of exotic spices from the Far East to flavour our own custards and pies! My own preference is to use native wild herbs and flowers in the cakes and pastries. The two I use most are dried meadowsweet and woodruff.

Oatmeal Biscuits

Preparation: 25 minutes, plus chilling time
Cooking: 15 minutes
Makes about 12 biscuits (cookies)

50 g/2 oz (⅓ cup) wholemeal
   (whole-wheat) flour
50 g/2 oz (⅓ cup) plain (all-purpose) flour,
   sifted, plus extra for dusting
125 g/4½ oz (1 stick plus 1 tablespoon) salted
   butter, room temperature
75 g/2¾ oz (¾ cup) rolled oats
50 g/2 oz (¼ cup) caster (superfine) sugar

Put the flours into a medium mixing bowl. Cut up the butter and rub it in with your fingertips until the mixture resembles breadcrumbs. Add the oats and sugar and combine with enough water to form a dough.

Refrigerate for 25 minutes.

Meanwhile, preheat the oven to 160°C/325°F/Gas Mark 3.

Line a baking sheet with baking (parchment) paper.

Roll out the dough on a lightly floured surface. Cut out 12 rounds with a cookie cutter (I use between 6–8 cm/2½ –3 inch) and transfer to the prepared baking sheet. Bake in the preheated oven for 15 minutes or until nicely browned.

Heather and Lavender Shortbread

Preparation: 25 minutes, plus chilling time
Cooking: 20 minutes
Makes about 30 biscuits (cookies)

200 g/7 oz (1¾ sticks) butter
100 g/3½ oz (½ cup) caster (superfine) sugar,
   plus extra for dusting
300 g/11 oz (2⅓ cups) plain (all-purpose)
   flour, plus extra for dusting
1 teaspoon mixed heather and lavender
   flowers (use dried if you can't find fresh)
a pinch of sea salt

Preheat the oven to 190°C/375°F/Gas Mark 5. Line a baking sheet with baking (parchment) paper.

Cream the butter and sugar together in a large mixing bowl. Sift in the flour. Finely chop the flowers and add with the salt. Combine together until a dough forms.

Roll out the dough on a lightly floured surface and cut into about 30 rectangular biscuits (cookies). Prick with a fork and dust with sugar. Transfer to the baking sheet and refrigerate for 20 minutes.

Bake in the preheated oven for 20 minutes or until pale golden brown. Cool on a wire rack.

My Mum's Gingerbread

Preparation: 25 minutes
Cooking: 20 minutes
Makes 8–10 muffins

120 ml/4 fl oz (½ cup) treacle (molasses)
60 g/2¼ oz (4½ tablespoons) butter, plus
   extra for greasing
4 tablespoons buttermilk
2 eggs, beaten
225 g/8 oz self-raising flour (1¾ cups
   all-purpose flour mixed with 2½ teaspoons
   baking powder)
60 g/2¼ oz (⅓ cup) caster (superfine) sugar
60 g/2¼ oz (generous ⅓ cup) sultanas
   (golden raisins)
60 g/2¼ oz (⅔ cup) ground almonds
   (almond meal)
1 teaspoon ground ginger
icing (confectioners') sugar, for dusting

This gingerbread makes a soft, cake-like muffin.

Preheat the oven to 180°C/350°F/Gas Mark 4. Grease the holes in a shallow 8–10-hole Yorkshire pudding or muffin pan.

Put the treacle and butter into a small pan over a medium–low heat and heat for about 3 minutes until melted. Remove from the heat. When cool, mix in the buttermilk and eggs.

Put all the dry ingredients (except the icing sugar) into a large mixing bowl and mix together. Fold the wet ingredients into the dry ingredients.

Fill the prepared pan with the batter and bake in the preheated oven for about 15 minutes until nicely browned. Remove from the oven and dust with icing (confectioners') sugar. Leave to cool in the pan.

Cakes, Pastries, Biscuits and Desserts

Ginger Biscuits

Preparation: 20 minutes, plus chilling time
Cooking: 12 minutes
Makes 12–16 biscuits (cookies)

225 g/8 oz (2 sticks) butter, softened
225 g/8 oz (1 cup firmly packed) brown sugar
450 g/1 lb (3⅔ cups) plain (all-purpose) flour,
   plus extra for dusting
1 tablespoon ground ginger
1 teaspoon salt
2 tablespoons treacle (molasses)
icing (confectioners') sugar, for dusting
   (optional)

Line a baking sheet with baking (parchment) paper.

Cream the sugar and butter together in a large mixing bowl.

Sift the flour, ginger and salt together, then fold into the butter-and-sugar mixture and add enough treacle to make a stiff dough.

Roll out onto a lightly floured surface and cut into 12–16 rounds using a 7-cm/3-inch cookie cutter.

Place the biscuits (cookies) onto the lined baking sheet and refrigerate for 15 minutes before baking.

Meanwhile, preheat the oven to 160°C/325°F/Gas Mark 3.

Bake in the preheated oven for 12 minutes or until firm to touch. Cool on a wire rack.

See opposite –>

Barm Brack

Preparation: 25 minutes, plus overnight soaking and standing time
Cooking: 2 hours
Serves 8

For the fruit mixture
375 ml/13 fl oz (1⅔ cups) black tea
175 g/6 oz (¾ cup firmly packed) soft
   brown sugar
140 g/5 oz (1 cup) sultanas (golden raisins)
140 g/5 oz (1 cup) raisins
25 g/1 oz (¼ cup prepared) lemon peel,
   chopped
25 g/1 oz (¼ cup prepared) orange peel,
   chopped

For the cake
rapeseed (canola) oil, for greasing
350 g/12 oz self-raising flour (2¾ cups
   all-purpose flour mixed with 3¾ teaspoons
   baking powder)
2 teaspoons mixed spice (apple pie spice)
a pinch of salt
1 egg, beaten
honey, for glazing

Barm brack (*bairín breac*) is a cake that is speckled with dried fruit. Before the advent of bicarbonate of soda (baking soda) or baking powder, it would have been made with the 'barm', the froth on fermenting malt liquor for spirits. The bread is sweet but not as sweet as a cake. It is often served with butter and tea.

The bread is associated with Halloween in Ireland. Traditionally, objects (such as a coin, a ring or a pea) would be placed in the bread. The finder of each object would have his fortune told through this object. Nowadays, commercially bought barm brack contains a ring. In *Dubliners* by James Joyce, there is a reference to bram bracks in the story 'Clay':

> The fire was nice and bright and on one of the side-tables were four very big barmbracks. These barmbracks seemed uncut; but if you went closer you would see that they had been cut into long thick even slices and were ready to be handed round at tea.

Warm the tea and sugar in a large pan over a low heat for a few minutes until the sugar dissolves. Add the fruit and peel and remove from the heat. Cover and allow to stand at room temperature overnight.

The following morning, preheat the oven to 160°C/325°F/Gas Mark 3. Grease a large 23-cm/9-inch-diameter cake pan and line it with baking (parchment) paper.

Sift the flour, spice and salt together in a large mixing bowl.

Combine the egg with the tea mixture and fold the wet ingredients into the flour.

Pour the batter into the pan and smooth the top. Bake in the preheated oven for 2 hours or until firm, glazing with a little honey 15 minutes before the end of baking.

Note
In some recipes, this cake was made with yeast. If using yeast, add 5 g/⅛ oz (¾ teaspoon packed) fresh yeast into the cake with regular plain (all-purpose) flour. You'll need to warm a little of the tea mixture to activate the yeast and allow the cake to rise for 1 hour before baking.

Cakes, Pastries, Biscuits and Desserts

Cakes, Pastries, Biscuits and Desserts

Hot Cross Buns

Preparation: 35 minutes, plus resting
and proving time
Cooking: 30 minutes
Makes 12 buns

300 ml/10 fl oz (1¼ cups) milk
1 tablespoon rapeseed (canola) oil
50 g/2 oz (4 tablespoons) butter
grated zest of 1 orange
1 teaspoon ground cinnamon
7 g/¼ oz (1 teaspoon) fresh yeast or 2.7 g
   (heaping ¾ teaspoon) fast action dried
   (active dry) yeast
500 g/1 lb 2 oz (4½ cups) spelt flour,
   plus extra for the crosses and dusting
100 g/3½ oz (⅔ cup) sultanas (golden raisins)
75 g/2¾ oz (⅓ cup firmly packed) soft
   brown sugar
1 egg, beaten
1 teaspoon salt
3½ tablespoons golden (light corn)
   syrup, to glaze

The origin of the hot cross bun goes back to medieval times, at least as far back as the fourteenth century. Seemingly, in 1361, a monk in St Albans developed a recipe called an 'Alban bun' and distributed the bun to the local poor on Good Friday in order to alleviate their suffering. The cross on the bun signified the Crucifixion while the spices in the bun recalled the embalming of Christ. Whether or not this is true, the buns have been associated with Easter and with an end to fasting after Lent ever since. In Ireland, hot cross buns are always available around Easter time. Even though we may have forgotten most of the complex symbolism that comes with them, they are still popular. Indeed, you can find them available throughout the year in certain places.

Put the milk, oil, butter, orange zest and cinnamon into a small pan over a low heat and warm. Cool to hand-hot temperature and crumble in the yeast.

Put the remaining ingredients (except the syrup) into a large mixing bowl and combine. Gradually pour in the milk mixture and combine to form a dough.

Turn the dough out onto a lightly floured surface and knead for 10 minutes. Add more flour if needed.

Return the dough to the bowl, cover with a cloth and allow to prove (rise) for 1 hour or until doubled in size.

Shape the dough into 12 balls. Cover and prove again until doubled in volume, about 30–45 minutes.

Preheat the oven to 180°C/350°F/ Gas Mark 4.

Mix a little spelt flour with water to make a paste. Put into a piping (pastry) bag and pipe a cross on top of each bun. Place in a pan and bake in the preheated oven for 20–25 minutes until golden brown.

Gently warm the golden (light corn) syrup and brush over the warm buns.

See opposite –>

Honey Spelt Cake and Sheep's Yogurt

Preparation: 30 minutes
Cooking: 40 minutes
Serves 8

200 g/7 oz (1¾ sticks) butter, softened
75 g/2¾ oz (⅓ cup firmly packed) soft
   brown sugar
75 g/2¾ oz (¼ cup) honey, plus extra to serve
4 eggs, beaten
300 g/11 oz (2¾ cups) spelt flour
2 teaspoons baking powder
3½ tablespoons sheep's milk

To serve
sheep's yogurt, hung in muslin (cheesecloth)
   to remove excess whey
icing (confectioners') sugar, for dusting

Preheat the oven to 140°C/275°F/ Gas Mark 1. Grease a 23-cm/9-inch-diameter cake pan.

Cream the butter, sugar and honey together in a large mixing bowl and fold in the eggs.

Sift the flour together with the baking powder and fold into the butter-and-sugar mixture. Stir in the milk, beating lightly.

Pour the batter into the prepared cake pan and bake in the preheated oven for 40 minutes until a skewer (toothpick) inserted into the centre of the cake comes out clean. Cool on a wire rack.

When the cake is cool, spread the sheep's yogurt over the top of the cake. Drizzle a little honey over the cake and dust with icing (confectioners') sugar.

Cakes, Pastries, Biscuits and Desserts

Gur Cake

Preparation: 30 minutes, plus chilling time
Cooking: 50 minutes
Makes 36 squares

For the shortcrust pastry
350 g/12 oz (2¾ cups) plain (all-purpose) flour
75 g/2¾ oz (⅓ cup) caster (superfine) sugar
175 g/6 oz (1½ sticks) cold butter, cubed
1 egg, beaten
a pinch of sea salt

For the cake
175 ml/6 fl oz (¾ cup) milk, plus extra
    for brushing
rind of 1 lemon, chopped (or use the zest)
2 eggs, beaten
350 g/12 oz (about 12 slices) leftover cake
    (I use sponge), broken up into small pieces
225 g/8 oz (1 cup firmly packed) muscovado
    (light brown) sugar
225 g/8 oz (1½ cups) raisins
75 g/2¾ oz (⅔ cup) plain (all-purpose)
    flour, plus extra for dusting
50 g/2 oz (4 tablespoons) butter, softened,
    plus extra for greasing
2 tablespoons mixed spice (apple pie spice)
1 teaspoon baking powder
icing (confectioners') sugar,
    for dusting (optional)

Gur cake is an interesting combination of pastry shell filled with a mixture of leftover cake or breadcrumbs with dried fruits and sugar. Originating in Dublin, it is also known as donkey's gudge in Cork, and a similar confection called Chester cake exists in Cheshire, England. The 'gur' in the name probably comes from 'gurrier', which is Irish slang for a ruffian. As a cheap cake made from leftovers, gur cake could be afforded by children skipping school. This led to the terms of 'gurrier' for the skiving children, and being 'on the gur' as the act of doing so. Gur cake is still a common sight around Ireland, being sold in bakeries in characteristic slabs. Depending on how sweet the leftover cake you're using is, you may want to reduce the sugar.

To make the pastry, combine the flour and sugar in a bowl and rub in the butter using your fingertips until the mixture resembles breadcrumbs. Add the egg and a little ice-cold water to form a dough. Rest the dough in the refrigerator for 1 hour.

Preheat the oven to 180°C/350°F/ Gas Mark 4.

Divide the pastry into two pieces and roll it out on a floured surface into two rectangles the same size as a rectangular 34 × 20-cm/13 × 9-inch baking pan. Place one piece of pastry on the base of the pan. Refrigerate the second piece of pastry until needed.

To make the cake, warm the milk with the lemon rind in a small pan over a low heat. Cool slightly and whisk in the eggs. Combine the rest of the ingredients in a large mixing bowl with the milk mixture. Spread the mixture evenly over the pastry in the pan and top with the other piece, tucking in any edges. Brush with a little milk.

Bake in the preheated oven for 45 minutes until the pastry is golden brown and the inside is bubbling. Allow to cool in the pan, then dust with icing (confectioners') sugar if desired and cut into squares or rectangles.

See opposite –>

Spiced Crab Apple Cake

Preparation: 30 minutes
Cooking: 45 minutes
Serves 8

200 g/7 oz (1¾ sticks) butter, softened
200 g/7 oz (1 cup firmly packed) soft
    brown sugar
2 teaspoons mixed spice (apple pie spice)
4 eggs
8 small crab apples
200 g/7 oz self-raising flour (1⅔ cups
    all-purpose flour mixed with 2½ teaspoons
    baking powder), sifted
3½ tablespoons buttermilk
1 teaspoon icing (confectioners') sugar,
    for dusting

Because crab apples are usually quite tart, they work well in a sweet and spicy cake. If you can't find crab apples, use a few large cooking apples.

Preheat the oven to 170°C/340°F/ Gas Mark 3½. Grease a 23-cm/ 9-inch-diameter springform pan.

Cream the sugar with the butter and mixed spice in a food processor or a large mixing bowl. Beat the eggs and add to the creamed butter, then grate the crab apples, add to the mixture and combine. Fold in the flour followed by the buttermilk.

Pour the batter into the prepared pan and bake in the preheated oven for 45 minutes. Allow to cool slightly before turning out of the pan and transferring to a wire rack.

Before serving, dust with the icing (confectioners') sugar.

Seed Cake

Preparation: 25 minutes
Cooking: 45 minutes
Serves 8

175 g/6 oz (1½ sticks) butter, softened
175 g/6 oz (¾ cup plus 2 tablespoons)
  caster (superfine) sugar
3 eggs
2 tablespoons whiskey
2 teaspoons caraway seeds
250 g/9 oz self-raising flour (2 cups
  all-purpose flour mixed with 1 tablespoon
  baking powder), sifted

Dating to the Middle Ages, seed cake is traditionally made with caraway seeds. At one time, caraway seed biscuits (cookies) were prepared to mark the sowing of the spring wheat. References to seed cakes appear in Chaucer's *Canterbury Tales* to Joyce's *Ulysses* (1922). Recipes for seed cake can be found in A. W.'s *A Book of Cookrye* (1591), *The English Huswife* by Gervase Markham (1615), Hannah Glasse's *The Art of Cookery Made Plain and Easy* (1747) and Isabella Beeton's *Book of Household Management* (1861).

Preheat the oven to 180°C/350°F/Gas Mark 4. Grease a 23 × 13 × 7-cm/9 × 5 × 3-inch loaf pan.

Cream the butter and the sugar together in a large mixing bowl. Add in the eggs, one at a time, and beat until combined. Add the whiskey, caraway seeds and flour and fold into the mixture.

Transfer to the prepared loaf pan and bake in the preheated oven for 45 minutes until a skewer (toothpick) inserted into the centre comes out clean. Leave to cool in the pan for 3 minutes and the transfer to a wire rack to cool completely.

See opposite –>

Simnel Cake

Preparation: 40 minutes
Cooking: 3 hours
Serves 10–12

175 g/6 oz (1½ sticks) butter, softened
175 g/6 oz (¾ cup firmly packed) soft
  brown sugar
4 eggs, beaten
225 g/8 oz (1¾ cups) plain (all-purpose)
  flour, sifted
225 g/8 oz (1½ cups) raisins
225 g/8 oz (1½ cups) sultanas (golden raisins)
75 g/2¾ oz (⅓ cup) glacé (candied) cherries
75 g/2¾ oz (scant ½ cup) mixed (candied) peel
50 g/2 oz (⅓ cup) almonds, finely chopped
50 g/2 oz (½ cup) ground almonds
  (almond meal)
grated zest of 1 orange
grated zest of 1 lemon
2 tablespoons whiskey
1 teaspoon mixed spice (apple pie spice)
½ teaspoon ground nutmeg

For the marzipan
450 g/1 lb (4¾ cups) ground almonds
  (almond meal)
225 g/8 oz (1 cup plus 2 tablespoons)
  caster (superfine) sugar
225 g/8 oz (1¾ cups) icing (confectioners')
  sugar, plus extra for dusting
2 eggs, beaten
2 tablespoons whiskey
1 teaspoon almond extract
1 egg white, lightly whisked, for brushing

Simnel cake is a light fruit cake that was traditionally baked and eaten during the pre-Easter period in Ireland. It is iced with marzipan and capped by a circle of eleven balls made of the same paste. These balls represent the eleven apostles. It was originally made for the fourth Sunday in Lent (Simnel Sunday). Traditionally, female servants would bake this fruit cake using all the ingredients that had to be used up before the fast and abstinence of Lent. They would give the cake to their mothers when visiting on this Sunday (also called Mothering Sunday). Darina Allen observes that the cake more than likely entered Ireland in Elizabethan times as a spiced bread and was transformed into a cake over time.

Preheat the oven to 140°C/275°F/Gas Mark 1. Grease and line a 23-cm/9-inch-diameter cake pan.

To make the marzipan, mix all the dry ingredients together in a large mixing bowl. Add the wet ingredients (except the egg white) and fold together to form a paste. Divide the paste into two. On a surface dusted with icing (confectioners') sugar, roll out two rounds from the marzipan, reserving a little for the balls.

To make the cake, cream the butter with the sugar in a mixing bowl and add the eggs a little at a time. Fold in the flour and then rest of the ingredients, mixing until everything is thoroughly combined.

Pour half the cake batter into the prepared pan and top with one of the marzipan rounds. Cover with the remaining cake batter. Bake in the preheated oven for 3 hours, covering the top of the cake if necessary to prevent it burning.

Allow the cake to cool completely. Brush it with a little egg white, then top with the second round of marzipan. Roll the reserved paste into eleven balls. Stick them to the top of the cake with additional egg white. Brown the top of the cake under a hot grill (broiler) or with a chef's blowtorch.

Cakes, Pastries, Biscuits and Desserts

Cakes, Pastries, Biscuits and Desserts

Coffee Cake

Preparation: 40 minutes
Cooking: 25 minutes
Serves 12

250 g/9 oz self-raising flour (2 cups
  all-purpose flour mixed with 1 tablespoon
  baking powder)
2 tablespoons (unsweetened) cocoa powder
a pinch of sea salt
250 g/9 oz (2¼ sticks) butter, softened,
  plus extra for greasing
250 g/9 oz (1 cup plus 2 tablespoons firmly
  packed) soft brown sugar
5 eggs, beaten
2 tablespoons coffee essence

For the icing
175 g/6 oz (1½ sticks) unsalted butter,
  softened
2 tablespoons coffee essence
350 g/12 oz (2¾ cups) icing
  (confectioners') sugar

To decorate
a few whole walnuts, roasted and cracked
  in half or pieces
roasted coffee beans

My great-aunt Betty always seemed to have a coffee cake to hand whenever we visited her in Bray, County Wicklow. A slice of coffee cake always takes me back there.

Preheat the oven to 180°C/350°F/ Gas Mark 4. Grease two 30-cm/ 12-inch-diameter cake pans.

Sift the flour, cocoa powder and salt together into a large mixing bowl.

In a separate mixing bowl, cream the butter with the sugar, then gradually add the eggs and the coffee essence.

Fold the wet mixture into the flour mixture. Divide the batter evenly between the two prepared cake pans and bake in the preheated oven for 25 minutes until a skewer (toothpick) inserted into the centre of the cakes comes out clean.

Remove from the oven and when cool enough to handle, turn out and cool further on a wire rack.

To make the icing (frosting), cream the butter with the coffee essence in a bowl and gradually fold in the sugar.

When the cakes are cold, sandwich them together with some of the icing. Spread the rest of the icing over the top (and sides if desired). Garnish with some walnuts and coffee beans.

See opposite –>

Porter Cake

Preparation: 40 minutes
Cooking: 50 minutes
Serves 12

450 g/1 lb (3 cups) raisins
zest and juice of 2 oranges
350 ml/12 fl oz (1½ cups) stout,
  3½ tablespoons reserved to pour on
  top of cake
225 g/8 oz (2 sticks) butter, softened,
  plus extra for greasing
225 g/8 oz (1 cup firmly packed) light
  soft brown sugar
3 eggs
500 g/1 lb 2 oz (4 cups) plain (all-purpose)
  flour, sifted
1 teaspoon baking powder
1 teaspoon ground nutmeg
2 teaspoons mixed spice (apple pie spice)
a pinch of sea salt

Though stout was produced in Ireland before Guinness began brewing in Dublin in 1759, the drink was always associated with the 'working man'. This cake has long been made with Guinness, but with the growth of the craft beer industry, there are many more Irish stouts on the menu. Chocolate stouts would give the cake a beautiful flavour. Galway Bay Brewery's Buried at Sea is a milk chocolate stout which is great in baking.

Preheat the oven to 160°C/325°F/ Gas Mark 3. Grease a 23-cm/9-inch diameter cake pan.

Soak the raisins in the orange juice and stout in a medium pan. After 30 minutes, bring the mixture to the boil and remove from the heat. Allow to cool.

Cream the butter with the sugar in a bowl. Gradually add the eggs and beat together until combined.

Sift the flour, baking powder, nutmeg, mixed spice (apple pie spice) and salt into the bowl.

Fold the dry ingredients into the sugar-and-egg mixture. Add the raisins and their cooking liquid and mix to form a batter.

Pour the cake batter into the pan and bake in the preheated oven for about 50 minutes, or until the core temperature of the cake is greater than 85°C/185°F on a meat thermometer.

Remove the cake from the oven, prick with a skewer and pour over the reserved stout.

Cakes, Pastries, Biscuits and Desserts

My Aunty Peg's Carrot Cake

Preparation: 25 minutes
Cooking: 45 minutes
Serves 10–12

300 g/11 oz (2⅓ cups) plain (all-purpose)
   flour, sifted
350 g/12 oz (1½ cups firmly packed) soft
   brown sugar
300 g/11 oz (2¾ cups prepared) carrots,
   peeled and grated
75 g/2¾ oz (½ cup) raisins
100 g/3½ oz (generous ¾ cup) walnuts,
   crushed
2 teaspoons baking powder
1 teaspoon ground cinnamon
½ teaspoon ground ginger
½ teaspoon ground nutmeg
1 teaspoon sea salt
4 eggs, beaten
300 ml/10 fl oz (1¼ cups) rapeseed
   (canola) oil

For the icing
250 g/9 oz (1 cup) cream cheese
150 g/5 oz (¼ cup) icing (confectioners') sugar
85 g/3 oz (6 tablespoons) unsalted butter,
   softened, plus extra for greasing
60 g/2¼ oz (½ cup) walnuts, roasted, to garnish

After coffee cake, carrot cake was probably the first cake I ever ate. It was a staple of my childhood. Although part of many European cuisines (even the Italians have one!), the combination of carrots, walnuts and cinnamon (another Eastern spice) is distinctly Irish. In our café Tartare, we make one without spices and dried fruit and flavour it with dried woodruff.

Preheat the oven to 160°C/325°F/ Gas Mark 3 and grease a Bundt cake pan or fluted ring (tube) pan.

Put all the dry ingredients into a large mixing bowl and mix together.

Combine the eggs and oil in a jug (pitcher) or small bowl. Gradually fold the wet ingredients into the dry ingredients.

Pour the batter into the prepared pan and bake in the oven for 45 minutes until firm. Remove from the oven and allow to cool, then transfer to a wire rack.

To make the icing (frosting), combine the sugar, cream cheese and butter and whip together. Ice the top of the cake and grate the walnuts over the cake (or leave them whole).

Strawberry and Rhubarb Tart

Preparation: 30 minutes, plus chilling time
Cooking: 45 minutes
Serves 8

For the pastry
400 g/14 oz (3¼ cups) plain (all-purpose)
   flour, sifted, plus extra for dusting
250 g/9 oz (2¼ sticks) butter, cubed,
   plus extra for greasing
50 g/2 oz (¼ cup) caster (superfine) sugar,
   plus extra for sprinkling
a pinch of sea salt
2 eggs

For the filling
350 g/12 oz (3 cups prepared) rhubarb,
   cut into small pieces
350 g/12 oz (2⅓ cups prepared) strawberries,
   hulled and halved
150 g/5 oz (¾ cup) caster (superfine) sugar
½ teaspoon ground ginger
juice of 1 lemon
freshly whipped cream or ice cream, to serve

Many other fruits can be used in this tart, such as blackberries, damsons (wild plums) or gooseberries.

To make the pastry, put the butter and flour into a large mixing bowl and rub together using your fingertips until the mixture resembles breadcrumbs. Add the sugar and salt and combine. Beat one of the eggs with a little ice-cold water and add to the bowl, then combine to bring the dough together. Wrap the dough in cling film (plastic wrap) and refrigerate for at least 1 hour.

Meanwhile, for the filling, combine the rhubarb, strawberries, sugar, ginger and lemon juice in a large mixing bowl.

Preheat the oven to 170°C/340°F/ Gas Mark 3½.

Divide the pastry into two and on a floured surface, roll into two rounds big enough to accommodate your pie dish using a rolling pin. Grease a 23-cm/9-inch-diameter pie dish and line with the pastry. Fill with the fruit mixture and top with the lid. Crimp the edges with your fingers. Beat the second egg and brush it over the lid, then sprinkle with sugar. Make a few slits in the pastry to allow steam to escape.

Bake in the preheated oven for about 45 minutes until golden brown. Sprinkle with sugar and serve with freshly whipped cream or ice cream.

See opposite –>

Cakes, Pastries, Biscuits and Desserts

Cakes, Pastries, Biscuits and Desserts

Apple and Hazelnut Tart

Preparation: 45 minutes, plus chilling time
Cooking: 55 minutes
Serves 8

1 kg/2¼ lb (about 7) cooking apples
90 g/3¼ oz (⅓ cup plus 1 tablespoon packed)
    soft brown sugar
100 g/3½ oz (¾ cup) hazelnuts, roasted

For the shortcrust pastry
250 g/9 oz (2 cups) plain (all-purpose) flour,
    sifted, plus extra for dusting
125 g/4½ oz (1 stick plus 1 tablespoon) cold
    butter, cubed, plus extra for greasing
a pinch of sea salt

For the crumble
200 g/7 oz (1⅔ cups) plain (all-purpose) flour
100 g/3½ oz (½ cup) caster (superfine) sugar
75 g/2¾ oz (5½ tablespoons) cold butter, cubed
1¾ tablespoons hazelnut oil (optional)

For the pastry, put the flour and butter into a large mixing bowl. Rub together with your fingertips until the mixture resembles coarse breadcrumbs. Add the salt and a little ice-cold water to bring the dough together. Do not overwork. Wrap in cling film (plastic wrap) and refrigerate for 30 minutes.

Meanwhile, to make the crumble topping, combine the flour and sugar with the butter and hazelnut oil (if using) in a large bowl and use your fingertips to make crumbles.

For the filling, peel and core the apples and cut into small wedges. Melt the sugar with 2 tablespoons of water in a medium pan over a medium–low heat, then add the apples. Cook for 1–2 minutes until the sugar coats the apples. Remove from the heat and allow to cool. Fold in the hazelnuts.

Grease a 23-cm/9-inch-diameter tart pan.

Roll out the pastry on a lightly floured surface until it is slightly bigger than the tart pan. Drape the pastry over the rolling pin and lay it across the pan. Press the dough into the corners of the pan using your fingers. Trim off the edges. Chill for 30 minutes.

Preheat the oven to 170°C/340°F/Gas Mark 3½.

Line the pastry case (shell) with a round of baking (parchment) paper and add baking beans (pie weights) or dried beans to weigh it down. Blind bake in the preheated oven for 15 minutes. Carefully remove the paper and weights and cook the pastry for a further 5 minutes.

Add the apple filling to the pastry shell and cover evenly with the crumble mixture. Bake for 30 minutes until the crumble mixture is golden brown. Remove from the oven.

Buttermilk and Elderflower Tart

Preparation: 45 minutes, plus chilling time
Cooking: 45 minutes
Serves 10

For the pastry
300 g/11 oz (2⅓ cups) plain (all-purpose)
    flour, sifted, plus extra for dusting
50 g/2 oz (⅓ cup) icing (confectioners') sugar
175 g/6 oz (1½ sticks) cold butter, cubed,
    plus extra for greasing
a pinch of sea salt
2 egg yolks

For the filling
200 ml/7 fl oz (scant 1 cup) buttermilk
200 ml/7 fl oz (scant 1 cup) double
    (heavy) cream
25 g/1 oz (¼ cup) plain (all-purpose) flour
6 eggs, beaten
75 g/3½ oz (½ cup) caster (superfine) sugar
100 g/3½ oz (7 tablespoons) butter, melted
3 tablespoons Elderflower Cordial
    (see page 390, or use shop-bought)
fresh elderflowers, to garnish

For the pastry, put the flour, sugar, butter and salt into a large mixing bowl. Rub together with your fingertips until the mixture resembles coarse breadcrumbs. Add the egg yolks and a little ice-cold water to bring the dough together. Do not overwork. Wrap in cling film (plastic wrap) and refrigerate for 1 hour.

Grease a 30-cm/12-inch-diameter loose-bottom fluted tart pan. Roll out the dough on a lightly floured surface. Line the prepared pan with the pastry and refrigerate for a further 1 hour. It's important that the pastry is cold when baking.

Preheat the oven to 160°C/325°F/Gas Mark 3.

Line the pastry case (shell) with a round of baking (parchment) paper and fill with baking beans (pie weights) or dried beans. Blind bake in the preheated oven for 20 minutes. Remove the weights and paper and return the pastry to the oven for a further 5 minutes.

Increase the oven temperature to 170°C/340°F/Gas Mark 3½.

To make the filling, blend all the ingredients together in a food processor and strain through a strainer. Remove any foam that remains on top. Place the tart shell on the baking sheet and pour the custard mixture into the tart shell and bake in the preheated oven for 25 minutes. There should still be a little wobble in the tart. Remove from the oven and cool for 1 hour, then garnish with some fresh elderflowers.

See opposite –>

Cakes, Pastries, Biscuits and Desserts

Apple Custard Pie

Preparation: 30 minutes, plus chilling time
Cooking: 35 minutes
Serves 8

For the pastry

400 g/14 oz (3¼ cups) plain (all-purpose)
  flour, plus extra for dusting
250 g/9 oz (2¼ sticks) butter, cubed,
  plus extra for greasing
50 g/2 oz (¼ cup) caster (superfine) sugar
a pinch of sea salt
1 egg, beaten

For the filling

750 g/1 lb 10 oz (7 medium) crisp apples,
  peeled, cored and sliced
2 tablespoons apple syrup (or use honey or
  maple syrup)
1 tablespoon whiskey

For the custard

250 ml/8 fl oz (1 cup) double (heavy) cream
2 eggs, plus 2 egg yolks
50 g/2 oz (4 tablespoons) butter
75 g/2¾ oz (⅓ cup) caster (superfine) sugar
freshly grated nutmeg, to taste
a pinch of sea salt

To make the pastry, sift the flour into a large mixing bowl, rub the butter into the flour using your fingertips and add the sugar and salt. Add the beaten egg and a little ice-cold water to bring the dough together. Wrap the dough in cling film (plastic wrap) and chill in the refrigerator for at least 1 hour.

Meanwhile, preheat the oven to 170°C/340°F/Gas Mark 3½. Grease a 23-cm/9-inch-diameter pie dish.

For the filling, put the apples with the syrup and whiskey into a medium pan over a medium–low heat and simmer for about 3 minutes until the apples are soft. Cool a little before filling the pie.

For the custard, blend the cream with the eggs, egg yolks, butter, sugar and nutmeg in a blender or food processor.

Roll out half the pastry dough for the base of the pie on a floured surface (you can freeze the other half). Lay the pastry in the preared pie dish. Tidy up the edges.

Add the apple mixture to the dish and pour the custard over the apples. Bake in the preheated oven for about 30 minutes until the custard is set.

See opposite –>

Upside Down Rhubarb and Ginger Cake

Preparation: 15 minutes
Cooking: 40 minutes
Serves 8

For the fruit

150 g/5 oz (¾ cup) caster (superfine) sugar
150 g/5 oz (1¼ sticks) butter, diced
2 tablespoons ginger syrup (from a jar of
  stem ginger, or make your own – see Note)
900 g/2 lb rhubarb, trimmed and cut
  into batons

For the cake batter

6 eggs
300 g/11 oz (2½ sticks) butter, softened
300 g/11 oz (1½ cups) caster (superfine) sugar
300 g/11 oz (1½ cups) plain (all-purpose) flour
2 teaspoons baking powder
2 teaspoons ground ginger

Preheat the oven to 180°C/350°F/Gas Mark 4.

Melt the sugar in an ovenproof cast-iron pan over a medium heat for about 10 minutes until it has caramelized. Remove the pan from the heat and stir in the butter and then the syrup. Arrange the rhubarb in the caramel.

Place all the cake ingredients into a food processor and blend into a batter. Alternatively, cream the butter with the sugar in a large mixing bowl, then add the flour, baking powder and ginger and fold in until combined.

Pour the batter over the rhubarb and caramel. Bake in the preheated oven for 30 minutes or until the cake is firm to touch. Allow the cake to cool for a minute or two before turning out. Don't wait too long because the sugar will cool and stick to the pan.

Note

To make a homemade coriander and ginger syrup, combine 250 ml/8 fl oz (1 cup) of water, 250 g/9 oz (1¼ cups) caster (superfine) sugar, 10 g/¼ oz peeled root ginger and 1 teaspoon of coriander seeds in a pan. Bring to the boil, simmer for 15 minutes and then cool.

Cakes, Pastries, Biscuits and Desserts

Cakes, Pastries, Biscuits and Desserts

My Great-aunt Kay's Fruit Crumble

Preparation: 15 minutes
Cooking: 35 minutes
Serves 4

500 g/1 lb 2 oz prepared fruit (about 4 cups)
  such as apple, rhubarb, plums or blackberries
100 g/3½ oz (½ cup) caster (superfine) sugar
150 g/5 oz self-raising flour (1¼ cups
  all-purpose flour mixed with 1¾ teaspoons
  baking powder)
75 g/2¾ oz (5½ tablespoons) butter

This is a fruit crumble (crisp) from my great-aunt Kay Clinch, who was born in the 1920s. It doesn't specify the fruit, so use whatever is in season. The only change I made was to use butter instead of margarine. My aunty Anne made this crumble many times and testifies to its deliciousness!

Preheat the oven to 180°C/350°F/ Gas Mark 4.

Coat the fruit with half the sugar and place in an ovenproof dish.

To make the crumble (crumb topping), rub the flour and butter together with your fingertips until the mixture resembles breadcrumbs. Fold in the rest of the sugar.

Cover the fruit with the crumble and bake in the preheated oven for 35 minutes until golden brown.

See opposite –>

Elderflower Custard and Hazelnut Crumble

Preparation: 40 minutes
Cooking: 2 hours 35 minutes
Serves 4

For the meringue
6 egg whites
325 g/11½ oz (1⅔ cups) caster (superfine) sugar
2 tablespoons Elderflower Cordial
  (see page 390, or use shop-bought)

For the custard
500 ml/17 fl oz (generous 2 cups) cream
3½ tablespoons Elderflower Cordial
  (see page 390) or use shop-bought
75 g/2¾ oz (⅓ cup) caster (superfine) sugar
3 egg yolks
1 leaf (sheet) gelatine

For the crumble
250 g/9 oz (2 cups) plain (all-purpose) flour
125 g/4½ oz (1 stick plus 1 tablespoon) butter
60 g/2¼ oz (⅓ cup) caster (superfine) sugar
60 g/2¼ oz (½ cup) hazelnuts, ground

For the meringue, preheat the oven to 110°C/225°F/Gas Mark ¼.

Whip the egg whites until soft peaks form. Gradually add the sugar, whisking constantly, until stiff, then finish by whisking in the elderflower cordial. Pipe the meringue or spread out flat onto silicone mats and bake in the pre-heated oven for about 2 hours until completely dried out. Alternatively, dry at 67°C/153°F in a dehydrator until firm.

Meanwhile, to make the custard, soak the gelatine in cold water for about 5 minutes until soft. Pour the cream and elderflower cordial into a small pan over a medium heat and bring to the boil.

Whisk together the egg yolks and sugar in a medium mixing bowl. Pour the cream over the egg mixture, whisking and adding gradually to avoid cooking the egg. Add the softened gelatine (squeezed of excess water) to the cream and whisk until incorporated.

Pour the custard into four ramekins or other suitable individual containers and chill.

For the crumble (crumb topping), preheat the oven to 180°C/350°F/ Gas Mark 4.

Rub the flour into the butter in a mixing bowl using your fingertips until the mixture resembles fine breadcrumbs. Mix in the sugar and ground hazelnuts. Transfer to a baking pan and bake in the preheated oven for 20–25 minutes until golden brown. Allow to cool.

When ready to assemble, remove the custard from the refrigerator 20 minutes before serving. Sprinkle a generous amount of crumble over the custard. Decorate with the meringue.

Cakes, Pastries, Biscuits and Desserts

Cakes, Pastries, Biscuits and Desserts

Plum and Cinnamon Roly-poly

Preparation: 25 minutes
Cooking: 35 minutes
Serves 6

125 g/4½ oz (generous ⅓ cup) Plum and Cinnamon Jam (see page 364)
whipped cream or custard, to serve

For the pastry
250 g/9 oz self-raising flour (2 cups all-purpose flour mixed with 1 tablespoon baking powder), plus extra for dusting
a pinch of sea salt
50 g/2 oz (4 tablespoons) butter, plus a little extra for greasing
50 g/2 oz (¼ cup) suet (available from butchers), chopped
150 ml/5 fl oz (⅔ cup) milk
1 teaspoon vanilla extract

Although jam roly-poly is a traditional British pudding, it appeared in many menus of 'big house' cooking in the nineteenth and twentieth centuries. It is a flat-rolled suet pudding, which is spread with jam and rolled up, then steamed or baked. Nowadays it is usually no longer made with suet. For a vegetarian version, replace the suet with vegetable fat (vegetable shortening).

Preheat the oven to 180°C/350°F/Gas Mark 4. Line a sheet of aluminium foil with greaseproof (wax) paper.

Put the flour, salt, butter and suet into a mixing bowl and rub together using your fingertips until the mixture is sandy. Add the milk and vanilla extract to form a dough.

Turn the dough out onto a floured surface and roll into a rectangle. Spread the jam over the dough, leaving a gap at the edges. Roll the dough and lift onto the greaseproof paper. Bring up the sides of the paper and foil to wrap the pastry and seal the edges.

Put an ovenproof dish on the bottom shelf of the preheated oven and then carefully fill it with boiling water. Place the roly-poly on a wire rack directly over the steaming water and bake for 35 minutes.

Once done, remove from the oven, unwrap and transfer to a plate. Serve warm, with lightly whipped cream or custard.

See opposite –>

Pavlova with Whiskey Caramel and Cream

Preparation: 20 minutes
Cooking: 2 hours, plus overnight drying time
Serves 8

6 egg whites
325 g/11½ oz (1⅔ cups) caster (superfine) sugar
1 teaspoon cornflour (cornstarch)
1 teaspoon white wine vinegar
250 ml/8 fl oz (1 cup) double (heavy) cream, to serve

For the whiskey caramel
100 g/3½ oz (½ cup) granulated sugar
2 tablespoons whiskey
2 tablespoons apple treacle (molasses)
25 g/1 oz (1¾ tablespoons) unsalted butter
80 ml/2¾ fl oz (⅓ cup) double (heavy) cream

Preheat the oven to 120°C/250°F/Gas Mark 2. Line two baking sheets with baking (parchment) paper.

For the pavlova, whisk the egg whites in a stand mixer fitted with the whisk attachment or a hand-held electric whisk until soft peaks form. Add the sugar, one spoon at a time, until it is all incorporated. Fold in the cornflour (cornstarch) and then the vinegar.

Create two meringue nests on the prepared baking sheets. Bake in the preheated oven for 2 hours, then turn off the oven and allow the meringue to dry out overnight.

To make the caramel, put the sugar, whiskey and treacle into a medium pan over a medium–low heat and heat for about 10 minutes until the sugar caramelizes. Remove from the heat and add the butter and then the cream, whisking until smooth.

To assemble, whip the cream. Spread the cream and most of the caramel over the base of one of the meringue nests and top with the other. Drizzle the top with the remaining caramel.

Cakes, Pastries, Biscuits and Desserts

Cakes, Pastries, Biscuits and Desserts

Sherry Trifle

Preparation: 30 minutes, plus 4 hours
30 minutes chilling time
Cooking: 5 minutes
Serves 8

1 × 135-g/4¾-oz package of raspberry
  jelly (Jell-O)
1 × 250-g/9-oz sponge cake (homemade
  or shop-bought)
150 g/5 oz (1 cup) strawberries, hulled and
  quartered or sliced, depending on their size
150 g/5 oz (1¼ cups) raspberries
75 ml/2½ fl oz (⅓ cup) Pedro Ximénez sherry
600 ml/20 fl oz (2½ cups) freshly made
  custard (see Warm Plums and Rose Custard,
  page 342, but omit the rose water), or use
  pre-made
450 ml/15 fl oz (scant 2 cups) double
  (heavy) cream, whipped

Every Christmas, my mother would make a sherry trifle. I think she always used pre-purchased sponge, a package of jelly (Jell-O) and Bird's brand custard. You can make your own sponge cake and your own custard or follow my mother's route. Come to think of it, I can't recall if she put sherry in – omit it if you'll be serving this to children. I do remember fruit cocktail in the pudding, which I didn't particularly like. In this recipe, I use strawberries and raspberries, but any canned fruit can be used.

Empty the jelly (Jell-O) into a heatproof bowl, pour over 600 ml/20 fl oz (2½ cups) of boiling water, and allow to stand for 2 minutes until dissolved. Alternatively, prepare according to package directions.

Place the sponge in the bottom of a large bowl with the fruit and sherry. Pour over the jelly and refrigerate for about 4 hours until set.

When set, pour the custard over the jelly, cover with cling film (plastic wrap) in contact with the custard (to prevent a skin forming) and refrigerate again for at least 30 minutes until set.

Before serving, cover the custard with the whipped cream.

Bread and Butter Pudding

Preparation: 25 minutes
Cooking: 30 minutes
Serves 6

1¾ tablespoons milk
250 ml/8 fl oz (1 cup) double (heavy) cream
1 teaspoon ground cinnamon
freshly grated nutmeg, to taste
3 eggs
75 g/2¾ oz (⅓ cup) caster (superfine) sugar
50 g/2 oz (4 tablespoons) butter, plus extra
  for greasing
10 slices of soft white bread
75 g/2¾ oz (½ cup) sultanas (golden raisins)
icing (confectioners') sugar, for dusting

One of the earliest published recipes for a bread and butter pudding is found in Eliza Smith's *The Compleat Housewife* (1727). Originally, bread and butter pudding was a way of using up leftover bread to make a warm and comforting dessert. The earliest bread and butter puddings used bone marrow and were often made with rice instead of bread, giving rise to the rice pudding in British and Irish cuisine. Many contemporary versions add whiskey for a more decadent touch. It is usually served with custard or a butterscotch sauce. However, despite its humble origins and simplicity of touch, bread and butter pudding will always hold a place in the Irish person's imagination when it comes to desserts. The recipe below serves six but I like to double the ingredients sometimes, as many will go back for a second helping.

Grease an ovenproof dish.

Put the milk and cream into a small pan over a medium heat and add the cinnamon and nutmeg. Bring to the boil, then remove from the heat.

Whisk the eggs with the sugar in a mixing bowl and pour the mixture over the cream. Stir to combine.

Butter the bread on both sides and lay the slices in the prepared dish, in layers with the sultanas (golden raisins). Pour the custard over the bread and allow to stand for 30 minutes.

Preheat the oven to 180°C/350°F/ Gas Mark 4.

Bake the pudding in the preheated oven for 25 minutes, until golden brown and the custard has set. Before serving, dust with a little icing (confectioners') sugar.

See opposite –>

Cakes, Pastries, Biscuits and Desserts

Cakes, Pastries, Biscuits and Desserts

Steamed Treacle Pudding

Preparation: 30 minutes
Cooking: 1 hour 30 minutes
Serves 8

175 g/6 oz (1½ sticks) butter, softened,
   plus extra for greasing
175 g/6 oz (¾ cup plus 2 tablespoons)
   caster (superfine) sugar
grated zest of 1 lemon
3 eggs, beaten
3 tablespoons whiskey
3 tablespoons treacle (molasses)
3½ tablespoons milk
175 g/6 oz self-raising flour (1⅓ cups
   all-purpose flour mixed with 2 teaspoons
   baking powder), sifted
a pinch of sea salt
whipped cream, to serve

Steamed puddings were very popular in Ireland. This one is made with treacle. I've used butter, but you can use beef suet instead, if desired.

Grease a pudding basin or bowl with a lip around its rim. Cut a double layer of greaseproof (wax) paper 5 cm/2 inches larger than the dish and make a pleat in the centre. Grease the paper. Cut a piece of aluminium foil to the same size. Cut a length of string to four times the dish's circumference.

Fill a large pan halfway with water, place a trivet or upturned heatproof saucer in the bottom and bring the water to the boil.

Cream the sugar and butter together in a large mixing bowl with the lemon zest. Add the beaten eggs, whiskey, treacle and milk and mix. Fold the wet ingredients into the dry ingredients.

Pour the batter into the greased dish, leaving a 2.5-cm/1-inch space below the rim. Cover with the greaseproof paper, butter side down, followed by the foil. Tie the string below the protruding rim of the dish, then make a loop to form a handle. Trim the paper just under the string and wrap the foil over it.

Use the handle to lower the pudding into the boiling water, cover and steam for 1 hour 30 minutes until cooked and a skewer (toothpick) inserted into the centre comes out clean. Top up with more water as necessary.

Serve with whipped cream.

See opposite –>

Plum Puddings with Brandy Sauce

Preparation: 40 minutes, plus soaking time
Cooking: 5 hours 15 minutes
Serves 8

450 g/1 lb (3⅔ cups) plain (all-purpose) flour
340 g/12 oz (1½ cups firmly packed) soft
   brown sugar
680 g/1½ lb (3⅓ cups) beef suet, chopped
340 g/12 oz (2 cups) raisins
340 g/12 oz (2 cups) dried currants
225 g/8 oz (1¼ cups) mixed (candied) peel
grated zest of 2 lemons
1 tablespoon mixed spice (apple pie spice)
1 teaspoon sea salt
4 eggs, beaten
350 ml/12 fl oz (1½ cups) milk
175 ml/6 fl oz (¾ cup) brandy

For the brandy sauce
55 g/2 oz (4 tablespoons) butter
55 g/2 oz (scant ½ cup) plain
   (all-purpose) flour
550 ml/18 fl oz (2½ cups) milk
4 tablespoons brandy or dark rum
55 g/2 oz (¼ cup) caster (superfine) sugar

According to Florence Irwin, this pudding should be made a month before Christmas. This allows the flavours of the cake and the alcohol to merge and develop. You can keep it moist by pouring brandy or whiskey over it once or twice a week. Though the tradition of making Christmas pudding had waned in the last few decades, it seems younger people are taking up the mantle again.

Mix all the dry ingredients together in a large mixing bowl. Make a well in the centre of the dry ingredients, add the wet ingredients and mix together. Leave to soak at room temperature for 1 hour.

Prepare eight 175-ml/6-fl-oz (¾-cup) pudding basins and a pan of water for steaming (see above). Pour the mixture into the greased basins and cover. Steam for 5 hours.

To make the sauce, melt the butter in a medium pan over a medium heat, stir in the flour and cook for 2 minutes to make a paste. Gradually add the milk, bring to the boil and simmer for about 10 minutes. Stir in the brandy and sugar and serve with the puddings.

Cakes, Pastries, Biscuits and Desserts

Cakes, Pastries, Biscuits and Desserts

Carrageen Moss Pudding

Preparation: 15 minutes, plus chilling time
Cooking: 15 minutes
Serves 8

15 g/½ oz (3 tablespoons) fresh carrageen
   (or 2 teaspoons dried)
1 litre/34 fl oz (4¼ cups) milk
2 egg yolks
3½ tablespoons honey, plus extra to serve
bee pollen, to serve (optional)

This famous seaweed pudding has appeared in many Irish cookbooks and on many Irish restaurant menus of the twentieth century, if not before. It is a variation of the classic blancmange, which was made with gelatin instead of carrageen. Most recipes use sugar, but I prefer to sweeten the pudding with honey. The recipes that Florence Irwin includes in her book *The Cookin' Woman* (1949) originates in Tory Island and South Donegal. Both include lemon zest to flavour. You can include it (or orange zest) if desired. Other recipes include whiskey, brandy and cinnamon. Serve with fresh seasonal fruit or with a little bee pollen.

Wash the carrageen if using fresh or rehydrate if using dried, following the package directions.

Heat the milk with the carrageen in a medium pan over a medium–low heat.

Beat the egg yolks and honey together in a small bowl, then pour the egg mixture into the milk and stir for about 10 minutes until it thickens.

Pour into moulds or bowls and refrigerate for a few hours until set.

To serve, drizzle with a little extra honey and sprinkle over some bee pollen, if using.

See opposite –>

Burnt Cream with Orange and Lemon

Preparation: 15 minutes, plus chilling time
Cooking: 15 minutes
Serves 6

1 litre/34 fl oz (4¼ cups) double
   (heavy) cream
2 cinnamon sticks
grated zest of 1 orange
zest of 1 lemon
6 egg yolks, beaten
100 g/3½ oz (½ cup) caster (superfine) sugar
50 g/2 oz (¼ cup packed) soft brown sugar,
   for dusting

In 2008, we opened a tapas bar called Cava in Galway City. One of the most popular desserts we serve is crèma Catalana, which is a Spanish version of the French crème brûlée. I was surprised to see an Irish version of 'burnt cream' in Darina Allen's *Irish Traditional Cooking*. She says the recipe came from the recipe book of Mrs Dot Drew of Mocollop Castle near Ballyduff in County Waterford. I also came across a recipe for set orange cream in an eighteenth-century manuscript. In homage to these recipes (and to the ways in which food flavours travel) I include our own version of the Irish/Spanish dessert that we serve in our Spanish Restaurant.

Put the cream, cinnamon and orange and lemon zests into a large pan over a medium heat, bring to the boil, then remove from the heat.

Whisk the eggs with the sugar in a large heatproof bowl. Pour the cream over the eggs, whisking all the time until it starts to thicken. Place the bowl over a pan of simmering water and stir for about 10 minutes until thick.

Pour into six ramekins and refrigerate for at least 1 hour until set and completely cold.

Before serving, dust with the brown sugar and caramelize for about 2 minutes under a hot grill or with a chef's blowtorch.

Cakes, Pastries, Biscuits and Desserts

339   Cakes, Pastries, Biscuits and Desserts

Rice Pudding

Preparation: 10 minutes
Cooking: 15 minutes
Serves 4

200 g/7 oz (1 cup) pudding (short-grain) rice
1 litre/34 fl oz (4¼ cups) milk
100 g/3½ oz (½ cup firmly packed) soft
    brown sugar, plus extra for sprinkling
2 cinnamon sticks
grated zest of 1 orange
50 g/2 oz (4 tablespoons) butter, cubed
1 teaspoon ground cinnamon

Put the rice into a large pan with the milk, sugar, cinnamon sticks and orange zest. Bring to the boil, then reduce the heat and simmer for 10–12 minutes, or according to the package directions, until the rice is tender.

Remove from the heat and whip in the butter. Pour into serving bowls and sprinkle with sugar and cinnamon.

Peach Creams

Preparation: 40 minutes
Cooking: 2 hours
Serves 6

For the meringue
6 egg whites
325 g/11½ oz (1⅔ cups) caster
    (superfine) sugar
grated zest and juice of 1 lemon

For the peaches
500 g/1 lb 2 oz (2½ cups) caster (superfine) sugar
1 cinnamon stick
1 teaspoon vanilla extract
6 peaches, a cross cut into the base of each one

To serve
300 ml/10 fl oz (1¼ cups) double
    (heavy) cream, whipped
fresh mint leaves

For the meringue, preheat the oven to 110°C/225°F/Gas Mark ¼.

Whisk the egg whites in a stand mixer fitted with the whisk attach-ment or a hand-held electric whisk until soft peaks form. Gradually add the sugar, whisking constantly, until stiff, then finish by whisking in the lemon juice and zest. Pipe into six nests on a silicone baking mat and bake in the preheated oven for about 2 hours until completely dry.

Meanwhile, for the peaches, put the sugar, 1 litre/34 fl oz (4¼ cups) of water, cinnamon and vanilla into a large pan and bring to the boil.

Add the peaches and simmer for about 10 minutes until the peaches are tender.

Remove the peaches from the liquid and return the liquid to the boil. Simmer for 20–30 minutes until reduced by half and syrupy.

Remove the skins from the peaches, quarter them and remove the stones (pits).

To serve, place the peaches and some syrup in each meringue nest and top with whipped cream and mint.

See opposite –>

Spiced Baked Apples

Preparation: 10 minutes
Cooking: 30 minutes
Serves 6

a pinch of ground cinnamon
a pinch of ground allspice
½ teaspoon freshly grated nutmeg
zest and juice of 1 lemon
100 g/3½ oz (½ cup firmly packed) soft
    brown sugar
3½ tablespoons brandy
100 g/3½ oz (7 tablespoons) butter, cubed
6 nice eating apples

Preheat the oven to 170°C/340°F/Gas Mark 3½.

Mix the dry spices together with the lemon zest and the juice.

Bring the sugar to the boil with enough water in a small pan over a low heat to make a syrup.

Add the brandy and spice-and-zest mix to the sugar and simmer for 5 minutes. Whisk in the butter until emulsified.

Place the apples on a roasting pan and pour the mixture over them. Bake in the preheated oven, basting occasionally, for about 20 minutes until the apples are soft.

Cakes, Pastries, Biscuits and Desserts

Warm Plums and Rose Custard

Preparation: 15 minutes
Cooking: 20 minutes
Serves 4

250 g/9 oz (1¼ cups) caster (superfine) sugar
1 kg/2¼ lb plums, pitted and halved
1 teaspoon lemon juice
a pinch of sea salt

For the custard
250 ml/8 fl oz (1 cup) double (heavy) cream
250 ml/8 fl oz (1 cup) milk
1 teaspoon rose water
5 eggs
5 tablespoons caster (superfine) sugar
sea salt

Traditionally, this dessert was made with greengage plums. Greengages are sweet green plums when at full ripeness.

To cook the plums, put the sugar in a large pan and cover with 750 ml/25 fl oz (3 cups) of water. Heat over a low heat until the sugar has dissolved, then increase the heat and boil for a few minutes until the mixture is a little syrupy. Add the plums and poach for about 5 minutes. Finally, stir in the lemon juice and salt.

To make the custard, warm the cream, milk and rose water in a small pan over a medium–low heat just until they come to the boil.

Whisk the eggs and sugar together in a heatproof bowl. Set the bowl over a pan of simmering water and add the milk and cream. Cook, whisking constantly, for about 10 minutes until the custard thickens.

Serve the custard with the plums.

See opposite –>

Gooseberry and Elderflower Fool

Preparation: 10 minutes
Cooking: 20 minutes
Serves 4

For the elderflower syrup
300 g/11 oz (1¼ cups) caster (superfine) sugar
1 bunch of fresh elderflowers, plus a few extra
   to garnish

For the fool
550 g/1¼ lb (3⅓ cups) green gooseberries,
   topped and tailed (trimmed)
300 ml/10 fl oz (1¼ cups) double
   (heavy) cream

Recipes for gooseberry fool appear over and over again in cookbooks on Irish food, from the eighteenth to twentieth century. It is a very simple summer dessert. Gooseberries and elderflower are in season at the same time, which is convenient as they make a great combination. If you're not able to make your own elderflower syrup, you can use cordial instead.

Put the sugar, 300 ml/10 fl oz (1¼ cups) of water and the elderflowers into a pan over a medium heat and bring to the boil. Remove from the heat and allow to infuse.

Add the gooseberries to a pan with the elderflower syrup and simmer for 15 minutes until the fruit begins to break down. Strain the berries through a strainer. Check the sweetness and add a little more sugar if the berries are too tart. Allow to cool.

Gently whip the cream. Spoon the gooseberry mixture into a bowl and top with the cream. Garnish with some fresh elderflowers.

Note
It's easy to make fools with all kinds of fruits. A popular variation is with rhubarb. Make a rhubarb purée by boiling 500 g/1 lb 2 oz chopped rhubarb with 150 g/5 oz (¾ cup) caster (superfine) sugar, 75 ml/2½ fl oz (⅓ cup) mead and ½ teaspoon dried meadowsweet or vanilla extract. Once soft, blend, and then use in the same way as the gooseberries above.

Cakes, Pastries, Biscuits and Desserts

Hay Ice Cream

Preparation: 15 minutes, plus chilling and freezing times
Cooking: 1 hour 15 minutes
Serves 4

a small handful of hay
300 ml/10 fl oz (1¼ cups) milk
6 egg yolks
90 g/3¼ oz (scant ½ cup) caster (superfine) sugar
a pinch of sea salt
300 ml/10 fl oz (1¼ cups) double (heavy) cream

Hay is not only for horses! It is a staple flavouring in our restaurant for savoury and sweet dishes. Smoking with hay is an age-old technique in Ireland but making dessert with it is relatively new. However, I urge you to try it as it is also fun. I've made hay mousse and custard at events abroad to showcase contemporary Irish desserts. While it may never compete with chocolate (which we don't use, as none is produced in Ireland), it does offer a beautiful, magical flavour that will remain in your mind.

Preheat the oven to 160°C/325°F/Gas Mark 3.

Toast the hay in a baking pan in the preheated oven for 30 minutes. Pour the milk into a small pan over a low heat and add the hay. Heat for 30 minutes to allow to infuse, but do not bring to the boil.

Cream the egg yolks with the sugar in a heatproof bowl. Strain the hay from the milk and pour the milk over the egg mixture, whisking all the time to avoid overcooking the eggs. Place the bowl over a pan of simmering water and whisk for about 10 minutes until the custard thickens enough to coat the back of a spoon. Transfer the custard to a container and chill in the refrigerator.

When the mixture is cold, gently whip the cream, then fold the cream into the mixture. Churn in an ice cream machine. Alternatively, transfer to a freezer-proof container and freeze, whisking about every 30 minutes until the ice cream is frozen in 2–3 hours.

Brown Bread and Whiskey Ice Cream

Preparation: 15 minutes, plus chilling and freezing time
Cooking: 35 minutes
Serves 4

100 g/3½ oz (2 cups) fresh brown breadcrumbs (from soda bread), torn into crumbs
75 g/2¾ oz (⅓ cup firmly packed) soft brown sugar
3½ tablespoons whiskey
300 ml/10 fl oz (1¼ cups) double (heavy) cream
300 ml/10 fl oz (1¼ cups) milk
6 egg yolks
90 g/3¼ oz (scant ½ cup) caster (superfine) sugar

Probably the most famous Irish ice cream. Like bread and butter pudding, this ice cream is made from leftover soda bread. It is made all over the country. I remember a particularly beautiful one served to me in Ballyvolane House in County Cork. Incidentally, they also made gin from milk!

Preheat the oven to 180°C/350°F/Gas Mark 4.

Combine the breadcrumbs and sugar in a baking pan and bake in the preheated oven for 15–20 minutes until the breadcrumbs are crystallized and golden.

Warm the whiskey, cream and milk in a small pan over a medium–low heat. Fill a separate pan with a little water and bring to a simmer.

To make the ice cream, whisk the yolks and sugar in a heatproof bowl until pale and yellow, about 3–4 minutes. Pour the cream mixture over the eggs and whisk until combined. Place the bowl over the pan of simmering water and whisk for about 10 minutes until the custard thickens enough to coat the back of a spoon. Allow to cool.

Freeze in an ice cream machine, following the manufacturer's instructions, adding the breadcrumbs in last 5 minutes.

Alternatively, transfer to a freezer-proof container and freeze for 3–4 hours, whisking the mixture every 30 minutes.

Roasted Barley Ice Cream with Irish Cream

Preparation: 20 minutes, plus soaking time
Cooking: 45 minutes
Serves 4

200 g/7 oz (1 cup) barley
350 ml/12 fl oz (1½ cups) milk
6 egg yolks
100 g/3½ oz (½ cup) caster (superfine) sugar
150 ml/5 fl oz (⅔ cup) double (heavy) cream, whipped
150 ml/5 fl oz (⅔ cup) Irish cream liqueur, to serve

Preheat the oven to 180°C/350°F/Gas Mark 4.

Roast the barley in a baking pan in the preheated oven for 10–15 minutes until dark and malty.

Put the barley and milk into a medium pan over a medium heat and simmer for 15 minutes. Remove from the heat and allow to soak for 1 hour, then strain.

Cream the eggs and sugar together in a heatproof bowl.

Return the milk to the boil then pour it over the eggs, whisking all the time. Place the bowl over a pan of simmering water and whisk for 10 minutes, until it thickens enough to coat the back of a spoon. Remove from the heat and allow to cool.

Fold in the whipped cream and churn in an ice cream machine. Alternatively, transfer to a freezer-proof container and freeze. Whisk every 30 minutes until frozen in 2–3 hours.

Serve doused in Baileys.

Sheep's Yogurt Ice Cream

Preparation: 15 minutes, plus freezing time
Serves 6

300 ml/10 fl oz (1¼ cups) double (heavy) cream, lightly whipped
300 ml/10 fl oz (1¼ cups) sheep's yogurt
200 g/7 oz (1 cup) caster (superfine) sugar
a pinch of sea salt
200 ml/7 fl oz (scant 1 cup) buttermilk

Combine the cream and sheep's yogurt in a bowl. Fold the sugar and sea salt into the bowl. Gradually pour in the buttermilk, folding all the time.

Freeze in an ice cream machine or transfer to a freezer-proof container and freeze. Whisk occasionally about every 30 minutes until frozen in 2–3 hours.

Extra Virgin Rapeseed Oil Ice Cream with Honeycomb

Preparation: 20 minutes, plus freezing time
Cooking: 25 minutes
Serves 4

225 ml/7½ fl oz (scant 1 cup) double (heavy) cream
225 ml/7½ fl oz (scant 1 cup) milk
5 egg yolks
125 g/4½ oz (⅔ cup) caster (superfine) sugar
a pinch of sea salt
100 ml/3½ fl oz (scant ½ cup) extra virgin rapeseed (canola) oil
honeycomb (see Honeycomb Yellowman, page 346, or use shop-bought), to serve
fresh herbs or flowers, to garnish

To make the ice cream, put the cream and milk into a small pan and bring to the boil. Whisk the yolks and sugar together in a heatproof bowl with the salt. Pour the cream-and-milk mixture over the yolks, whisking all the time. Place the bowl over a pan of simmering water and whisk for about 10 minutes until the mixture thickens enough to coat the back of a spoon. Put into an ice cream machine with the oil and churn until set.

Alternatively, transfer to a freezer-proof container with the oil, mix and freeze. Whisk occasionally about every 30 minutes until frozen in 2–3 hours. Keep in the freezer until required.

To serve, scoop some ice cream into a bowl, crush some honeycomb over it and garnish with some herbs and flowers.

Cakes, Pastries, Biscuits and Desserts

Toffee Apples

Preparation: 10 minutes
Cooking: 10 minutes
Serves 8

8 apples

For the toffee
400 g/14 oz (generous 1¾ cups firmly packed)
    soft brown sugar
50 g/2 oz (4 tablespoons) butter
4 tablespoons golden (light corn) syrup
1 teaspoon vinegar

I had completely forgotten about these apples (of which I ate many in my childhood) until I came across a recipe for them in Regina Sexton's *A Little History of Irish Food* (1998). As Sexton observes, 'nowadays toffee apples are a rare, if not extinct treat'. I recall eating them around Halloween when we would go out trick-or-treating.

Put the apples into a heatproof bowl and cover with boiling water. Allow to sit for 5 minutes, then remove from the water. Dry thoroughly and place on a wire rack over a baking sheet. Place a lollipop stick into the base of each apple.

For the toffee, put the sugar and 100 ml/3½ fl oz (scant ½ cup) of water into a pan over a medium heat and heat for about 5 minutes until the sugar has dissolved. Stir in the butter, syrup and vinegar. Bring to the boil for about 5 minutes until it reaches 150 °C/300 °F on a sugar (candy) thermometer.

Alternatively, pour a little toffee into a bowl of cold water – if it hardens immediately and is easy to break and brittle, the toffee is ready.

Pour the toffee over the apples (or dip the apples in). Give the apples two coats. Allow to cool on baking (parchment) paper.

See opposite –>

Honeycomb Yellowman

Preparation: 15 minutes, plus chilling time
Cooking: 15 minutes
Makes about 24 pieces

115 g/4 oz (1 stick) butter
225 g/8 oz (⅔ cup) treacle (molasses)
225 g/8 oz (scant 1 cup) golden
    (light corn) syrup
450 g/1 lb (2 cups firmly packed) soft
    brown sugar
2 tablespoons malt vinegar
1 tablespoon bicarbonate of soda
    (baking soda)

Yellowman (honeycomb, or sponge candy) was traditionally found on stalls at country fairs. It is usually associated with Northern Ireland, particularly the Ould Lammas Fair in Ballycastle, County Antrim, one of the oldest continuous fairs in Northern Ireland. It is a decidedly sweet treat and was often sold with dillisk (dulse, the purple seaweed). A folk ballad, written by John Henry MacAuley mentions the peculiar pairings: 'Were you ever at the Fair In Ballycastle-O? Did you treat your Mary Ann to some Dulse and Yellow Man.'

Line a baking pan with a sheet of greaseproof (wax) paper.

Melt the butter in a medium pan over a medium heat. Add the treacle (molasses), golden (light corn) syrup, sugar and vinegar. Bring to the boil and heat until it reaches about 149 °C/300 °F on a sugar (candy) thermometer. If you don't have a thermometer, test by dropping a little of the syrup

in a bowl of cold water. It should go crisp.

Remove from the heat and whisk in the bicarbonate of soda (baking soda). Be prepared for it to increase in volume and become frothy. Pour into the prepared pan. When cold, break into squares and store in an airtight container.

Cakes, Pastries, Biscuits and Desserts

pickling and preservation

Pickling and Preservation

'Years ago, preserving skills were essential for survival through our long winter months. A glut [bumper crop] in the garden provoked a frenzy of activity in order to harvest every bit. There was a great sense of urgency in the days before electricity as it was the only opportunity people had to lay down a store to get themselves through the fallow seasons. Preserving was acutely important in the rhythm of the year.'

Darina Allen, *Forgotten Skills of Cooking,* 2009

We have a long history of preservation in Ireland. Indeed, before the advent of refrigeration, every culture had methods of preservation. The recent return to this practice attests to our desire to engage with our culinary past, as a way of learning for the future but also of protecting past tradition. Old Irish recipe books reveal homemade vinegars, pickles and ferments as well as country wines (blackberry and elderberry). Up until the Industrial Revolution in the nineteenth century, all people were people of the land, whether they wanted to be or not. This meant that they had to preserve if they wanted ingredients outside the season.

While it is more difficult to assert what was going on before the advent of writing (sixth to eighth century), recipe books from the eighteenth and nineteenth centuries give us a flavour of how fruits, vegetables and meat were preserved. However, we need to be careful with written recipes of this time, in that they only reflect a portion of what society was doing. Of course, all recipes only represent those writing (or the community they are written in), but the use of sugar and spices for pickling and preservation may not have been accessible to all. Nonetheless, I have drawn inspiration from these recipes (and others from early periods). I have pulled back on the amount of spices (and rose water!) in the recipes, as I feel they do not reflect contemporary taste. It is important not to be bound too tightly to history.

Spices dominated European cooking from the Middle Ages to the twentieth century. Looking through old recipe books, it is hard to find a recipe without pepper, mace, ginger or the many other spices that were brought into countries like Ireland from the East. Because Ireland was ruled by England, it adopted many of the same culinary trends. 'Big house' cooking associated with the elite and aristocratic class used plenty of spices because it was also a sign of privilege. As spices became more affordable in the nineteenth century, they found their way into many dishes. But are they Irish? Do they represent Irish cooking? To a certain degree, they do.

We often overlook the role of spices in Irish cooking. In recent years their wholesale rejection has no doubt come about due to a 'return to the land' or to examining our own terroir. I am guilty of this, too. We use no spices at all at Aniar. But does this make our food more authentically Irish? Defining Irish food depends on where one stands. Spices have been a part of Irish cooking since the Vikings. Caraway and coriander seeds, cloves, nutmeg, mace, ginger: you'd imagine that these ingredients have more to do with the Middle East than Ireland's ancient East, but they have dominated cooking in this country for centuries. Of course, our Christmas pudding is laden with all sorts of spices sourced from many thousands of miles away. Every time you add nutmeg to your soup or your cheese sauce for your lasagne, you are engaging in a complex historical phenomenon that needs reflection. Irish food will never be what we want it to be unless we understand the historic forces that underlie its global complexity. You might think about that the next time you add a blade of mace to your eel soup.

Pickling and preservation with vinegar, fermentation or sugar is something I am passionate about in terms of Irish cooking. Not only does it provide us with a link to the past, but it also helps us maintain traditional practices of preservation. Allow your intuition to guide you through the seasons as you build up a larger supply of preserved goods that you can use at a later date.

Rapeseed Oil

Culinary rapeseed (canola) oil is the only food-grade oil produced in Ireland. We have used rapeseed oil in Aniar for the last seven years. We use an extra virgin oil for dressing and finishing food and a lighter, less flavoured rapeseed oil for frying. I love the floral, nutty quality of the oil and for me it gives our food a particular regional taste. In this day and age, every oil from around the world is available in most places, so it's important to seek out oil that is produced in your own area. Oil is often not considered as an ingredient in cooking but its use and value are extremely important. Don't just use any oil, or leave your oil in the press for months. Take care of your oil and your food will love you for it!

Herb Oil

Preparation: 5 minutes, plus soaking time
Cooking: 5 minutes
Makes 300 ml/10 fl oz (1¼ cups)

100 g/3½ oz (2½–4 cups packed) herbs
300 ml/10 fl oz (1¼ cups) light rapeseed
  (canola) oil

Most herbs can be used to make a nice green oil for seasoning your food. Perhaps the best ones are the greenest, so parsley, fennel, chive and dill work well. Use what is available to you. Wild herbs and flowers can also be used to make nice oils such as wild garlic (ramps), nasturtiums and wild leeks. You can also use seaweed to make an oil – for this, substitute the herbs for 25 g/1 oz (½ cup) dried milled seaweed. For soft herbs such as mint or basil, I like to blanch them beforehand as it makes a greener oil.

Blend the herbs in a food processor.

Transfer the herbs to a small pan over a low heat, add the oil and heat for about 5 minutes until the herbs and oil separate. The oil will begin to bubble.

Chill and leave to soak overnight.

Strain the following day and store in the refrigerator. Use within a week, or freeze for later use.

Burnt Hay Oil

To make the burnt hay, take a large handful of hay and set light to it in a metal bowl. When all the hay has burned, pour over enough oil to cover the hay. Cover and bake in a low oven for a couple of hours until the hay taste has permeated into the oil. Strain and use within 1 month.

Cider Vinegar

Apples lead to cider, which in turn lead to vinegar. Cider left at room temperature and exposed to the air will eventually (in a few weeks) turn to vinegar, though it won't be as acidic as the commercial kind. I use apple cider vinegar for pickling and seasoning all the time. Highbank Orchard produce a great organic vinegar. Pure unpasteurized cider vinegar is full of health-giving properties. Mixed with a little honey, it makes a great drink (that will keep your gut going).

How to Make Your Own Herb or Fruit Vinegar

There are two ways to make your own flavoured vinegar. First, by infusing ingredients into a base vinegar such as cider or white wine vinegar. I like to use fruit in season, such as blackberries and raspberries, or herbs such as tarragon, dill, sage and wild garlic. Simply infuse the herbs or fruit in warmed apple cider vinegar for about three weeks, giving the jar a shake each day. After maturation, you can strain the vinegar if desired.

The other way takes slightly longer. Sprinkle some sugar over the herbs or fruit and mash slightly. Cover with a little water and leave at room temperature to ferment. When all bubbling has ceased, strain the contents and leave the liquid exposed to turn to vinegar. Then bottle and refrigerate.

Celery Vinegar

Preparation and cooking: 15 minutes, plus maturing time
Makes 500 ml/17 fl oz (generous 2 cups)

1 head of celery, roughly chopped with leaves
300 ml/10 fl oz (1¼ cups) apple cider vinegar
150 ml/5 fl oz (⅔ cup) water
75 g/2¾ oz (¼ cup) honey

This is a simple infused vegetable vinegar. I love to use celery vinegar for dressing mackerel as an alternative to lemon or lime.

Combine all the ingredients in a medium pan over a medium heat and bring to the boil. Simmer for 5 minutes.

Transfer to a sterilized jar (see page 423) and age for 3 months.

See opposite –>

Seaweed Vinegar

Preparation and cooking: 15 minutes
Makes 750 ml/25 fl oz (3 cups)

300 ml/10 fl oz (1¼ cups) white wine vinegar
100 g/3½ oz (½ cup) caster (superfine) sugar
30 g/1 oz fresh kombu
30 g/1 oz fresh sugar kelp
10 g/¼ oz fresh dillisk (dulse)
1 teaspoon sea salt

I use fresh seaweed here, but you can use dried. Quarter the amount in that case. I use this instead of using lemon juice, especially on fish dishes.

Combine all the ingredients in a medium pan over a medium heat with 200 g/7 oz (scant 1 cup) of water. Heat for a few minutes until the sugar dissolves. Remove from the heat and allow to cool.

Transfer to a sterilized jar (see page 423). Do not decant the seaweed as the flavour will develop over time.

Wild Rose Vinegar

Preparation and cooking: 15 minutes
Makes 750 ml/25 fl oz (3 cups)

600 ml/20 fl oz (2½ cups) white wine vinegar
150 g/5 oz (8 cups) wild rose petals (or 25 g/1 oz/1 cup dried roses)

Bring the vinegar to the boil in a medium pan over a medium heat and add the rose petals. Return to the boil, then remove from the heat.

Transfer to a sterilized jar (see page 423) and store in a cool, dark place.

You can sweeten this vinegar with sugar or honey if you like.

Pickling and Preservation

Pickled Elderflowers

Preparation and cooking: 15 minutes
Makes 850 ml/30 fl oz (3½ cups)

10 bunches of elderflowers, stems removed
600 ml/20 fl oz (2½ cups) white wine vinegar
150 g/5 oz (¾ cup) caster (superfine) sugar
10 g/¼ oz (2 teaspoons) sea salt

These pickles are great with fish, chicken and vegetable dishes. Experiment with other flowers as well, such as gorse or nasturtium. Nasturtium flower vinegar is bright red and has a wonderful flavour.

Combine all the ingredients with 300 ml/10 fl oz (1¼ cups) of water in a large pan over a medium heat. Bring to the boil, then reduce the heat and simmer for 3 minutes.

Cool, transfer to a sterilized jar (see page 423) and store in a cool, dark place. Eat right away, or else use within a month.

See opposite –>

Pickled Lovage Stalks

Preparation and cooking: 10 minutes
Makes 350 ml/12 fl oz (1½ cups)

a handful of lovage stalks (stems),
   finely chopped
150 ml/5 fl oz (⅔ cup) apple cider vinegar
75 g/2¾ oz (⅓ cup) caster (superfine) sugar

Use these stalks as you would capers, with potato or fish dishes. Alexanders stalks can be pickled in the same manner.

Put the lovage stalks into a sterilized jar (see page 423).

Put the vinegar, 100 ml/3½ fl oz (scant ½ cup) of water and the sugar into a small pan over a medium heat and bring to the boil.

Pour the vinegar solution over the lovage stalks. Cool and refrigerate overnight. They are ready to eat the next day, and best used within a month.

Pickled Green Walnuts

Preparation: 20 minutes, plus 8–10 days
fermenting and drying time
Cooking: 10 minutes
Makes 2.5 kg/4½ lb

1 kg/2¼ lb (about 50) fresh and soft
   green walnuts
100 g/3½ oz (⅓ cup) sea salt
1 litre/34 fl oz (4¼ cups) malt vinegar
200 g/7 oz (scant 1 cup firmly packed)
   soft brown sugar
5 cloves garlic, peeled
25 g/1 oz (¼ cup) fresh ginger in one
   piece, peeled
1 blade of mace
1 teaspoon black peppercorns
1 teaspoon cloves

From the seventeenth century onwards, pickled green walnuts were extremely popular in Irish and British cooking. They go well with cheese and meat boards. The walnuts need to be picked in early summer before the shell forms. Though the process of making the walnuts is quite long (about 2 weeks), there isn't a lot of labour to it (unless you pick the walnuts yourself). I found this recipe in an eighteenth-century Irish cookbook and have adapted it for contemporary usage.

Prick the green walnuts all over with a fork and put into a large bowl. Cover with water and stir in the salt. Place a weight on top of the walnuts so they remain under the brine). Allow to ferment at room temperature for 4 days.

Remove the walnuts from the brine and place them on trays. Discard the brine. Dry outside in the sun or in a warm place until they are uniformly black – this will take about 24 hours.

Put the remaining ingredients into a large pan over a medium heat and bring to the boil. Add the walnuts and simmer for 5–10 minutes.

Transfer the walnuts into sterilized jars (see page 423), cover with the vinegar solution, ensuring they are properly covered, and seal. Leave in a cool, dark place for a few weeks before using.

To serve, remove the walnuts from the pickle and slice.

Pickling and Preservation

Pickled Seaweed

Preparation and cooking: 10 minutes
Makes 500 g/1 lb 2 oz

200 ml/7 fl oz (scant 1 cup) apple cider vinegar
50 g/2 oz (¼ cup) caster (superfine) sugar
100 g/3½ oz fresh seaweed (such as channelled
  wrack, sea spaghetti, sugar kelp)

Put the cider vinegar, sugar and 100 ml/3½ fl oz (scant ½ cup) water into a medium pan over a medium heat and bring to the boil. Remove from the heat and add the seaweed.

Allow to cool and transfer to a sterilized jar (see page 423). Store in the refrigerator and use within a month.

Serve with shellfish or roasted root vegetables such as carrots.

Pickled Ramsons

Preparation: 15 minutes, plus 3 months maturing time
Makes 500 g/1 lb 2 oz

500 g/1 lb 2 oz (2 cups) wild garlic (ramps)
  seed heads, separated from the stem
sea salt
malt vinegar

Wait until the final flowers have fallen from the bud and then collect as many seed heads as possible. Any seed heads such as those of elderberries or nasturtiums can be pickled in this way. These are my favourite pickles. Because wild garlic is native to Ireland, I feel we are somehow engaged in upholding an ancient tradition when we preserve these little seed heads.

Put the seed heads into a jar and lightly salt. Refrigerate overnight.

The next day, remove them from the jar, rinse and dry, then cover completely in malt vinegar. Mature for 3 months in the refrigerator.

Note
You can also pickle wild garlic flower buds. Cover 100 g/3½ oz buds with 300 g/11 oz (1¼ cups) malt vinegar warmed together with 75 g/2¾ oz (⅓ cup) sugar and 150 g/5 oz (⅔ cup) water.

Pickled Rock Samphire

Preparation and cooking: 10 minutes, plus 1 week maturing time
Makes 500 g/1 lb 2 oz

250 g/9 oz rock samphire (sea fennel)
250 ml/8 fl oz (1 cup) apple cider vinegar
100 g/3½ oz (½ cup) caster (superfine) sugar
1 bay leaf
½ teaspoon fennel seeds

Don't confuse rock samphire (*Crithmum maritimum*) with samphire (sea beans) from the salicornia plant (*Salicornia europaea*).

Put the rock samphire (sea fennel) into a sterilized jar (see page 423).

Put the vinegar, sugar, bay leaf and fennel seeds into a pan, bring to the boil, then remove from the heat.

Allow the vinegar solution to cool slightly and then pour it over the samphire. Top up with water if required and then seal. Refrigerate for one week before using. After this, best used within a month.

Pickled Cherries

Preparation and cooking: 15 minutes
Makes 1.5 kg/3¼ lb

1 kg/2¼ lb (7¼ cups) cherries
300 ml/10 fl oz (1¼ cups) apple cider vinegar
100 g/3½ oz (½ cup) caster (superfine) sugar
a few sprigs of rosemary and thyme
½ teaspoon sea salt

Put the cherries into sterilized jars (see page 423).

Put the vinegar, 200 ml/7 fl oz (scant 1 cup) of water and the sugar with the herbs and salt into a small pan and bring to the boil.

Allow to cool slightly, then pour the vinegar solution over the cherries and allow to cool. These can be eaten right away, and will last for 3 months in the refrigerator. Serve with grilled lamb or pork.

Pickling and Preservation

Pickled Mushrooms

Preparation and cooking: 15 minutes
Makes 1 kg/2¼ lb

250 g/9 oz mixed wild mushrooms
300 ml/10 fl oz (1¼ cups) beer
300 ml/10 fl oz (1¼ cups) white wine vinegar
1 cinnamon stick
1 blade of mace
2 bay leaves
a sprig of marjoram
sea salt

This recipe is based on an eighteenth-century recipe for pickling mushrooms. Pickled mushrooms, especially pickled wild mushrooms, are an ideal way of combating the short mushroom season. They are also great for adding flavour and acidity to many dishes. Try them with grilled steak or chicken with bitter leaves.

Poach the mushrooms in a little simmering water until soft. Season with salt and strain the liquid away. Transfer to a sterilized jar (see page 423).

Put the remaining ingredients into a small pan over a medium heat and bring to the boil. Pour over the mushrooms and store in a cool, dark place until needed. Best used within a month.

Pickled Heritage Carrots

Preparation and cooking: 15 minutes
Makes 1.5 kg/3¼ lb

750 g/1 lb 10 oz (12 medium) carrots,
   preferably heritage varieties
600 ml/20 fl oz (2½ cups) apple cider vinegar
200 g/7 oz (1 cup) caster (superfine) sugar
a few sprigs of thyme
25 g/1 oz (1 cup) chervil
1 teaspoon sea salt

Heritage carrots are more interesting not only because of their colours, but also because of their flavour. If you can't source heritage or heirloom carrots, use younger carrots for the best flavour.

Scrub the carrots clean and place upright in sterilized jars (see page 423).

Put all the remaining ingredients with 400 ml/14 fl oz (1⅔ cups) of water into a small pan over a medium heat and bring to the boil.

Pour the vinegar solution over the carrots. Eat once cool, or store in a dark, cool place until required. Best used within a month.

Pickled Cucumbers

Preparation and cooking: 10 minutes,
plus 3 weeks pickling time
Makes 1.5 kg/3¼ lb

6 small cucumbers
600 ml/20 fl oz (2½ cups) apple cider vinegar
200 g/7 oz (1 cup) caster (superfine) sugar
15 g/½ oz (¼ cup) dill
1 tablespoon fennel seeds
1 teaspoon juniper berries
1 teaspoon sea salt

Cucumbers have been pickled for centuries. There are many different recipes, some that include a variety of spices such as mace and nutmeg.

Put the cucumbers into sterilized jars (see page 423).

Put all the remaining ingredients with 400 ml/14 fl oz (1⅔ cups) of water into a medium pan over a medium heat and bring to the boil.

Pour the vinegar solution over the whole cucumbers. Cover and store in a cool, dark place for 3 weeks.

To serve, remove the pickles from the vinegar solution and slice thinly. Best used within a month.

Pickling and Preservation

Beer-pickled Shallots with Allspice

Preparation: 15 minutes
Cooking: 7 minutes
Makes 1 kg/2¼ lb

300 ml/10 fl oz (1¼ cups) malt vinegar
200 ml/7 fl oz (scant 1 cup) beer
50 g/2 oz (¼ cup) caster (superfine) sugar
1 teaspoon black peppercorns
1 teaspoon ground allspice
500 g/1 lb 2 oz shallots, peeled
sea salt

If you can't find shallots, use small onions, or large onions that have been quartered.

Put the vinegar, beer, sugar and spices in a medium pan over a medium heat and bring to the boil. Add the shallots and return to the boil. Simmer for about 5–7 minutes until the shallots are soft and remove from the heat.

Transfer the onions and the pickling liquid to sterilized jars (see page 423) and allow to cool. Best used within a month.

See opposite –>

Preserved Quinces

Preparation: 15 minutes
Cooking: 1 hour
Makes 2 kg/4½ lb

juice of 1 lemon
3 large quinces
400 g/14 oz (2 cups) granulated sugar
2 tablespoons rose water
1 cinnamon stick
5 cloves

Though not native to Ireland, quinces were popular in Irish cooking from the seventeenth century. Traditionally, they were prepared and preserved in sugar and spices. This recipe dates from the eighteenth century. Use preserved quinces instead of apples or pears in pork dishes. They can also be served with ice cream or meringue and fresh fruit for dessert.

Fill a bowl with water and add the lemon juice.

Peel and core the quinces and put into acidulated water (water with lemon juice) to prevent oxidation.

Place the remaining ingredients with 500 ml/17 fl oz (generous 2 cups) of water into a medium pan and bring to the boil.

Cut the quince into thick slices and place in the sugar solution. Simmer for 1 hour or until soft.

Transfer the fruit to sterilized jars (see page 423) with enough of the cooking liquid to cover. Store in the refrigerator and use within 3 months.

Brined Gooseberries

Preparation: 15 minutes, plus 1 week brining time
Makes 1.5 kg/3¼ lb

1 kg/2¼ lb (6⅔ cups) gooseberries, topped and tailed (trimmed)
sea salt

Use brined gooseberries with rich, fatty fish such as mackerel. They also work well with pork chops or chicken breast.

Put the gooseberries into sterilized jars (see page 423), leaving plenty of space for covering with the brine.

Make enough brine to cover the gooseberries, mixing 50 g/2 oz (3 tablespoons) of salt for each 1 litre/34 fl oz (4¼ cups) of water used and heating it in a pan over

a medium heat until the salt dissolves. Allow to cool.

Pour brine over the gooseberries and leave for at least a week. They can be left in for longer but be aware they will become saltier over time. Keep in the refrigerator for up to 6 months.

Pickling and Preservation

Pickling and Preservation

Preserved Damsons with Rose Water

Preparation: 5 minutes
Cooking: 5 minutes
Makes 1 × 1-litre/34-fl oz (4¼-cup) jar

450 g/1 lb (9 cups) damsons
200 g/7 oz (1 cup) caster (superfine) sugar
2 teaspoons rose water
a handful of wild roses (optional)

Damsons (wild plums) have been traditionally preserved in Ireland for many generations. Recipes include spices, particularly cloves. In this recipe, I use a combination of rose water and some wild roses and omit the cloves to give a lighter, fresher flavour. If you can't find damsons, regular plums will work just as well. Feel free to add whatever spices you want.

Put the sugar and rose water with 500 ml/17 fl oz (generous 2 cups) of water into a medium pan over a medium heat and bring to the boil. Add the damsons, reduce to a simmer and cook for 5 minutes until the damsons are soft. Remove from the heat and add the roses, if using.

Transfer to a sterilized jar (see page 423) and store in the refrigerator. Best used within a month.

Fermented Onions in Whey

Preparation: 10 minutes, plus fermenting time
Makes 1 × 1-litre/34-fl oz (4¼-cup) jar

6 onions, peeled and halved
½ teaspoon sea salt
500 ml/17 fl oz (generous 2 cups) whey

To get make your own fresh whey, hang yogurt or goat's curd in a muslin- (cheesecloth) lined sieve overnight. Otherwise, find yourself a cheese maker, who should gladly give you whey. I use organic onions for this.

Place the onions into a sterilized jar (see page 423) with the salt and cover with the whey. Add a little water if required – the onions should be covered.

Ferment for up to a week at room temperature.

Transfer to the refrigerator and use within a month.

Fermented Cabbage with Juniper

Preparation: 15 minutes, plus 5 days fermenting time
Makes about 1 kg/2¼ lb

2 heads of cabbage, outer leaves removed
1 teaspoon juniper berries, toasted
sea salt

Quarter the cabbages and remove the core. Slice thinly.

Sprinkle the bottom of a suitable container with salt. Place a layer of cabbage and a few juniper berries over the salt. Sprinkle a little more salt over the cabbage and then repeat the whole process until you have salted all the cabbage. Place a clean cloth over the cabbage and top with a heavy weight.

Ferment at room temperature for 5 days. If the cabbage requires a little water, pour a little water over the cloth. It is important the cabbage remains covered in the salted brine that is produced from the process of fermentation.

Transfer to sterilized jars (see page 423) and refrigerate. Best used within a month.

Fermented Celeriac

Preparation: 10 minutes, plus fermenting time
Makes 1 × 1-litre/34-fl oz (4¼-cup) jar

1 celeriac (celery root), peeled and sliced
 thinly on a mandoline
sea salt

Root vegetables, such as carrots, turnips, kohlrabi and Jerusalem artichokes (sunchokes) ferment particularly well. I love to use fermented celeriac with freshly picked crabmeat or pan-fried wild mushrooms.

Put the celeriac into a sterilized jar (see page 423) with 10 g/¼ oz (2 teaspoons) salt for every 500 g/ 1 lb 2 oz of vegetable. Cover with water and stir to dissolve the salt.

Ferment for 3–5 days at room temperature and then refrigerate. Best used within a month.

Pickled Oysters in Cider

Preparation and cooking: 20 minutes
Makes 750 g/1 lb 10 oz

12 oysters
250 ml/8 fl oz (1 cup) apple cider vinegar
250 ml/8 fl oz (1 cup) dry cider (hard cider)
100 g/3½ oz (½ cup) caster (superfine) sugar
2 teaspoons juniper berries, toasted
2 teaspoons fennel seeds, toasted

Pickled oysters can be eaten by themselves or served with rich beef dishes. They can also be blended into sauces to add additional salinity and acidity. Pickled oysters were popular in 'big house' cooking of the seventeenth and eighteenth century. A cod salad with anchovies and pickled oysters appears in the 'Smythe of Barbavilla Papers' (1621–1930). Housed in the National Library of Ireland, these are the papers of the Smythe family who lived in Collinstown, County Westmeath.

Fill a large bowl with ice-cold water.

Bring a large pan of water to the boil over a high heat, add the oysters and blanch briefly for 30 seconds in boiling water. Submerge them immediately in ice-cold water.

When the oysters are cold, shuck them. Ensure there is no grit or sand in and around the oyster.

Transfer the oysters to a sterilized jar (see page 423).

Meanwhile, put the remaining ingredients into a small pan over a medium heat and bring to the boil. Cool the liquid and then pour it over the oysters.

Chill and store in the refrigerator. Eat within a month.

Potted Herring

Preparation: 15 minutes, plus overnight
chilling time
Cooking: 10 minutes
Serves 4

50 g/2 oz (3 tablespoons) sea salt
500 g/1 lb 2 oz herring fillets, pin-boned
1 red onion, thinly sliced
20 g/¾ oz (⅓ cup prepared) dill, picked

For the pickling liquid
75 g/2¾ oz (⅓ cup) caster (superfine) sugar
450 ml/15 fl oz (scant 2 cups) apple cider vinegar
1 teaspoon mustard seeds
3 bay leaves

To make the brine, bring 750 ml/ 25 fl oz (3 cups) of water to the boil with the salt. Let the brine cool. Submerge the herring fillets in the brine in a suitable container and refrigerate overnight.

To make the pickle, bring the sugar, vinegar, 200 ml/7 fl oz (scant 1 cup) of water and both the spices to the boil and simmer for 5 minutes.

When the herring have brined, strain and lay them on a suitable tray with the dill and red onion. Pour over the cooled pickling liquid. Wait at least a day before eating. Store in the refrigerator in a sealed container for up to 1 month.

Pickling and Preservation

Jams and Preserves

The tradition of blackberry picking in Ireland every autumn (fall) is forever immortalized in Seamus Heaney's poem 'Blackberries'. In the poem, Heaney recalls how in 'Late August, given heavy rain and sun for a full week, the blackberries would ripen.' Eating the blackberries straight from the bush was 'like thickened wine'. Like the blackberries in the poem, our tradition of picking this wonderful fruit in the autumn and making jam, has begun to 'rot'. Blackberries were probably the first wild fruit I ever saw. I remember encountering them on my way to school. Walking past, I would taste them direct from the branch. Alongside blackberries, there are many other wonderful wild Irish fruits, such as elderberries, rose hips, crab apples, rowan berries and blueberries (*fraughans*). In the past, all these fruits were picked and preserved in jams, jellies, cordials (syrups) and other preserves. Down south, there is also a wonderful tradition of growing fruit. Wexford strawberries are world famous. Every year, from early summer on, you can purchase them from little stalls on the side of the road. Raspberries, blueberries, loganberries and many more are also commercially grown in Ireland and can be purchased in the summer and autumn. Unfortunately, jam making has declined in Ireland since the advent of industrialization and the birth of the modern supermarket. Still, many of the older generation will remember their mother or grandmother making jam every autumn. It is a tradition worth continuing. Indeed, in this digital age, autumn fruit has a way of reconnecting us with our local landscape.

☼ ᗡ � ⟁

Beetroot and Blackberry Chutney

Preparation: 30 minutes
Cooking: 45 minutes
Makes 1.5 kg/3¼ lb (4¾ cups)

450 g/1 lb (2 cups prepared) beetroot (beets), peeled and diced
450 g/1 lb (3 cups) blackberries
100 g/3½ oz (1 cup prepared) apples, peeled and chopped
200 ml/7 fl oz (scant 1 cup) malt vinegar
200 g/7 oz (1 cup) caster (superfine) sugar
2 onions, chopped
2 bay leaves
sea salt, to taste

Sterilize your jars and lids (see page 423).

Put all the ingredients in a large heavy-based pan over a medium heat and bring to the boil. Reduce to a simmer and cook for 45 minutes until the beetroot (beets) are soft.

Remove from the heat, transfer to the sterilized jars, seal and refrigerate.

Tomato Chutney

Preparation: 30 minutes
Cooking: 45 minutes
Makes 1.5 kg/3¼ lb (4¾ cups)

350 g/12 oz (1¾ cups) caster (superfine) sugar
500 ml/17 fl oz (generous 2 cups) apple cider vinegar
4 onions, diced
150 g/5 oz (1 cup) sultanas (golden raisins)
1 tablespoon mustard seeds
1 kg/2¼ lb (9 medium) ripe red tomatoes, skinned and chopped
sea salt

Sterilize your jars and lids (see page 423).

Put all the ingredients except the tomatoes into a large heavy-based pan and bring to the boil.

Add the tomatoes, reduce the heat and simmer for about 45 minutes until the chutney thickens.

Pour into the sterilized jars, seal and refrigerate.

Blackcurrant Jam

Preparation: 30 minutes
Cooking: 45 minutes
Makes 3 kg/7 lb (9½ cups)

2 kg/4½ lb (18 cups) blackcurrants, stems removed
1.5 litres/50 fl oz (6¼ cups) apple juice or water
3 kg/6½ lb (15 cups) caster (superfine) sugar

Sterilize your jars and lids (see page 423). If you don't have a sugar (candy) thermometer, put a few saucers in the freezer to chill.

For the jam, put the blackcurrants and apple juice into a large heavy-based pan over a high heat and bring to the boil. Reduce the heat and simmer for 15 minutes.

Add the sugar and return to the boil. Boil for 30–40 minutes, until the jam reaches the setting temperature of 105°C/220°F on a sugar thermometer. If you don't have a thermometer, test it by dropping a small spoon of the hot jam onto the cold saucer, then wait a couple of minutes before pushing it gently with your finger – if it wrinkles, your jam has reached setting point. Otherwise continue boiling for a few more minutes before testing again.

When set, remove from the heat. Spoon into the sterilized jars, keeping the jam away from the rims of the jars and leaving a slight gap of about 5 mm/¼ inch from the top. Seal with the lids and either store in a cool, dark place for up to 6 months or in the refrigerator for a few months.

Blackberry and Crab Apple Jam

Preparation: 30 minutes
Cooking: 35 minutes
Makes 2.5 kg/5½ lb (8 cups)

1 kg/2¼ lb crab apples, peeled and cored
1 kg/2¼ lb (7 cups) blackberries
1.5 kg/3¼ lb (7½ cups) caster (superfine) sugar

Sterilize your jars and lids (see page 423). If you don't have a sugar (candy) thermometer, put a few saucers in the freezer to chill.

Quarter the apples and add to a large pan with 250 ml/8 fl oz (1 cup) of water. Bring to a simmer over a medium heat and cook for 5–10 minutes until they turn to a pulp. Strain through a fine sieve.

Put the blackberries, half the sugar and 150 ml/5 fl oz (⅔ cup) of water into a large pan and simmer over a medium heat for about 5 minutes until the sugar has dissolved.

Add the apple pulp and the remaining sugar and bring to the boil. Boil rapidly for 10–20 minutes until the jam has set (see above). Skim and pour into sterilized jars.

See image on page 365.

Raspberry Jam

Preparation: 15 minutes
Cooking: 30 minutes
Makes 2.5 kg/5½ lb (8 cups)

1.5 kg/3 lb 5 oz (12 cups) raspberries
1.3 kg/2 lb 9 oz (6½ cups) caster
   (superfine) sugar

In her cookbook *Kind Cooking* (1955), Maura Laverty wrote of her raspberry-picking days, on the mitch (or playing truant) from school. The recipe below is based on the one in her book, which she acknowledges as her mother's recipe.

Sterilize your jars and lids (see page 423). If you don't have a sugar (candy) thermometer, put a few saucers in the freezer to chill.

Heat the fruit in a large heavy-based saucepan over a medium heat for 15 minutes until soft. Crush the fruit with a ladle to release its liquid. When the fruit starts to bubble, add the sugar. Stir continually to avoid the jam sticking or burning on the bottom.

Boil for 20–25 minutes until the jam reaches the setting temperature of 105°C/220°F on a sugar thermometer. If you don't have a thermometer, test by dropping a small spoon of the hot jam onto a cold saucer (see page 363). Skim off any impurities.

Remove from the heat and transfer to the sterilized jars.

See opposite –>

Plum and Cinnamon Jam

Preparation: 25 minutes
Cooking: 45 minutes
Makes 3.5 kg/7½ lb (11 cups)

2 kg/4½ lb (11¼ cups prepared) plums,
   pitted and halved
2 kg/4½ lb (10 cups) caster (superfine) sugar
2 tablespoons ground cinnamon

Cinnamon tells a tale of Irish food in relation to colonialism. It was used in Ireland from the eighteenth century by the elite Anglo-Irish classes and features in many recipes of preservation, from quinces to plums.

Sterilize the jars and lids (see page 423). If you don't have a sugar (candy) thermometer, put a few saucers in the freezer to chill.

Place all the ingredients into a large heavy-based pan over a medium heat and bring to the boil. You can add a little water to help the fruit break down.

Boil until the jam reaches the setting temperature of 105°C/220°F on a sugar thermometer (if you don't have a sugar thermometer see page 363).

Remove from the heat and transfer to the sterilized jars.

See opposite –>

Lemon Curd

Preparation: 15 minutes
Cooking: 20 minutes
Makes two 250-g/9-oz jars

200 g/7 oz (1 cup) caster (superfine) sugar
100 g/3½ oz (7 tablespoons) butter
grated zest and juice of 4 lemons
4 eggs and 1 egg yolk

Sterilize your jars and lids (see page 423).

Put the sugar, butter and lemon zest and juice into a heatproof bowl. Place the bowl over a pan of simmering water and stir for about 5 minutes until the butter has melted.

Whisk the eggs and the egg yolk and then stir them into the lemon mixture. Cook the mixture for a further 15 minutes, stirring occasionally. The mixture should be thick enough to coat the back of the spoon.

Pour into the sterilized jars, seal and store in the refrigerator.

Orange Marmalade with Whiskey

Preparation: 30 minutes
Cooking: 3 hours
Makes 3 kg/7 lb (8 cups)

1.5 kg/3 lb 5 oz (about 8) Seville oranges
juice of 2 lemons
3 kg/6½ lb (15 cups) caster (superfine) sugar
3½ tablespoons treacle (molasses)
100 ml/3½ fl oz (scant ½ cup)
Irish whiskey, preferably with a smoky
  or peat characteristic

There was a great tradition of making marmalade at home in Ireland throughout the twentieth century. I recall it being made in various households that we visited as children. The Irish have always had a penchant for Seville oranges for jam making, as their slightly bitter nature (with a coarser peel) makes a nicer marmalade. However, ordinary oranges can be used, though the marmalade will be slightly sweeter. Marmalade is not just for toast, as Darina Allen observes, it can also be used for many desserts, such as cheesecake and panna cotta. Feel free to use honey or maple syrup instead of treacle.

Sterilize your jars and lids (see page 423). If you don't have a sugar (candy) thermometer, put a few saucers in the freezer to chill.

Put the oranges and lemon juice into a large pan and cover with 3 litres/105 fl oz (12½ cups) of water. Bring to the boil over a high heat, then reduce the heat and simmer for 2 hours.

Remove the oranges from the water and put into a large bowl. When cool enough to handle, cut in half and scoop out the flesh and piths and return them to the water. Cut the peel into strips and reserve.

Bring the water back to the boil and simmer for 30 minutes.

Remove the pan from the heat and push the entire contents through a sieve.

Return the strained liquid to the pan (cleaned, of course) with the sugar, treacle (molasses) and peel. Bring back to the boil and boil until the marmalade reaches the setting temperature of 105 °C/220 °F on a sugar thermometer. If you don't have a thermometer, test by adding a spoon of the hot jam onto a cold saucer (see page 363).

Remove the marmalade from the heat and stir in the whiskey. Pour the marmalade into the sterilized jars, stirring to ensure the peel is distributed evenly. Seal and store.

See opposite –>

Cherry 'Marmalade'

Preparation: 30 minutes
Cooking: 45 minutes
Makes 2 kg/4½ lb (6½ cups)

1.8 kg/4 lb (13 cups) cherries, stoned (pitted)
  and halved
450 g/1 lb (2¼ cups) caster (superfine) sugar

This recipe is adapted from the oldest known collection of Irish recipes, written by Dorothy Parsons (born in Birr Castle, County Offaly) in 1666.

Sterilize your jars and lids (see page 423). If you don't have a sugar (candy) thermometer, put a few saucers in the freezer to chill.

Put the cherries and sugar into a large heavy-based pan over a high heat and bring to the boil. Reduce the heat and boil, stirring all the time, for 20 minutes.

Squash the fruit with a potato masher. Continue to boil for

25 minutes until the jam reaches the setting temperature of 105 °C/220 °F on a sugar thermometer. If you don't have a thermometer, test by dropping a small spoon of the hot jam onto a cold saucer (see page 363).

When set, remove from the heat. Transfer to the sterilized jars, seal and store.

Pickling and Preservation

Pickling and Preservation

Salt

It's difficult to think about cooking without salt, but for the first few thousand years the first immigrants into Ireland did not use salt. It was only with the arrival of the agricultural revolution that people needed additional salt in their diet. The first salt was most likely produced only in coastal regions by trapping water in 'pans' and allowing it to evaporate. A map of County Mayo drawn in 1817 by William Bald shows salt pans at Polranny, near where the bridge to Achill Island now stands. The Celts (and Romans) were experts in mining salt in Central Europe, so we can only assume that they brought their technology of salt production to Ireland. The Celts knew the value of salt (from which the word 'salary' derives) and it was used in Ireland as a currency. The eighth-century text *Conall Corc and the Corco Luigde* records that the Aran Islanders paid a tribute of salt to the King of Cashel. Another method of salt production gives details of burning seaweed and boiling it with seawater. The resulting ash was used to season and cure foodstuffs. In the Middle Ages, English salt was imported into Ireland by the Anglo-Norman elites. English salt was seen (and still is to a certain degree – think of Maldon) as being a superior salt.

Though it is unclear whether the Celts mined Ireland for salt, modern salt mines do exist, but they mostly produce salt for gritting the roads. However, in the last few years Ireland has started to produce excellent sea salt to rival its English and French counterparts. My favourite is produced by Achill Island Sea Salt. Their flaky crystals are some of the finest in the world. Good-quality flaky salt comes from low and slow evaporation of the water. Oriel Sea Salt is another fine salt produced in County Louth. I hope this new small-scale salt production blooms into a world-renowned industry. As many coastal place names reveal, salt production is in our heritage. Down the road from me lies Salthill, which is now a part of Galway but used to be a coastal town.

Herb or Seaweed Salt

Preparation: 5 minutes
Makes 250 g/9 oz (1¼–1½ cups)

50 g/2 oz (1¾–2 cups packed) herbs, large stems removed, or 25 g/1 oz (½ cup) milled dried seaweed
200 g/7 oz (¾ cup) sea salt

I use many herb salts, both for seasoning and curing. Fresh woody herbs work best, such as rosemary, oregano, sage and thyme (or a combination of all four). Saying that, for curing, you can blend salt with softer herbs such as fennel or dill. You can also make a great salt with dried seaweed. Of all the flavoured salts, seaweed salt is my favourite. Dried seaweed has an intense umami quality and mixed with salt it provides a deep saline flavour. Seaweed salt is good on roast chicken or leg of lamb. You can also play around with adding additional spices to your seaweed salt, such as paprika (for colour) or black pepper (for extra pungency).

Put the herbs or seaweed and salt into a food processor and blend until smooth.

Sift through a sieve if desired.

Store in a cool, dark place.

Salted Ling

Preparation: 10 minutes, plus curing,
drying and desalinating times
Serves 4

4 ling fillets, skin on
sea salt

The practice of salting fish dates back to at least the Vikings. Whether or not they invented this process or collaborated with the Basque people (one bringing the fish, the other bringing the salt) is not known. However, we can surmise that the Vikings introduced the practice of salting fish to the Irish. Though cod was the most popular fish to salt, in truth any fish can be salted for later use.

Though not as famous as its counterpart (salted cod), salted ling has long been a staple of rural Irish fishing communities due to the availability of the fish. In his 1948 essay 'The Ling in Irish Commerce', published by *The Journal of the Royal Society of Antiquaries of Ireland*, Arthur E. J. Went cites examples from 1364 (Ballycotton, County East Cork) and later in 1537 (Dungarven, County Waterford) of the importance of this fish. During the seventeenth century, ling was exported from Galway to England and Spain. The ling is, according to Went, 'an ancient Irish food' and 'is part of the Irish heritage'. As with cod, ling was preserved by salting and drying the fillets. In this way, it kept for a long time. Though the practice of salting ling has all but died out due to refrigerating and freezing, it is still sometimes sold in Cork. If you cannot find your own salted ling, it is easy to make.

Cover the ling fillets liberally with sea salt. Leave to cure for 5–7 days.

Strain the fish and rinse under cold running water. Hang in a cool, dry place for 7–10 days until firm.

To use, desalinate by covering the fish in cold water and leaving to soak for between 12 and 24 hours, depending on the dryness of the ling.

Spiced Beef

Preparation: 45 minutes, plus curing
and pressing times
Cooking: 3 hours
Serves 8

1 teaspoon cloves
1 teaspoon ground mace
1 teaspoon black peppercorns
1 teaspoon ground allspice
500 g/1 lb 2 oz (2¼ cups) coarse (kosher) salt
60 g/2¼ oz (3 tablespoons) treacle (molasses)
50 g/2 oz (¼ cup firmly packed) soft
  brown sugar
4 shallots, chopped
4 bay leaves, crushed
1 teaspoon chopped thyme
1 tablespoon pink (curing) salt
3 kg/6½ lb beef silverside (bottom round
  or rump roast)

Spiced beef is a variation of corned beef. Spices may have been introduced to offset the salty flavour or to hide a putrid smell, but more likely they were a way of adding an exotic touch to a cheaper cut. The addition of pink salt (potassium nitrate) would have helped preserve the beef. Spiced beef is popular in the south of Ireland, especially Cork, but it is also widely eaten at Christmas time around the country. However, it is available all year round. In recent years, it has made a return in the form of an Irish Reuben sandwich due to its similarity to pastrami. You'll find many a good Reuben sandwich in Ireland.

Put all the spices in a mortar and grind with a pestle.

Put all the other ingredients except the beef into a large mixing bowl and combine to make a curing mix.

Place the meat on a tray and rub in the curing mix. Allow to cure for a week, rubbing in the mix every day.

After a week, roll and tie the meat neatly with kitchen string (twine).

Put into a large pan, cover with water and bring to the boil over a high heat, then reduce the heat and simmer gently for 2–3 hours until cooked.

Strain the water. Put the beef in a tray, lay a plate over the top and weigh the plate down with a heavy weight. Leave to press overnight in the refrigerator. Serve cold.

Corned Beef

Preparation and cooking: 3 hours 30 minutes, plus brining time

Makes 1 × 1.5-kg/3¼-lb corned beef

1 × 1.5-kg/3¼-lb beef brisket

For the spice mix
1 tablespoon black peppercorns
1 tablespoon mustard seeds
1 tablespoon coriander seeds
1 tablespoon allspice berries
½ teaspoon ground mace
½ tablespoon cloves

For the brine
250 g/9 oz (1 cup) sea salt
65 g/2½ oz (⅓ cup) caster (superfine) sugar
15 g/½ oz (1 tablespoon) pink (curing) salt
2 cloves garlic
½ cinnamon stick
1 bay leaf

To cook the corned beef
a bunch of herbs tied together such as thyme, rosemary, sage and parsley
2 onions, one studded with cloves
1 carrot

Corned, or salted, beef is a famous Irish tradition for the preservation of beef. Its first recorded mention dates back to the eleventh century in *Aislinge Meic Con Glinne*. In later centuries, Irish merchants traded with their French counterparts and imported salt to Cork and Waterford to make this unique product. Cork was the centre for corned beef production from the seventeenth to nineteenth centuries. During that period, it was shipped to many areas all over the world, including the West Indies to feed the slave populations working in the plantations. Cuts of beef used to produce corned beef are brisket, topside and silverside (bottom round or rump roast). You can use regular salt instead of curing salt, but the beef won't be as pink.

For the spice mix, put all the ingredients into a coffee grinder and blend until smooth. Reserve 2 heaped tablespoons for the brine, and save the rest for another time.

For the brine, put all the ingredients into a large pan and cover with 5 litres/175 fl oz (21 cups) of water. Add the 2 tablespoons of the spice mixture and bring to the boil. Allow to cool.

Place the brisket in the cooled brine and refrigerate for 5 days, turning every day.

When you are ready to cook the corned beef, discard the brine and rinse off the brisket, then put the brisket into a large pan of water with the herbs, onions and carrot. Bring to the boil and simmer for 2–3 hours until the beef is tender.

Remove from the pan and allow to rest. Thickly slice against the grain to serve.

Charcuterie

Over the last fifteen years, Ireland's charcuterie has developed into a world-class industry. McGeough's and Gubbeen are two examples of this recent revolution, but there are many more now. Though these modern Irish traditions of air-dried lamb, salamis and coppa seem altogether new, they do have precedent in the food history of Ireland. The practice of drying and smoking meat and fish is an age-old tradition in Ireland, as it is in many other Northern European countries such as Germany and the Nordic countries. Because of the damp climate, fish and meat would be salted and dried to preserve it for leaner times. Smoking gave the produce additional flavour. Oak and beech proliferated in Ireland and helped contribute to the tradition of smoking meat and fish. As well as consuming it themselves, the Irish have exported cured salmon, smoked fish (eel, mackerel and kippers/herrings), and salted (corned) beef for many centuries.

Cured Leg of Lamb

Preparation: 30 minutes, plus 6 months
1 week curing and drying time
Cures 1 leg of lamb

25 g/1 oz (½ cup prepared) meadowsweet,
    dried and milled
750 g/1 lb 10 oz (3 cups) sea salt
1 leg of lamb

In this recipe I use meadowsweet, but I've also used woodruff and milled seaweed. In fact, you can use any dried or milled herb you like. You can also add spices to the curing mix.

Combine the meadowsweet with the salt. Rub the salt into lamb.

Place the lamb on a tray and cure in the refrigerator for at least a week, turning it every day.

After a week, rinse off the salt and hang the leg in the refrigerator, uncovered, for 6 months to dry.

Cured Duck with Juniper and Gin

Preparation: 30 minutes, plus 2 weeks 2 days
curing and drying times
Serves 4

300 g/11 oz (1¼ cups) sea salt
200 g/7 oz (1 cup) caster (superfine) sugar
5 g/⅛ oz (1 tablespoon) juniper berries, toasted
a few sprigs of thyme
4 duck breasts
3½ tablespoons gin

To make a curing mix, put the salt, sugar, juniper berries and thyme into a food processor and pulse briefly.

Lay the duck on a bed of the curing mix and then cover. Refrigerate and allow to cure for 2 days, turning the duck breasts regularly.

Rinse the duck and allow to dry, uncovered, on a wire rack over a tray of salt in the refrigerator for 1–2 weeks.

At regular intervals during the drying, baste the duck with a little gin.

Cured Pork Neck with Seaweed

Preparation: 30 minutes, plus curing and
drying times
Cures 1 pork neck

1 pork neck
200 g/7 oz (1 cup) caster (superfine) sugar
300 g/11 oz (1¼ cups) sea salt
2 teaspoons pink (curing) salt
2 tablespoons milled sugar kelp

Seaweed is a great addition to cured meats. It lends a subtle umami quality to the finished product.

To make a curing mix, combine the sugar, salts and seaweed in a small mixing bowl.

Lay the pork neck on a tray and rub the curing mix into it. Turn the neck over and repeat the process on the other side.

Refrigerate and allow to cure for 5–7 days, turning the neck every day and ensuring that the curing mix covers all areas of the neck.

After the curing time is complete, rinse the neck and dry in the refrigerator for 6–8 weeks until firm.

Making Your Own Lardo

Preparation: 30 minutes, plus curing time
Cures 4 × 250-g/9-oz pieces

300 g/11 oz (1¼ cups) sea salt
4 cloves garlic
a few sprigs of rosemary and thyme
1 tablespoon black peppercorns
1 tablespoon juniper berries
1 bay leaf
1 kg/2¼ lb pork back fat, skin off, cut into
    4 equal pieces

Lardo is the cured back fat from a pig. You really need heritage pigs to make it, as the modern pigs are just too thin! Originally an Italian process, lardo is now widely made by many chefs and producers in Ireland. Fingal Ferguson makes a great one! Lardo takes six months to make, so be prepared for the wait. When making the lardo in Aniar, I leave out the black pepper (we don't use pepper in the restaurant), but feel free to play around with the spices, adding coriander or cumin seeds if desired. Furthermore, feel free to play around with wild herbs as well, such as woodruff.

To make a curing mix, put the salt with the garlic, herbs and spices into a food processor and blend until thoroughly combined.

Rub the curing mix into the pork fat on all sides. Cover with cling film (plastic wrap) and refrigerate for 6 months, turning occasionally.

See opposite –>

Beef Heart 'Ham'

Preparation: 30 minutes, plus 1 week
brining time
Cooking: 2 hours
Serves 2

1 beef heart
1 carrot
1 onion
1 clove garlic
1 bay leaf
a sprig of thyme
horseradish cream, to serve

For the brine
125 g/4½ oz (½ cup) sea salt
125 g/4½ oz (⅔ cup) caster (superfine) sugar
5 g/⅛ oz (1 teaspoon) pink (curing) salt
    (Prague powder #1)
1 teaspoon juniper berries

This beef heart is delicious served with horseradish cream, made from fresh horseradish mixed with sour cream.

Put all the brine ingredients into a large pan and cover with 2 litres/70 fl oz (8½ cups) of water. Bring to the boil, then remove from the heat and allow to cool.

Trim the excess fat off the heart and open. Remove any arteries or gristle. Place the heart in a bowl and cover with the brine until submerged. Leave for 1 week in the refrigerator.

Meanwhile, remove the heart from the brine and rinse. Put it into a large pan with the vegetables and herbs and cover with water. Bring to the boil and simmer for about 2 hours until tender.

Remove the heart from the pan and carve. Serve with some horseradish cream.

Pickling and Preservation

Pickling and Preservation

Stocks, Sauces and Condiments

Stocks, Sauces and Condiments

Stocks (broths) are the base of so much cooking. A great stock or broth makes a good sauce taste even better. I love to play around with stocks in terms of adding different vegetables and herbs. I especially love to use dried seaweed in my stock, whether milled or whole. This not only gives them a slight salinity but also increases the umami flavour in the stock, as well as the vitamin and mineral content. The Japanese have been using seaweed to make dashi for centuries, and I think it's about time we learned how to use our seaweed effectively. I personally love adding seaweed to everything! Only season your stock or sauces at the very end. Often when you reduce a salted stock, it becomes unpalatable.

Many old Irish recipes, particularly from the coast, specify cooking fish or shellfish in seawater. For me, this is a wonderful way to bring the life of the sea into our cooking. Be careful not to salt again after cooking, as the water will be salty enough. Potatoes as well as clams and mussels cooked in seawater are popular in many parts of Europe. A little seaweed won't go astray either!

In terms of sauces, I've included the classics (Parsley Sauce) and the contemporary (Whey Sauce) to give an insight into the range of today's Irish cooking. As an island, we have much outside influence. But that's not to say we don't create a few recipes of our own!

Condiments have long had a central place on the Irish table, from apple sauce with ham to bread sauce with game. There are many more traditional and contemporary condiments that I wish I could have included, but hopefully this gives you a flavour of Irish cooking.

Vegetable, Cider and Seaweed Stock

Preparation: 15 minutes
Cooking: 1 hour 30 minutes
Makes 5 litres/170 fl oz (21 cups)

2 tablespoons rapeseed (canola) oil
2 onions, chopped
2 leeks, sliced
3 carrots, chopped
1 fennel bulb, chopped
1 clove garlic, chopped
1 bay leaf
350 ml/12 fl oz (1½ cups) cider (hard cider)
15 g/½ oz dried sugar kelp

This is an alternative to a basic vegetable stock. The cider gives it a little bit more body and an apple flavour and the seaweed provides depth.

Fry the vegetables in batches: heat 1 tablespoon of the oil in a large pan over a medium heat, add the onions and leeks and fry for about 5 minutes until soft and translucent. Remove from the pan and set aside. Heat the remaining oil in the pan, add the carrots, fennel and garlic and fry for about 5 minutes until tender.

Return the reserved vegetables to the pan, add the bay leaf and cover with the cider. Simmer for about 20 minutes until reduced by half.

Cover everything with water, bring to the boil and then reduce to a simmer. Add the sugar kelp and simmer for 1 hour.

Allow to cool, then strain.

Chicken, Fennel and Seaweed Stock

Preparation: 30 minutes
Cooking: 4 hours
Makes 5 litres/170 fl oz (21 cups)

1 chicken, cut into pieces (breasts reserved for another use)
2 tablespoons rapeseed (canola) oil
2 fennel bulbs, chopped
1 onion, chopped
1 leek, chopped
350 ml/12 fl oz (1½ cups) cider (hard cider)
15 g/½ oz dried sugar kelp

Preheat the oven to 180°C/350°F/ Gas Mark 4.

Put the chicken pieces into a roasting pan and roast in the preheated oven for about 1 hour until brown.

Heat the oil in a large pan over a medium heat and fry all the vegetables until brown. Add the cider and bring to the boil.

Add the chicken and seaweed to the pan and cover with water. Bring to the boil, reduce the heat and simmer for 2–3 hours, skimming occasionally.

Strain the stock through a sieve and reduce further if desired. Chill the stock and skim off the fat when cold.

Ham and Seaweed Stock

Preparation: 20 minutes
Cooking: 3 hours
Makes 5 litres/170 fl oz (21 cups)

2 ham hocks (hock ends of 2 half hams)
1 carrot, chopped
1 onion, chopped
1 clove garlic, crushed
10 g/¼ oz sea spaghetti
10 g/¼ oz dried dillisk (dulse)
a few sage leaves
10 g/¼ oz dried kelp
10 g/¼ oz dried sugar kelp

Use ham stock (or the leftover water after cooking your ham) for meat or chicken dishes. As the hams are salted, be careful not to add any additional salt to a dish that you are using this stock for.

Put all the ingredients except the kelps into a large pan over a high heat, cover with water, bring to the boil, then simmer for 2 hours. Strain the liquid into another pan. Discard the vegetables and reserve the ham for another dish.

Place the seaweeds in the pan and simmer for 1 hour. Strain through a piece of muslin (cheesecloth) and store in the refrigerator.

Stocks, Sauces and Condiments

Brown Chicken Stock

Preparation: 30 minutes
Cooking: 3 hours 30 minutes
Makes 5 litres/170 fl oz (21 cups)

1 chicken, cut into pieces (breasts reserved
   for another use)
1 tablespoon rapeseed (canola) oil
2 onions, sliced (skins reserved)
2 carrots, roughly chopped
2 celery stalks, chopped
375 ml/13 fl oz (1⅔ cups) white wine
1 star anise
3 apples, quartered
1 bay leaf
a few sprigs of thyme and rosemary
   (or any other hardy herb)

Use this recipe for game birds, too. Reduce to use as the base for sauces.

Preheat the oven to 180°C/350°F/
Gas Mark 4.

Put the chicken pieces and onion skins into a roasting pan and roast in the preheated oven for about 1 hour until browned. Remove the chicken and deglaze the pan with a little water. Retain the liquid.

Heat the oil in a large pan over a medium–high heat, add the onions and fry for about 10 minutes until browned. Add the carrots and celery and cook for a further 5 minutes until browned.

Add the white wine, reserved liquid and star anise and bring to the boil. Add the chicken pieces and bones, apples, herbs and enough water to cover the stock. Bring the stock to the boil, then simmer for 2 hours, skimming off any impurities.

Strain the stock through a piece of muslin (cheesecloth).

Beef Stock

Preparation: 30 minutes
Cooking: 3 hours 30 minutes
Makes 5 litres/170 fl oz (21 cups)

1.5 kg/3¼ lb beef bones
4 tablespoons rapeseed (canola) oil
500 g/1 lb 2 oz diced beef shoulder
2 onions, sliced
1 star anise
6 carrots, chopped
1 leek, sliced
2 celery stalks, chopped
2 cloves garlic, crushed
375 ml/13 fl oz (1⅔ cups) red wine
1 bay leaf
a few sprigs of rosemary and thyme

Preheat the oven to 180°C/350°F/
Gas Mark 4.

Rub the bones in some oil, put into a roasting pan and roast in the preheated oven for 1 hour.

Meanwhile, heat 2 tablespoons of the oil in a large pan over a medium–high heat and when smoking hot, brown the meat in batches. Remove the beef from the pan and deglaze it with a little water. Set aside the liquid.

Heat the remaining oil in the same pan over a medium–high heat, add the onions and star anise and fry for about 10 minutes until the onions are brown. Add the carrots, leek, celery and garlic and cook for 5 minutes until soft.

Add the red wine and herbs and reduce by half. Add the beef bones, the deglazing water and enough water to cover. Bring the stock to the boil then simmer for 2 hours, skimming off any impurities.

Strain the stock through a piece of muslin (cheesecloth) and leave to rest overnight. Skim off any fat that remains. Reduce to use in sauces.

Fish and Seaweed Stock

Preparation: 20 minutes
Cooking: 1 hour 25 minutes
Makes 5 litres/170 fl oz (21 cups)

2 kg/4½ lb fish bones, cleaned
2 leeks, chopped
2 fennel bulbs, chopped
1 clove garlic, crushed
35 g/1¼ oz dried seaweed (I like to use
   kombu or sugar kelp)

Put the fish bones, vegetables and garlic into a large pan and cover with water. Bring to the boil, reduce the heat and simmer for 45 minutes.

Strain through a piece of muslin (cheesecloth), return the liquid to a clean pan and add the seaweed. Simmer for a further 30 minutes.

Chill and strain again.

Stocks, Sauces and Condiments

Lamb Jus

Preparation: 20 minutes
Cooking: 2 hours 20 minutes
Makes 5 litres/170 fl oz (21 cups)

1 tablespoon rapeseed (canola) oil
500 g/1 lb 2 oz diced lamb shoulder
250 ml/8 fl oz (1 cup) cider (hard cider)
a few sprigs of thyme
5 litres/170 fl oz (21 cups) lamb stock
tarragon vinegar (see Herb or Fruit Vinegar,
   page 352), to taste (optional)
sea salt

During game season, you can also use this method to make venison jus. Some chefs like to swap out the cider for wine and add in juniper berries and black peppercorns. Feel free to change as you prefer.

Heat the oil in a large pan over a medium heat, add the diced lamb and fry for about 5 minutes until nicely browned. Strain the lamb and discard the fat. Deglaze the pan with the cider and simmer for about 10 minutes until reduced by half.

Return the meat to the pan with the herbs and cover with the lamb stock. Simmer for 2 hours, skimming occasionally.

Strain through a piece of muslin (cheesecloth) and reduce if desired. Season with salt and vinegar.

Cider and Honey Sauce

Preparation: 5 minutes
Cooking: 20 minutes
Serves 6–8

500 ml/17 fl oz (generous 2 cups) cider
   (hard cider)
1 shallot, diced
1 clove garlic, crushed
a sprig of thyme
50 g/1¾ oz (2½ tablespoons) honey
200 g/7 oz (1¾ sticks) butter, cubed
apple cider vinegar, to taste
sea salt

Use this sauce for grilled vegetables, fish or chicken.

Put the cider, shallot, garlic and thyme into a medium pan over a medium–low heat and simmer for about 15 minutes until reduced by half.

Strain through a sieve, then add the honey and heat until it dissolves. Whisk in the butter and season to taste with salt and vinegar.

Whey Sauce

Preparation: 10 minutes
Cooking: 30 minutes
Serves 6–8

500 ml/17 fl oz (generous 2 cups) whey
100 ml/3½ fl oz (scant ½ cup) white wine
1 shallot, finely diced
1 clove garlic, crushed
a sprig of thyme
250 ml/8 fl oz (1 cup) single (light) cream
100 g/3½ oz (7 tablespoons) butter, cubed
Herb Vinegar (see page 352), to taste (optional)
sea salt

Whey sauce is a light, acidic butter sauce that goes well with vegetables (such as celeriac/celery root) and fish (such as cod). You can make your own whey by straining yogurt, or ask a friendly cheesemaker.

Put the whey into a medium pan over a medium–low heat with the wine, shallot, garlic and thyme. Simmer for about 15 minutes until reduced by half and strain through a sieve.

Add the cream, bring to the boil and simmer for about 15 minutes until reduced by half. When the sauce has a nice viscous quality, remove it from the heat and add the butter. The sauce should be thick and luscious. Add more butter if required.

Season with a little herb vinegar and salt if required.

Parsley Sauce

Preparation: 5 minutes
Cooking: 15 minutes
Serves 6–8

500 ml/17 fl oz (generous 2 cups) milk
50 g/2 oz (4 tablespoons) butter
50 g/2 oz (⅓ cup) plain (all-purpose) flour
250 ml/8 fl oz (1 cup) bacon, ham or vegetable stock (broth)
a small handful of parsley, leaves picked and chopped
sea salt

Parsley sauce is a traditional accompaniment for bacon and cabbage. Essentially, it is a béchamel (white) sauce containing chopped parsley. There are many different variations in many Irish cookbooks, containing white pepper, mace, bay leaf and garlic as additional seasonings. Feel free to change the herbs as desired.

Warm the milk in a small pan.

Melt the butter in a separate small pan over a low heat and stir in the flour. Cook for 2 minutes to form a paste. Slowly add the warm milk until it is all incorporated into the mixture.

Bring to a simmer and cook for 5–10 minutes until thickened. Whisk in the stock (broth). Add the parsley and season with sea salt.

See opposite –>

Bread Sauce

Preparation: 10 minutes
Cooking: 30 minutes
Serves 8–10

600 ml/20 fl oz (2½ cups) milk
1 bay leaf
6 whole black peppercorns
4 cloves
50 g/1¾ oz (2½ tablespoons) butter
1 onion, diced
150 g/5 oz (3 cups) fresh breadcrumbs
sea salt

This sauce goes well with game, and is also traditionally served with roast turkey at Christmas.

Pour the milk into a small pan over a medium heat and add the bay leaf and spices. Bring to the boil and remove from the heat. Allow to infuse for 20 minutes, then strain through a sieve.

Melt the butter in a medium pan over a medium heat and fry the onion for about 5 minutes until translucent. Add the breadcrumbs and cook for 1 minute. Gradually add the milk and whisk until the mixture has a sauce consistency. Season to taste.

Redcurrant Sauce

Preparation: 5 minutes
Cooking: 30 minutes
Makes 500 ml/17 fl oz (generous 2 cups)

200 g/7 oz (1 cup) caster (superfine) sugar
200 ml/7 fl oz (scant 1 cup) red wine vinegar
3½ tablespoons port
250 g/9 oz (2¼ cups) redcurrants
sea salt

This sauce goes well with game and pâtés.

Bring the sugar, vinegar and port to the boil in a medium pan over a medium heat, then add the redcurrants. Boil for a few minutes and then reduce to a simmer.

Simmer for about 25 minutes until the redcurrants burst and the sauce has a nice jam-like consistency.

Season with a little sea salt.

Stocks, Sauces and Condiments

Stocks, Sauces and Condiments

Apple Sauce

Preparation: 15 minutes
Cooking: 10 minutes
Serves 8

4 cooking apples, peeled, cored and sliced
50 g/1¾ oz (¼ cup firmly packed) soft
    brown sugar
1 cinnamon stick
1 teaspoon grated orange zest
25 g/1 oz (1¾ tablespoons) cold butter, cubed
sea salt

Apple sauce accompanies Michaelmas (29 September) goose, but it also works well with confit pork belly or roasted duck.

Put the apples into a small pan over a medium heat with the sugar, cinnamon and 3½ tablespoons of water. Simmer for about 5 minutes until the apples are completely soft. Discard the cinnamon stick.

Strain through a fine sieve. Return to the pan, add the orange zest and simmer for a few minutes. Season and whisk in the butter.

Elderflower Sauce

Preparation: 10 minutes
Cooking: 30 minutes
Makes 350 ml/12 fl oz (1½ cups)

200 ml/7 fl oz (scant 1 cup) chicken
    stock (broth)
200 ml/7 fl oz (scant 1 cup) cider (hard cider)
1 large head of elderflowers
200 ml/7 fl oz (scant 1 cup) double
    (heavy) cream
apple cider vinegar, to taste
sea salt

This sauce can be served with fish or chicken.

Bring the chicken stock (broth), cider and elderflowers to the boil in a large pan, then reduce the heat and simmer for about 20 minutes until reduced by half.

Strain through a sieve, add the cream and simmer for about 10 minutes until reduced to a sauce consistency. Season to taste with salt and vinegar.

Horseradish Sauce

Preparation: 10 minutes
Cooking: 10 minutes
Serves 6–8

250 ml/8 fl oz (1 cup) double (heavy) cream
1 teaspoon mustard
1 teaspoon lemon juice
2 tablespoons freshly grated horseradish
finely chopped chives

Though horseradish sauce is typically served with beef, it can also be served with fish, chicken or shellfish, such as oysters.

Pour the cream into a small pan, add the mustard and lemon juice and bring to the boil. Reduce the heat and simmer for about 10 minutes until slightly thickened.

Whisk in the fresh horseradish and chives.

Mushroom and Whiskey Sauce

Preparation: 10 minutes
Cooking: 30 minutes
Serves 6–8

50 g/1¾ oz (3½ tablespoons) butter
150 g/5 oz (2 cups prepared) button
   (white) mushrooms, sliced
a sprig of thyme
3½ tablespoons whiskey
3½ tablespoons beef stock (broth)
250 ml/8 fl oz (1 cup) double (heavy) cream
1 teaspoon chopped tarragon
sea salt

This robust sauce will match steak or chicken.

Melt half the butter in a frying pan (skillet), over a medium heat, add the mushrooms and thyme and fry for about 5 minutes until nicely coloured, then season to taste.

Add the whiskey and heat for a few minutes to burn off the alcohol, then add the stock (broth) and cream.

Simmer for about 15 minutes until reduced and the sauce coats the back of a spoon. Whisk in the remaining butter. Fold in the chopped tarragon and season.

Anchovy Sauce

Preparation: 5 minutes
Cooking: 15 minutes
Serves 6–8

250 ml/8 fl oz (1 cup) double (heavy) cream
100 ml/3½ fl oz (scant ½ cup) white wine
1 teaspoon anchovy paste
lemon juice, to taste
sea salt

This sauce goes well with oily fish such as mackerel, and vegetables.

Put the cream and white wine into a small pan and simmer over a low heat for about 15 minutes until reduced by half.

Stir in the anchovy paste, then season to taste with lemon juice and sea salt.

Wild Garlic Mayonnaise

Preparation: 10 minutes
Makes 225 ml/7½ fl oz (scant 1 cup)

2 egg yolks
2 tablespoons apple cider vinegar
225 ml/7½ fl oz (scant 1 cup) wild garlic oil
   (see Herb Oil, page 351)
sea salt

Put the egg yolks into a medium mixing bowl with the vinegar. Whisk them together, then begin to add the oil, a little at a time, whisking constantly. Don't go too fast. Only add a little more when the previous oil is incorporated. Finish with a tablespoon of water and adjust the seasoning to taste.

For Hazelnut Mayonnaise
Make the above mayonnaise with 150 ml/5 fl oz (⅔ cup) of regular rapeseed (canola) oil along with 3½ tablespoons hazelnut oil. Serve this with grilled vegetables such as asparagus, and meats such as venison, beef and chicken.

For Seaweed Mayonnaise
The same method as the Wild Garlic Mayonnaise but use a seaweed oil (see Herb Oil, page 351). You can also add dried/fresh seaweed into the mayonnaise. If using dried, rehydrate it first. Serve with fish or vegetables.

For Watercress Mayonnaise
Make a standard mayonnaise with 225 ml/7½ fl oz (scant 1 cup) regular rapeseed (canola) oil. Chop 50 g/1¾ oz (1½ cups prepared) watercress and fold into the mayonnaise with a little lemon juice. Serve with poached fish.

See image on page 218.

Stocks, Sauces and Condiments

Salad Cream Dressing

Preparation: 5 minutes
Makes about 200 ml/7 fl oz (scant 1 cup)

150 ml/5 fl oz (⅔ cup) double (heavy) cream
2 hard-boiled egg yolks
1 tablespoon English mustard
2 tablespoons apple cider vinegar
2 teaspoons soft brown sugar
lemon juice, to taste
sea salt and freshly ground white pepper,
    to taste

Before the advent of olive oil, salad cream was popular in Ireland. Of course, this arrival came earlier is some places, but by and large it was not until the late 1970s that olive oil made an appearance in any considered way. Growing up in the 1980s, my grandmother would always dress salads with salad cream (though I can't remember her making it, I think it came out of a bottle!).

Put all the ingredients into a food processor and blend until smooth.

Adjust the seasoning as desired.

Mushroom Ketchup

Preparation: 15 minutes
Cooking: 1 hour 15 minutes
Makes 750 ml/25 fl oz (3 cups)

1 tablespoon rapeseed (canola) oil
1 onion, diced
2 cloves garlic, very finely chopped
½ teaspoon ground mace
½ teaspoon groud nutmeg
1 bay leaf
600 g/1 lb 5 oz mixed mushrooms, sliced
75 g/2¾ oz (⅓ cup firmly packed) soft
    brown sugar
75 ml/2½ fl oz (⅓ cup) apple cider vinegar
3½ tablespoons apple balsamic vinegar
sea salt and freshly ground black pepper

Mushroom ketchup entered the lexicon of Irish food during the sixteenth or seventeenth century as part of the 'new English' foods then appearing in places in the Pale (the English-governed part of Ireland, now mostly Dublin). This recipe can be made with cultivated or wild mushrooms. You can also add some dried mushrooms (just rehydrate them in warm water) into the recipe.

Heat the oil in a medium pan over a medium heat. When the oil is hot, add the onion, garlic and spices and bay leaf. Season with salt and pepper. Fry for 7–8 minutes until the onion is nicely caramelized.

Add the mushrooms, cover and fry, stirring occasionally, for about 5 minutes until they begin to break down and release their liquid.

Add the sugar and vinegar and reduce the heat to low. Cover and cook for 1 hour, adding a little water if required.

Remove the bay leaf and blend the ketchup in a food processor. Adjust the seasoning and consistency as desired.

Gooseberry Ketchup

Preparation: 15 minutes
Cooking: 15 minutes
Makes 1 litre/34 fl oz (4¼ cups)

500 g/1 lb 2 oz (3⅓ cups) gooseberries,
    topped and tailed (trimmed)
250 ml/8 fl oz (1 cup) malt vinegar
250 g/9 oz (1 cup plus 2 tablespoons
    firmly packed) soft brown sugar
1 onion, chopped
1 clove garlic, crushed
1 bay leaf
5 juniper berries
sea salt

This ketchup pairs well with grilled oily fish such as salmon or mackerel.

Put all the ingredients into a medium pan over a medium heat and simmer for about 15 minutes until soft.

Remove the juniper berries and bay leaf. Blend in a food processor or with an immersion blender until smooth. Strain if desired through a fine sieve.

Stocks, Sauces and Condiments

Apple Stuffing for Goose or Duck

Preparation: 15 minutes

Cooking: 5 minutes

Makes enough for 1 goose or large duck

25 g/1 oz (1¾ tablespoons) butter

450 g/1 lb (about 3) cooking apples, peeled, cored and sliced

3½ tablespoons chicken stock (broth)

25 g/1 oz (2 tablespoons) granulated sugar

1 teaspoon each of finely chopped sage and thyme leaves

1 egg (to help bind, optional)

75 g/2¾ oz (1⅔ cups) fresh breadcrumbs

sea salt

Melt the butter in a small pan over a medium heat. Add the apples along with the stock (broth), sugar and herbs. Cover and cook for about 5 minutes until the apples have completely broken down.

Remove from the heat and stir in the egg, if using, and the breadcrumbs. Season to taste.

Any leftovers will freeze well.

Sausage Stuffing

Preparation and cooking: 15 minutes

Makes enough for 1 bird

25 g/1 oz (1¾ tablespoons) butter

1 onion, finely diced

450 g/1 lb sausage meat

120 g/4 oz (2⅔ cups) fresh breadcrumbs

1 teaspoon finely chopped sage

sea salt

This stuffing is great for poultry but also for making your own sausage rolls with ready-made puff pastry, which is widely available. You can freeze this stuffing if you have too much for one bird.

Melt the butter in a small pan over a medium heat and fry the onion for about 5 minutes until soft and translucent. Remove from the heat and allow to cool.

Combine the onion, sausage meat, breadcrumbs and sage in a large mixing bowl. Season with a little sea salt and use as desired.

Chestnut Stuffing for Poultry

Preparation: 10 minutes

Makes enough for 1 bird

500 g/1 lb 2 oz (3¼ cups) chestnuts, cooked

100 g/3½ oz (2 cups) fresh breadcrumbs

3½ tablespoons double (heavy) cream

25 g/1 oz (1¾ oz) butter

1 teaspoon each of finely chopped sage and thyme leaves

sea salt

Put all the ingredients into a food processor and blend until smooth.

Season to taste.

Stocks, Sauces and Condiments

Drinks, Shrubs and Syrups

Drinks, Shrubs and Syrups

'The most important things to do in the world are to get something to eat, something to drink and somebody to love you.'

Brendan Behan, *The Wit of Brendan Behan*, 1968

When it comes to drink, the global reputation of Ireland is somewhat ahead of its food. Our relationship to alcohol is well known. Departing visitors always comment on our love of the 'black stuff' (Guinness). But drinks in Ireland are a lot more diverse than that. As the quote on the left by Irish writer Brendan Behan (who did enjoy a drink or two) suggests, food, drink and hospitality have always been at the forefront of the Irish experience. However, I think the latter two have played a more pivotal role in shaping attitudes towards Ireland for the last two hundred years. Hospitality in particular, since the medieval period, has been a part of the Irish experience for visitors. From Guinness to Baileys and a myriad of fine whiskeys, the reputation of the Irish alcohol industry is second to none.

Before tea arrived in Ireland, buttermilk, cider and oat milk were common everyday drinks. Bull's milk was a drink made from oats soaked in water. The mixture was left to ferment for three days and then drank. It was not stirred up again before drinking. The leftover oats were used to make sowans, a dish similar to porridge but with a sour taste.

But these are not the only drinks I would like to discuss here. There is another tradition of Irish drinks that is intimately connected to its landscape. These drinks, from cider to beer, to wine and liqueurs, are all made with wild herbs and fruit. This tradition has waned a little, but it now seems to be on the rise again, due to people's renewed interest in their local landscape and an interest in alternative drinks such as kefir and kombucha (both of which are made and drunk in Ireland now). In truth, these drinks can be made anywhere in the world, given that many of Ireland's wild ingredients are native to other countries as well. For a long time, country wines, made from blackberries, haws and elderberries, and herb beers, made from nettles and dandelions, were common to many households all over the country.

I have also included in this section some syrups and shrubs. Syrups, including cordials, were a way of preserving the flavour of fruit, which could then be used to make meringue or flavour cakes or drinks. Shrubs were country tonics or 'drinking vinegars' (both acidic and sweet and often alcoholic) to take when ailing. Shrubs can be made according to a hot and cold process and with or without alcohol, depending on your preference. I have included examples of all the methods here, but any fruit or spices can be used. Just use my recipes as a guide when making your own. Shrubs provide a great way of adding a sweet and sour flavour to certain dishes. Sharon Greene of Wild Irish Foragers produces many syrups and shrubs from her wild farm in Offaly.

Blackberry Shrub

Preparation: 10 minutes, plus 2 days
standing time
Makes 1.25 litres/40 fl oz (5 cups)

450 g/1 lb (3 cups) blackberries
450 g/1 lb (2¼ cups) caster (superfine) sugar
450 ml/15 fl oz (scant 2 cups) apple
   cider vinegar

Mix all the ingredients together in
a bowl. Cover and allow to stand
for 2 days at room temperature.

Strain through a sieve, transfer to a
sterilized bottle (see page 423) and
store in the refrigerator.

The shrub will be ready to use
immediately, and will keep for
3–6 months.

Rhubarb and Ginger Shrub

Preparation and cooking: 15 minutes
Makes 750 ml/25 fl oz (3 cups)

450 g/1 lb (3⅔ cups prepared) rhubarb, sliced
250 g/9 oz (1¼ cups) caster (superfine) sugar
250 ml/8 fl oz (1 cup) apple cider vinegar
1 teaspoon freshly grated ginger

Put all the ingredients along with
250 ml/8 fl oz (1 cup) of water into
a medium pan over a medium heat
and simmer for about 10 minutes
until the rhubarb is soft.

Allow to cool, then strain through
a sieve, transfer to a sterilized
bottle (see page 423) and store in
the refrigerator.

It is ready to use immediately, and
will keep for 3–6 months.

Rum and Orange Shrub

Preparation: 10 minutes, plus fermenting
and maturing time
Makes 750 ml/25 fl oz (3 cups)

750 ml/25 fl oz (3 cups) rum
75 g/2¾ oz (⅓ cup) caster (superfine) sugar
juice of 3 oranges
juice of 1 lemon

This recipe is based on an eighteenth-century shrub recipe.

Mix all the ingredients in a
container, cover and store for
3 weeks, stirring occasionally.

After 3 weeks, transfer to
a sterilized bottle (see page 423)
and age for 2–3 months in the
refrigerator.

Raspberry Syrup

Preparation: 15 minutes, plus soaking time
Cooking: 30 minutes
Makes 1.25 litres/40 fl oz (5 cups)

500 g/1 lb 2 oz (4 cups) raspberries
500 g/1 lb 2 oz (2½ cups) caster
   (superfine) sugar

You can use any berries for the recipe below. I like to use blackberries,
strawberries and blackcurrants.

Put the raspberries, sugar and
500 ml/17 fl oz (generous 2 cups)
of water into a large pan over a
medium heat and bring to the boil.
Reduce the heat to low and simmer
for 25 minutes.

Mash the fruit with a fork or potato
masher. Remove from the heat and
allow to macerate for a few hours,
then strain through a sieve. If you
want the syrup to be extra clear,
strain through a piece of muslin
(cheesecloth). Chill.

Drinks, Shrubs and Syrups

Birch Syrup

Preparation: 10 minutes
Cooking: 30 minutes
Makes 1.25 litres/40 fl oz (5 cups)

5 litres/175 fl oz (21 cups) birch sap
500 g/1 lb 2 oz (2½ cups) caster
  (superfine) sugar

Use for glazing meats or flavouring desserts.

Put the birch sap into a large stewpot over a high heat and bring to the boil. Reduce the heat and simmer for about 30 minutes until reduced to 500 ml/17 fl oz (generous 2 cups).

Add the sugar, increase the heat and boil until the syrup coats the back of a spoon. Cool, then store in refrigerator.

Elderflower Cordial

Preparation: 15 minutes
Cooking: 10 minutes
Makes 2.5 litres/85 fl oz (10½ cups)

1 kg/2¼ lb (5 cups) caster (superfine) sugar
12 elderflower heads
2 lemons, zest removed and quartered
30 g/1 oz citric acid (optional)

Dilute the cordial (syrup) with sparkling water to serve as a drink.

Place all the ingredients into a large pan with 1.5 litres/50 fl oz (6¼ cups) of water and heat for about 5 minutes until the sugar dissolves. Remove from the heat and allow to cool.

Strain through a sieve, transfer to sterilized bottles (see page 423) and refrigerate.

Rose Hip Cordial

Preparation: 15 minutes
Cooking: 25 minutes
Makes 1.25 litres/40 fl oz (5 cups)

1 kg/2¼ lb (8 cups) rose hips, seeds removed
500 g/1 lb 2 oz (2½ cups) caster
  (superfine) sugar

Rose hip cordial is a nice to drink with sparkling water or add to desserts.

Put all the ingredients into a large pan with 1.5 litres/50 fl oz (6¼ cups) of water and bring to the boil. Reduce the heat and simmer for about 25 minutes until the rose hips are soft.

Strain through a sieve (or a jelly bag if you want a clear cordial/syrup – you can leave the rose hip seeds in if you do this). Store in the refrigerator.

Carrageen, Milk and Honey

Preparation: 5 minutes
Cooking: 20 minutes
Serves 4

1 litre/34 fl oz (4¼ cups) milk
15 g/½ oz dried carrageen
45 g/1½ oz (2 tablespoons) organic honey

Put all the ingredients into a large pan over a medium heat and bring to the boil. Reduce the heat and simmer for 15–20 minutes until the carrageen becomes gelatinous and begins to break up. Remove from the heat and strain through a sieve.

You can drink it straight away or pour it into moulds and refrigerate for a few hours until set.

Almond Milk

Preparation: 5 minutes
Makes about 1 litre/34 fl oz (4¼ cups)

200 g/7 oz (1⅓ cups) almonds, peeled
honey, to sweeten

Almond milk was popular in Ireland and appeared in recipe books from the seventeenth to nineteenth century. It was often made with barley water first, which was then mixed with almonds and herbs (such as strawberry leaves and rosemary) before being sweetened (with honey or sugar). Wild herbs such as meadowsweet or woodruff can also be used to flavour the milk.

Put the almonds into a blender with 800 ml/28 fl oz (3⅓ cups) of cold water and blend until smooth.

Strain through a piece of muslin (cheesecloth) and sweeten to taste.

Woodruff Tea

Preparation and cooking: 15 minutes
Serves 1

a large handful of dried woodruff leaves
a few fresh woodruff leaves and flowers
woodruff oil (see Herb Oil, page 351, optional)

The role of wild plants in the Mesolithic diet is hard to assess because there is little archaeological evidence left behind from the consumption of plant material. However, we do know that plants were part of the hunter-gatherer diet and there is some evidence (in Belderrig, County Mayo) that points towards the use of plant material for some type of herbal drink. This may have been drunk for their health and medicinal properties. Any wild herbs make wonderful infusions. Outside Ireland, hunter-gatherers have eaten plants for thousands of years, so it's safe to assume that their equivalent in Ireland brought those traditions with them when they arrived on these shores.

To make the tea, pour 250 ml/ 8 fl oz (1 cup) hot water (82°C/ 180°F) over the dried woodruff leaves and allow to infuse for 10 minutes. Strain through a sieve.

To serve, put a few woodruff leaves and flowers into a small cup, pour over the tea and decorate with a few drops of woodruff oil, if using.

Blackcurrant Leaf Tea

Make in the same way as the woodruff tea. Pour hot water (82°C/180°F) over a handful of blackcurrant leaves and allow to infuse for 4–5 minutes before serving.

Birch and Pineapple Weed Tea

Fill a teapot with baby birch leaves and a small quantity of pineapple weed heads. Pour hot water (82°C/180°F) over them and allow to infuse for 4–5 minutes before serving.

Drinks, Shrubs and Syrups

Cider

Preparation: 45 minutes, plus fermenting
and maturing times
Cooking: 30 minutes
Makes 8 × 750-ml/25-fl oz (3-cup) bottles

3 kg/6½ lb (about 16 medium) apples,
  washed and unpeeled
juice of 3 lemons
25 g/1 oz (¾-inch piece) fresh ginger
3.5 kg/7¾ lb (17½ cups) caster
  (superfine) sugar

The tradition of making cider (hard cider) grew along with the apple orchards of the many monastic sites that dominated Ireland in the early Middle Ages. When I was growing up, the cider industry in Ireland was dominated by Bulmers, an off-dry cider produced in Tipperary. However, recent years have seen an explosion of craft ciders in Ireland with many different styles being produced. It is really a drink we should work on developing more because it is the closest we have to a wine industry in Ireland. With the rise of food tourism, more orchards should be prepared to welcome visitors to showcase what they do to the outside world. The experience of making the drink goes hand in hand with the experience of drinking it. Highbank Orchard in Kilkenny, who also make gin and brandy from apples, are at the forefront of this revolution.

Making traditional cider requires a small cider press (or juicer). The flavour of the cider arises from the interaction of the pure juice with the flavour of the crushed pips (seeds). In pure cider, no sugar is added, but this depends on the type of apples you are using. If you're making cider with crab apples, you'll need to use sugar. Some recipes allow for a spontaneous fermentation while others add yeast and a nutrient. The recipe below is based on the one in Theodora FitzGibbon's *Irish Traditional Food* (1983). For me, it's more of a country apple wine.

Cut the apples into pieces and put them into an earthenware or glass/plastic container (metal will taint the cider).

Bring 7 litres/245 fl oz (30 cups) of water to the boil and pour it over the apples. Cover and leave to ferment for 2 weeks somewhere warm, stirring daily and pressing the fruit against the sides.

Strain the juice through a sieve into a large stewpot and add the lemon juice and ginger. Measure the liquid and add 225 g/8 oz (1 cup plus 2 tablespoons) of sugar for every 450 ml/15 fl oz (scant 2 cups) of liquid. Bring the liquid to the boil for a few minutes until the sugar dissolves. Cover again and allow to ferment for a further 12 days.

Skim the scum off the top and the sides of the pot, transfer to a demijohn (see opposite) with an airlock and leave for a further week.

Siphon into sterilized bottles and age for 2–3 months before drinking.

Blackberry Liqueur

Preparation: 10 minutes, plus maturing time
Makes about 1 litre/34 fl oz (4¼ cups)

150 g/5 oz (1 cup) blackberries
50 g/1¾ oz (¼ cup) caster (superfine) sugar
750 ml/25 fl oz (3 cups) brandy
a few mint leaves, torn

Put the berries, sugar, brandy and mint leaves into a sterilized glass jar (see page 423).

Seal and store in a cool, dark place for 2 months, shaking from time to time to help the sugar to dissolve.

Strain and store in a cool, dark place before serving. The soaked fruit can be dried in a low oven (55°C/130°F) for 4 hours and eaten with ice cream.

Mead

Preparation: 10 minutes, plus fermenting
and maturing times
Makes 5 × 750-ml/25-fl oz (3-cup) bottles

3 litres/105 fl oz (12½ cups) filtered water
1 kg/2¼ lb (3 cups) honey
7 g/¼ oz (2¼ teaspoons) wine yeast (1 sachet)

Mead is a honey wine with ancient origins. It is produced when honey and water ferment. This would have occurred naturally before humans learned how to produce it. The drink is common to many cultures across Europe and most likely has its origins in Africa or Asia. The Bell Beaker people may have been the first to produce it (see page 17). The Celts and the Vikings also enjoyed mead and they too may have popularized it on the Island before the production of cider began in the monastic settlements due to the production of apples from the orchards.

Combine the ingredients in a large bowl or pan and stir. Cover with a clean cloth and allow to ferment for 2–4 days, stirring occasionally.

Pour into a demijohn (a large narrow-necked bottle) with an airlock and ferment for 2–3 weeks.

Drink immediately or siphon into sterilized bottles (see page 423) and age for up to 6 months.

Dandelion Beer

Preparation: 30 minutes, plus fermenting
and maturing times
Cooking: 30 minutes
Makes 8 × 750-ml/25-fl oz (3-cup) bottles

500 g/1 lb 2 oz (9 cups chopped)
    dandelion leaves (greens)
juice and grated zest of 2 lemons
10 g/¼ oz (about 5 slices) fresh ginger
1 kg/2¼ lb (5 cups) caster (superfine) sugar
25 g/1 oz (3 tablespoons) cream of tartar
7 g/¼ oz (2¼ teaspoons) yeast (1 sachet)

Both beer and wine can be made with dandelions. Before carbonation stones, cream of tartar was used instead of yeast to carbonate drinks.

Put the dandelions with the lemon zest and ginger into a large stewpot and cover with 4.5 litres/158 fl oz (19 cups) of water. Bring to the boil, reduce the heat and simmer for 15 minutes.

Strain through a sieve and add the sugar and the cream of tartar. Allow to cool, then add the yeast and the lemon juice.

Transfer the mixture to a demijohn (see above) with an airlock and ferment for 3 days.

Siphon into sterilized bottles (see page 423) with screw-top lids and leave for 1 week in a cool place before drinking.

Nettle Wine

Preparation: 30 minutes, plus cooling
and maturing times
Cooking: 45 minutes
Makes 5 × 750-ml/25-fl oz (3-cup) bottles

2 litres/70 fl oz (8½ cups) young nettle tops
1 lemon, halved, plus the juice from
    1 × 15-g/½-oz (⅜-inch piece) fresh ginger
1.5 kg/3¼ lb (7½ cups) caster (superfine) sugar
7 g/¼ oz (2¼ teaspoons) yeast (1 sachet)
yeast nutrient (follow package directions)

Put the nettles, the lemon halves and the ginger into a large pan and cover with water. Bring to the boil, reduce the heat and simmer for 45 minutes.

Strain the water through a sieve into another pan and top it up so the total amount of water is 4.5 litres/158 fl oz (19 cups). Add the sugar and the juice of the remaining lemon and allow to cool.

When cool, add the yeast and yeast nutrient.

Pour the mixture into a demijohn (see above) with an airlock and allow to age for 6 months.

Siphon into sterilized bottles (see page 423) and age for a further 6 months.

Sloe Gin

Preparation: 15 minutes, plus maturing time
Makes 1 litre/34 fl oz (4¼ cups)

225 g/8 oz sloe berries
125 g/4½ oz (⅔ cup) caster (superfine) sugar
750 ml/25 fl oz (3 cups) gin

In recent years, Ireland has undergone a veritable gin revolution. There are now so many gins on the Irish market that I have lost count of them. Some of the more interesting ones are made with seaweed and wild ingredients. In the restaurant, we make our own herbal infusion using a base gin. Sloe (or sloeberry) gin is the original of these 'wild' liqueurs but any fruit can be used, depending on your taste and preference.

Place the berries, sugar and gin into a large sterilized glass jar (see page 423).

Store in a cool, dark place for 2 months, shaking intermittently to help the sugar to dissolve.

Once matured, strain into bottles and refrigerate.

See opposite –>

Birch Wine

Preparation: 45 minutes, plus fermenting and maturing times
Cooking: 15 minutes
Makes 8 × 750-ml/25-fl oz (3-cup) bottles

5 litres/175 fl oz (21 cups) birch sap
1.5 kg/3¼ lb (7½ cups) sugar
4 lemons, halved
7 g/¼ oz (2¼ teaspoons) wine yeast (1 sachet)
yeast nutrient (follow package directions)

In the *Donovan Family Recipe Book* (1713), Mary Ogle writes 'In the latter end of March or the beginning of April make a hole in a birch tree…'. Though few (if any) of us tap birch trees now, the practice still continues in a few parts of Ireland. In Aniar, we get birch sap from the trees and reduce it to a syrup (see page 390) to glaze pork and tuna. The syrup can also be used for ice creams and other desserts. Collecting birch sap is a job in itself and takes time and practice. We're lucky to know a forager (Brian Gannon) who collects it for us. Making your own wine is a big project, but if you have the time and inclination it can be rewarding. I recommend reading up on some basic techniques before first attempting it.

Pour the birch sap into a large stewpot with the sugar and lemons and bring to the boil. Remove from the heat and strain through a fine sieve or muslin (cheesecloth).

When cool, add the yeast and then the yeast nutrient, cover with a lid and allow to ferment at room temperature for 4–5 days.

Siphon the liquid into a demijohn (a large narrow-necked bottle) with an airlock and leave in a cool place for 2 months.

Rack off (see below) into a fresh demijohn after 1 month and again after the second month.

Bottle the wine when clear. Age for up to 6 months.

Note
The term 'rack off' refers to using a food-grade hose or racking tube to siphon the wine must from the bottle into a clean bottle, leaving the sediment behind.

Drinks, Shrubs and Syrups

Whiskey Punch

Preparation: 10 minutes
Cooking: 10 minutes
Serves 4

750 ml/25 fl oz (3 cups) whiskey
225 g/8 oz (1 cup plus 2 tablespoons) caster (superfine) sugar
grated zest and juice of 2 oranges
grated zest of 2 lemons, plus lemon slices, to serve
3 cloves
1 cinnamon stick

Punch (*Puins*) was traditionally made with whiskey or brandy, but it was also made with poteen or rum if none of the former could be found. It is usually served at Christmas time as well as to many weary travellers in hotels around the country. In her *Irish Traditional Food* (1983), Theodora FitzGibbon recounts William Thackery's observation in his *Irish Sketch Book* (1843) that 'for a sum of twelve shilling any man could take his share of turbot, salmon, venison and beef with port and sherry and whiskey punch'.

Place 500 ml/17 fl oz (generous 2 cups) of water with the sugar, orange zest and juice, lemon zest, cloves and cinnamon into a large pot over a medium heat and bring to the boil.

Remove from the heat and allow the liquid to cool slightly before adding the whiskey. Serve with some lemon slices.

Irish Whiskey Cream

Preparation: 5 minutes
Serves 8

200 ml/7 fl oz (scant 1 cup) whiskey
250 ml/8 fl oz (1 cup) double (heavy) cream
2 tablespoons sugar syrup

Most people now know Irish whiskey cream or Irish cream liqueur as Baileys, one of the most successful drinks ever produced in Ireland. It is now exported all over the world. There are many other brands on the market, but it is a cocktail you can make yourself at home. Most of the recipes I have come across contain chocolate, vanilla and coffee. Below is a much simpler version. The sugar syrup can be flavoured if desired.

Mix the whiskey, cream and sugar syrup together, pour into glasses and serve.

Baby Guinness

Preparation: 5 minutes
Serves 2

60 ml/2 fl oz (4 tablespoons) coffee liqueur
30 ml/1 fl oz (2 tablespoons) Irish cream liqueur

A Baby Guinness is short cocktail usually drunk as a shot (in one mouthful). It is usually made with Baileys and Kahlúa, but it can also be made with Tia Maria and Black Sambuca.

Fill two shot glasses two-thirds full with the coffee liqueur, then gently pour the Irish cream liqueur over it.

Use the back of spoon, so the cream liqueur rests on top of the other liquid, like a head of a pint of Guinness.

Irish Coffee

Preparation: 5 minutes
Serves 2

20 g/¾ oz (1½ tablespoons packed)
 soft brown sugar
150 ml/5 fl oz (⅔ cup) whiskey
300 ml/10 fl oz (1¼ cups) hot coffee
4 tablespoons double (heavy) cream,
 very lightly whipped

Irish coffee has its modern origins in Foyne in Shannon, County Clare. It was invented by Joe Sheridan in Shannon Airport in 1947, when transatlantic flights recommenced after World War II. However, a combination of whiskey with coffee as a cocktail has been part of both Irish and European culture for much longer. In nineteenth-century Vienna, coffee houses served coffee cocktails topped with cream.

Warm the glasses with hot water.

Add the sugar, pour in the whiskey and stir. Pour over the hot coffee and stir again, ensuring the sugar has dissolved.

With the aid of the back of a spoon, pour the lightly whipped cream over the top of the coffee.

Scalteen

Preparation and cooking: 10 minutes
Serves 2

550 ml/18 fl oz (2½ cups) milk
40 g/1½ oz (2 tablespoons) honey
120 ml/4 fl oz (½ cup) whiskey

This recipe is based on the one that appears in Myrtle Allen's *Cooking at Ballymaloe House* (1990). Allen notes that the drink is referred to in *The Diaries of Humphry O'Sullivan*, an account written by a Kilkenny schoolteacher in the 1830s. A different recipe appears in Diarmuid Ó Muirithe's book *Words We Don't Use (Much Anymore)* (2011) attributed to a man from Tipperary: 'Add half a bottle of whiskey, two whisked eggs and a lump of butter to a pint and a half of strained beef broth to which salt and black pepper has been added. Heat the mixture well but do not boil.' Allen's is more an after-dinner drink, while the latter seems to be more a meal.

Warm the milk and honey in a small pan over a low heat.

Add the whiskey, stir and serve warm.

Sack Posset

Preparation: 10 minutes
Cooking: 10 minutes
Serves 4

850 ml/30 fl oz (3½ cups) single (light) cream
100 g/3½ oz (½ cup) caster (superfine) sugar
1 cinnamon stick
1 blade of mace
grated zest of 1 orange
6 egg yolks, plus 2 egg whites
250 ml/8 fl oz (1 cup) sack (or dry sherry)
3½ tablespoons orange juice

A posset was a popular drink in wealthier Irish households in the seventeenth and eighteenth centuries. It was usually taken for curative purposes, but drinking it nowadays I wonder how they thought that this mixture could cure anything. I imagine it would be good to have on a cold winter's evening, sitting by the fire.

Pour the cream into a medium pan over a medium heat and add the sugar, spices and orange zest. Simmer for about 5 minutes until the cream is hot.

Whisk the eggs with the sherry and orange juice in a large mixing bowl. Pour the hot cream over the egg mixture, whisking all the time.

Return the mixture to the pan and heat gently for a few minutes until warm, whisking all the time to avoid the mixture curdling. Pour into glasses and serve warm.

Drinks, Shrubs and Syrups

An Index of Wild plants, Seaweed and Fungi

An Index of Wild Plants, Seaweed and Fungi

The following information is provided as a guide, with harvesting seasons given for Ireland. Availability and seasons will vary depending on where you live. Consult a local guide for specific information. Exercise caution when picking wild ingredients, and any foraged ingredients should only be eaten if an expert has deemed them safe – this is especially true for mushrooms. Only pick mushrooms that are young, fresh, healthy and whole. All herbs, shoots, flowers and leaves (greens) should be picked fresh, from a clean source. When foraging for any produce, be aware of the environment in which it grows. Pick berries that are high up and out of reach of wild animals, and avoid gathering herbs by the roadside or near fields of cultivated crops which may use pesticides.

Wild Herbs and Flowers

Since the arrival of the earliest settlers on the island, wild herbs and flowers formed an important part of the diet of Irish people in terms of food and medicine. However, our contemporary attitude towards wild food is nebulous at best. With the advent of modernism and consumer culture that brought with it processed food, wild food gradually became less important in the Western world in the twentieth century, though it is probably only in the last seventy-five years that we have turned our backs wholesale on wild food. This is a great shame. Every year, literally tonnes of wild food goes to waste. What was once a necessity (rose hips to help with chesty coughs) has now turned into an occasional pastime for the few. How did this all happen? Even before the last century, before the refrigerator and the freezer, farming and the industrial revolution had changed people's eating habits. This gradual letting go of the wild meant that each new generation had a little less knowledge than the last one. As food became easier to acquire, we would travel less into the wood or forest in search of our daily bread. As I have mentioned elsewhere, perhaps the greatest threat to wild food is the idea that it is for people who cannot buy their food. While this may seem like a crazy idea, following the famine in Ireland, wild food was associated with the lower classes, people who could not produce or purchase food themselves. Picking berries and herbs was looked down upon by many, particularly as more and more people migrated to the cities to live. While the tradition of picking fruits continued in the countryside throughout the twentieth century, it is now almost non-existent. However, perhaps a revival is in order.

It is important we realize the central place of wild food in the canon of Irish food. It has sustained us for thousands of years. Only in this way can we celebrate it and return to using it in our daily lives. But to do this, we must acquire lost knowledge and get out into the open to explore our surroundings. How to begin? Probably with dandelions or nettles, or even wild garlic. All these plants are easy to identify and are even easier to use in your daily life of cooking. This is how I began. From this point, it is just a matter of identifying a few plants every year and adding them to your larder (pantry). In no time, you'll have a host of wild food at your disposal. The list below is by no means exhaustive and represents just the most common wild herbs I use in my cooking. There are many more and I hope that this list gives you an insight into the culinary aspects of Irish wild herbs and flowers.

Alexanders

Irish name: *Lusrán grándubh*
Latin name: *Smyrnium olusatrum*
Flowering period: March to June

Wild alexanders, also called horse parsley, abound in the south of the country. I've encountered them in the city of Cork and in the hedgerows along the small roads of east Cork. They can also be found in coastal regions as well as on the Aran Islands, particularly Inis Mór. It was introduced into Ireland possibly around 500 BC and subsequently flourished in monastic settlements. Alexanders are not used too frequently nowadays. With the introduction of celery in the nineteenth century, the heady days of this wild herb were numbered. I love its celery-scented flavour and its bright yellow-green flower heads. Its leaves are distinctly shiny so you can use that to identify it among the other umbellifers. In terms of eating, the whole plant is up for grabs. From its leaves (nicely pickled or added to salads) to its stalks (stems) and hollow shoots (blanched as any vegetable, or pickled), it is perhaps a little paradise for the cook. I've paired it with crab and it's excellent. In the autumn (fall), you can also dry the seeds and use them as a substitute for pepper or mix them with salt for a celery-tasting seasoning. You can use the plant to flavour stock (broth) and stews. Drying the leaves and blending them with salt or sugar produces a nicely saline-aromatic sweetener that can be used for meringue and marshmallow. Alexanders sugar in strawberry jam is a nice touch. As with many wild herbs, it can be added to different spirits such as vodka and gin to make a flavoured liqueur.

Angelica, wild

Irish name: *Gallfheabhrán*
Latin name: *Angelica sylvestris*
Flowering period: July to September

Angelica (sometimes called woodland angelica) is found all over Ireland, particularly on riverbanks and in damp grassy meadows and woods. In the summer, its sweet white flowers open into a soft white umbel that smells like anise. As with Alexanders and lovage, the plant has a variety of uses from savoury to sweet. Icelandic chef Gunnar Karl Gíslason has a wonderful recipe for pickled stalks (stems) that can be used with poached or salted white fish. They also combine well with braised fennel because the flavours complement each other.

In the past, crystallized strips of young angelica stalks and leaves were sold as cake decoration material (they are hard to find now), but they were also enjoyed on their own as a sweet treat. I have come across candied angelica in Ballymaloe House in East Cork. Candied angelica is made by blanching the stalks and then cooking them in sugar syrup before drying them.

The roots and seeds were sometimes used as an alternative to flavour gin and other liquors. A coastal variety, called seacoast angelica, was used as an alternative to wild celery. In herbal medicine, a lot of the plant was used to treat a variety of ailments, from heartburn and arthritis to nervousness.

Asparagus, wild

Irish name: *Lus súgach*
Latin name: *Asparagus officinalis* subsp. *prostratus*
Flowering period: June to August

Though a native procumbent species, wild asparagus is extremely rare in Ireland and occurs mainly in the south-east of the country. It is listed as endangered in the UK, so it should not be harvested. However, the more upright garden asparagus (*Asparagus officinalis*) can be found in the wild due to the fact it escaped from constant cultivation. It was introduced to England by the Romans and was planted in Ireland by subsequent settlers. So, if you're lucky enough to find this one, pick away!

Bittercress, hairy

Irish name: *Searbh-bhiolar giobach*
Latin name: *Cardamine hirsuta*
Flowering period: February to November

Though looked upon by many as a common garden weed, this peppery bitter herb in the cress family packs a beautiful punch when added to salad leaves (greens) or used as a garnish with beef or pork. It can be found growing up the sides of walls, in fields and along waste ground. Because the flowers are available most of the year, they are also nice to use on canapés as a micro leaf (green). There are a number of bittercresses that grow in Ireland, and all are in the cabbage (brassica) family.

Bog myrtle

Irish name: *Raideog*
Latin name: *Myrica gale*
Flowering period: April to May

Bog myrtle (or sweet gale) is a native deciduous shrub with flowery catkins of different colours, depending on the sex of the plant. The female plant has yellow-green flowers, while the male flowers are red-brown. Though unremarkable in its appearance, its flowers are decidedly fragrant. Because of its strong scent, which can travel a great distance, it has a high place in much Irish folklore. As its name indicates, it is found in bogs, heaths or on the edges of lakes. In the west of Ireland, it can be seen all over Connemara. In the *Lebor Gabála Érenn (Book of Invasions of Ireland)*, the first Irish brewer is said to have used bog myrtle to flavour his ale. Though this is perhaps questionable, there is a tradition of using it in the brewing of beer (instead of hops) in Ireland and Great Britain. From the branches to the leaves

and flowers, all aspects can be used to flavour beers and ales. In the Irish Brehon laws, bog myrtle is a protected plant, probably because of its use as a dye. Bog myrtle fruit can be used in stews, like juniper berries, to add a floral flavour and aroma. In terms of its medicinal use, the Vikings used it as a cure for depression. As an essential oil, it can be used to treat ailments of the skin.

Borage

Irish name: *Borráiste gorm*
Latin name: *Borago officinalis*
Flowering period: April to September

Borage is found in grassy places and on waste ground. Its little blue flower has five petals. Borage, also called starflower, is not native to Ireland but grows wild now after escaping the many nineteenth-century gardens where it grew. In his book *The Flora of County Dublin* (1904), Irish botanist Nathaniel Colgan called the plant a 'garden outcast'. Borage leaves have a faint taste of cucumber and can be used in tea or infused into cream. The flowers and young leaves are a great addition to salads and to many drinks and juices. The seeds contain an edible oil, but because of their size they are difficult to harvest. Combined with dried woodruff, dried borage leaves make a nice powder, which is useful for enhancing desserts such as ice cream and tarts.

Burdock, lesser

Irish name: *Cnádán*
Latin name: *Arctium minus*
Flowering period: July to September

The young leaves of this common scrub, which occurs all over Ireland, can be used as spinach. They need to be cooked because they are quite bitter. The roots of burdock have been used in the past, both as a vegetable (dug up, scrubbed clean, boiled and fried in butter) and for making beer. The roots can also be infused with cream or in alcohol, like other wild roots.

Cabbage, wild

Irish name: *Cabáiste fiáin*
Latin name: *Brassica oleracea* var. *oleracea*
Flowering period: May to August

Wild cabbage is a hard one to find because of its rarity and the fact that it grows at the base of cliffs. I thought I found it once near Galway, but I was mistaken (it was sea kale). It can be found in the west of Ireland though, in Sligo and Mayo. Apart from growing at the base of cliffs, it can be found on stone beaches where the soil is chalky or limestone (i.e. alkaline soils). Use as you would cabbage leaves, steaming them or cooking in a little butter and water. Due to the scarcity of wild cabbage, it should be harvested with respect, taking only a small portion of leaves from each plant.

Wild Herbs and Flowers

Campion, sea

Irish name: *Coireán mara*
Latin name: *Silene uniflora*
Flowering period: June to August

Though technically a sea herb too, this plant can be found inland in sandy mountainous areas. Its green waxy leaves are great in salads or on potato dishes. It is slightly saline, with aromatic, vegetal qualities.

Carrot, wild

Irish name: *Mealbhacán*
Latin name: *Daucus carota*
Flowering period: June to August

Between June and August, little umbels of small white or pinkish flowers appear in the hedgerows, by the bogs and beaches and in the fields. It's also called Queen Anne's lace (due to the story that she pricked her finger making lace and bled onto the top of the flower, hence its red central flower). The flowers and leaves have a faint carrot taste and are nice in salads or as a garnish for fish. Roots of the younger plant are small but can be eaten because they are quite tender. However, older plants have very woody roots. The seeds of the flower head are great and taste a little like caraway. It was the Romans who first cultivated carrots around 500 AD. Looking at the cultivated orange carrot nowadays, it's a wonder how we got to this point, considering the paucity of the wild root (which is white).

Celery, wild

Irish name: *Smaileog*
Latin name: *Apium graveolens*
Flowering period: June to August

Due to its resemblance to hemlock, wild celery is probably one to avoid for the novice forager. Though hemlock leaves smell unpleasant, I would still be wary given the highly poisonous nature of hemlock. Wild celery is not as big as its cultivated counterpart, but it can be used in the same manner. Use leaves as a herb or in a cream sauce. Stalks (stems) can be pickled or use to make a broth. Dry leaves and blend with salt to make a nice wild herb salt. The seeds can be used as a spice.

Chamomile

Irish name: *Camán meall*
Latin name: *Chamaemelum nobile*
Flowering period: June to August

I often confuse chamomile (or Roman chamomile) with scentless mayweed, which seemed to grow in abundance around the west coast. However, mayweed grows upright instead of creeping. Chamomile is much more aromatic and the whole plant exudes a 'chamomile' smell. Dry the heads to use for desserts, from sugar syrups to ice creams and sorbets. You can use the leaves for tea or to flavour cream for custards or set creams such as panna cotta. While it is rare in Ireland, it has been found in the south-west of the country.

Charlock

Irish name: *Praiseach bhuí*
Latin name: *Sinapis arvensis*
Flowering period: May to August

Charlock, also known as charlock mustard or wild mustard, was once eaten all over Ireland, especially among the country people. Today many regard it as a troublesome weed, but it was once held in high esteem. Several Irish herbalists such as John K'eogh and Caleb Threlkeld have observed its use in past times. Boiled with nettle and yellow meal, it provided sustenance to many during the famine (nettles, charlock and seaweed were the three foods that saved many from hunger during the famine). After boiling, the resulting water would be drunk as a tonic. The leaves can be added to soups or stews. In the absence of grain, the seeds were ground for bread (*reuthie*).

Chervil, bur

Irish name: *Peirsil bhog*
Latin name: *Anthriscus caucalis*
Flowering period: June to August

Bur chervil is a diminutive form of wild chervil (*Anthriscus sylvestris*; also called cow parsley) but is much softer and sweeter. You can use this plant like chervil in sauces, soups and beef tartare. It has a nice anise fragrance. Combine with other wild greens such as watercress and wild garlic to make a delicious pesto or salsa verde.

Chickweed

Irish name: *Fuilig*
Latin name: *Stellaria media*
Flowering period: March to October

Chickweed is a gardener's and farmer's nightmare. It pops up everywhere, all year round, especially where you don't want it, in fields and even in footpaths. My father-in-law was amazed the day I told him you could eat it. He asked me to clear his driveway of it! It pairs well with beef in a salad, lending a crisp bitterness to the dish. In fact, you can toss it through any salad. The flowers are particularly beautiful, and I love using them to garnish dishes. Chickweed is a hardy green, so you can forage for it all year around. In herbal and folk medicine, it was traditionally used as a remedy to treat itchy skin conditions and pulmonary diseases. Due to its high iron content, it can help people who suffer from iron deficiency. As a herb that has been in Ireland longer than people, we should really give it more respect.

Cleavers

Irish name: *Garbhlus*
Latin name: *Galium aparine*
Flowering period: June to August

This plant goes by many names and it's one that nearly everyone knows. Sticky back, sticky willie or goose grass will cleave to your clothes when you brush past it. But did you know it is an ancient edible? The seeds may have been used to make a porridge in Mesolithic period. Baby cleavers can be eaten raw and are a great garnish for raw fish. I've used the tops to garnish raw scallops in the restaurant. Young cleavers are best pan-fried with a little butter, like spinach. Stay away from the mature cleavers because they are too bitter and astringent.

Cuckoo Flower/Lady's Smock

Irish name: *Biolar gréagáin*
Latin name: *Cardamine pratensis*
Flowering period: March to June

We use the flowers of this plant on several dishes, especially with potatoes. The plant is in the brassica family, so the leaves can be used too. However, they do have a particular taste so use with care and use sparingly. Miles Irving describes it as a little like horseradish but with a 'strange medicinal overtone'. You can use the flowers to flavour desserts such as set creams. The flower takes its name from the cuckoo's song because it appears in late spring. The flowers appears in several old Irish tales, such as *Mad Sweeney*.

Daisy, ox-eye

Irish name: *Noínín mor*
Latin name: *Leucanthemum vulgare*
Flowering period: June to September

Though ox-eye daisies and their smaller counterpart (*Bellis perennis*) are edible, it is difficult to find evidence in Ireland of anyone eating them. They play an important part in our mythology and folklore in terms of signalling the beginning of spring and making daisy chains. Use the flower petals in salads or to garnish your dishes. The heads are a little bitter so don't use too many of them (even though they look pretty). The leaves can be cooked in a little butter and water, but you'll need to collect a lot to feed the family!

Dandelion

Irish name: *Caisearbhán*
Latin name: *Taraxacum officinale* agg.
Flowering period: March to October

Dandelions are the gateway herb for foragers. Their ubiquity makes them readily noticeable and, with few exceptions, it would be hard to find an Irish person who would not recognize a dandelion. Edible in its entirety, the plant takes its common name from the French *dent-de-lion* (meaning 'lion's teeth') because of the shape of its leaves. The plant has a singularly distinct yellow flower head. It has about three hundred subspecies, all of which are edible. It has a long history as a food and medicine, and it has been traced back to all the ancient cultures (Chinese, Egyptian, Greek, Roman). It was mostly likely eaten in Ireland since hunter-gatherer tribes came to the island. Since the Bronze Age, it was used as a diuretic medicine to help with kidney problems. Most people find the dandelion a little too bitter to eat raw, but it is full of vitamins and minerals in its raw state. You can briefly blanch it as you would spinach and toss it with nuts and garlic. There is also a tradition in Ireland of making wine and beer with the flowers (often combining them with citrus flavours). Dandelion root is used to make a coffee substitute and root beer. Finally, dandelion flowers are extremely important for bees, particularly in terms of producing nectar and pollen early in the season. The resulting floral and aromatic honey demonstrate the vital necessity of this 'noxious weed'.

Elderflower

Irish name: *Trom*
Latin name: *Sambucus nigra*
Harvesting period: May to July

The heads of sweet-scented creamy-white flowers are the first fruit that the native elder tree gives us. They usually spring up at the end of May and flower until July. Then they're followed by the edible berries (see page 411). Elderflowers are famous in the UK in a cordial (syrup), but I love to pickle them. Every year, around May, we collect as many as we can to preserve them (see page 354). These flowers work wonderfully with white fish such as halibut or turbot, lightly poached and sprinkled with the little sparks of floral acidity. In this way we can keep that wonderful floral scent and impart it into different dishes, even in the winter. Dried elderflowers are good as a seasoning. I have used them in the past to season roasted chicken. Just dry in a dehydrator and blend with salt. Use the salt when roasting a whole chicken or barbecuing legs and thighs.

Fat hen

Irish name: *Praiseach fhiáin*
Latin name: *Chenopodium album*
Flowering period: July to October

Fat hen is a form of wild lentil. The name seemingly comes from people feeding the seeds to their hens to fatten them (it is also known as lambs quarters and white goose foot). It is often found on pre-Norman archaeological sites and appears to have been an important part of the diet. Unfortunately, today it is considered a weed and is pulled up from many a potato field. The whole plant is edible, particularly its leaves, shoots when

young, and the black seeds or grains that it produces. Harvesting the seeds by hand is extremely difficult and gives you a glimpse into the labour of hand-harvesting pulses (legumes) and grains. The leaves are easy to harvest and can be used as a substitute for spinach in cooking, or basil in a pesto. The young shoots can be treated like Tenderstem (baby) broccoli or pickled like lovage stalks (stems).

Fennel

Irish name: *Finéal*
Latin name: *Foeniculum vulgare*
Flowering period: July to October

Fennel is a garden escape (planted for many years then went wild) and now grows across the country on waste ground, roadsides and coastal areas. As well as being a garden escape, it may be left over from past cultivation. Use as you would cultivated fennel herbs: fronds are great for making fennel oil or sauce. The flowers are perhaps the best thing about wild fennel. These little yellow pollen bombs are great in salads or as a garnish. In the past, we have used them to garnish onion and other vegetable dishes. You can also dry this 'pollen' and then blend it to a fine powder to sprinkled over white fish. Or infuse it into cream for making ice creams. Finally, you can dry the seeds and use as an alternative to pepper or folded into bread.

Field pennycress

Irish name: *Praiseach fhia*
Latin name: *Thlaspi arvense*
Flowering period: May to October

Another small cress in the brassica family that grows prolifically in gardens, roadsides and on waste ground. As with other small wild cresses (such as hairy bittercress), the leaves pack a little fiery punch. Use as a salad leaf (green) or as a garnish. The flowers have a nice piquant flavour; you can use them on fish dishes. Finally, you can use chopped leaves as a substitute for chives or parsley in butter-based sauces.

Garlic, wild

Irish name: *Creamh*
Latin name: *Allium ursinum*
Flowering period: March to May

Wild garlic, also known as ramsons or bear garlic, grows plentifully on ancient woodlands all over Ireland. While its green leaves pop their head through the moist soil in early spring, it is not until late spring that their white flower blossoms can be seen in full bloom. It is then that the air surrounding them fills with a garlic-like scent. It was a favourite of the bear and wild boar until they were hunted to extinction. In the Middle Ages, wild garlic was used to flavour bread, butter and stews. It was also recommended for colds, coughs and asthma. The flowers

are wonderful sprinkled over soups and salads, their tiny white tendrils offset by beautifully luscious green soups such as spinach and pea. From their leaves, a pesto can be made. Finally, and perhaps most importantly, the seed heads of wild garlic can be preserved and used later like an Irish caper. In Aniar, we usually use ours in the autumn (fall). These little pickled buds pair wonderfully with wild game, lamb and roast fish. *Allium tricoccum* is a similar wild species found in the United States, where it is commonly called ramps, that has identical culinary uses.

Garlic mustard/Jack-by-the-hedge

Irish name: *Bóchoinneal*
Latin name: *Alliaria petiolata*
Flowering period: March to July

Use young leaves in salads and the flowers for garnish. You can use the leaves to make a green sauce as an alternative to mint. Combine them with wild garlic to make a pesto or fold through mashed potato (blanch first to remove their bitterness). Use the seeds as you would mustard seeds. It has been used for medicinal purposes in the past to assuage sore throats and mouth ailments.

Goat's-beard

Irish name: *Finidí na muc*
Latin name: *Tragopogon pratensis*
Flowering period: June to August

Practically all of this plant (which is also known as Jack-go-to-bed-at-noon and meadow salsify) is edible, from its roots to its flowers. You can use the stalks (stems) as you would use asparagus, and treat the roots like salsify – peel, then blanch in water and butter.

Good King Henry

Irish name: *Praiseach bhráthar*
Latin name: *Blitum bonus-henricus*
Flowering period: April to July

Introduced from England by the monastic orders, it is a great alternative to spinach. Like sorrel, the leaves are high in oxalic acid, so they are quite sharp to taste. Also called poor man's asparagus, the shoots can be used like asparagus, though they are smaller and take a little time to prepare. Traditionally grown as a pot herb, it was called monk's spinach in Ireland.

Goosefoot, red

Irish name: *Blonagán dearg*
Latin name: *Oxybasis rubrum*
Flowering period: July to October

This plant is a little bitter to use by itself, though it works well as a vegetable with acidic ingredients such as yogurt, or fatty ones such as bacon. Fry in pork fat.

Wild Herbs and Flowers

Gorse

Irish name: *Aiteann gallda*
Latin name: *Ulex europaeus*
Flowering period: all year round

In spring, the light lingers longer into the early evening and the gorse flowers bloom all over the countryside. Their little flower petals are like yellow headlights that brighten up the landscape. Picked from their thorny green stems, the flowers have a distinct smell of coconut. Gorse wine is perhaps the first thing that springs to mind when thinking of this flower. This full-bodied drink has a wonderful sweet vanilla aftertaste and has a history of being made in the country. Though to make a batch you need 5 litres/175 fl oz (21 cups) of these little yellow petals and about 9 months of waiting to mature the wine. Gin and vodka can also be flavoured with gorse flowers. It is very simple and only takes 3–4 weeks to macerate. Get a jar of gorse flowers. Cover with gin or vodka. Seal. Wait. Drink. Gorse vinegar is another ingredient that adds a nice acidity to the many white fish that can be found in Irish waters.

Ground elder

Irish name: *Lus an easpaig*
Latin name: *Aegopodium podagraria*
Flowering period: May to July

Ground elder was introduced to England by the Romans and thus made its way to Ireland. It was once a staple in many gardens, but its invasive tendency let it go out into the wild. Personally, I think the best time to use this herb is in April and May, when it is still quite small. The little leaves make an excellent garnish for raw shellfish. Perhaps one of the most memorable dishes that we have produced in Aniar was a dish of raw scallops and ground elder. It has a sharp, nutty flavour that cuts wonderfully through the richness of the scallop. You can use the large leaves like spinach and eat the shoots as a vegetable. Cook similarly to garlic scapes or asparagus.

Ground ivy

Irish name: *Athair lusa*
Latin name: *Glechoma hederacea*
Flowering period: March to June

Ground ivy can be found around the many coastal counties of Ireland, in woods and hedgerows. Its leaves can be used as a herb or in salads, but collect them before flowering because they become bitter afterwards. Use large leaves in soups or stuffing. Before the introduction of hops, ground ivy was used in beer making (hence one of its many other names: ale-hoof). Tea was once made by infusing the dried herbs in boiling water. You can use the flowers as a garnish.

Heather

Irish name: *Fraoch mor*
Latin name: *Calluna vulgaris*
Flowering period: July to September

Heather grows plentifully among the bog lands, mountains and moors. It is especially prevalent in Connemara, where it can be seen in abundance during its flowering period. This herb is usually associated with poverty, because it thrives on poor acidic soil. However, because it survives on rough terrain it is also a symbol of independence and resilience. It features in many medieval Irish legends and in the Brehon laws. Clearing a field of heather was an offence according to these medieval Irish laws.

The flowers can be dried to make a clear herbal tea. The flowers are also rich in nectar, and honey produced from bees gathering nectar from the flowers is a beautiful, rare Irish product. Beer and wine has been made from the flowers for many centuries. Often the shoots of the heather plant replace hops in beer and ale making, which can be seen in several contemporary craft beers. In terms of cooking, heather is a component that can be added in a small amount when baking full pieces of lamb or beef. It pairs well with hay in smoking food to bring a subtle floral aroma to the finished product.

In Irish history, the branches have been used to make a variety of things, from brooms to bedding, to roofing, dying yarn yellow, binding turf and feeding cattle and other animals. As a herb, it also featured in 'Garland Sunday', an event usually held on hilltops on the last Sunday in July to celebrate the start of the summer harvest. In many countries, many people would pick heather, wear it or place it by the door to bring good luck.

Hedge mustard

Irish name: *Lus an óir*
Latin name: *Sisymbrium officinale*
Flowering period: April to October

Another wild member of the brassica family, the leaves of hedge mustard have a cabbage taste. You can use small leaves raw as a garnish or in salads. Larger leaves need to be cooked: steamed or blanched is best. The flowers make a nice garnish for white fish.

Herb Robert

Irish name: *Ruithéal rí*
Latin name: *Geranium robertianum*
Flowering period: March to October

Herb Robert is a geranium with many traditional uses in folk medicine, from the treatment of diarrhoea to inflammation of the kidney and preventing the formation of kidney stones. It is said to take its name from Saint Robert, founder of the Cistercian order of monks, who used the herb for many medical purposes. Both the leaves and flowers are good for eating. We use the leaves to garnish beef tartare when they're in season. You can also use the leaves to make a herbal tea.

Honeysuckle

Irish name: *Táthfhéithleann*
Latin name: *Lonicera periclymenum*
Flowering period: June to September

My friend Sharon Greene of Wild Irish Foragers uses honeysuckle to make syrups and shrubs. These are made by extracting the nectar from the flowers. Long ago, children would suck the nectar straight from the flowers, hence its name! Honeysuckle has a long history of use as a medicine, being used to cure or alleviate asthma and other respiratory ailments, as well as illness of the mouth. Bark, leaves and flowers were all used effectively in folk medicine. However, the berries are poisonous so stay away from them.

Knotweed, Japanese

Irish name: *Glúineach bhiorach*
Latin name: *Reynoutria japonica*
Flowering period: August to October

The jury is out concerning this invasive species. On the one hand, we could forage and eat it forever. On the other, every time you cut it, it grows, thus taking over its environment. Is there a way to keep both camps happy? The foragers and the conservationists? I hope so. Japanese knotweed was introduced as a garden plant and is a great vegetable that can be pickled or steamed. It straddles savoury and sweet uses. Some people make jam or compote from it. Noma, the renowned restaurant in Denmark, has used it to make sorbet. The vegetable is used for medicinal purposes, particularly in Japan.

Leek, Babington's

Irish name: *Cainneann*
Latin name: *Allium ampeloprasum* var. *babingtonii*
Flowering period: July to September

It is uncertain whether these wild leeks arose as a garden escape or as a relic of cultivation. Our forager Brian Gannon drops them in every year, and we pickle them immediately. We use the subsequent vinegar for flavouring the butter we make in the restaurant. We also use the pickled leeks for a variety of other dishes. Due to their wild nature, they are often very astringent, so I generally leave them a couple of months in the vinegar before using. However, if you get tender ones, they can be poached in butter and water until tender.

Wild Herbs and Flowers

Leek, three-cornered

Irish name: *Creamh garraí*
Latin name: *Allium triquetrum*
Flowering period: March to May

The three-cornered leeks, also called three-cornered garlic, have come to populate the roadside verges (shoulders) near my house. They are a wonderful little white flower and emit a deep garlic smell when pressed to the nose. Upon picking them the other day, my morally conscious seven year old told me to stop stealing them. She thought I had reversed into someone's driveway and got out to invade their garden. Many people have these leeks in their garden but mistake them for white flowered bluebells. If in doubt, give it a smell. These guys are unmistakable. According to British forager Miles Irving, three-cornered leeks have been cultivated in the British Isles since 1759. Following cultivation, they quickly colonized much of the verges, edges and banks of roads and fields. Going back two hundred years ago in Ireland, it is said that peasants hung this plant outside their door to keep the vampires away. Unfortunately, I don't think they took pleasure in eating it. As well as using the flowers in a spring salad, the flowers also pair well with shellfish. A nice light dish of some dressed crab would benefit from a sprinkling of these flowers and some extra virgin rapeseed (canola) oil. You can use the leaves of this plant in a similar way to chives, though be careful with their flavour because they are more robust. Thinly sliced and pan-fried with some fish is the way to go. Just add them at the end of cooking with a little butter and cook very briefly. Both the flowers and the stems work well with lightly grilled oysters. To take the garlicky edge off the stems, quickly blanch them in boiling water and then refresh in iced water. Finely chop and fold into room temperature butter. Place a little knob (pat) of butter on top of a native oyster and grill until it melts. Be careful not to overcook the oyster. Finally, a potato and three-cornered leek soup should keep any cold at bay.

Lovage, Scots

Irish name: *Sunais*
Latin name: *Ligusticum scoticum*
Flowering period: April to October

This wild plant (also known as Scottish licorice-root) has a distinct celery flavour and aroma and was once used widely before the introduction of celery into Ireland. Cultivated lovage is a different species (*Levisticum officinale*) but both can be used in the same manner. Pickled lovage stems are one of my favourite pickles. I use the leaves to make sauces, usually cutting the sauce with spinach as the taste of lovage often overpowers. Other uses include wrapping the larger leaves around fish before steaming, using the leaves in a potato and lovage soup, and lovage oil (blend the herb with twice as much oil, then heat and strain).

Marjoram, wild

Irish name: *Máirtín fiáin*
Latin name: *Origanum vulgare*
Flowering period: July-September

Similar to the Mediterranean native oregano, wild marjoram is native to Ireland. However, its flavour is quite strong so use sparingly or combine with thyme and rosemary. Wild marjoram is good with lamb or game such as pheasant and pigeon as well as for stuffing in chicken, but again, be careful not to use too much. Traditionally, it was used in Ireland to make a medicinal herbal tea that would be drunk to help ease indigestion, coughs and other ailments.

Marsh marigold

Irish name: *Lus buí Bealtaine*
Latin name: *Caltha palustris*
Flowering period: March to May

A member of the buttercup family (many of which are poisonous) and also called kingcup, the flower heads can be pickled, and the stems and leaves can be steamed or fried. Both parts of the plant need to be cooked because they contain toxic protoanemonin and helleborin.

Mayweed, scented

Irish name: *Fíogadán cumhra*
Latin name: *Matricaria chamomilla*
Flowering period: June to August

Occasionally found in Ireland, but most often you will find sea mayweed or scentless mayweed (which have no aroma). You can use scented mayweed, sometimes known as German chamomile, like chamomile (see page 402).

Meadowsweet

Irish name: *Airgead luachra*
Latin name: *Filipendula ulmaria*
Flowering period: June to September

Meadowsweet, or queen of the meadow, is a member of the rose family. Its creamy white flowers dominate the hedgerows between June and September. For me, it is a wild herb that characterizes the summer months in Ireland. We use the flowers mainly for dessert, first drying them, then sifting them to a fine powder. This aromatic sweet powder can be used to make ice cream, sorbet and jellies (Jell-O). Mixing the powder with sugar provides a good flavouring for sweet pastries and cakes, lending them a decidedly floral character. As woodruff, meadowsweet was used to make floors and rooms smell more pleasant. The Druids considered it a sacred herb and it was used in ceremonies. In the Middle Ages, the herb was used to flavour beer in Ireland. Its name derives from it being used to perfume the honeyed alcoholic drink mead, hence its Anglo-Saxon equivalent: 'mead-sweetener'.

For herbalists, meadowsweet is good for helping to treat many aliments such as fever but also diarrhoea and dysentery. You can use its leaves and stalks (stems) to produce a vinegar by infusing with apple cider vinegar. Infusing its leaves in gin will produce a nice drink. In terms of its health benefits, drinks made with the flowers are supposed to be good for skin disorders.

Mint, round-leaved

Irish name: *Mismín cumhra*
Latin name: *Mentha suaveolens*
Flowering period: August to September

Due to crossbreeding, there are many wild mints, but all are edible. Use round-leaved mint, often known as apple mint, in the same way as cultivated mint. The herb works well with lamb and peas, strawberries and other summer fruits, and in sorbets and drinks. Round-leaved mint is native to England but was introduced into Ireland. It can be found around Dublin on roadsides and waste grounds.

Mint, spear

Irish name: *Cartlainn gharraí*
Latin name: *Mentha spicata*
Flowering period: July to October

A lot more common than round-leaved or apple mint, I know of a few places where spearmint grows in Galway. Once it establishes itself it takes over, which is why many see mint as a pest. Use as for round-leaved mint above, but it is also great in tea or with fish. With a selection of other wild herbs, it makes a nice salsa verde. Mint is immortalized by Irish poet Seamus Heaney in his poem 'Mint', though I don't know which mint he meant, but I assume it was this one: 'Let the smells of mint go heady and defenceless, like inmates liberated in that yard. Like the disregarded ones we turned against, because we'd failed them by our disregard.' It is found in many dumps and ditches, waste grounds, and on the banks of streams and rivers.

Nasturtium

Irish name: n/a
Latin name: *Tropaeolum majus*
Flowering period: June to October

Nasturtium are a garden escape that, like mint, take root wherever they find space. Alongside elderflower and wild garlic, we probably get more from this plant than many others. The peppery small leaves are great to garnish fish and shellfish. You can use the large leaves for purées, soups, oils, sorbets and ice creams. The seeds can be pickled (in a 3-2-1 solution of vinegar, water and sugar) and used to flavour tartare and meat sauces. Use the flowers for decorating desserts, flavouring rum or gin (to make a nasturtium liqueur) and pickling.

Wild Herbs and Flowers

Nettle

Irish name: *Neantóg*
Latin name: *Urtica*
Flowering period: June to August

Nettles have a rich practical and mytho-logical significance in Irish cooking. As well as a nutritious foodstuff, they also have a tradition of being used for making cloth since the Bronze Age. There are many Irish customs associated with nettles. One, from Galway in the west of Ireland, involves people drinking the juice of freshly pressed nettles to give them strength for the year ahead. Nettles abound around towns among waste grounds. Indeed, they sometimes are hard not to encounter. Because of this, it has been a symbol of desolation in many Irish myths. Nettle soup or 'potage' has a long history dating back to at least the eighth century in terms of written record. We can only assume that it has been a foodstuff for the preceding centuries. For me, along with oysters and seaweed, it is one of the central historic foods of Ireland. The eighth-century monk Saint Colmcille reportedly lived on nettle soup. In terms of nutrition, nettles are very good for blood circulation. The best time to pick nettles is in the spring and summer before they flower. Use the small leaves to make a wonderfully rich green purée or blanch them and add to salads. I always blend nettle with spinach because by itself it tends to be a little coarse. Nettle soup is a traditional Irish soup and is usually made with potatoes or oats.

Parsley, cow

Irish name: *Peirsil bhó*
Latin name: *Anthriscus sylvestris*
Flowering period: April to June

Cow parsley is another name for wild chervil. It can be confused with fool's parsley (*Aethusa cynapium*) and poison hemlock (*Conium maculatum*) so it is really one for the experienced forager. The leaves of cow parsley have a mild aniseed taste and can be used as you would cultivated chervil. We use it with beef tartare in the restaurant. Larger leaves are a little bitter, so they are better suited for infusions.

Parsnip, wild

Irish name: *Cuirdín bán*
Latin name: *Pastinaca sativa*
Flowering period: July to August

The yield of wild parsnip root is so small that it is difficult to justify digging it up. However, they can be cooked and taste great. The leaves, though coarse, can be infused into cream, syrups and oil to extract the flavour. Parsnip-leaf ice cream is a good one to try. Use the flowers in salads and to garnish. Finally, the seeds can also be used. As with any seed, use as a spice to enliven sauces.

Pennywort, wall

Irish name: *Carnán caisil*
Latin name: *Umbilicus rupestris*
Flowering period: June to September

Wall pennywort (or navelwort) grows in many old walls all over Ireland. I recall finding an abundance in the monastic walls in Glendalough. Use the round leaves in salads or to garnish fish (turbot) or vegetable dishes (celeriac/celery root).

Pignut

Irish name: *Cúlarán*
Latin name: *Conopodium majus*
Flowering period: May to June

In the past, the roots of the pignut were eaten. The roots have a tuberous shape and can be eaten raw or cooked. For me, their taste lies somewhere between a hazelnut and Jerusalem artichoke.

Pineapple weed

Irish name: *Lus na hiothlann*
Latin name: *Matricaria discoidea*
Flowering period: May to November

Pineapple weed, also known as disc mayweed and wild chamomile, is an aromatic flower that exudes a pineapple-chamomile scent when its leaves and flower head are crushed. It is not native to Ireland and was only first found in Dublin as recently as 1894. It grows widely in the countryside and on well-trodden ground. I've found it in abundance in farms, both vegetable and poultry. It has a cone-shaped flower head that is composed of densely packed yellowish-green corollas. The flowers can be used in salads and in herbal teas, though late in the season the flowers tend to become quite bitter. When picking, crush the flower head and ensure it gives off a pleasant aromatic aroma. Pineapple weed was used for medicinal purposes, including for the relief of gastrointestinal upset, infected sores and fevers. In terms of cooking, I like to infuse it into sauces for white fish or poultry. Finally, pineapple weed works well in gin and can be infused to make a herbal liqueur.

Pink-sorrel

Irish name: *Seamsóg ghlúineach*
Latin name: *Oxalis articulata*
Flowering period: May to September

You can use the flowers and leaves like its cousin wood sorrel (see page 408). They add a nice acidic touch to savoury and sweet dishes from pork belly to desserts, such as meringue.

Plantain, buck's-horn

Irish name: *Adharca fia*
Latin name: *Plantago coronopus*
Flowering period: May to July

All the plantains are great wild edibles and it is a pity we ignore them so much. The small leaves have a beautifully mild taste and we use them a lot to garnish, often cooking them lightly in brown butter. To harvest, trim small leaves from the rosettes.

Plantain, greater

Irish name: *Cuach Phádraig*
Latin name: *Plantago major*
Flowering period: June to October

Also known as common plantain, the large leaves of greater plantain are a little tough, so go for smaller ones. Use as you would spinach or Swiss chard, in salads or lightly cooked. The leaves are high in calcium. Blend with oil as a dipping sauce.

Plantain, ribwort

Irish name: *Slánus*
Latin name: *Plantago lanceolata*
Flowering period: April to October

Use the long narrow leaves of ribwort – or narrowleaf – plantain as you would greater plantain.

Primrose

Irish name: *Sabhaircín*
Latin name: *Primula vulgaris*
Flowering period: December to May

A beautiful native perennial whose flowers make a great garnish and can be candied for desserts. The leaves can also be used, raw or cooked. They have a peculiar honey flavour that lingers after eating. The flowers have also been used to make country wine in the past.

Radish, wild

Irish name: *Meacan raidigh*
Latin name: *Raphanus raphanistrum* ssp. *raphanistrum*
Flowering period: May to September

A yellow and white flowered cabbage plant. Use it the same way as sea radish (see page 416). The leaves are coarse so they need to be cooked. You can pickle the seed pods in vinegar.

Rape, wild

Irish name: *Ráib*
Latin name: *Brassica napus*
Flowering period: May to August

Use the leaves and flowers like wild radish, though the leaves are a little more tender. The stalks (stems) can be blanched and charred and used as a vegetable.

Wild Herbs and Flowers

Salad burnet

Irish name: *Lus an uille*
Latin name: *Sanguisorba minor*
Flowering period: May to September

This is a small bittercress herb with leaves that can be used in salads and soups. It is also known as small burnet.

Sheep's sorrel

Irish name: *Samhadh caorach*
Latin name: *Rumex acetosella*
Flowering period: May to August

A smaller, more diminutive form of common sorrel, sheep's sorrel is used in a similar manner. It is good in salads. We've used it to garnish ice cream in the restaurant because its acidic nature cuts through the richness of the cream.

Shepherd's purse

Irish name: *Lus an sparáin*
Latin name: *Capsella bursa-pastoris*
Flowering period: January to December

A member of the cabbage (Brassicaceae) family, this small bittercress is good as a garnish or in salads. The herb takes its name from the resemblance of the seed cases to a purse. It has been used in folk medicine to alleviate bleeding and kidney trouble. You can infuse it in boiling water to make a tea.

Silverweed

Irish name: *Briosclán*
Latin name: *Potentilla anserina*
Flowering period: May to August

Though perhaps not the most exciting wild herb in terms of flavour, silverweed (or silverweed cinquefoil) is rich in vitamins and minerals and has a long history of use. Indeed, it has provided sustenance in times of scarcity and famine. However, Miles Irving observes that silverweed was 'systematically harvested' for its roots. The roots were used in Ireland as a vegetable before the introduction of the potato. A twelfth-century text mentions its use. The roots were also used to make flour. They were dried and blended to a powder. The leaves don't taste of much but my forager friend puts them into smoothies because of their nutritional value.

Sorrel, common

Irish name: *Samhadh bó*
Latin name: *Rumex acetosa*
Flowering period: May to June

The phrase 'lemon of the north' refers to the simple common sorrel (it is also known as garden sorrel or, simply, sorrel). The delicate acidity in sorrel marries beautifully with poached fish. I've found it on a clifftop in County Cork when

I went foraging with Darina Allen many moons ago. The most beautiful months to forage it are between May and September. Sorrel has been consumed in Ireland for many centuries and used as an ingredient for soups, sauces and pies. In her book *Traditional Irish Cooking* (1995), Darina Allen includes a sorrel pie that was made on the Inis Mhic Uibhleáin, one of the Blasket Islands. Sorrel sugar syrup is great for making sorbets and cocktails.

Sweet cicely

Irish name: *Lus áinleoige*
Latin name: *Myrrhis odorata*
Flowering period: April to July

Sweet cicely (sometimes known as anise) is a large aromatic plant that offers much in the realm of food. To start, the leaves can be used as a herb in both savoury and sweet dishes, adding an anise touch to vegetables and fruits. The roots can be boiled and eaten as you would a tender baby carrot. The flowers can be used to garnish desserts and tarts, from apple to gooseberry. In the autumn (fall), you can use the green seeds to give a sauce an aniseed taste. The stalk (stem) can be pickled or candied. To make sweet cicely sugar, simply pick the sweet cicely leaves from its stalk and blend with sugar. Do not blend too fine. For a longer-lasting sugar, dry the herb first and then blend (the reduced moisture will help keep the sugar fresh). Store in a cool, dark place. Use in pastries or for making jelly candies.

Swine cress

Irish name: *Cladhthach*
Latin name: *Lepidium coronopus* (syn. *Coronopus squamatus*)
Flowering period: June to September

This plant has mustardy leaves that can be used to garnish or season sauces. Due to its bitter quality, it is best combined with other wild herbs if using in a salad.

Swine cress, lesser

Irish name: *Cladhthach mhín*
Latin name: *Lepidium didymus* (syn. *Coronopus didymus*)
Flowering period: June to September

A smaller version of the above plant with beautiful pungent, mustardy leaves. The leaves are nice with pork.

Thistle, milk

Irish name: *Feochadán Muire*
Latin name: *Silybum marianum*
Flowering period: June to September

There are many varieties of thistle, but I find the milk thistle is the most recognizable and the most useful in terms of foraging. As a young plant, the leaves can be picked and the prickles removed,

though I feel with our busy lives, I can't imagine too many people doing this nowadays. The flower heads can be eaten too (prepared in a similar way to globe artichokes) but they do require time. In the past, milk thistle was also used to curdle milk.

Thyme, wild

Irish name: *Tim creige*
Latin name: *Thymus polytrichus*
Flowering period: May to September

Look for wild thyme on sandy dunes and dry grassland. You can use it in the same ways as cultivated thyme, but wild thyme is not as powerful as its cultivated cousin, so you'll have to use more. It is great as an aromatic herb in stocks (broths) and sauces and in stuffings and sprinkled over roasts, especially lamb.

Toadflax, ivy-leaved

Irish name: *Buaflíon balla*
Latin name: *Cymbalaria muralis*
Flowering period: May to September

Also known as Kenilworth ivy, this herb grows on walls and rocks all over the west of Ireland and I encounter it every day. The leaves have a slight bitter, peppery quality. I like to use them to garnish fish dishes, particularly raw ones such as scallops or langoustines (Dublin bay prawns).

Turnip, wild

Irish name: *Tornapa fiáin*
Latin name: *Brassica rapa*
Flowering period: April to October

Like wild carrot, wild turnip is picked more for its leaves and flowers than its root. The leaves, especially the younger ones which are less bitter, are good for adding to salads or for garnishing fish. However, larger leaves can be steam or charred. The flowers and the flower buds can also be used and remind me of sprouting broccoli.

Vetch, bush

Irish name: *Peasair fhiáin*
Latin name: *Vicia sepium*
Flowering period: April to September

Vetch grows abundantly on hedge banks and in meadows. The shoots of common vetch can be used in salads or as a garnish for fish. In medieval times, varieties of vetch seeds were used to make bread. However, contemporary accounts of the period state the bread was only good in cases of starvation or famine. One monk wrote, it was 'of such miserable quality' that he lamented each time he had to eat it. Thankfully, we no longer must endure this. Vetch was also used as fodder for animals. Today, I like just to use the shoots fresh for their taste, texture and beautiful

Wild Herbs and Flowers

tendril appearance. One nice combination of these wild pea tendrils is with briefly charred mackerel. There is a particular type of vetch that grows in shingle beaches called the 'sea pea' (see page 416). When young, the peas have a beautiful saline quality. Dress with a little oil and vinegar and serve with a piece of charred mackerel. If you can't find any sea peas, the garden variety will do! But please, keep the mackerel mostly raw. Bitter vetch has an edible tuber but it can be difficult to dig up, unless in an area where it is extremely plentiful. In ancient times, it was dried and chewed as a foodstuff. Common vetch, which looks very similar to bush vetch, was introduced to Ireland but now grows wild also, particularly in the south and east of the country. I have spotted it growing in County Offaly.

Watercress

Irish name: *Biolar*
Latin name: *Nasturtium officinale* (syn. *Rorippa nasturtium-aquatica*)
Flowering period: June to September

In folklore of the British Isles, watercress occupies an important place. In Ireland and Scotland, it was said that when used as a charm, watercress could take the goodness out of people's milk. Considering milk was an important aspect of the Irish diet, drinking milk with goodness taken out was a frightful position to find oneself in. But it wasn't all bad. Watercress could alleviate depression and increase a person's intelligence. In Cork at Little Christmas, water was turned into wine and watercress into silk! As a foodstuff, watercress appears in many mythological tales from *The Cattle Raid of Cooley* to *Sweeney Astray* and the twelfth-century manuscript *The Colloquy of the Old Men*. It seems Fionn mac Cumhaill and his merry Fiánna subsisted on watercress as they pottered around Ireland in search of the mad and magical. The herbs played an important role in the monks' diet alongside barley and rye bread. They would eat it raw or add it to soups or broths. In the olden days (when I was young, according to my daughter), watercress was sold in the spring market in Dublin. This was done not only to purge the blood after the winter but also to prevent scurvy. I would imagine it was the latter that was more important! Probably the most traditional manner of eating watercress in Ireland is with fish, namely smoked salmon or trout. The piquancy of the watercress marries well with the rich fattiness of the smoked fish. When serving with the leaner trout, you may want to include a little crème fraîche or cream.

White waterlily

Irish name: *Bacán bán*
Latin name: *Nymphaea alba*
Flowering period: June to August

The seeds and roots of this plant were eaten by earlier hunter-gatherers in Ireland during the Mesolithic period. Archaeological evidence from Mount Sandel (County Derry) points to their importance in the diet of these first settlers. The roots need to be peeled of the outer layer and then the inner can be boiled. You can grind the seeds into flour and use it as a thickener. A drink can also be prepared from roasted, ground seeds.

Wood sorrel

Irish name: *Seamsóg*
Latin name: *Oxalis acetosella*
Flowering period: April to June

Wood sorrel is one of my favourite wild plants to use, whether in a salad or eaten by itself. The intense lemony flavour of the leaf makes it a wonderful substitute for lemons on fish dishes or anything else requiring a gentle acidity. Wood sorrel also works well on desserts to help balance fat and sweetness. Because of its size, it is not suitable to use in soups or hot dishes. Common or sheep's sorrel is much better to add because they are much bigger and hardier. Wood sorrel has several mentions in old Irish literature, particularly in the poem *Sweeney Astray*. Adrift in the wild, the king feeds off wood sorrel to quell his hunger. Wood sorrel is supposed to be the original shamrock that Saint Patrick used to explain the holy trinity to the pagan Irish, though this is questionable due to the absence of any concrete evidence. In Irish folk medicine, wood sorrel was used to alleviate stomach and digestive ailments.

Woodruff

Irish name: *Lus moileas*
Latin name: *Galium odoratum*
Flowering period: May to June

Woodruff is a small upright plant with sweetly scented flowers that grows in forests. It's a relative of cleavers (or what most people in Ireland call 'sticky backs'). It's beautiful dried and used in both savoury and sweet ways. Woodruff is a nice addition to cream, sugar and salt. When dried, the herb has a faint almond scent and often reminds me of marzipan. Because of its sweet-smelling nature, the herb was used to sweeten homes – it is also known as sweetscented bedstraw. It was strewn on floors, stuffed into pillows and placed between sheets. Woodruff tea has its roots in medicine, where it was used as a cure for colds and fevers. It has purportedly been drunk as a tea since Neolithic times. In late spring, its flowers can be picked and used to garnish myriad different tarts and desserts. They are nice pickled because they give off a hint of vanilla. Because of its woodland location, I like to pair it with game in the autumn (fall), adding it to sauces for venison and wild duck. Finally, woodruff tea is a pleasant aromatic drink that has possible ancient origins. If making tea, combine with borage for a sweet-scented beverage.

Yarrow

Irish name: *Athair thalún*
Latin name: *Achillea millefolium*
Flowering period: June to September

Yarrow is a perennial wild herb found on many pastures, roadsides and waste grounds. Though small, its long bushy clumps of feathery green leaves make it easy to identify. Yarrow is deeply embedded in our own folklore. People travelling on a long journey were instructed to pick ten leaves of the yarrow, then throw one away and put the nine others into a white cloth and tie it with a string around your neck. This would ward off the evil spirits that you may encounter along the Irish country roads. The medicinal properties of yarrow were well known to previous generations and it was used regularly as a remedy for colds and fevers. In Romania, it is still used for its anti-inflammatory effects and to help blood circulation disorders. As well as being good eaten raw in a salad of different leaves (greens), yarrow makes a wonderfully refreshing tea. It also pairs really well with most white fish. I usually just clean the little leaves in water and then dress them with some oil and lemon juice. A pinch of sugar will help draw out the aromatic flavour. Grilled brill dressed with yarrow and some boiled and buttered new potatoes would make a nice light lunch. You could also dress the potatoes instead with some chopped yarrow because its leaves taste similar to rosemary. You can tell your guests that yarrow is the new rosemary and inspire them all to do a little foraging and cook more with our wild perennials.

Wild Herbs and Flowers

Wild Fruits, Nuts and Trees

'To what meals the woods invite me
All about! [...] All that one could ask for comfort Round me grows, There are hips and haws and strawberries, Nuts and sloes. And when summer spreads its mantle What a sight!

'The Hermit's Song', eighth century

From its first settlers to many of those still living in the countryside, wild fruit and nuts from trees – along with other parts of the trees such as leaves, needles and sap – have sustained a countless number of people on this island. However, though foraging for fruits and nuts is now on the increase, it is not practised by the majority of the population. Many of us will have memories of picking blackberries or crab apples and using them to make jams and tarts, but unfortunately this is no longer the norm and today is the preserve of professional foragers collecting these wild delights for restaurants. However, all is not lost. There is still time to relearn and re-engage with our local landscape, following the seasons and using its bounty, even in a small way.

Picking wild strawberries in the summer or hazelnuts in the autumn (fall) is a wonderful activity that can reconnect us with the natural flow of each season. This section also includes some information on the trees of Ireland which were of central significance to the early settlers in terms of the mythology that they inscribed upon them. One interpretation of the first written language in Ireland, 'Ogham' (possibly beginning from the fourth century), sees each of its letters being ascribed to a particular tree. Surviving examples of the Ogham alphabet are inscribed on stones, many of which are in the south of Ireland (in the province of Munster). While the theory that this alphabet (and language) is tied to the names of trees is contested by scholars of the primitive Irish language, it does demonstrate the importance of the trees for the native Irish.

Apple

Irish name: *Abhail*
Latin name: *Malus domestica*
Fruiting period: autumn (fall) to winter

Though this tree was introduced to Ireland, it is similar to the native crab apple but not as sour. Apple trees can be found in the wild and are often relics of cultivation or have grown from discarded apple cores.

Arbutus

Irish name: *Caithne*
Latin name: *Arbutus unedo*
Fruiting period: October

Arbutus, or the strawberry tree, is very rare in Ireland nowadays, occurring mainly in the south-west, particularly in Cork and Kerry. This is due to a combination of climate change and human intervention (it was used to make charcoal). The berries can be eaten but are not very palatable. However, Niall Mac Coitir observes in his *Ireland's Trees: Myths, Legends and Folklore* (2003) that baskets of the fruit were on sale in Killarney in the nineteenth century. Syrups or shrubs were possibly made for medicinal purposes. The Straits Salish people of Vancouver Island in Canada used arbutus bark and leaves to create medicines. It is not difficult to imagine that the native Irish would have used it for a similar purpose. In Portugal, I encountered a liqueur made from the fruit, some of which was aged for decades. In Spain, they make a fruit liqueur called *madroño* (the Spanish name for the tree). The British forager Miles Irving notes that alcoholic drinks and confectionery from the fruit have long been produced in Europe so the tradition is by no means exclusive to the Iberian Peninsula. We may have produced all these things in Ireland in the past. 'My Love's an Arbutus' is the title of a poem by the Irish writer Alfred Perceval Graves (1846–1931).

Ash

Irish name: *Fuinseog*
Latin name: *Fraxinus excelsior*
Fruiting period: autumn (fall)

Ash is one of the most common trees in Irish hedgerows and is also found in many ancient woods. Mythologically speaking, the ash has a rich significance in Irish folk culture. W. B. Yeats, the Irish poet and Nobel laureate, mentions it in his *Fairy and Folk Tales of Ireland* (1918). In terms of eating, it is the seeds (clumps of winged keys) that you should be on the lookout for. Pickle them in hot pickle with whatever spices you like and leave to mature for at least 3 months. The pale dense timber makes good hurley sticks (the traditional Irish field sport played with a wooden stick and a small ball).

Beech

Irish name: *Fáidhbhile*
Latin name: *Fagus sylvatica*
Fruiting period: September to October

Though not a native tree to Ireland, beech trees are noticeable in the woodlands both for their stature and their grey-silvery bark. They also have distinct, small, bright- green leaves. They are seldom used today, but in the past its spring leaves were eaten as a salad leaf (green). I like to pickle the baby leaves and use them to add acidity to fish. We pickle the leaves in the spring and keep them to use in autumn (fall) and winter. Its nuts (called beechnuts or mast), which can be harvested in autumn, were a common fodder for pigs. The leaves also make a great liqueur, and adding them to gin has its origins in both France and England. Oil can be extracted from the nuts, a practice that still occurs in several European countries. In their book, *Wild and Free* (1978), Cyril and Kit Ó Céirín note that butter was once made from the nut oil. The buds themselves can also be eaten, raw or cooked, though due to their size, they are often overlooked. Beech wood is excellent for smoking foodstuffs, particularly hams and cheeses. Beech leaf tea is a good detoxifying drink and can be made with the leaves and twigs.

Bilberry

Irish name: *Fraughan*
Latin name: *Vaccinium myrtillus*
Fruiting period: August

Bilberries are wild blueberries. In Ireland, they were called *'fraughans'*. They grow wild in acidic soil and can be found among the many mountain ranges in Ireland, such as the Comeraghs to the Galtees. Probably the nicest way to eat them is to sprinkle them with sugar and serve with some whipped cream. They are a good source of vitamin C. In the restaurant, we preserve them in sugar syrup and keep them for the winter. Jelly can also be made from bilberries. They were traditionally picked in August (around the feast of Lughnasa to celebrate the harvest season). In her book, *Traditional Irish Cooking* (1995), Darina Allen writes of 'Fraughan Sunday', the first Sunday in August, where the whole community would partake in gathering the berries. Using fraughans in cakes, pies and tarts was also popular in the past.

Birch, silver

Irish name: *Beith gheal*
Latin name: *Betula pendula*
Flowering period: April to May

In April, we like to tap silver birch trees to retrieve the sap from inside. Though this practice is rare nowadays, it has a tradition in many parts of Ireland and in the British Isles. A country wine can be made from the sap (see page 394), as illustrated in the many cookbooks from the eighteenth and nineteenth centuries. Today, Evan Doyle, who runs Brooklodge in Macreddin Village, makes a liquor from the sap. Sap needs to be reduced by one-tenth to obtain a syrup, but it can be reduced less if making wine or tea. Twigs and baby leaves can be used to make tea. I've used the syrup to glaze pork belly and tuna. It can also be used for desserts and over ice creams, from vanilla to dillisk (dulse). As a native tree of Ireland, its wood was important in boat making and other implements, from shoes to parchment. Birch is associated with the Ogham (ancient Irish alphabet inscribed in stones) letter *beith*, which translates as birch.

Blackberry

Irish name: *Sméara dubh*
Latin name: *Rubis fruiticosus*
Fruiting period: autumn (fall)

Blackberries are a truly ancient fruit that have been consumed in Ireland for thousands of years. There are many Irish language phrases that indicate their widespread consumption. Though the tradition of blackberry picking has waned in recent years, it is seeing a resurgence due to people's desire to reconnect with their local landscape. Blackberry bushes are easily found all over Ireland in hedgerows and along walkways. The most traditional way to preserve blackberries is to make jam or to stew them for pie filling, but I also like to infuse them in gin and vinegar. When you go back a few months later, you get a wonderful surprise. Blackberries make a nice cordial (syrup) and even a wine! By collecting blackberries in autumn (fall), you engage in a wonderfully long tradition that has occupied children, families and even whole towns. Often, they were picked straight from the bramble and mixed with cream or milk and a little sugar. Before their use in the production of jams and tarts, blackberries were eaten in oat porridge. Blackberry seeds have been found in the stomachs of Neolithic peoples, which indicates their ancient consumption. As well as a food, the berries and the rest of the plant were used for dying cloths and alleviating digestive ailments.

Blackcurrant

Irish name: *Cuiríní dubha*
Latin name: *Ribes nigrum*
Fruiting period: July to August

These berries are famously associated with Ribena (a cordial drink/syrup that every Irish and British child who grew up in the 1980s and before was weaned on). The berries are great raw and make a nice jam or syrup. They can also be mixed with other fruits when making sweet pies. Blackcurrant ice cream is a nice treat if you collect enough. The berries make a nice liqueur: add to gin or brandy and leave for a few months. Blackcurrant vinegar is nice in salads: infuse berries in apple cider vinegar for a few weeks, then strain. The leaves of the blackcurrant bush are edible, and I love using them. The smaller leaves can be eaten raw or used to garnish savoury and sweet dishes. The larger leaves are great for wrapping fish and shellfish and for stuffing (like grape vine leaves). Blackcurrant twig broth can be made with the smaller twigs with the aromatic characteristics of the twigs coming through. In folk medicine, a leaf tea was made to help with many inflammatory ailments.

Blackthorn/Sloe

Irish name: *Draighean*
Latin name: *Prunus spinosa*
Fruiting period: autumn (fall)

The berry of the blackthorn tree is famous for being infused in gin (see page 394). It was the first wild infusion I made, and it led me to experiment with many other wild berries and spirits made in Ireland such as whiskey, poitín, gin and now vodka. Place the berries in gin for at least 2 months before using. Wine can also be made and was often made at Halloween. The wood of the tree has a long mythological significance and is woven into many folk beliefs and customs. It was also used as a weapon for men attending country fairs who were looking for a fight.

Cherry, wild

Irish name: *Silín*
Latin name: *Prunus avium*
Fruiting period: July to August

The fruit of the wild cherry tree has been gathered in Ireland for centuries. Cherry stones (pits) have been unearthed during excavations in County Offaly that date to the late Bronze Age. To our modern palate, we may find the fruit rather dry or tart, but they can be eaten raw. Because of their high pectin count, cherries make excellent preserves and jellies. Cherry wine and liqueur can also be made. If making wine, the high pectin content requires a clarifying agent. Wild cherry brandy can be made with 250 g/9 oz (generous 2 cups firmly packed) brown sugar, a bottle of brandy and 500 g/1 lb 2 oz (3 cups) of wild cherries. It will be a little like sloe gin. The sugar is not essential and can also be added after the maturation. Often, I add simple syrup instead. The cherry tree appears many times in Celtic mythology, as well as the history of the British Isles. It has been seen as a symbol of love outside wedlock, and fleeting youth.

Crab apple

Irish name: *Crann fia-úll*
Latin name: *Malus sylvestris*
Fruiting period: August to October

All cultivated apples stem from this small wild apple. It has sustained people for thousands of years in Ireland. For our modern palate, raw crab apples are often a little too bitter, but you will find edible ones that are not so bitter! I have fermented and pickled them with great success, but the traditional method was to stew them to make jelly or to fill pies. The ancient Irish and British also made an alcoholic drink from the juice of these apples that predates the production of cider in monastic Ireland. It may have been more like a rough apple wine. In Europe, especially France, there is a tradition of making verjuice from the apple. One would assume that vinegar was also made from them in Ireland, but we have no record of this before the cultivation of apples in orchards. Apples were cultivated before the arrival of the monastic orders and occupy a place in the Brehon laws. Crab apples can also be used to make black apples (the same process as black garlic). Just place the apples in a rice cooker on its lowest setting for at least 8 weeks. The resulting apples will make a nice black apple purée and the liquid can be used to make black apple vinegar.

Dog rose

Irish name: *Feirdhris*
Latin name: *Rosa canina*
Flowering/fruiting period: from early summer for flowers to autumn (fall) for fruit

In terms of Irish history, the dog rose plant has been prized as an important source of food. In the Brehon laws, it is classified as one of the 'bushes of the wood', according to Mac Coitir. It seems the fruit has been consumed since ancient times in Ireland, as referenced to in both Celtic and Viking mythology. The flowers are great in salads, especially with beetroot (beets). They can also be used to make jellies or decorate desserts. Rose petal syrup has a long tradition in the British Isles. During the Elizabethan period, rose petals were used to flavour both water and butter. The hips of the dog rose are a lot smaller than the Japanese rose (see page 412). The seeds (which are a major irritant if eaten), need to be removed before cooking. However, I don't always do this when making syrup because I hang the liquid in a jelly bag to stop the seeds going through. Jam, purée and syrup are all good to make from the fruit. If making jam, you may want to add apples because the hips are very small and need a lot of work. Rose hip tea and wine can also be made with the hips. Rose hip gin makes a wonderful alternative to sloe gin. When collecting flowers, only remove the petals so the fruit can still form.

Douglas fir

Irish name: *Giúis dhuchlais*
Latin name: *Pseudotsuga menziesii*
Flowering/fruiting period: n/a

The Douglas-fir is named after the Scottish botanist David Douglas, who first introduced the tree to Europe from North America in 1827. I have found no record of it being used as a food or flavour source in Ireland in the past, but we have used it a lot in the restaurant for the last eight years. As with Scots pine and spruce, the young needles can be eaten raw and have citrus orange notes. I like to freeze them first because this helps tenderize them. The young needles can also be pickled (for savoury dishes) or preserved in sugar syrup (for sweet dishes). A flavoured oil can be made with the older needles. I usually blend the needles with three times their weight in oil and then heat to pasteurize. The needles can be infused in sauces and stocks such as in milk or any game stock. The flavour of fir works particularly well with venison and game birds. The cones of the fir are edible. North American indigenous people have long used them for culinary purposes, even grinding them into a flour and mixing them with fat. The bark of pine trees has been used as a food source by the Sami, the indigenous people from northern Scandinavia. The inner bark is a rich source of vitamin C and helped prevent scurvy in the community.

Elder

Irish name: *Trom*
Latin name: *Sambucus nigra*
Fruiting period: August to September

It came as a surprise to me when I first discovered that in the past the elder tree was a symbol of anxiety for many farmers and country folk. It is claimed that Judas hung himself from an elder tree and that if you cut one down, the fairies would come and get you. The elder tree is indigenous to Ireland and, apart from being a sign of a cursed piece of land, it offers us an abundance of flowers (see page 403) and berries that we can use to cook with and make wine. The flowers usually bloom in June and July and the berries are in full swing in September. If you've never picked elderberries before, I encourage you to do so because they can be used in so many ways in the kitchen. From soups to jams, from syrups to sauces, elderberries are extremely versatile. Make sure your elderberries are plump and ripe, although if you can still find some green unripe ones, you can pickle them and use them like capers. Remove the stalks (stems) from the berries, cover them with a good-quality sea salt and leave for 3 weeks. Rinse, then cover with warm cider vinegar. You can use them after 6 weeks. They are good with pickled fish such as mackerel or herring. With the ripe berries, I like to make vinegar and sauces for our wild game dishes in Aniar. There is nothing as nice in the autumn (fall) as combining wild duck with an elderberry sauce. If you can't get wild duck, there are many great duck farmers in Ireland and elsewhere, so it won't be hard to find a local one. Saying that, elderberries pair well with any wild game, from venison to pheasant and partridge.

Gooseberry

Irish name: *Spíonán*
Latin name: *Ribes uva-crispa*
Fruiting period: July to September

You're a gooseberry! To be honest, I never dwelt on the significance of the meaning of these words. I just knew they weren't good; an everyday insult meant to demean. Every summer, our kitchen is full of green gooseberries. You may know gooseberry jam. Equal quantities of berries and sugar brought to the boil until setting temperature is achieved. I prefer to pass it through a fine sieve, though the seeds are edible. For birds, perhaps. Fold this jam into whipped cream and smashed meringue for a nice alternative to strawberry fool (whip). If you get sweeter gooseberries (more often than not, they're as tart as hell), fold them in as well. Sprinkle with icing (confectioners') sugar. If you have less of a sweet tooth, I'd pair the gooseberry jam with a nice Irish sheep's cheese, such as Cáis na Tíre. This is a beautiful cheese from Tipperary that rivals manchego. On the more savoury side, I like to pair these tart berries with fish. This may seem unorthodox, but it

is a combination I have come across in Spanish cooking, in particular from Elena Arzak, one of the few female chefs in the world to hold three Michelin stars. Gooseberries are great pickled, too, and will keep for the whole year.

Hawthorn

Irish name: *Sceach gheal*
Latin name: *Crataegus monogyna*
Flowering/fruiting period: from summer for flowers to early autumn (fall) for fruit

The buds of flowers of the hawthorn emerge in late spring and are good to eat along with the young leaves. A tea can be made with the young leaves. The berries, which can be picked in the late summer and early autumn (fall) are quite astringent and need to be cooked. They make a nice jelly. We have fermented them but with little success because they remain extremely tart! In the past, the berries were infused in brandy or whiskey to make a country liqueur. Wine can also be made from the berries. Haw wine (made with the addition of sultanas/golden raisins and lemon) has also been made in the past. Also called the 'May bush' to indicate the arrival of May and the summer, the tree was associated with the fairies and was regarded in Irish folk culture with both fear and respect.

Hazel

Irish name: *Coll*
Latin name: *Corylus avellana*
Fruiting period: September to October

As with salmon and oysters, hazelnuts represent some of the first foods eaten in Ireland by its original inhabitants. When I crack these nuts today, I still marvel at what they mean to our food culture. As well as bearing fruit (its nuts), the whole hazel tree was a valuable commodity in ancient Ireland. Its branches were used to create weirs and wattle fences (to catch salmon, eels and other fish). In Irish mythology, the hazel tree was a symbol of knowledge. Indeed, the salmon of knowledge seems to have got his powers from eating nine hazelnuts that fell from a tree beside the river Boyne (another sacred site). Hazel rods were used to protect people against evil spirits as well as for making wands and water divining. Forked hazel twigs are still used by water diviners today. As these tales illustrate, the hazel tree was an important part of Irish food and culture for thousands of years. In the late autumn (fall), the nuts can be eaten straight from the tree (or on the ground as they fall off when ripe). Store in a cool dry place in single layers to avoid mould. Roasted hazelnuts are a gorgeous meal in themselves. Charred shells have been found in many ancient fire pits. I love to use them in sweet and savoury dishes, from adding them to crumble toppings for tarts and pies to shaving them over ham hock terrines and barley dishes. To make a simple praline, heat equal quantities of

Wild Fruits, Nuts and Trees

sugar and hazelnuts until they caramelize, then pour onto a silicone mat or baking (parchment) paper. When cool, crack and eat. When blended, the praline makes an ideal crumb for cheesecake. Hazelnut oil is a good source of vitamins and great in dressings. Perhaps the nicest way to eat hazelnuts is to toast them and serve them with whipped fermented cream. Try toasting them in pork fat for an extra depth of flavour. Hazelnuts can also be soaked in whiskey for a delicious flavoured nut (and a nice drink).

Japanese Rose

Irish name: *Rós rúscach*
Latin name: *Rosa rugosa*
Flowering period: June to July

The Japanese rose bush, also known as the beach or seaside rose, is probably the most common wild rose bush that you will encounter in Ireland. Originally a garden escape, it has now become naturalized as a wild plant. There is one in the grounds of my daughter's school and I love to watch it gradually flower in spring and then produce its wonderful fruit in autumn (fall). I love making vinegar with the petals. They really have an intensity that is unmatched with regards to the roses that you find in the shops. As with the fruit of the dog rose, the fruit was used to make both jams and syrups, though wine was also made from the hips. Rose hips were often combined with crab apples (to give volume) in the making of jam. Pickled rose hips are a way of preserving the fruit. However, the seeds of the rose hip cause irritation to both the skin and the bowels, so be sure to remove them before cooking. Rose hip tea is a good source of vitamin C and can be made by combining crushed hips with boiling water. Strain through muslin (cheesecloth) to ensure no seeds pass into the tea. When picking the hips, try to wait for the first frost because this will soften the fruit and make it easier to cook. For savoury use, I find rose hip purée works well with fish and shellfish, especially langoustines (Dublin bay prawns) and scallops. If you want to use the purée for dessert, just combine it with the same volume of sugar and cook until the sugar dissolves.

Juniper

Irish name: *Aiteal*
Latin name: *Juniperus communis*
Fruiting period: September to February

The flavour of juniper is known to most of us as one of the key aromats that gives gin its distinct taste. Though classified as a tree, juniper is generally no bigger than a shrub. It is found on rocky limestone, in bogs and often in woodlands rich in pine and birch trees. Juniper is one of the few native evergreens growing in Ireland. The fruit is best dried and can be used in many game dishes. I like to pick the fruit just before it is fully ripe and dry the berries overnight in a cool dry

space. There are many classic Irish game dishes that include the dried berries. As well as contributing flavour to many Irish game dishes, juniper is also good for adding flavour to pickles. The berries are a common addition to pickled or fermented cabbage. They pack a punch, so use sparingly.

Larch

Irish name: *Learóige*
Latin name: *Larix*
Flowering/fruiting period: n/a

The larch tree was introduced to Ireland in the early seventeenth century and was planted on many country estates. The young needles are suitable to eat, and I have pickled them in the past. As with other pine-like trees, the needles can also be used to flavour sugar syrup and oil. The bark of the tree has medicinal qualities and can be ground into a flour to make cereal or bread.

Lichens

I didn't grow up wandering through the woods, eating lichen off the tree. Did anyone in this country? It is strange how different countries adopt different food practices even though they may have the same foodstuff. I suppose Japan would be a good example in terms of what they have done with seaweed. Another one is how the Nordic countries use lichen. But in the Nordic countries this is a recent discovery (that coincides with its use in restaurants). For other ethnic groups such as the Inuit of Lapland and Greenland, eating lichen off the tree is an age-old pastime. However, as with mushrooms, not all lichen is edible. Part fungus, part algae, 6 per cent of Earth's land surface is covered by lichens and there are about twenty thousand known species. Several notable edible liches are: *Cetraria islandica* (Iceland moss), *Cladonia rangiferina* (reindeer moss or lichen), *Parmelia perlata* (Kalpasi or the black stone flower), *Umbilicaria* (rock tripe), *Tillandsia usneoides* (Spanish moss), and *Evernia prunastri* (oakmoss). Reindeer and oakmoss are the two most common lichens we use in Aniar. Lichen has a bitter astringent quality, so it needs to be cooked first. In Iceland, they would boil the lichen in water with added bread soda. I find steaming the lichen and then drying it makes it the most palatable. You can also fry it oil. In Noma, the renowned restaurant in Denmark, they spray the lichen with chocolate as part of their 'forest' dessert (which includes a cep/porcini mushroom covered in chocolate). While we have yet to embrace lichen as a nation (or re-embrace it, if our ancient ancestors ate it), I do believe it will make its way into our food culture eventually.

Medlar

Irish name: *Meispealchrann*
Latin name: *Mespilus germanica*
Fruiting period: late autumn (fall)

The fruit from this tree is best picked after the first frost because it tends to soften. It is recommended that the fruit is stored until nearly rotten (this is called 'bletted'). You can then eat the fruit raw, simply sprinkled with sugar or baked. The fruit makes good jelly and jam as well as liqueurs. It is referred to as 'dog's arse (ass)' due to its shape. Darina Allen includes a recipe for apple and medlar sauce (with plenty of spices and cider) in her book *Grow, Cook, Nourish* (2017). In the past, the fruit was also used for medicinal purposes in Ireland, being infused into liquid and drunk to alleviate digestive ailments.

Oak

Irish name: *Dair*
Latin name: *Quercus robur*
Fruiting period: autumn (fall)

Though the acorns of the oak are extremely bitter, they have been used as food in the past. They were buried in the ground until the following spring and then eaten. Miles Irving observes that some oak trees produce acorns that are not bitter, so he recommends sampling the output of the oak trees in your area. Acorns have long been a food for pigs and pigs fed on acorns are now a prized part of Spanish food (the Iberian pig is fed on acorns). In the past, wild pigs would have naturally eaten the acorns. The meat from these pigs is beautifully marbled and extremely tasty. Oak flour can be produced from the acorns, but they need a lot of cooking first to remove the bitter quality.

Raspberry

Irish name: *Sú craobh*
Latin name: *Rubus idaeus*
Fruiting period: June to July

Like the wild strawberry (see opposite), the wild raspberry is a diminutive thing. These little berries are beautiful raw, and this is perhaps the best way to eat them due to their size. Wild raspberry vinegar is a great way of preserving their flavour – just place them in a jar with some white wine vinegar. Alternatively, you can make a cordial or sugar syrup from the berries.

Redcurrant

Irish name: *Cuirín dearg*
Latin name: *Ribes rubrum*
Fruiting period: July to August

These berries are great to eat raw or cooked in jam or jelly. Redcurrants are wonderful to ferment (use a 2 per cent brine solution, see page 361) and go well with game, especially small birds such as quail, woodcock or snipe. Redcurrants can also be used in desserts, sprinkled with sugar and served with custard, or folded into a pudding mixture and steamed.

Rowanberry

Irish name: *Caorthann*
Latin name: *Sorbus aucuparia*
Fruiting period: August to November

The rowan tree (or Mountain-ash) is native to Ireland. Its berries have long been used in jams, jelly and syrups. Though the berries can be eaten raw, they are very acidic and may upset your digestive system, so I would avoid them. The berries can be used to make a country wine and there is mention of rowan wine in medieval Irish literature. However, it seems the 'Celtic' people of Ireland flavoured their mead long before this point. They have a low pectin count so apple is often used to help them set in a jam or jelly. Recently, a variety of rowan tree with sweet berries has been produced. Traditional dishes in Ireland are rowanberry and apple jelly, rowanberry wine and rowanberry syrup. A shrub would also have been made with the syrup with the addition of apple cider vinegar.

Scots pine

Irish name: *Giúis / péine albanach*
Latin name: *Pinus sylvestris*
Fruiting period: n/a

A native tree of Ireland, the stumps of the oldest pine trees date to more than seven thousand years ago. However, most of the Scots pine trees in Ireland date from a few hundred years ago and were largely imported from Scotland. Because of its resinous nature, it was used to make torches or 'candles' to navigate through ancient mines. In the past, logs were burned around Christmas time to provide light in the darkness of winter. This is perhaps the origins of our association of Christmas with the pine tree. Historian A. T. Lucas (who wrote about the Irish diet before the potato) observed how winter fires of pine logs were lit in the south of the country. The resin from the tree was collected and used for waterproofing boats and preserving wood. Despite its edible nature, there is very little record of its use as a food. The baby flowers (little pine cones) from both the male (yellow) and female (red) trees can be used as food (though they are bitter raw). We preserve them in honey and apple cider vinegar and use them with pork. They are like a citric caper and are great to cut through fat. Pair them with black garlic on toast for a very contemporary take on Irish food! To make a syrup, combine 250 g/9 oz of the needles with 1 kg/2¼ lb (5 cups) of caster (superfine) sugar and 1 litre/34 fl oz (4¼ cups) of water. Pine-flavoured oil can also be made but you may want to add parsley for colour. Pine soaked in apple cider vinegar will make a nice citric dressing. The young cones, which appear in late spring and early summer, can be cooked in sugar syrup until soft and make a delicious sweet treat. Finally, pine gin is a nice one to have in your larder (pantry). I use the flowers, but the needles can also be used.

Spruce, Norway

Irish name: *Sprús*
Latin name: *Picea abies*
Fruiting period: n/a

Every spring I await the appearance of the beautiful green and tender tips of the spruce tree. Spruce trees can be found in most counties in Ireland. I found some recently while out walking in Mayo. The tips are excellent eaten raw and pair well with poached white fish. In the restaurant, we try to preserve as many as we can because their citrus flavour lends our cooking a distinct flavour. The spruce shoots freeze well and will keep their beautiful green colour. We also pickle them in a 3-2-1 solution of vinegar, water and sugar, then use them on pork and vegetable dishes. As with the rest of the pine family, spruce shoots can be used to flavour sauces (especially game), marinades, gin, vinegar and sugar syrups. Spruce cordial (syrup) is great to make, too. In regards to nutrition, spruce is high in vitamin C and was used in folk medicine for alleviating coughs and sore throats.

Strawberry, wild

Irish name: *Sú talún fhián*
Latin name: *Fragaria vesca*
Fruiting period: July to August

The wild strawberry is one of Ireland's beautiful native berries. In the summer, its little white flowers can be seen popping up among its coarse green leaves. The flavour of the fruit is intense and often it is far better than many cultivated varieties. They are best picked straight from the stalk (stem) and eaten. If you're not eating it there and then, be very gentle with the fruit because it easily bruises. Carry them in a little container and only pick what you need. As well as eating them raw (with loads of cream!), the strawberries are great in a liqueur. I like to soak them in vodka or gin with some sugar. Leave them in a cool place for a few months and then decant.

Sweet chestnut

Irish name: *Cnó capaill milis*
Latin name: *Castanea sativa*
Fruiting period: September to November

Not to be confused with the horse chestnut, which is much more common and not edible, sweet chestnuts have a much pricklier shell and contain up to three nuts. While sweet chestnut trees are found mostly in the east and south (which is usually warmer and drier), they can also be found in the west of the country. Some nuts have weevil larvae inside, so do inspect each nut as you remove it from its shell. Chestnuts are best roasted, but they can also be poached and then grated. I like to grate chestnuts over chicken. Make sure to peel off the skin of the nut because it is quite bitter. Chestnuts are also great for stuffing and making purée. I have also come across chestnut soup in the course of my research in older recipe books.

Walnut

Irish name: *Gallchnó*
Latin name: *Juglans regia*
Fruiting period: October to November

The walnut tree was supposedly first planted in County Waterford by Sir Walter Raleigh in the seventeenth century, though they may have been in the country before that. Walnut trees are few and far between in Ireland and are mostly located in the south of the country because they need more heat to fruit. However, they do appear in other places, dotted around the country. Young green walnuts can be picked from July and used for ketchups or syrups. The pickling of green walnuts (see page 354), which subsequently go black, was a common enough tradition in England and Ireland, particularly among the landed classes. Several recipe collections from the seventeenth and eighteenth centuries have recipes for pickled walnuts. In October, brown walnuts can be picked. Use raw, roasted or in salads.

Sea Herbs

'We stop to pick some rock samphire, the green stalky plant that King Lear sees being gathered on the English coast. At his urging, I taste it sceptically: it is crisp and salty as a cashew.'

Fintan O'Toole, *Irish Times*, 19 August 2013

Like seaweeds, sea herbs have a rich tradition of use in Irish cooking, particularly in coastal areas. However, looking through all the Irish recipes books of the past century you would imagine that we had no tradition of using these wild herbs. Apart from sea beet being used in soup, or samphire (sea beans) cooked in butter, it's hard to find other recipes. I don't know if this is because cookbooks exclude their use due to availability or because they weren't part of a specific written tradition. As with seaweeds, just because we have no written record that doesn't mean they have no part in our food culture in the past. Hunter-gatherers would have certainly consumed them, and they provide an important part of the diet in terms of vitamins and minerals. I use all of these wild sea herbs daily in our restaurant and they have become a very important part of my own personal cuisine. This is not to say that these herbs are exclusive to Ireland. The grow in many countries along the same latitude as ourselves. But it is how each region uses them that makes them specific to their own terroir, or their sense of place. Due to their coastal nature, they pair well with fish and shellfish, but feel free to experiment with them. I know that many go well with lamb, especially marsh lamb that is reared on the coast. This list is not exhaustive and only lists the main sea herbs that I have found the most useful in my kitchen.

Arrowgrass

Irish name: *Barr an mhilltigh mara*
Latin name: *Triglochin maritima*
Flowering period: June to September

Arrowgrass is a native Irish seagrass that grows on the coast and in salt marsh areas. It is quite prolific in the west of Ireland and we pick it from April to September. The taste of the grass reminds me of coriander (cilantro). It's one of my favourite sea herbs in terms of its subtle flavour. Often, we use it raw to garnish white fish or in place of fresh herbs in shellfish dishes, especially oysters and mussels. It's also good to finely chop it and use instead of chives in a crab salad. If blanching, it only takes a second in boiling water because it starts to deteriorate very quickly. Only take the tender tops of the grass when you are out foraging. Use a pair of scissors to remove them. This will also allow the plant to keep growing.

Buck's-horn plantain

Irish name: *Adharca fia*
Latin name: *Plantago coronopus*
Flowering period: May to July

As with ribwort and sea plantain, buck's-horn is quite bitter raw. However, blanched in water or fried in butter, it becomes quite succulent. Its young shoots are delicious. Older leaves tend to be fibrous. Plantain is vitamin and mineral rich and also contains protein. Best used for a garnish when young.

Horseradish

Irish name: *Meacan ragaim*
Latin name: *Armoracia rusticana*
Flowering period: May to June

Horseradish is not a native wild plant but rather what one would call a garden escape (planted for many years then went wild). It doesn't grow prolifically around Ireland, but it can be found on certain coasts in the east and south-east. Horseradish is in the brassica family (like cabbage, broccoli, mustard, wasabi) and it is its root that is the most useful as a spice. Intact, the root has very little aroma, but when grated, it releases its pungency. Grated horseradish was traditionally mixed with vinegar as a condiment for beef or fish. In his book *The Herball, or Generall Historie of Plantes* (1597), the English botanist John Gerard observes:

> '[T]he Horse Radish stamped with a little vinegar put thereto, is commonly used among the Germans for sauce to eat fish with and such like meats as we do mustard.'

The vinegar helps preserve its heat and pungency. Grated horseradish can also be mixed with cream or buttermilk. Creamed horseradish is commonly served with roast beef in Ireland and features in many traditional recipes. Grated horseradish can also be blended with oil to produce a spicy oil. Personally, I love to use it in buttermilk with raw fish or shellfish, or in a buttermilk ice cream for a little heat.

Monk's beard

Irish name: *Lus an tsalainn*
Latin name: *Salsola soda*
Flowering period: June to September

Monk's beard (or saltwort, barilla plant or oppositeleaf Russian thistle) is another type of edible seagrass. In the market, it is commonly referred to by its Italian name *agretti*. Taste wise, it is located somewhere between samphire (sea beans) and arrowgrass. Depending on how old the grass is when picked, it can be either extremely delicate or woody. It can be blanched in boiling water or lightly fried in butter.

Orache

Irish name: *Eilifleog leathan*
Latin name: *Atriplex prostrata*
Flowering period: July to September

There are several species of orache that grow on the coasts of Ireland, of which spear-leafed is the most common (or the easiest to find). They all have little triangular leaves that have a wonderful saline taste. The other varieties (frosted and Babington) have a pretty colour and texture and, used together, create an attractive garnish for fish or vegetables. In the spring, the leaves do not need any cooking, but as they grow into the summer and autumn (fall), they may need a quick blanch in boiling water. The small tender leaves are wonderful with raw fish such as tuna or cod. The large leaves blanched pair well with roasted monkfish and turbot. In the winter months, I often use them to garnish roasted vegetables, such as carrots or celeriac (celery root). Their salinity and slight bitterness complement the fattiness of vegetables roasted in butter or oil.

Rock samphire

Irish name: *Craobhraic*
Latin name: *Crithmum maritimum*
Flowering period: April to June

The rock samphire (also known as sea fennel) grows – as you may have already guessed – on rocks. It's easy to spot, dotted among sea cliffs and shingled beaches, growing out of the sandy dunes. Some describe its taste as unpleasant due to its bitter quality and petroleum notes. It is an acquired taste. It is traditional to pickle it in many European countries, the pickle being used to accompany lamb, game and cheese. In terms of cooking, it can be steamed or blanched in boiling water, then tossed in a little butter. The flowers can also be used in fish dishes. Its leaves and seed pods are nice pickled and can be used in chicken and fish dishes to add an acidic note. Rock samphire appears several times in English literature, most notably in Shakespeare's *King Lear*. In the sixteenth century, herbalist John Gerard wrote, 'The leaves kept in pickle and eaten in sallads with oile and vinegar is a pleasant sauce for meat'. He could not have been more right!

Samphire/Glasswort

Irish name: *Lus na gloine*
Latin name: *Salicornia europaea*
Flowering period: August to September

Samphire (sea beans), the beautiful wild green vegetable that grows by the sea, is best picked in July and August. All in all, there are six varieties in Ireland. You'll find it on marshy ground, usually just over the dunes. It's plentiful in the west of Ireland. I usually head out past Salthill to places like Barna and Spidéal and look for wet damp ground behind the beach head. Most of us are familiar with marsh samphire, which looks a little like baby asparagus. Eaten raw, it has a nice crisp texture and salty taste. It goes well in broths; either a simple clear seaweed soup (such as a Japanese dashi) or a roast fish bone broth. These broths are really easy infusions to make and are full of minerals and other good stuff for the body. Saying that, nothing can quite beat samphire fried in foaming golden butter.

Scurvygrass

Irish name: *Carrán creige*
Latin name: *Cochlearia danica*
Flowering period: February to June

A peppery little leaf that gets its name from preventing scurvy. It is usually found on coastal roads, sea cliffs and on the edge of salt marshes and beaches. It packs quite a punch so use sparingly. Use raw in salads or blanch briefly for adding to stews and soups. It makes a piquant purée, though it is necessary to cut with spinach as the flavour overpowers everything. In recent years, I've made a fluid gel by blending it into a little blanching liquid and then straining and thickening with agar agar. Its small white flowers can be used as a garnish for fish dishes but again be mindful of their strength – too many can destroy a good fish dish. It can be combined with other sea vegetables such as sea beet for a lovely green maritime soup.

Sea aster

Irish name: *Luibh bhléine*
Latin name: *Tripolium pannonicum*
Flowering period: July to October

Sea aster belongs to the Asteraceae family, of which the daisy flower is also a part. As well as being able to eat the succulent salty leaves, you can also eat the flowers. I like to use them to garnish seafood salads and fish buffets. However, the bees and butterflies do love this flower, so if using, always make sure there's plenty left for them. The plant is short lived during the summer months. You'll usually find sea aster among the host of other salt marsh plants, so it's nice to combine them with samphire (sea beans), orache and sea beet to make a sea herb salad. The leaves pickle and ferment well and can also be used to give colour to any green sauce such as parsley or watercress. I often make an oil-based green sauce with sea aster, combining it with everything I find in the marsh: sea marsh pesto!

Sea beet

Irish name: *Laíon na trá*
Latin name: *Beta vulgaris* subsp. *maritima*
Flowering period: July to September

Sea beet is an ancient sea herb that grows in coastal areas of Ireland. It can be found on rocky shingle beaches or areas of salt marsh. Modern beetroot (beets), sugar beet and Swiss chard stem from the same family. Its leaves are triangular, shiny and dark green. During its flowering period, it has tiny green, sometimes reddish, petal-less flowers. I love to use sea beet with fish dishes, briefly blanched and then dressed in sea salt and vinegar. It can also be served raw. Baby leaves pair well with fresh oysters and charred mackerel. Because of its salinity, it tends not to need salt. I tend to avoid large leaves because they have a waxy and woody texture. However, the large leaves work well in soup. Potato and sea beet soup pops up now and then in Irish cookbooks of the past. Evidence of eating the root, in the form of barbecuing it, is found in Neolithic Denmark, about seven thousand years ago. Of all the sea herbs, it is probably the easiest to identify and one of the best to start with in terms of seaside foraging.

Sea blite

Irish name: *Blide mhara*
Latin name: *Suaeda maritima*
Flowering period: July to September

Sea blite (aka seepweed) can be very salty because it absorbs salt from the salty soils it grows in. If it is very salty, soaking it in fresh water helps lessen the salinity. Sea blite can be eaten raw, or else it is good fried or blanched. It is also nice as a salty seasoning for meat or fish dishes or in salad. I often combine it with samphire (sea beans) and sea lettuce when making a sea salad; or use it to garnish spring lamb as the sprigs are reminiscent of rosemary. The younger shoots can be pickled in vinegar and made into a tangy relish.

Sea buckthorn

Irish name: *Draighean mara*
Latin name: *Hippophae rhamnoides*
Flowering period: March to April

Sea buckthorn was introduced to Ireland in coastal areas to prevent erosion. The fruit from the tree, a bright orange tart berry, is vitamin and mineral rich and has a taste akin to an orange or a mango. It usually appears around September. The berries can be juiced and used for ice cream or sorbets or cooked to make jams, syrups or jellies. Though the berry has a long history of use going back to the Greeks, it was René Redzepi of Noma who revived it (after reading about its uses in a survival guide) in terms of its contemporary use. His scallop and sea urchin dish with sea buckthorn, as well as his carrot and sea buckthorn, are now classics of contemporary cooking. In the west, we source ours from County Mayo and Sligo and use it in various ways, as a purée with pork belly or langoustines (Dublin bay prawns) or as a granita with sheep's yogurt.

Sea carrot

Irish name: *Mealbhacán mara*
Latin name: *Daucus carota* subsp. *gummifer*
Flowering period: June to July

Sea carrot is a subspecies of wild carrot (which can also be found in coastal areas). Its appearance in Ireland is rare, though it can be found in the south and east of the country. Flowers and young succulent leaves make a pretty garnish. Use like wild carrot.

Sea holly

Irish name: *Cuileann trá*
Latin name: *Eryngium maritimum*
Flowering period: June to August

To look at, this prickly sand plant does not seem to be the most inviting thing for one's palate, but it does has several food uses. Seemingly, its roots were popular in the seventeenth and eighteenth centuries,

Sea Herbs

both as a food and a medicine. The roots were roasted as a vegetable. When young, its leaves can be blanched. They have a similar taste to asparagus (which is also a type of grass). I was told coastal people used the flowers of the plant to make cheese. I assume this process is similar to making cheese from milk thistle flowers, where the flowers are dried and then the stamens (the purplish threads from each flower head) are used to split the milk into curds and whey. Thistle rennet is best for young cheeses.

Sea kale

Irish name: *Praiseach thrá*
Latin name: *Crambe maritima*
Flowering period: June to August

I first came across sea kale in the late Myrtle Allen's *Ballymaloe Cookbook* (1977). It is, as many other sea vegetables and herbs, a rare one to find. It grows mostly in the south (hence its use in Ballymaloe, which is located in County Cork). To cook sea kale, trim the stalk (stem) and rinse under running water. Blanch in salted boiling water and serve with a little melted butter and sea salt. Its flowers can also be used as with other members of the brassica family.

Sea lungwort

Irish name: *Lus na sceallaí*
Latin name: *Mertensia maritima*
Flowering period: March to June

It is the leaves of this plant that are the most important for culinary use. Its little leaves have a subtle oyster taste (hence its other name: oyster plant). It is extremely rare and is listed as protected. In Ireland, it can be found in the south-east and in the north of the country. It favours gravelly ground. Because of the popularity of its leaves, it is now widely cultivated. It is best not to pick this one in the wild!

Sea pea

Irish name: *Peasairín trá*
Latin name: *Lathyrus japonicus* subsp. *maritimus*
Flowering period: July to August

Like sea lungwort, sea pea (also known as beach pea or beach vetchling) is protected due to its rarity. It resembles vetch in appearance, which grows in abundance.

Sea plantain

Irish name: *Slánlus mara*
Latin name: *Plantago maritima*
Flowering period: June to August

As with the other varieties of plantain, sea plantain (also known as goose tongue) is a common enough occurrence in coastal and marshy areas. The leaves can be eaten raw, used as a garnish or added to salads.

However, taste them first – they pack a bitter, astringent punch (like sea radish). Cook young leaves in brown butter and finish with a little sea salt.

Sea purslane

Irish name: *Lus an Ghaill*
Latin name: *Atriplex portulacoides*
Flowering period: July to September

Slightly salty, this wonderful sea herb pairs beautifully as a garnish with white fish. Coastal, sandy or muddy salt marshes are its favourite habitat. Often it tends to sprawl and spreads its way across marshy areas behind the beach head. Other than a useful food stuff, the plant also helps stop coastal erosion. So, when picking its leaves, be careful not to uproot it. Briefly blanched is perhaps the best way to use it, but it's also nice raw in salads or as a garnish. The buds are also good to pickle, adding a delicate salinity to any dish.

Sea radish

Irish name: *Meacan mara*
Latin name: *Raphanus raphanistrum* subsp. *maritimus*
Flowering period: May to July

Sea radish is another coastal plant with bristly leaves and yellow flowers. It is usually found on rocky beaches, dunes or at the base of cliffs. The cultivated radish is a related species. Because of its bristly leaves, it is not great eaten raw; however, if thinly sliced, it does have some raw uses as a garnish for shellfish or sprinkled into broths. It is probably at its best briefly blanched and simply dressed. The root is edible and can be used as horseradish root. In Aniar, we have fermented the roots with some success. The resulting liquid has a beautiful piquant flavour. Place the roots in a 2 per cent brine (see page 361) and leave at room temperature for 5–7 days. You can also ferment the stalks (stems) in the same manner and then dry them. Blending the dried leaves produces a nutty aromatic powder and can be used as a seasoning. Its yellow flowers are a great garnish, but they die quickly. Finally, in the autumn (fall), its pods can be pickled and used in place of capers.

Sea sandwort

Irish name: *gaineamhlus mara*
Latin name: *Honckenya peploides*
Flowering period: May to August

The first time I was told that sea sandwort tasted like cucumber, I was a bit sceptical. But just as arrowgrass has notes of coriander (cilantro), sea sandwort is the closest you'll get to replicating a 'sea' cucumber flavour. It is delicate, subtle and crunchy, and I love using it raw on fish dishes. It is best eaten when young, because the older stalks (stems) and leaves get a little woody. Blend with a mix of other green sea herbs for a nice Irish salsa

verde. You can also blanch and serve with a little melted butter and sea salt. Or serve over raw oysters with a dash of Irish gin!

Wild cabbage

Irish name: *Cabáiste fiáin*
Latin name: *Brassica oleracea*
Flowering period: May to August

Wild cabbage is probably the rarest wild plant in Ireland, to be found at the base of sea cliffs (with chalky or limestone soils), dotted around the country, from County Derry to County Mayo. You can use the plant as you would regular cabbage. The leaves are great – just remove the stalk (stem) before wilting in a little butter and water. Serve with white fish such as cod, hake or John Dory.

Seaweed

In terms of terroir, seaweed is a vital ingredient for Irish cooking. It has a long history of use since prehistoric times and continues to inform the direction of contemporary Irish cooking. For me, seaweed is the unsung hero of Irish food and, along with oysters, represents our two national foodstuffs. In recent history, the potato has overshadowed it, but hopefully the tide is turning for these wonderful algae. Recent books by Prannie Rhatigan and Sally McKenna demonstrate its use and diversity, not only in the context of Irish food, but also the other seaweed traditions that exist elsewhere in the world. Seaweed makes a wonderful flavoured oil and vinegar because of its rich umami characteristics. I love to use it to dress fish and shellfish as well as vegetable dishes. Nori, dillisk (dulse) and kelps are some of my favourites, but do experiment yourself with the other seaweeds. All will add a slightly different subtlety to the finished dish. Milled seaweed or seaweed salt brings a wonderful saline flavour to anything you're seasoning. Though it may seem strange, seaweed salt works well with meat: lamb rump, beef brisket, roast chicken. Seaweed is a great conduit for flavour. All cuts will work with different types of seaweed salt. Though I always use dried seaweed in making oil, vinegar and salt, fresh seaweeds work well for certain oils and vinegars. However, it is really the dried seaweed that has the best umami potential. If you live near the sea, look up your local seaweeds. Find people who pick them. Seaweed is a great vehicle to bring you back in touch with your environment.

Alaria

Irish name: *Láir/láracha*
Latin name: *Alaria esculenta*
Location: lower tidal zone
Harvesting period: mid-spring to summer

'Alaria' is Latin for 'wings', due to the wing-like appearance of the base of the seaweed – it is also known as winged kelp (and badderlocks). It is easily identified due to the central midrib that runs through the entire seaweed. When eating the seaweed raw, I usually remove the midrib because it can be tough. However, if it is very young, the rib should be tender. As a young leaf, it is great in a salad. The young leaves can also be dressed with oil and vinegar and served with lamb or goat. The older leaves give a sweet flavour to broths and soups. In her book *Irish Seaweed Kitchen*, Prannie Rhatigan has some great recipes for using alaria, such as miso. As we learn more techniques and ways of using seaweed from the Japanese, I hope our consumption increases.

Bladderwrack

Irish name: *Feamainn dhubh / cosa cruadha*
Latin name: *Fucus vesiculosus*
Location: middle tidal zone
Harvesting period: all year round

Bladderwrack is commonly found all over the shore, along with eggwrack (*Ascophylum nodosum*). Both seaweeds have a tradition of being used to fertilize the land, especially land that grew potatoes. By leaving it on the soil over the winter and then digging it through in the spring, it gives necessary nitrogen and other essential elements to the soil. Bladderwrack is also used for seaweed baths. If you have never had a seaweed bath, then I suggest you give it a go. It does wonders for your skin. In terms of eating, I recommend picking the smaller branches in the spring and early summer. It's good for broths, soups and dashis. Add to a bouquet garni of herbs for an interesting addition to stocks (broths).

Carrageen moss

Irish name: *Carraigín*
Latin name: *Chondrus crispus*
Location: lower tidal zone
Harvesting period: spring to autumn (fall)

Carrageen (from the Irish *carraigín*, meaning 'little rock') moss, otherwise known as Irish moss, is perhaps the most famous of Irish seaweeds, being used as a gelling agent for the once popular dessert Carrageen Moss Pudding (see page 338). In its original form, carrageen is purple, but it is often sold bleached so as not to add a colour to the foodstuff that it is thickening. Many drinks are made with carrageen, some for health benefits such as soothing a sore throat. In the past, it was added to alcoholic cocktails to give the drink texture. Though I have never found a recipe that used it raw, I love to add it to dishes at the last minute. Personally, I like its crunch with freshly cooked shellfish, such as mussels or clams. Because of its gelatinous nature, you can't leave it sitting in a liquid too long or it becomes slightly sodden and slimy. Finding it in the wild is often easier than looking for pepper dulse because it tends to shine when under water. In its powdered form, it can be used to make fluid gels and thicken ice creams. Jimmy's Ice Cream, a company in Connemara, use carrageen to thicken their ice cream. In this state, it is very useful as a substitute for flour in sauces; Iota and kapa (two commercially available seaweed powders) are both derived from carrageen and are used a lot in molecular cooking.

Channelled wrack

Irish name: *Dúlamán*
Latin name: *Pelvetia canaliculata*
Location: upper shore and splash zone
Harvesting period: spring to autumn (fall)

Channelled wrack is a small seaweed that can be found on the rocks at the top of the tide line. Its little fronds form a channel shape. In the spring and summer, it begins life as a bright yellow colour and then turns to a dark green-brown by autumn (fall). It is easy to harvest with a pair of scissors by cutting the tips off the top. Be careful not to uproot any of the plant from the rock as this will diminish its ability to regrow the following year. It can be added to any shellfish dishes such as mussels or clams. It not only has an enjoyable texture but its slightly saline flavour contributes to the overall dish. It pickles well, and I love to use it with freshly poached shellfish to lend it a gentle acidity. Simply heat a 3-2-1 solution of vinegar, water and sugar and pour it over the seaweed. Add it to an oyster instead of lemon juice the next time you're eating one. In terms of nutrition, it is quite high in vitamin C. Irish seaweed expert Prannie Rhatigan notes that animals who live by the shore tend to graze on seaweed. Feeding cattle seaweed could also reduce greenhouse gases.

Dillisk

Irish name: *Duileasc*
Latin name: *Palmaria palmata*
Location: mid to lower tidal zone
Harvesting period: spring to autumn (fall)

Dillisk (dulse) is common on Irish coasts and one of the most popular for culinary uses. It can be harvested at low tide. It is usually found in the lower tidal zone, beside and under many other seaweeds, clinging to the rocks. Dillisk can be eaten raw, straight off the strand. I usually wash it and season it lightly with sea salt, oil and a little vinegar and add it to fish dishes as a garnish. It can be blanched in boiling water but it loses its beautiful purple colour, so if blanching, do so lightly. Puréed cooked dillisk goes well with steak.

Dried dillisk is a great addition to soups, especially potato soup. I love to add it to a traditional potato and leek soup to give it more of a maritime and saline taste. Dillisk is a great addition to broth and to flavour vinegars as well. In some parts of the country, it is often added to mashed potato to create a 'dillisk champ'. When it has been dried and milled to a powder, it has many uses as a seasoning. Mix it with one part salt to create a 'dillisk salt'. This keeps indefinitely and is great sprinkled over a leg of lamb before roasting. In Northern Ireland, the tradition of eating dillisk goes back centuries (if not thousands of years). In her book *The Cookin' Woman: Irish Country Recipes* (1949), Florence Irwin includes a recipe for stewed dillisk: the dillisk is stewed with milk, butter, salt and pepper for 3–4 hours and then served with oatcakes or brown bread. Coastal communities have long used dillisk as a foodstuff, and before the introduction of the potato it was a vital source of nutrition for those that lived by the sea. 'Dillisk girls' were women who collected the dillisk at low tide to sell it at the market, both as a food and a fertilizer. In her *Irish Traditional Cooking* (1995), Darina Allen includes a note about dillisk sandwiches told to her by an old man in Antrim.

Kelp

Irish name: *Ceanna slat/murach bealtine*
Latin name: *Laminaria hyperborea*
Location: sub-tidal zone
Harvesting period: spring to autumn (fall)

Kelp is a large brown seaweed that grows in huge forests under the sea. Kelp is the generic name for many different types of large seaweed that make up the Laminariales family. Traditionally, kelp was harvested to produce sodium carbonate and iodine. Kelp was burned to create an ash that could be used as a

fertilizer and in soap and glass production. Farmers would spread burned kelp ash on their land to help the potatoes grow. Alginate is derived from kelp and is used in many ice creams and other foodstuffs that need a gelling agent.

Every spring, when the kelp forest begins to grow again, their old fronds are cast up on the shore. These are called 'may weed' and are easy pickings as a nutritious foodstuff. Some of the earliest evidence of seafood consumption includes the harvesting of foods such as limpets, periwinkles and mussels, all of which are associated with kelp forest habitats. There are several theories that kelp forests facilitated the migration of humans to North America. This is called the 'Kelp Highway Hypothesis'. Primitive islanders and coastal communities all over the world used kelps as a foodstuff, if only to gather the tiny shellfish that lived off it.

I love to use kelps to flavour broths, stocks and soup. It is also beautiful cooked and prepared as noodles. Monkfish wrapped in kelp and steamed is wonderful. Of course, it pairs well with all shellfish, but you can also experiment with pork and beef. After cooking for an hour in water, we pan-fry it in butter and cider as a great garnish for meats, such as pork belly or chicken. The limit of kelp in Irish food is only the limit of your imagination.

Kelp is the seaweed associated with the discovery of the 'fifth taste' *umami* in 1908. Kelp-fed lamb is considered a delicacy. Paired with clams and sea vegetables, it represents the beauty of Irish coastal cuisine.

Nori

Irish name: *Sleabhac*
Latin name: *Pyropia*
Location: middle tidal zone
Harvesting period: summer and winter

Nori is a type of seaweed that can be found clinging to large rocks at low tide. It has a smooth and silky texture and a delicate appearance. Known to most people as the seaweed that is used for making sushi, in Ireland and Wales it goes by the name laver. It is the chief ingredient in laverbread, a traditional seaweed bread. Laver cultivation as food is thought to be very ancient and is common to all cultures on the British Isles.

To harvest nori, it is plucked from the rocks and given a preliminary rinse in seawater. Because of its location, laver needs to be repeatedly washed to remove the excess sand that is among its folds. For laverbread, it is usually boiled for hours until it becomes a stiff, green paste. This paste could also be potted or kept in a cool, dark place. In this way, nori can be preserved for about a week. During the eighteenth century, the green paste was packed into crocks (earthernware dishes) and sold as potted laver. The paste also pairs well with lamb, mutton and bacon.

As with most seaweeds, nori is high in vitamins and minerals. Interestingly, it was a British woman, psychologist Kathleen Mary Drew-Baker, that saved nori production in Japan following the Second World War. She had been researching the *Porphyria umbilicalis*, which grows in the seas around Wales and was traditionally harvested for making laverbread. Her work was subsequently discovered by Japanese scientists who applied it to artificial methods of seeding and growing nori, rescuing the industry and thus saving the tradition of growing nori for future generations. Kathleen Drew-Baker was hailed as the 'Mother of the Sea' in Japan and a statue was erected in her memory.

Oarweed

Irish name: *Fearmainn dubh*
Latin name: *Laminaria digitata*
Location: extreme lower tidal zone
Harvesting period: spring and summer, but found all year round

Oarweed is a variety of kelp and is often confused with 'may weed' (*Laminaria hyperborea*). It is commonly found tossed up on the shore. Golden brown, it looks like a large hand. At extremely low tides, the seaweed can be found attached to rocks. As with other varieties of kelp, the seaweed in its dried form is a great flavour addition to soups and broths. It can also be added in powdered form to the base of a sauce. I like to add it to onions and garlic when I'm cooking a soup or stew. When tender, the fresh fronds can be added to salads. If you have to buy it dried, and you want to add it to salads, place in water and slowly simmer for an hour until tender.

Pepper dulse

Irish name: *Míóbhán*
Latin name: *Osmundia pinnatifida*
Location: middle and lower tide zone
Harvesting period: spring to winter

Probably the smallest and most beautiful of all the Irish seaweeds, pepper dulse packs a wonderful peppery and umami punch. I usually look for pepper dulse on the base of rocks when the tide is out, but if you're lucky, you may find a whole colony in little rock (tide) pools. If the pepper dulse remains under water, it retains its black colour. Often it can be bleached by the heat of the sun.

Pepper dulse is called the 'truffle of the sea' due to the sweet-savoury flavour that it imparts. Because of its minute size, it is best used as a garnish. It does need to be cleaned and picked through for loose stones and sand. As with all other seaweeds, you can dry pepper dulse and grind it into a powder using a coffee mill. It has a short shelf life, so it is best to dry it after the second day or it wilts and loses flavour. If you're lucky enough to find a patch, be careful to harvest it sustainably. Use with cooked and shelled mussels and clams or to dress pan-fried scallops.

Sargassum

Irish name: n/a
Latin name: *Sargassum muticum*
Location: middle to lower tidal zone
Harvesting period: spring to autumn (fall)

Sargassum, also known as wireweed, is a large brown invasive seaweed from the Pacific. The Sargasso Sea is named after the algae, because it hosts a large amount of free-floating sargassum. For most, this seaweed is a pest and competes with native seaweeds and chokes them into extinction. It can be found all along the Irish shore. Sargassum reproduces by itself when pieces break off and float away. In this capacity, it is a planktonic species. Because of its invasive character, sargassum does not need to be sustainably harvested. In China, they make herbal tea with the seaweed in powdered form. Its air pockets provide a nice crunch to salads.

Seagrass

Irish name: *Glasan/lineáil ghorm*
Latin name: *Ulva intestinalis*
Location: lower tidal zone (and in rock/tide pools)
Harvesting period: spring and summer

From a distance, seagrass (grass kelp) looks much like sea lettuce. Upon closer inspection, you will notice that it is made up of tiny pale green tendrils. Indeed, it also goes by the name of gut weed because it resembles an intestine. It is extremely common in Ireland as well as on other Atlantic shores. It can be used in a similar way to sea lettuce, raw on salads or lightly blanched and served with poached white fish. Dried, it produces a wonderful green powder, which is a nice garnish for eggs.

Sea lace

Irish name: *Ruálach*
Latin name: *Chorda filum*
Location: lower tidal zone
Harvesting period: summer

Sea lace looks like very young sea spaghetti and is often confused with it by the novice harvester. It is also known as dead men's ropes and mermaid's tresses. It can be used as sea spaghetti (see below) though as it is smaller and more delicate be careful with the cooking of it. Use as a garnish for raw shellfish and fish, such as scallops and cod.

Sea lettuce

Irish name: *Glasán*
Latin name: *Ulva lactuca*
Location: lower tidal zone
Harvesting period: spring to autumn (fall), but can be found all year round

Sea lettuce is an edible green algae that is common on the Irish coastlines. It is an ancient foodstuff for many peoples, from China and Japan to Scandinavia and Ireland. It is perhaps the easiest seaweed to identify and can be eaten straight out of the water. It's located along the lower tidal zone, so like dillisk (dulse), it is best found at low tide, floating in the water, as it dries out quickly on the sand. It's great raw in salads or lightly steamed as an accompaniment for fish such as softly poached turbot. If you find large sheets of sea lettuce, it can be used to wrap whole pieces of fish. Sea trout wrapped in sea lettuce is a good dish. Chopped with other seaweed, it makes an excellent seaweed salsa for shellfish. I have read of people adding it to sandwiches, though I have never tried that myself!

Sea spaghetti

Irish name: *Imleacán cloch*
Latin name: *Himanthalia elongata*
Location: lower tidal zone (and in rock/tide pools)
Harvesting period: spring to autumn (fall)

Spaghetti de mer, tangle, thong weed or sea thong? I know what sounds more attractive! Sea spaghetti is an extremely popular seaweed. Coastal families gave it to babies when teething. Sea spaghetti grows from 'buttons' attached to the rocks. It is important that you don't remove these parts, which would otherwise impede the reproduction of the seaweed. Cut the seaweed a few centimetres (an inch or so) from its base. In spring and early summer, the younger shoots are tender enough to eat raw. It is beautiful dressed with some extra virgin rapeseed (canola) oil and Seaweed Vinegar (see page 352). In the autumn (fall), I steam or boil it to tenderize it. It can also be deep-fried from fresh to make a little seaweed snack. Because of its popularity, it's usually quite easy to find it in dried or powdered form. Soak overnight or rehydrate in warm water before using as fresh. Thinly sliced, it makes a nice addition to any salsa or sauce served with fish. Try sea spaghetti hollandaise or beurre blanc with chives.

Sea truffle

Irish name: *Olann Dhearg*
Latin name: *Vertebrata lanosa*
Location: middle tidal zone
Harvesting period: spring to autumn (fall)

Whereas most seaweed grows on rock, sea truffle grows on other seaweeds. Sea truffle is not the 'real' common name of the seaweed – which is wrack siphon weed – but most people I know call it this because of the intense 'truffle' taste that comes from the seaweed when dried. The best way to use this seaweed is to clean it, dry it and then blend it into a fine powder. It is wonderful sprinkled over shellfish, butter or on vegetables. It can be used fresh but use sparingly due to its intensity. I like it with shelled mussels in a light broth. Mix dried sea truffle with sea salt flakes for a delicious seaweed salt.

Serrated wrack

Irish name: *múrach dubh*
Latin name: *Fucus serratus*
Location: lower to low intertidal zone
Harvesting period: spring to autumn (fall)

Serrated wrack (also known as saw wrack or toothed wrack) is traditionally used in seaweed baths. Its bitterness makes it a little unpalatable.

Sugar kelp

Irish name: *Madraí rua/cupóg na gCloch*
Latin name: *Saccharina latissima*
Location: sub-tidal zone
Harvesting period: spring to autumn (fall)

Sugar kelp goes by several different names, though all hint at the underlying sweetness of this seaweed. Also known as sweet kombu or sugar wrack, sugar kelp can grow up to 3 metres (10 feet) long. It has a distinctive wavy appearance. I use sugar kelp as a standard addition to our broths. Often, in the restaurant, we re-use the soft sugar kelp that we strain from the broth as a vegetable to go with pork belly. When choosing your sugar kelp, pick younger plants because these will be more tender. These are usually a sandy-yellow to olive-brown colour. The stalks (stems) of the younger plant also make for good eating. In Japan, they dry it for months and then use it to flavour dashi. I have aged sugar kelp for a year and subsequently used it. Its flavour becomes much rounder and more developed. Try hanging it on your own wall for a year!

Velvet horn

Irish name: *Beanna veilbhite*
Latin name: *Codium tomentosum*
Location: sub-tidal zone
Harvesting period: spring to autumn (fall)

Velvet horn is a species of green seaweed in the family Codiaceae. It is small and green (it grows up to 30 centimetres/12 inches long) with branched, cylindrical fronds that remind me of slender fingers. It is also called spongeweed due to its spongy or silky texture. It occurs mainly in the north and south-west of Ireland. Due to pollution in places, it is becoming quite rare. We get ours from Mungo Murphy in Rossaveal in Connemara. As with the other seaweeds, it can be used in stock, but I find it's best as a tempura. Simply dip in batter and fry in hot oil for a crunchy seaweed snack. Irish seaweed expert Prannie Rhatigan recommends using it in salads or making tea from it.

Wild Mushrooms

Going for a 'mushroom hunt' was not something I explored in early youth. There seemed to be a fear of wild food. Thankfully, recent years have changed this attitude. There is no better woman than Mary White to educate you on mushrooms in Ireland. She regularly runs courses in Carlow (www.blackstairsecotrails.ie). I would never recommend going out and eating wild mushrooms on the spot, especially if you live in a country where it is hard to tell apart mushrooms that are safe to eat from poisonous mushrooms. Either pick them with an expert, or better yet, in a guided group.

Wild mushrooms have a wonderful legacy in Irish food history. As with many other wild foods, people have eaten them on the island for as long as people have lived here. Before the advent of farming, they provided an important part of the hunter-gatherer diet, along with nuts and herbs. As farming grew to dominate over the following centuries, much common knowledge of which wild mushrooms one could eat was lost. This is not the case in many European countries. More than likely, the constant warring with the English and the gradual dispossession of land resulted in a further loss of knowledge. The nineteenth and twentieth centuries put a veritable end to that knowledge with the establishment of industrial farming and the subsequent rejection of wild food as something for the poor. Of course, this was not the case everywhere and pockets of knowledge remain, but overall we have lost our ability to engage with the wild. Furthermore, I was told that many country people in Ireland would not go near mushrooms as they believed the fairies used them as houses, and to take them up would result in the wrath of the fairies! Whatever the truth of this tale, myth and superstition play an important part in Irish food culture. Growing up, I was afraid of fairies, so I can only imagine what it was like 100 years ago!

The following is in no manner a complete guide to the wild mushrooms of Ireland, and I am by no means an expert – it represents only those that I favour in terms of cooking and the ones I have used in our restaurants. If you're interested in learning more about Irish mushrooms look up Bill O'Dea (based in County Wicklow) and Dr Lucy Deegan and Mark Cribbin of Ballyhoura Mountain Mushrooms (County Limerick and Cork).

Beefsteak

Latin name: *Fistulina hepatica*
Found: July to October

Growing on the lower trunks of trees, these mushrooms are best eaten when young because they turn very woody when old. Traditionally, strips were soaked in milk overnight to remove the astringency. The best cooking method is frying or grilling, but they can also be added to stews or soups. They can be eaten raw, but slice them as thin as possible. Pairs well with berries and hazelnuts.

Brown birch boletes

Latin name: *Leccinum scabrum*
Found: July to October

There are many species of boletus (of which the cep/porcini is one), some are more edible, or palatable, than others.

Aside from the cep, which is one of the most prized wild mushrooms, the brown birch and the summer boletus are my two preferred ones. We occasionally get deliveries into the restaurant from one of our foragers, Brian Gannon. Larger mushrooms need to be cut in half to check for insects. Use as you would use ceps, sliced thinly and fried by themselves with some butter and thyme, or in soups and stews. The mushrooms dry well. From the dried mushrooms, you can make oil, vinegar and powder for flavouring other dishes.

Cauliflower fungus

Latin name: *Sparassis crispa*
Found: July to October

As their name suggests, these mushrooms loosely resemble a head of cauliflower. They grow in coniferous woods, normally at the base of pine trees. Our forager Brian Gannon has dropped them in on occasion. Though they can be fried, I prefer to pickle them whole and then use the pickled pieces for different dishes such as salads or a garnish. The mushroom also dries well and then can be used to flavour stocks (broths) and sauces.

Ceps

Latin name: *Boletus edulis*
Found: June to November

Penny bun, ceps as the French call them, or porcini if you go by their Italian name, are a member of the boletus family. They were first classified in 1782 by the French botanist Pierre Bulliard. They grow widely across Ireland but are difficult to cultivate, which is why most people know them as a dry ingredient. Ceps are most commonly sold dried and are wonderful rehydrated in warm water and added to risotto (which I make with barley – don't tell the Italians that I told you). Dried ceps can also be blended into a powder. I often use it to dust over white fish such as cod and monkfish. A whole monkfish roasted on the bone and dusted with cep powder is a real treat. Buy yourself an icing (confectioners') sugar shaker and fill it with cep powder. Keep in a cool, dry place and it should last you for months. The powder can also be frozen or given to your friends as presents. Fresh ceps are harder to come across, but it's worth seeking them out, whether in the woods or from the many farmer's markets across the country. Ulrich Hoeche, one of the many mushroom foragers in Galway, always finds a few for us at Aniar. They make a wonderful purée, but I like to just fry them in duck fat and thyme and finish with a little sea salt.

Chanterelles

Latin name: *Cantharellus cibarius*
Found: July to October

Chanterelles are probably the most common mushroom I come across. Both in the fields and the farmer's markets. We use them in the restaurant from the late summer into the winter. Of all the wild mushrooms, I find chanterelles the most accessible, especially to people who have not tried wild mushrooms before. Chanterelles are found in woods, especially with beech, birch or pine trees. If you forage from these trees in spring, it's useful to remember to return in the late summer and autumn (fall). Though they have a few lookalikes, chanterelles are probably one of the easiest mushrooms to identify. They are yellowy-orange with a cap that has a central depression and a wavy margin. Their distinct feature is evenly spaced ridges that run from under the cap to the stalk (stem). They cook well on their own (in butter or duck fat) and are great with egg dishes. Chanterelles also pickle well. I often pickle the smaller ones; they make a nice garnish later, particularly on pork belly or beef. If drying, it's best to blend to a powder. The powder goes extremely well with white fish, especially monkfish.

Chicken of the woods

Latin name: *Laetiporus sulphureus*
Found: April to November

Like the beefsteak mushroom, this mushroom grows on broad-leaved trees such as oak and sweet chestnut. Growing in semi-circular brackets, its bright orange tends to lighten in colour near the edges. Amazingly, its texture and flavour resembles chicken! I like to slice it into steak-like pieces and fry in duck fat or clarified butter. Some people like to blanch the pieces beforehand because of the mushroom's natural acidic taste. Chicken of the woods is great in sandwiches because of its meaty nature, but it also works well as a mix with other wild mushrooms in soups and stews.

Finally, the mushrooms are great pickled or fermented. I pickle them in apple cider vinegar, a little water and some fresh herbs and garlic. To ferment, use a 2 per cent sea salt solution (see page 361).

Dryad's saddle

Latin name: *Polyporus squamosus*
Found: July to November

This is a 'bracket' fungus found on broad-leaved trees such as beech, sycamore and elm – 'bracket' refers to the way they project from the trees. Like chicken of the woods, use younger mushrooms. The surface of the mushroom is yellow and brown. Use as you would chicken of the woods – fried or pickled is best.

Field mushroom

Latin name: *Agaricus campestris*
Found: July to November

Called *beacán* in Irish, these are the only wild mushroom I ever remember anyone eating from my youth. Field mushrooms, or meadow mushrooms in North America, often grow among other non-edible or poisonous mushrooms, but the field mushroom is fairly distinct with its flattened white, creamy coloured cap. Modern fertilizers seem to have impacted negatively on the mushroom and its growth is somewhat lessened in fields that are sprayed.

The mushroom's gills are deep pink to a browny-black. When cut open, it has a white flesh and a pleasant smell. Pick in the morning and fry by themselves or use in a mix for a wild mushroom soup. In the past, people placed butter in the cap and cooked them over hot coals. They dry well: remove the caps and dry in a low oven or a dehydrator. Finally, mushroom ketchup or fermented relish can be made with these mushrooms. Layer a preserving jar with the mushrooms, liberally salting each one. Leave in a cool place until the mushrooms break down and become a black paste. Blend, strain and season as desired. In the past nutmeg, mace and a host of other spices would have been added to balance the potent taste of the relish. 'Mushrooms to keep a year' is a recipe from the Mrs A. W. Baker collection (1810).

Hedgehog fungus

Latin name: *Hydnum repandum*
Found: June to November

Also called urchin of the woods, this woodland mushroom is one of my favourites to pick because of its distinct spiny layer, which is found underneath its cap. I like to remove all the spines before cooking (because sometimes little creatures live in there) but not everyone does this. It's great fried by itself or pickled for later use. It does need plenty

of liquid though, so I usually fry it in butter and cider (or white wine) with some fresh thyme. In Cava (our tapas bar), we use it in a mix for our mushroom paella.

Hen of the woods

Latin name: *Grifola frondosa*
Found: August to October

Hen of the woods, also called maitake (by the Japanese) grows in clusters at the base of trees such as oak, beech and ash. Originally native to North America, China and Japan (where it is prized for its medical and culinary qualities), it can now be found in Ireland, but with some difficulty. The mushroom has a sweet and pleasant taste, so I find it's best to fry by itself with thyme and garlic. Try with pork fat! Because it dries well, it can also be purchased dried and rehydrated. It makes a good stock or broth. I love to fry them, place on some buttered toast with goat's cheese and then grill (broil) until the cheese melts.

Horn of plenty/Black trumpet

Latin name: *Craterellus cornucopioides*
Found: August to October

I was first introduced to black trumpets in their dried form. In many of the restaurants I have worked in over the years, they were used dried as an addition to risotto or soup. Because of their intense flavour and colour, they give a wonderful pronounced taste. Like chanterelles, they occur in woodlands, mainly beech and oak. They grow in clusters and have a distinct funnel or trumpet-like cap. They do need a good clean because they grow underneath the falling leaves. Cut them in half and brush with a pastry brush. When dried and blended to a fine powder, they work well with white fish. In my opinion, they are best dried, but they can be fried fresh as most other mushrooms. They are best added to a mix of yellow chanterelles and winter chanterelles. Do fry very lightly because they are quite leathery.

Morel

Latin names: *Morchella elata/M. esculenta*
Found: March to May

There is one spring wild mushroom that is most highly prized by mushroom lovers: the morel. This little brown and black honeycombed mushroom has a distinct cap of sophisticated ribs, almost like the vault of a Late Gothic cathedral. Morels are part of what mushroom hunters call the 'foolproof four'. Alongside morels, the others are: hen of the woods, chanterelles and puffballs. Though these mushrooms do have a few false look-a-likes, they are distinct. The false morel will not do you too much damage: probably only an upset stomach. All true morels need to be cooked, because uncooked they can also cause a few digestive problems. It is also important to clean them because they grow in sandy areas and there may be a few insects inside. I like to use an old toothbrush or pastry brush when cleaning wild mushrooms. Try pairing them with other things in season such as lamb or asparagus (a French classic). How about a fried duck egg with some freshly blanched asparagus and pan-fried morels in duck fat? Nice with a glass of pinot noir, me thinks. Morels also make a nice barley risotto. Finally, morels are great dried and used in teas and broths. Try mixing them with dried seaweed for a magical broth.

Orange peel fungus

Latin name: *Aleuria aurantia*
Found: August to November

A small bright orange mushroom commonly found in woodlands. It looks a little like a discarded orange peel (hence its name). The outer surface of the mushroom is white and covered with small scales. The fruit body is cup shaped. It breaks down a lot in cooking, so it's best to dry it first. However, I have mixed it with other mushrooms when frying. It can be eaten raw. Slice thinly and add to autumnal salads. Pairs well with roasted squash or pumpkins with toasted seeds and goat's curd.

Oyster mushrooms

Latin names: *Pleurotus cornucopiae/ P. ostreatus*
Found: August to November/all year round

Oyster mushrooms grow on tree stumps or fallen trunks, especially oak, beech and elm. Though the branched oyster mushroom (*Pleurotus cornucopiae*) only occurs in the late autumn (fall) and early winter, the common oyster mushroom (*P. ostreatus*) can be found all year around. Collect both when young. Oyster mushrooms fry well by themselves or in a mix. They are also good pickled in oil and can be dried for later use.

Pig's ears

Latin name: *Peziza badia*
Found: August to November

Pig's ear mushrooms are little small reddish-brown cup mushrooms found on soil and clay banks. These mushrooms need to be cooked. Cooked simply in a little oil or butter, they develop a slight nutty taste. They are nice in a mix for any mushroom dish or in egg dishes, such as omelettes or scrambled eggs. I love them pickled with juniper. They are also great dried. In this way, they can be added to stews, soups or risottos or turned into a powder and used as a seasoning. When mixed with salt, this seasoning is lovely with pork.

Puffball

Latin names: *Bovista plumbea/Calvatia gigantea/Lycoperdon perlatum*
Found: June to December

There are many variations of this family and I'll only deal with three here: dusty (or grey/paltry) puffball (*Bovista plumbea*), giant puffball (*Calvatia gigantea*), and the common puffball (*Lycoperdon perlatum*). There are at least five or six others, all of which can be used in similar ways. Slice the puffball (if large) and fry in oil and butter with herbs. Use in stews or different wild mushroom mixes. They can be dried, but I find the resulting flavour a bit disappointing. Small to medium puffballs are best for flavour.

Saffron milkcap

Latin name: *Lactarius deliciosus*
Found: August to November

The saffron milk cap is one of many milk caps, such as the sweet-milk cap and the coconut-milk cap. The fruit body of this mushroom has a reddish-orange cap that stains the hands when cut. Young mushrooms are best because the older ones are prone to insects. The mushrooms need a little more cooking than others, due to their bitter quality. Best used as a mix. Can be used in dishes that already have saffron in them such as paella.

Scarlet elf cup

Latin name: *Sarcoscypha coccinea*
Found: January to April

Part of the 'ascomycete' family (along with orange peel fungus and pig's ears). Found in forest woodland, hiding under the fallen leaves of beech and hawthorn trees. Their inside surface is bright scarlet. The scarlet elf cap is one of the few mushrooms that is available in the early winter months. It can be eaten raw or cooked and it dries well. Because of its colour, it's nice in winter salads or served pickled as an accompaniment to pork or chicken.

St George's mushroom

Latin name: *Calocybe gambosa*
Found: April to June

St George's mushrooms are a late spring and early summer mushroom that are found on chalky soil in pastures, woodland and even sometimes in hedgerows. The flesh of the mushroom is thick and white. Traditionally, they were eaten on the 23rd of April, which is the day of St George. The mushrooms are wonderful cooked with a little butter, salt and thyme, or in chicken or fish dishes. In addition, they're great fried on sourdough bread with cheese. I like to pickle or dry them and use them later in the season. When dried, I like to blend them into a powder and use them in egg dishes.

Summer boletus

Latin name: *Boletus reticulatus*
Found: June to August

The summer boletus, as its name suggests, pops up in the summer. It looks very similar to a cep (porcini). They usually appear between June and August. Though the flavour is not as pronounced as a cep, they can be used in the same way: sliced thinly and served with fresh hazelnuts and dressed with oil, lemon juice and salt or pan-fried in butter or duck fat with rosemary and thyme. They dry well and can be used in soups or stocks (broths).

Winter chanterelle

Latin name: *Craterellus tubaeformis*
Found: August to November

Though not much to look at from a distance, this little edible is one of my favourite late autumn (fall) and early winter mushrooms. Akin to the large yellow chanterelle, these little grey and yellow mushrooms are a rich delicacy. With a browny-grey cap and a yellow stem, they are often found under fallen leaves. However, because they grow in groups, if you find one, you should find a lot! Not the best eaten raw, I love to mix these together with hedgehogs, yellow chanterelles and oyster mushrooms to create a rich forest melody. They dry well and are very good pickled or preserved in oil. Fried in a little butter and thyme, they are great with wild duck or venison, with which they also share the same season.

Wood ear

Latin name: *Auricularia auricula-judae*
Found: all year round

This fungus goes by a few common names including jelly ear and Jew's ear. It grows on dead branches of broad-leaved trees, particularly the elder tree (which gives us both flowers and berries). Its fruit body resembles an ear, though it is a reddish-brown colour. It has a crunchy-jelly texture that can be a bit off-putting at first. I like to pickle them in vinegar or dry to use in stews or soups.

Wood/field blewit

Latin names: *Lepista nuda/L. saeva*
Found: September/October to December

As the name indicates, the wood blewit is found in woods, while the field blewit is found in pastures and other grassy areas. The wood blewit has a blue-grey cap, while the field is a little browner. They are best picked on dry days because they absorb water. Use as a mix or in stews. Pickle in vinegar or under oil. Do not dry due to disappointing results. I like the wood blewits fried with white fish and chicken, with plenty of herbs and butter.

Conclusion

'If you were an Irish tomato, how would you like to be smothered in foreign French dressing...'

Myrtle Allen, *The Ballymaloe Cookbook*, 1977

For me this book is only the beginning; the beginning of the wholesale recovery of Irish food and its revaluation on a national and international stage. I hope it will inspire young chefs, cooks and individuals to go out into their own environment and find again the beautiful food that surrounds them. All we have is what surrounds us: our local environment made up of its landscape and the community that enriches it. Each time we eat, each time we put something in our mouth, we engage with our food culture. Of course, sometimes this eating is out of necessity or out of boredom. However, there are occasions that when we eat, we know we are consuming the past – that in every mouthful of what we eat we can reach back and taste that lost connection to previous periods of time. This book forges ahead while looking back. It draws on many sources and authors. History is vital for understanding where we come from and how we eat. The history of Irish food is the history of conflicts, both big and small. Food comes in, takes over, replaces other food. While the above quotation from Myrtle Allen, the grande dame of Irish food, can be taken as a little tongue in cheek, it does demonstrate how we continually wrestle with the notion of what is ours and what is not in terms of food and its influence. It would be naive to think there was such an unchanging thing as 'Irish food'. It is perpetually in flux. It is as different now as it was in the past or will be in the future. I welcome the new ways in which Irish food is changing, the way that it grows more confident and adapts to what is to hand (in terms of both produce and people) and the ways that it has yet to interpret the vibrant past of our ten thousand-year food heritage.

Recipe Notes

Butter is unsalted, unless specified otherwise.

All milk is whole (full-fat) milk, unless specified otherwise.

Herbs are fresh, unless specified otherwise.

Eggs are assumed to be large (US extra large) and preferably organic and free-range.

Onions are medium yellow onions, unless specified otherwise.

Potatoes are floury, unless specified otherwise – try Rooster, Maris Piper or Russet varieties.

Individual fruits and vegetables, such as onions and pears, are assumed to be medium sized, unless specified otherwise, and should be peeled and/or washed.

When using the zest of citrus fruit, buy unwaxed or organic.

Fish are assumed cleaned and gutted.

Cooking and preparation times are for guidance only, as individual ovens vary. If using a convection (fan) oven, follow the manufacturer's instructions concerning oven temperatures.

Exercise a high level of caution when following recipes involving any potentially hazardous activity including the use of high temperatures, open flames and when deep-frying. In particular, when deep-frying, add food carefully to avoid splashing, wear long sleeves and never leave the pan unattended.

When deep frying, heat the oil to the temperature specified, or until a cube of bread browns in 30 seconds. After frying, drain fried foods on paper towels.

Exercise caution when foraging for ingredients; any foraged ingredients should only be eaten if an expert has deemed them safe to eat, and should be cleaned well before use.

Some recipes include raw or very lightly cooked eggs, meat or fish, and fermented products. These should be avoided by the elderly, infants, pregnant women, convalescents and anyone with an impaired immune system.

When sterilizing jars for preserves, wash the jars in clean, hot water and rinse thoroughly. Heat the oven to 140°C/275°F fan/Gas Mark 1. Place the jars on a baking sheet and place in the oven to dry.

When no quantity is specified, for example of oils, salts, and herbs used for finishing dishes or for deep-frying, quantities are discretionary and flexible.

All spoon and cup measurements are level, unless otherwise stated. 1 teaspoon = 5 ml; 1 tablespoon = 15 ml. Australian standard tablespoons are 20 ml, so Australian readers are advised to use 3 teaspoons in place of 1 tablespoon when measuring small quantities.

Cup, metric and imperial measurements are used in this book. Follow one set of measurements throughout, not a mixture, as they are not interchangeable.

Bibliography

Allen, Darina. *Irish Traditional Cooking* (London: Kyle Books, 2008) [first published 1995]

Allen, Darina. *Forgotten Skills of Cooking* (London: Kyle Books, 2009)

Allen, Darina. *Grow, Cook, Nourish: A Kitchen Garden Companion in 500 recipes* (London: Kyle Books, 2017)

Allen, Myrtle. *The Ballymaloe Cookbook* (Dublin: Gill & Macmillan, 1984) [first published 1977]

Allen, Tim. *The Ballymaloe Bread Book* (Dublin: Gill & Macmillan, 2001)

Andrews, Colman. *The Country Cooking of Ireland* (California: Chronicle Books, 2009)

Armstrong, Alison. *The Joyce of Cooking* (Barrytown, New York: Station Hill Press, 1986)

Armstrong, Cathal and David Hagedorn. *My Irish Table: Recipes from the Homeland and Restaurant Eve* (Berkeley: Ten Speed Press, 2014)

Barnard, T. C. *A New Anatomy of Ireland: The Irish Protestants, 1649–1770* (New Haven and London: Yale University Press, 2003)

Blake, Carla. *The Irish Cookbook* (Cork: Mercier Press, 1971)

Bowes, David. *Real Irish Food: 150 Recipes from the Old Country* (New York: Skyhorse Publishing, 2012)

Burrows, Ian. *Food from the Wild* (London: New Holland Publishers, 2005)

Cashman, Dorothy. 'An Investigation of Irish Culinary History Through Manuscript Cookbooks, with Particular Reference to the Gentry of County Kilkenny (1714–1830).' (Dublin: unpublished PhD thesis, 2016)

Cashman, Dorothy. 'Ireland's Culinary Manuscripts.' In Darina Allen, *Irish Traditional Cooking* (2012): 14–15

Clarkson, L. A. and E. Margaret Crawford. Eds. *Feast and Famine: Food and Nutrition in Ireland 1500–1920* (Oxford, 2001)

Coolin, Joseph. *Ireland: A Short History* (London: Oneworld, 2014)

Corrigan, Richard. *The Clatter of Forks and Spoons* (London: Fourth Estate, 2008)

Cullen, Louis M. *The Emergence of Modern Ireland 1600–1900* (London, Batsford, 1981)

Cullen, Louis M. 'Comparative aspects of the Irish Diet, 1550–1850', in *Hans J Teuteberg, Ed. European Food History: A research review* (Leicester, London and New York, 1991)

Danaher, Kevin. *In Ireland Long Ago* (Cork: Mercier Press, 1962)

Dundon, Kevin. *Full on Irish: Creative Contemporary Cooking* (Epicure Press, 2006)

Dundon, Kevin. *Kevin Dundon's Modern Irish Food* (Mitchell Beazley, 2013)

FitzGibbon, Theodora. *A Taste of Ireland* (Boston: Houghton Mifflin Company, 1969)

FitzGibbon, Theodora. *Irish Traditional Food* (Dublin: Gill & Macmillan, 1983)

FitzPatrick, Elizabeth and James Kelly. Eds. *Food and Drink in Ireland* (Dublin: Royal Irish Academy, 2016)

Galvin, Gerry. *The Drimcong Food Affair* (Galway: McDonald Publishing, 1992)

Galvin, Gerry. *Everyday Gourmet* (Dublin: The O'Brien Press, 1997)

Geraghty, Siobhán. *Viking Dublin: Botanical Evidence from Fishamble Street* (Dublin: National Museum of Ireland, 1996)

Hickey, Margaret. *Ireland's Green Larder: The Definitive History of Irish Food and Drink* (London: Unbound, 2018)

Irving, Miles. *The Forager's Handbook: A Guide to the Edible Plants of Britain* (London: Ebury Press, 2009)

Irwin, Florence. *Irish Country Recipes* (Belfast: The Northern Whig, 1937)

Irwin, Florence. *The Cookin' Woman: Irish Country Recipes* Belfast: Blackstaff Press, 1986) [first published 1949]

Jackson, Peter Wyse. *Ireland's Generous Nature: The Past and Present Uses of Wild Plants in Ireland* (Missouri: Missouri Botanical Press, 2014)

Kelly, Fergus. *Early Irish Farming: A study based mainly on the law-tract of the 7th and 8th centuries AD* (Dublin: Dublin Institute for Advanced Studies, 1997)

Kohl, Johann Georg. *Ireland* (New York, 1844)

Lalor, Brian. Ed. *The Encyclopaedia of Ireland* (Dublin: Gill & Macmillan, 2003)

Laverty, Maura. *Full & Plenty: Classic Irish Cooking* (The Irish Flour Millers' Press, 1986) [first published 1960]

Laverty, Maura. *Never No More* (London: Virago Press, 2004) [first published 1942]

Laverty, Maura. *Kind Cooking* (Tralee: The Kerryman, 1955)

Lennon, Biddy White and Georgina Campbell. *Traditional Cooking of Ireland* (London: Anness Books, 2017)

Lewis, Ross. *Chapter One: An Irish Food Story* (Dublin: Gill & Macmillan, 2013)

Lovell, M.S. *The Edible Mollusca of Great Britain and Ireland* (London: L. Reeve & Co., 1892)

Lucas A. T. 'Irish Food Before The Potato'. *Gwerin: A Half-Yearly Journal of Folk Life*. Vol. 3:2 (1960) 8–43

Lucas A. T. *Irish-Norse Relations: Time for a Reappraisal* (Cork, 1966)

Lucas A. T. Ed. *Cattle in Ancient Ireland* (Kilkenny: Boethius Press, 1989)

Mac Coitir, Niall. *Ireland's Wild Plants: Myths, Legends and Folklore* (Cork: The Collins Press, 2015)

Mac Coitir, Niall. *Ireland's Trees: Myths, Legends and Folklore* (Cork: The Collins Press, 2015)

Mac Coitir, Niall. *Ireland's Animals: Myths, Legends and Folklore* (Cork: The Collins Press, 2015)

Mac Coitir, Niall. *Ireland's Birds: Myths, Legends and Folklore* (Cork: The Collins Press, 2015)

Mac Con Iomaire, Máirtín. 'The History of Seafood in Irish Cuisine and Culture'. *Proceedings of the Oxford Symposium on Food and Cookery* (Devon: Prospect Books, 2005): 219–233

Mac Con Iomaire, Máirtín. 'Exploring the "Food Motif" in Songs from the Irish Tradition.' (Dublin, 2014).

Mac Con Iomaire, Máirtín and Pádraic Óg Gallagher. 'The Potato in Irish Cuisine and Culture', *Journal of Culinary Science and Technology*, Vol. 7 (2–3) (2009): 152–167

Mac Con Iomaire, Máirtín and Pádraic Óg Gallagher. 'Irish Corned Beef: A Culinary History' *Journal of Culinary Science and Technology*, Vol. 9 (1), (2011): 27–43

Mac Con Iomaire, Máirtín and D. Cashman. 'Irish Culinary Manuscripts and Printed Cookbooks: A Discussion', *Petits Propos Culinaires* 94 (2011): 81–101

Mac Con Iomaire, Máirtín and E. Maher, Eds. (2014). *'Tickling the Palate': Gastronomy in Irish Literature and Culture* (Oxford, Peter Lang, 2014

McDonnell, Hector. *Ireland's Other History* (Dublin: The Lilliput Press, 2012)
McKenna, Sally. *Extreme Greens: Understanding Seaweed* (Durrus, Cork: Estragon Press, 2013)

Mahon, Bríd. *Land of Milk and Honey: The Story of Traditional Irish Food and Drink* (Dublin: Poolbeg Press, 1991)

Mallory, J. P. *The Origins of the Irish* (London: Thames & Hudson, 2013)

Miller, Ian. *Reforming Food in Post-famine Ireland: Medicine, Science and Management, 1845–1922* (Manchester: Manchester University Press, 2014)

Morris, Nicki and Paula Borton. *The Great Fish Book: A Wonderful Collection of Recipes from the Finest Restaurants in Great Britain and Ireland* (Bath: Absolute Press, 1988)

Murphy, Margaret and Michael Potterton. *The Dublin Region in the Middle Ages: Settlement, Land-use and Economy* (Dublin: Four Courts Press, 2010)

Ó'Céirín, Cyril and Kit. *Wild and Free: Cooking from Nature* (Dublin: The O'Brien Press, 1978)

Piatti-Farnell, Lorna and Donna Lee Brien. Eds. *The Routledge Companion to Literature and Food* (London: Routledge, 2018)

Rhatigan, Prannie. *Irish Seaweed Kitchen* (Holywood, Down: Booklink, 2009)

Rhatigan, Prannie. *Irish Seaweed Christmas Kitchen* (Sligo: Inishmurray Ink Publishing, 2018)

Sexton, Regina. *A Little History of Irish Food* (London: Kyle Books, 1998)

Sexton, Regina. 'Food and Culinary Cultures in pre-Famine Ireland.' *Proceedings of the Royal Irish Academy: Archaeology, Celtic Studies, History, Literature,* Vol. 115 (2015): 257–306

Sexton, Regina and Cathal Cowan. *Ireland's Traditional Foods: An Exploration of Irish Local and Typical Foods and Drinks* (Dublin: Teagasc, 1997)

Shanahan, Madeline. *Manuscript Recipe Books as Archaeological Object: Text and Food in the Early Modern World* (London: Lexington Books, 2015)

Sheridan, Monica. *The Art of Irish Cooking* (New York: Gramercy, 1965)

Skehan, Donal. *The Pleasures of the Table: Rediscovering Theodora FitzGibbon* (Dublin: Gill & Macmillan, 2014)

Taylor, Patrick. *An Irish Country Cookbook* (New York: Tom Doherty Associates, 2017)

Thomson, George L. *Traditional Irish Recipes* (Dublin: The O'Brien Press, 1982)

Waddington, Paul. *Seasonal Food* (London: Transworld, 2004)

Uí Chomáin, Máirín. *Cuisine le Mairin* (Cork: Attic Press, 1992)

Uí Chomáin, Máirín. *Encore Cuisine* (Cork: Attic Press, 1994)

Uí Chomáin, Máirín. *Irish Oyster Cuisine* (Dublin: A & A Farmar, 2004)

Index

W

Y

Phaidon Press Limited
Regent's Wharf
All Saints Street
London N1 9PA

Phaidon Press Inc.
65 Bleecker Street
New York, NY 10012

phaidon.com

First published 2020
© 2020 Phaidon Press Limited

ISBN 978 1 83866 056 7

A CIP catalogue record for
this book is available from the
British Library and the Library
of Congress.

Commissioning Editor: Ellie Smith
Project Editor: Lucy Kingett
Production Controller:
Sarah Kramer
Photography and Styling:
Anita Murphy and Zania Koppe
of Ginger and Sage
Typesetting: Michael Wallace

Designed by Julia Hasting

Printed in China

The publisher would like to thank
Theresa Bebbington, Vanessa
Bird, Jane Ellis, Sophie Hodgkin,
Lesley Malkin, João Mota, Adelaide
Mueller, Anna Nightingale, Lisa
Pendreigh and Tracey Smith.

Jp McMahon

Jp McMahon is a chef, restaurateur
and author. He is culinary director
of the EatGalway Restaurant
Group and runs the Aniar Boutique
Cookery School. Founding chair
and director of the Galway Food
Festival, Jp is an ambassador for
Irish food. He organises 'Food on
the Edge', an annual international
chef symposium in Galway and
writes a weekly column for
The Irish Times.

Author's Acknowledgements

To the women who stoked my
fire for Irish food: Florence
Irwin, Theodora FitzGibbon,
Maura Laverty, Monica Sheridan,
Myrtle and Darina Allen, Bríd
Mahon, Regina Sexton, Georgina
Campbell, Biddie White Lennon,
Máirín Uí Chomáin, Prannie
Rhatigan, Sally McKenna and
Margaret Hickey. And, of course,
my mother, grandmother and
my nana. I thank you all. You
gave me the gift of cooking and
sharing food.

Many have helped me along the
way in writing this book over the
last three years. I have had so many
conversations with so many people
that it would be impossible to list
each and every name. However, the
people below have stood by me
throughout and it would not have
been possible without them:

My wife, Drigín, and our two
daughters, Heather and Martha:
you are my shining lights.

My parents, Carol and Gerard, and
the rest of my family.

My sister Edel, for all her help with
editing and designing the initial
proposal that became this book.

Abigail and Laura, for all their
assistance with the project (and
everything else).

All of our staff at our three
restaurants (Aniar, Cava Bodega
and Tartare).

The Food on the Edge team,
including Ruth and Olivia.

Anita and Zania, for their beautiful
photography.

The many chefs that I have worked
with over the years, who have
helped me hone my craft.

Atilla and Claudio for their
assistance is testing the recipes.

Regina Sexton, Máirtín Mac Con
Iomaire and Darina Allen for your
many conversations and insights.
Without your own writings, this
book would not exist.

Prannie Rhatigan, for all her
seaweed knowledge.

Lucy, and everyone else at Phaidon:
a good editor is a great thing
indeed!

To all the farmers, fisherman and
food producers in Ireland (without
you, there would be no 'New Irish
Cuisine').